Michael Grant is an eminent historian who has held many
distinguished academic posts. He was formerly a Fellow of
Trinity College, Cambridge, Professor of Humanity at
Edinburgh University, and the first Vice-Chancellor of the
University of Khartoum. From 1959 to 1966 he was
President and Vice-Chancellor of the Queen's University,
Belfast. Among his many published books on the history and
culture of the ancient world are *Myths of the Greeks and
Romans, The Civilisations of Europe, Gladiators, The World of
Rome, The Ancient Mediterranean, The Ancient Historians, Roman
Myths, Julius Caesar, Herod the Great* and *Nero*

Also in this series and available in Cardinal

HISTORY OF CIVILISATION

THE CLIMAX OF ROME

Michael Grant

To Steven Runciman

CARDINAL edition published in 1974
by Sphere Books Ltd
30/32 Gray's Inn Road, London WC1X 8JL

First published in Great Britain
by Weidenfeld & Nicolson Ltd 1968
Copyright © Michael Grant 1968

Set in Monotype Baskerville

Printed in Great Britain by
Cox & Wyman Ltd,
London, Reading and Fakenham

ISBN 0 351 16534 7

CONTENTS

LIST OF ILLUSTRATIONS

ACKNOWLEDGEMENTS

The author and publishers would like to thank the following for supplying photographs for use in this volume: Alinari, Plate 23, British Museum, Plates 1, 3, 10; Cincinnati Art Museum, Plate 4; Deutsches Archäologisches Institut, Rome, Plate 9; Fototeca Unione, Rome, Plates 20, 22; Giraudon, Plate 2; Landesmuseum, Trier, Plates 25, 26; Libyan Ministry of Education, Plate 8; Louvre, Paris, Plate 19; Mansell Collection, Plates 2, 16, 17, 19, 23, 24, 28, 29; National Museum, Rome, Plates 5, 17; Ny Carlsberg Glyptotek, Copenhagen, Plate 7; Radio Times Hulton Picture Library, Plate 27; Scala, Plate 18; Thomson Newspapers Ltd, Plate 21; Vatican Museums, Plate 6.

LIST OF MAPS

FOREWORD

This book gives an account of Rome and the lands under its rule between the accession of Marcus Aurelius and the death of Constantine the Great (A.D. 161–337). My aim has been to combine in a single volume a discussion of the most important political and economic events and the outstanding cultural and religious developments, with some attention to their backgrounds and aftermaths.

Not only was the empire converted to Christianity during this epoch, but it was also extraordinarily rich in other happenings. Many of them, however, have been neglected by all but specialists, because the original sources are often obscure and difficult to interpret, and most of all because the period seems to belong neither to antiquity nor to the Middle Ages. That is indeed one of its peculiar fascinations. Spanning the gulf between two worlds, it is a time of rapid transition comprising changes which could scarcely have been more far-reaching and decisive. But the idea that this is therefore a mere no-man's-land, a trough between the ages, would be quite mistaken. The attribution of that somewhat shadowy, interim character to the period was encouraged by Edward Gibbon, who believed that the happiest age of mankind ended with the death of Marcus Aurelius, and that afterwards came decline and fall.

Such a view, developed by Gibbon with incomparable brilliance, had classical authority. Ever since the earliest empire, Roman writers had been airing the view that Rome was getting old. When the historian Dio Cassius came to the end of Marcus' reign, he paused in order to observe that his work "now descends from a kingdom of gold to one of iron and rust, as affairs did for the Romans of that day". And in the next century St. Cyprian, though one of the Christians whom Gibbon did not like, agreed with him in feeling upon all sides the chilly touch of impending death.

This is too incomplete and negative a view of the period. Politically and economically, it is true, gloom was justified. For insecurity and anxiety were more acute and desperate than they had ever been, and there was a rapid growth of government by autocratic force. Yet political and economic distress does not always prevent cultural and spiritual triumphs, and sometimes breeds them. In the later Roman empire, great positive, personal achievements of the mind and spirit accompanied and often resulted from such adversities and governmental oppressions. Indeed, these achievements were so outstanding, in a variety of fields, that the epoch to which they belong is one of the most important in the history of the world; and because it shows what human beings can do in harrowing conditions it is also one of the most heartening.

And so I have called this book *The Climax of Rome*. After surveying the field, I shall point in the epilogue to the reasons which exist for claiming that this title, however unexpected in relation to the period, is justifiable, or inevitable (p. 320). Nevertheless a further element of paradox remains in the word Rome. The men who made the age were Romans in the sense that they lived in the Roman empire. But the greatest of them did not come from Rome itself, or even from Italy. In particular, my book has a lot to say about the east, since this eastern bias, though perhaps unusual in western students of history, seems to me to reflect the importance of that area in the third- and fourth-century world. Eternal Rome was more than a geographical term; it had become a concept or series of concepts, the emotive symbol of a great society comprising many races and cultures. Such, then, is the Rome of which this age is the climax.

I acknowledge with gratitude permission to quote from copyright works:

A. H. Armstrong and Messrs. Allen and Unwin for *Plotinus*, the executors of M. Hadas and Bobbs-Merrill Co. for *Three Greek Romances*, Everyman's Library for *Heliodorus: Ethiopian Story*, E. C. Echols and University of California Press for *Herodian of Antioch's History of the Roman Empire*, E. R. Dodds and the Cambridge University Press for *Pagan and Christian in an Age of Anxiety*, the Cambridge University Press for *Cambridge Ancient History*, A. H. M. Jones and Messrs. Longmans for *The Decline of the Ancient World*, Messrs. William Heinemann for translations from Achilles Tatius, Galen (*On the Natural Faculties*) and Tertullian (*Apology*) in the Loeb

Classical Library, M. Staniforth and Penguin Books for *Marcus Aurelius' Meditations*, P. Turner and Penguin Books for *Lucian's Satirical Sketches*, G. R. S. Mead and Penguin Books for "Hymn of Soul" in F. C. Happold's *Mysticism*, P. Jay and "Oxford Magazine" for *Pervigilium Veneris*, E. O'Brien and Mentor Books for *The Essential Plotinus*.

I owe thanks to Professor A. H. M. Jones and Professor F. W. Walbank for allowing me to read works of theirs before publication. But neither they nor anyone else, apart from myself, can be held responsible for the numerous inadequacies which my attempt to cover so wide a field is certain to have produced. I want to express appreciation to the library staff at the Queen's University, Belfast, to Mr. Anthony Burton, Mr. Julian Shuckburgh and Mrs. Patricia Vanags of Messrs. George Weidenfeld and Nicolson Ltd, to Mrs. W. Bernstein who collected the illustrations, and to Dr. Ursula Pietsch of Verlag C. H. Beck. Acknowledgements are also due to the University of Saskatchewan, which has published a lecture of mine on this general theme, and to *Horizon* (New York), *Mankind* (Los Angeles), and *History Today* (London), for which I wrote preliminary studies relating to the recovery of the empire, the triumph of Christianity, and the Gnostics and Manichaeans.

I am also grateful to my wife for very much invaluable assistance.

Gattaiola, 1973   MICHAEL GRANT

PART I

The World of Rome Transformed

I

The History of the Later Empire

Historical Sketch

The Roman empire extended from Britain in the north to the Sahara desert in the south. But its principal and most sensitive frontiers were those which stretched for thousands of miles along the Rhine, Danube and Euphrates, and along the borders of a few advanced territories beyond certain sectors of those three great rivers.

At the time with which this book begins, most of the unified state had long been at peace. Augustus (d. A.D. 14), who had replaced the inadequate government of the Republic by an autocracy elaborately concealed beneath traditional forms, laid a firm basis for the Pax Romana by a thoroughgoing overhaul of the entire administration, which was henceforward able to control the nearly thirty (later nearly fifty) provinces with efficiency, honesty and increasing mildness. The empire's backward social structure makes it difficult to agree with Gibbon that the human race, in these regions, has never again enjoyed the happiness and prosperity of the second century A.D. (p. 11). And yet the emperors of that period brought all these peoples the blessing of profound, durable peace, such as had not been seen over so large an area before and has never been seen again.

Although peace brought with it a certain atrophying of originality, the reign of Marcus Aurelius was distinguished by four authors whose gifts show how misleading it is to dismiss this period patronisingly (as is done, for example, by our educational systems) as post-classical. These are the scintillating Latin novelist Apuleius from north Africa, and, among writers in Greek, the razor-sharp, scoffing Lucian from the Euphrates area, Galen from Asia Minor "the medical pope of the Middle Ages", and the emperor himself, whose *Meditations* reveal one of the most complex and thoughtful men ever to occupy a throne.

And yet it was in the reign of Marcus Aurelius and his fellow-emperor Lucius Verus that the military situation grew sharply and permanently worse, with results which demolished the Roman Peace for ever. A recurrence of the usual expensive military operations against Rome's eastern neighbour on the Euphrates, Parthia, was followed by threats of a gravity never hitherto experienced from the Teutonic and Iranian tribes, Germans and Sarmatians, who lived beyond the Rhine and Danube. These consequent campaigns, which were accompanied by an epidemic of plague and followed by many further wars during the century to come, are depicted with a new sense of horror and pathos on the Arch of Marcus Aurelius. The fighting cost sums so large that their exaction from the subjects of the empire put an end to the relative comfort and ease of the middle classes. A second factor which contributed substantially to their impoverishment was the recurrence, after well over a century's intermission, of a constant series of civil wars caused by disputed imperial successions resulting in the assassination of one ruler after another. The death of Marcus' unconventional, deranged son Commodus (180–92), during whose reign eastern religious tendencies made much headway and gladiatorial games enjoyed imperial participation, was followed by four ruinous years of such warfare, in which the survivor of five claimants to the imperial throne was Septimius Severus (193–211).[1,2]

Trajan (d. 117), of Romano-Spanish origin, had been the first emperor who was not an Italian, and that was a pointer to the future, in which very few rulers came from Italy; the country lost its political and economic importance and became a mere framework for the prestige of eternal, subsidized Rome. Septimius, on the other hand, was the first of a number of non-Europeans, for his homeland was north Africa, which was also the only area still producing a distinguished Latin literature. But his influential wife Julia Domna came from Syria, which, through the medium of its Hellenized writers and artists, contributed an even greater share of the empire's talents and achievements. Indeed Syrian and other oriental literary, artistic and spiritual themes now began to encroach more and more upon the traditions of Greece and Rome, thereby forming the

18

distinctive amalgam that is characteristic of this later empire. Though Septimius maintained the fiction that he belonged (through adoption by Marcus Aurelius) to the tradition of the Antonine Golden Age, his exceptional ability and clear-sighted ruthlessness qualified him perfectly for the task, in which he was aided by the most famous jurists in legal history, of developing his rule into an absolute autocracy. For there now had to be painful adjustments to a new and grimmer age of intensified, forcibly collected taxation, in kind as well as cash; while people forgot these troubles, when they could, by reading the best of the ancient romantic novelists, Longus and Heliodorus.

Septimius' neurotically ambitious, boorish son Caracalla (211–17) eliminated his father-in-law, the praetorian prefect,[3] and then his own brother Geta, but only survived the latter by five years. His successor, Macrinus, was a Mauretanian whose elevation to the throne displayed the growing weakness of the senate, since he was the first emperor not to have been a member of that body. He soon succumbed to the first Syrian to occupy the throne, Elagabalus (218–22), a fourteen-year-old Sun-priest and sexual invert who belonged to the family of Julia Domna. Elagabalus' attempt to introduce Rome to thoroughgoing religious orientalization was tactless and premature, and yet under his younger cousin Severus Alexander (222–35), whose mother Julia Mamaea acted as regent, the religious tendencies of the previous reign continued to make headway in less extreme and obtrusive forms. Severus Alexander, unlike his predecessor, tried to appear as a Roman traditionalist who respected the senate. But it was not possible to revert to an old-fashioned constitutionalist régime, since the financial needs of the empire had suddenly become very much greater than they had been before. This was due to the replacement of Rome's eastern enemy Parthia—the only sizeable political unit on the imperial borders—by a far more dangerous foe, the Sassanian Persians.

The emergence of this major foreign power unhappily coincided with the deterioration of Rome from Military Monarchy into Military Anarchy. For the next half century the empire was almost continuously convulsed by internal wars of succession. Advantage of this weakness was taken both by Persia and by the increasingly formidable German and other tribes operating from beyond the

Danube frontier. The huge peasant-born Danubian Maximinus I might have dealt effectively with these latter attacks if he had not handled his own subjects with methods of particular severity, which led to his death (238).

In that single year the empire saw the coinage of no fewer than seven Caesars. These included three successive pairs of murdered colleagues, ruling jointly, in pursuance of ancient consular precedents, in order to spread the imperial burden.[4] The survivor of the seven was Gordian III (238–44), a youth of thirteen whose praetorian prefect Timesitheus became his all-powerful minister. The Persians were now ruled by their most aggressive expansionist, Shapur I; and the empire during the next twenty years also experienced the maximum intensification of German invasions. A series of soldier-emperors, whose careworn faces have come down to us in portrait busts of unrivalled quality, seemed unlikely to be able to save the Roman world. Philip the Arab (244–9) distracted attention by celebrating the millennium of Rome; Decius (249–51) and Valerian (253–60),[5] amid pestilence and increasing currency debasement, blamed their catastrophes upon the growing sect of the Christians. These, who had now produced educated apologists in Alexandria and elsewhere, were soon able to show in their turn how Decius was killed in battle against the Germans (Goths) and Valerian suffered the appalling ignominy of capture by the Persians. While these successive, unprecedented blows prompted one Roman general after another to declare himself emperor in the provinces, Valerian's son, colleague and successor Gallienus (253–68) was confronted by a breakaway of the western provinces under Postumus. Moreover, faced by currency collapse, price inflation and over-whelming attacks on both main fronts—involving the permanent loss of the upper Rhine-Danube re-entrant—Gallienus was also obliged to concede virtual independence to a large eastern princedom under Odenathus of Palmyra. Odenathus' widow and successor Zenobia conquered all Rome's oriental provinces; and the emperor of Rome now controlled only the precarious central strip of an empire which seemed to be in full disintegration.

And yet, at an incalculable expense of human resources and human happiness, the long haul towards military recovery had begun. Despite the fearful disasters of his reign—and a dubious reputation as a cultured Hellenist who was not sufficiently anti-

Christian—Gallienus started to stem the tide by establishing a new mobile cavalry army, with which he apparently won a major victory over the Goths. After him, in a period which witnessed the successive deaths of the two greatest teachers of the age, Plotinus the Platonist and mystic in Campania and Mani, founder of the Manichaeans in Persia, three emperors of the Danubian peasant stock which now formed the backbone of the army, Claudius II Gothicus (268–70), Aurelian (270–5) and Probus (276–82), directed almost miraculous feats of strategical skill and endurance which eliminated the menace on the northern frontiers.[6]

In order to achieve this result, Aurelian took the exceptional step of stabilizing his frontier by deliberately and permanently evacuating a province (trans-Danubian Dacia). Yet he brought back under his rule the western and eastern "empires" that had defected. At the same time he sought to revive official paganism, in the face of its Christian and other competitors, on the basis of the Sun-worship which had become an almost monotheistic cult, with the stern faith of Mithraism as its off-shoot.

Carus (282–3) restored the situation on the eastern frontier. Then his sons adopted the practice, sometimes resorted to earlier, of dividing the empire on a geographical basis,[7] and this arrangement was placed on what was intended to be a permanent basis by Diocletian (284–305). While himself ruling the eastern provinces from Nicomedia (Izmit), he raised Maximian, an Illyrian peasant like himself, to be his co-Augustus in the west, based on Mediolanum (Milan); Rome was no longer an imperial capital. Furthermore, this was to be a Tetrarchy, in which each emperor had an imperial coadjutor intended to be his heir—Galerius in the east, and Constantius I Chlorus in the west.

Diocletian, who combined Roman conservative patriotism with unflinching systematic insight into power-structures and long-term planning, gathered together all the threads which were tending towards absolutism, and formalized his autocratic government with ceremonial reminiscent less of Augustan Rome than of Sassanian Persia. The accompanying hieratic art, too, had moved a long way from classical ideals. It was housed in palaces of unprecedented splendour, architectural originality and expense. Greater cost still fell on the crushingly taxed citizens of the empire when Diocletian's analysis of imperial obligations caused him not only to institute a large-scale expansion of the civil service but to double the size of the army. The requirements of this huge force were provided by converting the exactions in kind, which had been a feature of the previous century, into a regular system. The methods employed to collect these materials, extortionate though they were, at least showed everyone where they stood, because the empire's needs were publicly announced each year in the first known annual budgets of history. But Diocletian, confronted like his predecessors with galloping inflation, showed the weakness of the ancient world in economic theory when he failed to control rising prices by his currency reform or his unprecedented edict enforcing maximum prices.

In rapid progression towards a totalitarian state, Diocletian decided to rally the peoples of the empire behind the traditional gods, and his desire to make their worship obligatory led him to the severest of all persecutions of the Christians (303). This outlasted the abdication of Diocletian (305) by eight confused years, during which the Tetrarchy broke down among a welter of joint, competing occupants of the throne.[8] But Galerius, who had abetted or instigated Diocletian's persecution, called the anti-Christian campaign off from his deathbed (311). Though his successor Maximinus II Daia (d. 313) then undertook a further attempt to reinforce paganism as a counterweight to Christianity, Constantine the Great, hitherto a determined adherent of Sun-worship, declared that his conquest of Italy from Maxentius (312) had been achieved under Christian auspices. Then, intensifying his dedicated, if theologically somewhat muddled, endeavours to Christianize the empire, he transformed the church from a national enemy into a heavily subsidized state religion subordinate to the emperor, with superb new churches for its worship.

Meanwhile Constantine, a man of impetuous, wide-ranging energy who was convinced of his god-sent mission, suppressed his eastern co-ruler Licinius, and thus became the sole survivor of six rival emperors and the only occupant of the throne (324–37). He completed a massive reorganization of the army on more mobile lines than hitherto, stabilized all frontiers and still further expanded the bureaucracy. Constantine's tightening of the authoritarian, autocratic and theocratic state is echoed in the transcendent immobility of his statues, which proclaim the death of humanism.

Since the emperor had to be within reach of the Danube and Euphrates frontiers and the resources of the eastern provinces, which by now far exceeded those of the west, Constantine selected Byzantium on the Bosphorus as his capital, renaming it Constantinople (324–30). After the empire had become permanently partitioned by a north-south line running west of Singidunum (Belgrade) (395), its western regions disintegrated into new German countries and ceased to have their own emperor (476). But the eastern territories, retaining the name of the Roman empire, continued the rule of Rome from Constantinople for nearly a thousand years after the last emperor had ruled in Italy.

The Sources of Information

The ancient sources of information for this tangled, confused succession of events are very numerous indeed, and one of the historian's principal problems is to detach what is important from a mass of detail. And yet all these sources are too fragmentary to be adequate. "The period is like a dark tunnel, illumined from either end, and by rare and exiguous light wells in the interval."[9] Those words were written about the central half-century of the epoch (235–84), but even the illumination from either end, though perhaps bright in contrast with the obscurity in the middle, is only fitful and flickering.[10] Knowledge of what happened has to be built up by a process of jigsaw puzzle and inference far more difficult than reconstructions of the earlier world of Rome or the later empire of Constantinople.

The most serious deficiency is the absence of any comprehensive account by an ancient historian of distinction. The earlier years are to some extent covered by surviving portions of the account written in Greek by Dio Cassius of Nicaea (Iznik) in Asia Minor. A senator and holder of high office, he wrote a history of Rome from its beginnings to A.D. 229, in eighty books. But for the last hundred and eighty-three years (except for incomplete versions of the two final books) we possess his history only in the form of an eleventh-century compendium,[11] and that too is lacking at times. Dio Cassius was a contemporary and eye-witness of events after 180;[12] he is anecdotal and reminiscent and undetached, and that is both his value and his weakness. Herodian, a Hellenized Syrian, wrote an eight-book history of the years 180–238. Repetitive, pompous, superficial and inaccurate, he has preserved a certain amount of street-corner gossip and gives us a third-century view of the passing of the Antonine Golden Age. There are also other Greek historians of later times who incorporate a good many isolated facts and events that would otherwise be lost.

The Latin *Historia Augusta*, ostensibly the work of six authors supporting the senatorial aristocratic tradition, is a collection of lives of emperors from Hadrian to the accession of Diocletian (117–284), though the sections from A.D. 244 to 253 are missing. Several of the biographies purport to be dedicated to Diocletian and Constantine, but internal evidence suggests that the work, at least in the form in which it has come down to us, is later than their age by half a century, or a century, or even two centuries. Although this indication that the ostensible authorship is false makes the whole work highly unreliable as a historical source, the major second-century Lives in the *Historia Augusta* include in haphazard form much material, not found elsewhere, which may tentatively be regarded as factual. Probably this goes back in large part to Marius Maximus, the author of a sequel to Suetonius' *Twelve Caesars*, who has been identified as one of Septimius Severus' generals. The *Historia* contains a disproportionately long biography of Severus Alexander (222–35) which may be a remodelled account of the life of Julian the Apostate (361–3); and most of the other third-century lives, especially those of the more transient figures, seem from what contemporary evidence we can collect to be stuffed with fiction, including alleged documents that are manifestly forged.

The last great doctor, Galen, speaks for himself, at great length. He writes in Greek; and so, except for the marvellous Latin of Apuleius, do the novelists. The outstanding philosophers Marcus Aurelius and Plotinus—the latter in his *Enneads*, published by a pupil Porphyry—likewise use the Greek language. On religion, pagan and Christian alike, there are innumerable authors in a variety of languages, the outstanding historical work on the Christian side being the *Ecclesiastical History* written in Greek by Eusebius (260–340).[13] An immense amount of historical information can be disinterred from the *Digest* of Justinian, of which a large proportion was derived, with or without modification, from jurists of Severan times. The thirteenth book of the so-called "Sibylline Oracles" throws light on eastern events in the third century.

Papyri, revolutionizing our comprehension of the history of the ancient novel, and illustrating almost innumerable aspects of public and private life, have been found in Egypt in their thousands.[14] Archaeology and art provide their usual abundant aids, and epigraphic evidence of bewildering quantity and variety includes the military calendar of Dura Europos (*Feriale Duranum*), more than sixty fragments of Diocletian's Edict of Prices found in thirty-two different places, and the Sassanian inscription of Shapur I in the Kaaba of Zoroaster (Naksh-i-Rustam), which counterbalances equally propagandist Roman accounts of Romano-Persian hostilities and, in particular, the inscriptions on imperial Roman coins. For this is the epoch, above all others, in which the designs and circulation and mintage of coins (augmented by commemorative medallions) have a far-reaching significance which spans the fields of politics, publicity, war, economics, religion and art. Occasionally coins even depict and name self-styled Augusti and the relatives of Augusti whose very names are otherwise totally unknown.[15] "It is beyond doubt that in the coins lies a treasure, partly won, partly awaiting further study as a condition of its full exploitation; a treasure which, failing new discoveries of inscriptions or manuscripts, offers almost our only chance of penetrating the thick darkness that still envelops so much of the history of the third century."[16]

NOTES

1. Pertinax and Didius Julianus (Rome, 193), Pescennius Niger (east), Clodius Albinus (Gaul)
2. For the succession of emperors and their dates, see the list at the end of the book
3. For this office see p. 105
4. Maximinus I and his son Maximus Caesar, Gordianus I Africanus and his son Gordianus II Africanus (Carthage), Balbinus and Pupienus (Rome)
5. Trebonianus Gallus ruled 251–3, Aemilius Aemilianus 253
6. There were also short reigns of Quintillus (270), Tacitus (275–6), Florian (276)
7. Carinus and Numerian (283–4)
8. Including also Constantius I Chlorus (father of Constantine) (305–6), Severus II (306–7), and Maximian (attempted returns to throne, 306–8, 310)
9. A. H. M. Jones
10. E.g. we learn chiefly about Diocletian from Lactantius, who hated him
11. Johannes Xiphilinus
12. Dio LXXIII, 4, 2

13. Eusebius, *V. Const.*, contains imperial decrees and letters
14. Minutes of town-councils, official correspondence, military activities, tax records, wills, marriages, divorces, lawsuits, sales, leases, private letters and accounts
15. E.g. Uranius (Sulpicius) Antoninus II, Dryantilla, Cornelia Supera
16. H. Mattingly

PART II

The Later Roman State

2

The Military Achievement

Crisis within the Empire

Between the accession of Marcus Aurelius in A.D. 161 and the death of Constantine the Great in 337, approximately eighty men bore the title of emperor (Augustus), either at the capital or in some other part of the empire. Between 247 and 270 alone thirty emperors were proclaimed. Therein lay one of Rome's most grievous and expensive problems. Distinctions between emperors on the one hand, and usurpers or pretenders on the other hand, are misleading, for most of the emperors who managed to assert their claims to the throne were just as much usurpers or pretenders as those who failed to do so.

The old custom by which emperors were created by the senate had become a threadbare farce. Throughout the period that body, though still deeply respected, only made two or three attempts to take the lead in establishing the succession, in each case with exceedingly impermanent results.[1] For emperors were now almost invariably created by one of the armies. When the new Augustus had been acclaimed by his troops, he usually wrote to the senate informing them of his appointment and requesting senatorial approval. Under threat of coercion, the senate agreed, willingly or otherwise according to circumstances. The motives of the armies were selfish; they hoped for the huge gifts which on these occasions were extravagantly provided (p. 71). Since local recruitment was prevalent, they were stronger in parochial *esprit de corps* than in patriotism. Accordingly, with the backing of the large civilian populations of their areas, they declared new emperors with deplorable frequency; and the ruler whom they superseded was almost always killed.

This totally unstable situation regarding the succession paralysed the empire's defence system, with correspondingly grave results for its economy. There were constant, costly civil wars; time after time a military effort on the frontiers had to be called off because emperors felt obliged to defend or assert themselves against a rival Roman army commander. "What", as Herodian demanded, "was the use of barbarians being annihilated when greater slaughter took place in Rome itself and in the provinces?" Germans and Persians were, of course, well aware of this situation: how far they acted in collusion with one another is not known, but inevitably they exploited Rome's internal preoccupations.

On certain occasions, when the troops themselves took the initiative, the commanders had little alternative to assuming the purple, since refusal of the offer would have meant immediate assassination. Occasionally, too, a leader seized power in order to fulfil a local and urgent need to shore up a frontier. But nearly always the lure, however obviously impermanent, was the throne of the Augusti. The result is to be seen today in the extraordinarily large number of different persons portrayed on the coinage. For after a man had been declared emperor, wherever he might be, he had to reward his supporters by an immediate issue of money.

One of his early concerns thereafter was to try, usually in vain, to establish some arrangement about the succession to the throne, in the hope of creating confidence and warding off the almost inevitable blow. There were two ways of doing this. In the first place, like Septimius Severus, Philip, Decius, Valerian and many others, he could rapidly bring forward and promote his own son or sons or some other close relative, so that if the emperor himself died there might be a chance of a smooth take-over within the family. The armies, in theory, liked a dynastic succession of this kind, although their emotional loyalty to the heir often wore off quickly if he proved parsimonious, or too juvenile and inexperienced to make an effective commander. The senators, on the other hand, preferred a second method by which the ruler nominated and adopted a suitable, competent heir from outside the family. For then they could be consulted, and the man proposed for the succession would be some worthy member of their own order—whom they might continue to influence. This adoptive solution was scarcely available to men conducting rebellions on the frontiers. But in Rome, during the stable second century, such methods had been employed to produce four successive emperors of exceptional talent, the last of them being Marcus Aurelius. A century later, Diocletian was a convinced adherent of the doctrine that the emperor should ignore the claims of birth and choose the best man available as his heir, and his elaborate arrangement of the Tetrarchy was based on this principle. Yet the rulers of both periods were to a large extent making a virtue of necessity, owing to the lack of sons of their own; and in both periods again they took the precaution of bringing their adoptive heirs into their own families by marriage.[2]

After the first of these series of adoptions, Marcus Aurelius designated his son Commodus as his successor. Indeed, following the precedent by which he himself had possessed an imperial colleague (Lucius Verus), he even elevated the young man to be a fellow-Augustus, relying on experienced henchmen to support his claim to the succession. Commodus was the first ruler whose legitimacy and consequent divine favour were derived from his "birth in the purple". Coins and medallions stress his special *nobilitas*, and when he married in 177 his father issued a medallion dedicated to father and son alike as dynastic founders (PROPAGATORIBVS IMPERII). The youth turned out to be very erratic, or at least so anti-traditional that disaster was inevitable. But whether or not Marcus ought to have known that this would be so, the rejection of his son's claims in favour of someone else would almost certainly have involved one of the civil wars which were to proliferate so disastrously around future successions.

The murder of Commodus (192) created just such an occasion. The praetorian guard, recalling its initiatives in the previous century, sponsored two successive emperors who were both killed within five months.[3] But meanwhile the provincial armies were taking a hand, and, although the praetorian guard continued on occasion to seek the throne for its commanders,[4] this legionary initiative set the pattern for a century. In the Civil Wars of A.D. 68–9 the legions of Spain, Germany and Syria had put up their rival candidates. In 193 there were similar assertions by the armies of the Danube provinces, Syria and Britain.[5] After four years of bloodshed and expenditure, the Danubian candidate, Septimius Severus,[6] was victorious. On becoming established as emperor he took precautions against future usurpations (like his own) by limiting the total regular force under any one provincial governor to a maximum of two legions.

The Danubian armies were by far the largest in the empire, and during the recurrent civil strife of the third century it was their candidate, more often than not, who gained the throne. A turning-point was reached in 235 when a Danubian unit on the upper Rhine successfully proclaimed an ex-ranker from the area, Maximinus I. The Danube armies also put forward the usual quota of would-be rulers who failed to establish themselves.[7] But in addition to these a whole series of emperors who successfully asserted their claims were themselves Illyrians, originating from Danubian and Balkan territories. Decius, born in this area to a family of Italian origin, had a short reign full of disasters. But Claudius II Gothicus (268–270), Aurelian, Probus, Diocletian and Constantine, all of Danubian peasant family, were men of exceptional force and military talent who, against all probabilities, staved off the collapse of imperial defence (pp. 52ff).

The vital frontier provinces, which bound together the western and eastern parts of the empire, were Upper and Lower Pannonia, comprising eastern Austria, western Hungary and northern Yugoslavia. Farther east, Moesia extended to the mouth of the Danube. These were the regions which now produced not only the most able Roman emperors but the best Roman soldiers; and a great many of these soldiers served in the large armies which manned their own territories. Fortunately, they were filled with the frontiersman's intense Italian, Roman patriotism. They had in their hearts an image of eternal Rome as the inseparable associate of their own homeland—their defence of the Danube frontier simultaneously protected Italy and their own country.

In Pannonia, which supported the bulk of this responsibility, the process of Romanization had not extended very far beyond the upper class in the towns; and the territory was scarcely Hellenized at all. Before the Romans took over, it had already been launched on a modest economic development, and its artistic monuments continued to show strong regional characteristics. And yet the coinage of Decius, honouring the two Pannonias and the Genius of the Illyrian army, tells how conscious of their specific Roman role and contribution these peoples and soldiers had become. From their stock came few senators, but it produced the officers who were the most powerful element in the army, and with the backing of their compatriots some of them became outstanding emperors of Rome.

The Rhine armies were now smaller and less important than the armies of the Danube. But they had to meet terribly severe German raids (p. 52), and they felt neglected by Rome in favour of the Danube legions, and impeded from carrying out their vital task of defence. It seemed to these officers and soldiers, in a time of grave crisis, that the only solution was to have an emperor of their own. And so they supported Postumus, governor of one of the German provinces along the river, in a rebellion against Gallienus, whose son was put to death by Postumus at Colonia Agrippinensis (Cologne) (259/60). This revolt was only one among many, but it had particularly far-reaching repercussions. Postumus was joined not only by Gaul but by Britain and Spain, and for a time he even controlled parts of north Italy.[8] For fourteen years western Europe was a large separatist state, confronting Rome in a cold war which broke occasionally into open hostilities.

Gallienus issued gold medallions to his own officers and friends, explicitly on account of their loyalty against Postumus (OB FIDEM RESERVATAM). Postumus for his part inaugurated his coinage with a few specific references to German aspects of Hercules—whom he adopted as his divine patron—and with a description of himself as Restorer of the Gauls. This was aimed at increasing Gallic self-consciousness, but thereafter the coins show no trace of a nationalist policy; a later issue calls him Restorer of the World. Postumus saw himself as thoroughly Roman, and at Augusta Trevirorum (Trier)— one of the German business cities that had replaced cities farther from the front as political centres—he set up his own consuls and senate, independent from those of Rome. Racked by external and internal strains, the empire was breaking up into separate parts. Gallienus' coin-type "Peace Everywhere" and Postumus' traditional "Happiness of the Age" are both extraordinary examples of wishful thinking.

The uncomfortable dilemma of the central emperor was clearly illustrated by the concluding stages of his relationship with this Gallic empire. In order to hold Postumus off while at the same time maintaining readiness against external threats, Gallienus had set up a mobile strategic force at Mediolanum (p. 59). But this was such an impressive army that its general was a security hazard. Indeed, its very first commander, the capable Aureolus, deserted from Gallienus to Postumus, and was subsequently proclaimed emperor himself (268); and in the same year the next commander of the corps, Aurelian, was one of the leaders of a successful plot to murder Gallienus. An emperor could not command everywhere, and an effective military unit must mean a dangerous rival. The failure to find a solution to that internal problem was one of the principal reasons why the empire seemed doomed to succumb to its external enemies.

After Postumus' last successor Tetricus had come over to Aurelian during the decisive battle between their armies (274), there were unpleasant aftermaths of these troubles in Gaul. Under Probus two further revolts broke out. Moreover, as had also happened a century earlier, hordes of desperate and destitute men—expropriated peasants and fugitives, and the army deserters who had abounded for nearly a century—banded together under two chiefs who may have had wider ambitions (285–6).[9] These gangs were crushed by Diocletian's colleague Maximian. But immediately afterwards a more serious breakaway in the same western provinces almost repeated the pattern established by Postumus. Carausius, a naval officer of humble sailor origin from the lands of the Rhine-Scheldt estuary, was entrusted by Maximian with the defence of Britain against German pirates, but set himself up as independent emperor there instead (286/7–293/4).[10] He defeated Maximian and secured some measure of reluctant official recognition, which he celebrated on coinage showing himself as co-ruler of the whole empire. Carausius also temporarily controlled north-eastern France, but lost Gesoriacum (Boulogne) to Maximian's lieutenant Constantius I Chlorus, and was then killed and succeeded by his own chief minister Allectus. Three years later, Constantius brought Britain back into the empire.

Although Carausius, desiring to trade with Frisia and the Rhineland, struck a coin of much better silver than had been seen in the central empire for many years, this British separatist state, like the government of Postumus, favoured slogans which were pronouncedly Roman in style. Carausius was hailed as Restorer of Britain, but there is no nationalist sentiment. A very large proportion of his coins celebrate the Imperial Peace (PAX AVG.); and he was no doubt

34

proud of his ability to keep invaders out of Britain. Yet, even if such local rulers had their successes against the barbarians, these internal dissensions within the empire, requiring precautions and battles by one Roman army against another, could only add to the enormous and unprecedented burden of imperial defence.

The east, garrisoned by a Roman force second only to the Danube army in size and effectiveness, was not slow in putting forward emperors of its own choice. Avidius Cassius, governor of Syria and virtual ruler of the east, who at a time when such rebellions were unusual rebelled against Marcus (175), was the protégé of his Syrian compatriots in the eastern armies; and after that revolt the emperor indicated that in future no man should govern the province of his origin. Another Syrian nominee was Elagabalus (218–22). Thereafter a number of emperors were proclaimed by these eastern garrisons,[11] including Philip, who was himself the son of an Arabian sheikh (244). Further claimants were backed by the archers of Osrhoene (Mesopotamia), at home or on the other fronts where they were serving.[12]

But the most vigorous, longstanding and dangerous of these dissident movements was sponsored by that other recruiting-ground for eastern bowmen, the oasis city of Palmyra (Tadmor). Palmyra was strategically placed because it possessed valuable wells and access to a winter tributary of the Euphrates, and was located at a desert crossroads between Syria and Mesopotamia. By the first century B.C. it had captured the trade between those two countries, and was organizing and protecting caravan routes straight across the desert. Annexed by Rome in c. A.D. 17, the town was subsequently linked by road to the Euphrates (75), and throve on the collection of frontier dues. Since early in the second century it had been occupied by a strong Roman garrison. Septimius and his family staked a good deal on Palmyra. The place was raised to the status of a Roman colony, but the loss of military independence which this change officially entailed meant more rather than less power for Palmyra, since henceforward many of its quasi-autonomous formations of mounted archers were stationed not far from their own city, as important elements in the imperial forces along the Parthian frontier.

When Parthia was superseded by the more formidable Sassanian power (p. 41), the part played by Palmyra in the Roman defence system became indispensable. Psychologically, however, its role was equivocal. It is true that Palmyra favoured certain Greco-Syrian trappings of architecture and costume which looked towards the empire. But its vigorous artistic styles, with their rigid hieratic frontality foreshadowing Byzantium, show a more natural orientation towards Parthian and Sassanian Babylonia and the urban centres of that country, such as Seleucia (Tell Omar) which stood on the Tigris opposite the capital of Ctesiphon (S.E. of Baghdad) and was the third greatest city in the world. Artistic parallels to Palmyra are also to be found farther east still, for example at Shami in the Persian mountains north of Susa.

So, culturally at least, Palmyra was more closely related to the eastern than to the western power. Another reason for good relations with the Sassanians was political: namely their new domination of the river mouths on the Persian Gulf, which endangered Palmyrene trade. So when Shapur I overran Rome's eastern provinces and captured Valerian (p. 43), the chieftain of Palmyra Odenathus (Odainath) made approaches to the invader (c. 260). But Odenathus encountered a contemptuous rebuff. This was one of Shapur's mistakes which, despite all his successes, he had good reason to regret. For henceforward Odenathus staunchly supported the Romans. Indeed, in the desperate situation in which Gallienus found himself, the defence of the whole region was very soon in Odenathus' hands. Supported by his Palmyrene and Osrhoenian archers and by heavy cavalry, he was even strong enough to advance upon the Persian capital and then to repeat the attempt. The vacuum created by Rome's preoccupations elsewhere gave Palmyra the opportunity to assert its control from the Taurus mountains to the Red Sea. Moreover, Odenathus was virtually in charge of the entire Roman armies of the east. As a challenge to Persia, he was even allowed by Gallienus to call himself King of Kings.[13] Moreover, to the annoyance of Roman provincial governors—who regarded him as a barbarian—he was also awarded the titles of Corrector of the Orient, Leader of the Romans and *Imperator*.

But then Odenathus, turning back from Babylonia to face a Gothic invasion of Asia Minor, was murdered (266/7); and his gifted and erudite widow Zenobia (Bat Zabbai), with the leading Greco-Syrian scholar Cassius Longinus as her chief minister,[14] set out to achieve total independence. Indicating her admiration for Cleopatra, she seized Egypt, and most of Asia Minor fell into her hands.[15] Zenobia's possessions extended from Mesopotamia to a point almost within reach of Europe. Then, either just before or just after the accession of Aurelian (270), she disclosed her new plans. Although anti-Roman elements must have been in the ascendant at Palmyra, her son, who had inherited his father's titles, was in Roman fashion declared *Augustus*, and she herself became *Augusta*. Even the Palmyra that now, as a new power, refused to serve Rome any longer could not get clear of the Roman track on which it had so long been running.[16]

When Aurelian was seen to have accepted the challenge, Zenobia's propaganda attempted a last minute compromise: her coins give her son his old titles only, and show Aurelian on the other side. But it was too late for such diplomacy, for Aurelian, proclaiming himself Restorer of the East, recaptured Asia Minor and Egypt, and defeated the queen's leading general outside Antioch and Emesa. Palmyra itself fell to him, rebelled, and fell again. Zenobia, together with Tetricus (the last break-away ruler of the west), was kept to walk in golden chains in Aurelian's Triumph. Her city was devastated. To the inconvenience of Rome, which now had to do the work of the caravan police, Palmyra relapsed into the desert village it once had been, until Diocletian made it into an important centre again (p. 139).

Between the years 266 and 274 the Roman empire had been divided into three independent parts, with separate rulers at Augusta Trevirorum in the west and Palmyra in the east, while the metropolitan emperor controlled only what lay between the two. Although the western and eastern rulers made contributions to external defence, their threat to the central power seemed to Aurelian, even at a time when every effort was needed on the frontiers, to necessitate his expensive expeditions, first against Zenobia, and then against Tetricus. When reunification had with great difficulty been achieved, he at last set out against Persia, which had fortunately been suffering from internal dissensions and therefore did little to help Zenobia. But on the way, like so many before and after him, he succumbed to the dagger of an assassin.

There had been many earlier rebellions and usurpations, and they continued, particularly in Egypt where Greek or Hellenized writers had long been attacking Rome's injustice, tyranny, avarice, weakness and bad government, calling its emperors uncultured, lecherous Jew-lovers.[17] But in many other provinces, too—and often without any such anti-Roman overtones—similar accounts of subversions and fleeting imperial aspirations could be recorded. Few territories were without their own splinter movements and candidates for the throne. This chaotic, anarchic situation, which Diocletian sought to prevent by doubling the number of provinces and multiplying *official* emperors (pp. 95–6), was a paralysing handicap the Roman government had to suffer inside its frontiers, while simultaneously facing outwards in order to shoulder the massive and ever-increasing burden of the military activity conceived necessary in the interests of imperial defence.

Crisis on the Frontiers

Defence measures were needed on many borders, but the only major foreign power among Rome's enemies had long been its eastern neighbour. Until the third century A.D. semi-feudal Iranian Parthia, under its ruling house the Arsacids, controlled Iraq and Persia and, more loosely, some of the lands to Persia's north and east. The Parthians adjoined the Roman empire along the Euphrates, and this region, too near the Mediterranean for comfort, was the most sensitive part of Rome's oriental frontier.[18]

Although actual hostilities, accompanied as they were by vast expense, only occupied about one-sixth of the time, the relations between the two empires were perpetually strained. The Parthians raided Syria, and Rome, where there was always a militaristic party urging emperors to behave like Alexander the Great, launched a considerable number of invasions into Parthian territory. Sometimes these were disastrous; at Carrhae (Haran) Crassus lost his army and his life (53 B.C.). Sometimes, on the other hand, the expeditions appeared to be successful. For example Trajan captured the Parthian capital Ctesiphon and Seleucia across the Tigris (A.D. 115) (and even presented the Parthians with a monarch, REX PARTHIS DATVS, p. 39). But such successes, though very costly in men and money, were always short-lived in their effects. The only lasting solution would have been the total destruction of one of these powers by the other, and this was beyond the bounds of military and financial possibility.

The general aim of Roman policy was to control the northern dependencies of Parthia. For a long time the major bone of contention was the huge mountainous land of Armenia, which without clearly defined frontiers extended to the north of Mesopotamia as far as the Caucasus, while its western flanks around the upper Euphrates adjoined the extremities of the Roman empire. Each of the two empires, for centuries, invaded Armenia and fomented internal revolutions there, so as to have a puppet monarch who would serve its policy and prestige; and each also continued to feel that an Armenia belonging to the other was a dagger pointing at its own heart. But in spite of all these exertions neither side ever achieved its purpose for more than fleeting durations. Diplomatic settlements, such as those attempted by Augustus and Nero, had to be cautiously handled, because important sections of public and aristocratic and military opinion in Rome required not an equal settlement but victory. The designs of imperial coins make it clear that glory weighed more heavily than practical advantage. Indeed, an emperor who proved unable or unwilling to pursue large-scale frontier warfare might soon be killed by his own side, as the fates of at least three emperors showed.[19] And so attempts at a diplomatic solution were rare, cautious and impermanent in their results.

Meanwhile it was becoming evident to Roman leaders that the key to the conquest of the Armenian highlands and to the elimination of Parthia as a major power was Mesopotamia. By this was meant not the whole land between the Euphrates and Tigris but its north-western region, which now comprises parts of Iraq and Asiatic Turkey. That area, which had been colonized extensively by the heirs of Alexander the Great, formed an important political and commercial link between Syria and the deserts beyond. Furthermore, its occupation would enable Roman forces, first, to advance half-way to the leading Parthian cities without leaving their own possessions, and secondly to invade Armenia from two sides instead of from one. Accordingly Trajan annexed the country as a new province of Mesopotamia, and took over Armenia, not in accordance with normal policy as a puppet kingdom, but as a further Roman province. This convinced imperialist also annexed Assyria (Adiabene) beyond the Tigris, and gave the southern part of the land between the rivers a puppet "King of the Parthians". His intention was that these should be protective outpost areas beyond the main lines of defence. But when Trajan died, Hadrian decided that such annexations were no solution to the problem, and reverted to the old idea of a buffer state of Armenia ruled by a pro-Roman monarch. Another client-king was to be supported on the throne of Mesopotamian Edessa (Urfa), the capital of Osrhoene immediately beyond the Euphrates. Hadrian may have been right to decide that the permanent control of Mesopotamia would be too expensive to be practicable. For Parthians could move upstream to invade the area with the protection of the desert on their right, but it was hard for Romans, who were not in possession of the Persian mountain ranges beyond, to maintain the occupation of such a province. Nevertheless, since Hadrian did not feel able to relinquish control altogether, his decision meant a reversion to the constant nagging warfare of previous centuries.

When Parthia launched one of its periodical *coups d'état* in Armenia, the governor of Marcus Aurelius' Anatolian frontier province Cappadocia was defeated and killed, and Marcus felt obliged to send his colleague Lucius Verus to direct a series of large-scale campaigns (163–6). As before, the Parthian capital met with destruction, and Edessa was re-established as a protectorate. It was probably at this stage that the Romans captured, fortified and garrisoned Dura (Salahiye), situated on the Euphrates a little below its tributary the Khabur. This originally Greek but now largely Parthianized town, a melting-pot of many languages and artistic styles, now became the southern frontier post of Rome's Mesopotamian province.[20] However ultimately inconclusive, the fighting had at least brought a peace which lasted for nearly thirty years.

Hostilities broke out again when the Parthians, profiting by Roman civil war, invaded Mesopotamia in 195. Three years later the Romans, under Septimius, sacked the enemy capital yet again, and, although he could not capture the Arab desert-fortress of Hatra, the province of Mesopotamia was reannexed. At least four settlements of Roman ex-soldiers were planted in order to hold the region down. The historian Dio Cassius, though no enemy to Septimius, criticized these expensive efforts at conquest.[21] But Caracalla, obsessed by a desire to rival Alexander the Great, took the opposite view. These ambitions also gave him the idea, original for a Roman emperor, of marrying the daughter of the Parthian king, Artabanus V. But that monarch did not fancy the suggestion, which consequently became one of history's might-have-beens. Caracalla reverted to the usual plans for conquest, assisted, in this case, by the kidnapping of the kings both of Edessa and of Armenia. Caracalla crossed the Tigris into Assyria, but before the campaign could develop further he was murdered (217). His successor Macrinus presented the Armenian diadem to Parthia's nominee; this was so pacific and sensible that it probably contributed to his desertion by his own troops, and subsequent execution.

But now there occurred, to Rome's lasting disadvantage, one of the decisive events of the age. During the previous century Parthia had been declining in strength. The process was accelerated by its warfare against Rome, and particularly by the invasion of Septimius.[22] Such recurrent crises weakened the hold of the Parthians over their feudal dependencies. Among these was Persepolis, whose prince Ardashir (Artaxerxes), ruler of a large area extending from the Persian Gulf to Isfahan, now invaded Parthia and overthrew Artabanus V,[23] setting up throughout the entire empire his own Sassanian dynasty, named after his grandfather Sassan (223/6).

The capital of the new régime was still Ctesiphon, but its holy city was at ancestral Istakhr near Persepolis. Nearly eight centuries earlier, when the glorious Achaemenid Persians had displaced the Medes, the centre of power had shifted from northern Iranian tribes to southern princes; and now the pattern repeated itself. Sassanians were eager to emphasize this ancient inheritance, and yet their institutions and culture also took over a great deal from their immediate Parthian predecessors. But the new state was far more formidable than Parthia. In spite of continuing Greek influences, the abandonment of Greek models for the new empire-wide coinage was a sign of intensely nationalistic policies.[24] Centralization was greatly increased, both in the powerful, intolerant state church and in the government. The Sassanian monarchs built up a stable bureaucracy and, while respecting the ancient families, created a new and powerful class of lesser nobles directly dependent on the crown.

Establishing closer and more fruitful relations with the peoples of outer Iran, they saved the Greco-Roman world from the nomad hordes compelled to remain outside their far-off northern and eastern frontiers. Like the Romans, they were subject to barbarian pressures on their borders; and like them again, they were from time to time immobilized by internal dissensions. Nevertheless their heightened efficiency confronted Rome with a military threat at least as dangerous as anything that the very largest concentrations of Germans could provide, and probably more perilous still because of superior Persian co-ordination. For the Sassanian army, reinforcing the traditional mail-clad horsemen by recruitment from new nobles, was the most up-to-date attacking force of the age. The Romans paid it the compliment of imitation (p. 59), but they had lost the chance either of reducing their eastern neighbour to insignificance or of bringing it to a workable settlement. Rome's eastern military activities, hitherto something of a luxury, had now become a grimly urgent and immensely expensive necessity.

For the Sassanians were not only powerful; they were also aggressively inclined to expansion. Claiming the restoration of the ancient Persian frontiers, they interpreted this to require the absorption of all Roman territory as far west as the Aegean sea. Such was the menace which the young Severus Alexander, by no means a military expert, had to encounter. Although the desert fortress of Hatra, which was now garrisoned by Roman troops,[25] held out against the Sassanians, Ardashir overran Mesopotamia (230), and there were mutinies among Rome's eastern garrisons. Severus Alexander attempted an ambitious three-pronged invasion. Suffering severe casualties from the climate, his armies were less than successful. Yet their losses were matched by Persia's, and the Mesopotamian province was temporarily reannexed. But only six years later, in the time of Maximinus I, it was overrun again, and Nisibis (Nüsaybin) and Carrhae fell into Persian hands.

The full, unprecedented burden which would now fall upon Roman armies began to be clear when Shapur I (Sapor)(? 239–70) was crowned with the provocative title of "King of Kings of Iran and non-Iran". Next to Hannibal, Shapur was the most dangerous enemy Rome ever had. In addition to yearly raids into the Roman provinces, he launched three major campaigns, the first in the time of Gordian III (242/4), the second at some date between 250 and 256, and the third which brought the reign of Valerian to an end (259 or 260). Shapur's account of what happened, engraved in three languages at Naksh-i-Rustam near Persepolis,[26] differs from anything we learn from the scrappy accounts of Greek or Roman writers. But his claim to have captured thirty-seven cities is probably justified. The Mesopotamian towns that fell into his hands included Carrhae, Nisibis (?*c.* 254), Dura (255/8),[27] Edessa (*c.* 260) and Hatra. Shapur recorded a major victory over the Romans at Barbalissus south-east of Aleppo. Moreover, not only Mesopotamia but also Armenia was lost to Rome. Shapur even captured Antioch, certainly once and possibly twice,[28] and in retaliation for Trajan's "king given to the Parthians" he set up a puppet Roman emperor there. He even took Caesarea (Kayseri) in Cappadocia, devastating both Asia Minor and Syria with a roughness which suggests that, despite his claims, he did not intend their permanent annexation. This ferocity discouraged the enemies of Rome from welcoming Shapur's leadership. Although he was reputed to be brave, liberal and interested in the things of the mind and spirit, he made mistakes; another was his rejection of the proffered assistance of his strongest potential ally in the region, Palmyra (p. 36).

Five Persian reliefs carved on the mountainside of Fars shows three Roman emperors in various degrees of defeat and degradation.[29] Roman coins, on the other hand, continued at intervals to report victories. But the young Gordian III, as unqualified for warfare as Severus Alexander before him, lost his life in Mesopotamia during a Persian campaign (244). Shapur, on one of his monuments, shows Gordian in a prostrate position, implying he fell in battle; or his own troops may have lynched him. There was also a strong suspicion that Philip, his praetorian prefect and successor, was responsible for his death. In any case Philip did not fight on. He arranged to retain the Mesopotamian province, but tacitly abandoned Armenia and paid Shapur a considerable sum of money. Although there were advantages in this course, Mesopotamia was not easy to hold without Armenia, and it was a penalty of diplomacy that the Persians chose to regard his action as implying recognition of their claims; the relief which shows Gordian as fallen displays Philip as a suppliant. But far worse was the fate of Valerian, who fell into Shapur's hands. The traditional story tells of a Persian trap, though there remains the alternative possibility that he was taking refuge from his own mutinous army. Together with many soldiers who were settled by the Persians and made to work for them, Valerian remained permanently their prisoner. This event, the most inglorious in all Roman history, is emphasized over and over again in Persian propaganda. Valerian's son Gallienus either did not succeed in rescuing him or did not try. His father's name and memory were obliterated from the records.

After the death of Shapur, the Sassanians retained Armenia and Mesopotamia, but internal troubles caused their impetus to weaken. For example, they took little effective advantage of Palmyra's break-away from Roman rule (p. 37). When Palmyra had been brought to heel, the emperor Carus recaptured the Mesopotamian province and seized the enemy capital, but soon succumbed to lightning or more probably conspiracy (283). Then the Persian king Narses (293–302) declared war against Rome, defeated Diocletian's lieutenant Galerius, and recovered Mesopotamia.[30] However, a subsequent important victory by Galerius in Armenia, which resulted in the capture of Narses' wives, forced the Persians to abandon the newly gained territory and sue for peace. The treaty confirmed Rome's claim to the region, not quite as far as the precarious old southern frontier of Dura but down to Circesium (near Bassira), which still remained the border in Mohammedan times. The Romans had temporarily regained the superiority, and Narses was obliged to recognize their spheres of influence in Armenia and the Caucasian lands to its north.

Still, however, the settlement was not permanent. The old tug of war was renewed, though now with the larger Roman forces which the strength of the Sassanian power necessitated. Shapur II (310–79), a strong monarch after a period of internal confusion, was provoked by Armenia's conversion to Christianity into occupying the country, but soon lost it again to a young relative whom Constantine placed on the Armenian throne. But this new policy of keeping the country directly under the imperial dynasty was not successful, and the struggle over both Armenia and Mesopotamia continued. Armenia was partitioned (384/7), but in the seventh century each territory fell to the Moslem Arabs, who succeeded to the control of Sassanian Iran and of the eastern parts of the Byzantine empire—gravely weakened as they were by a relationship of cold war, sometimes breaking into open hostilities, that had lasted for seven centuries.

The frontier was heavily guarded. Along the desert border, which ran through Palmyra and Bostra to Petra, Diocletian built or reconstructed powerful forts with square towers and posterns, served

44

by new roads and arms factories.[31] Farther to the north also, where the land between the great rivers was divided between Romans and Sassanians, there were powerful Roman defences. A massive earthwork extended, with some interruptions, for 470 miles. The Persian side, too, had elaborate fortifications; this was a sealed-off barrier between two worlds. And yet the peoples on either side of the boundary had a great deal in common—and wherever the line was fixed the same would have been true. Indeed the emperor and king themselves would have recognized many similarities in the elaborate etiquettes of one another's courts, and during rare moments of comparative friendliness they spoke of one another as Brothers. Yet each side rejected peaceful relations (with their possibilities of a luxury trade that Palmyra, Petra and Alexandria would have welcomed), in favour of the prolonged confrontation.

While the Parthians were ruling, there had been an element of the war-game in this; campaigns trained the Roman troops and gave the emperors honorific titles and applause. But when the Sassanian monarchy came to power, the war-game turned to deadly earnest. Even after Rome's traumatic experiences at the hands of Shapur I had subsided into the old bickering for Armenia and Mesopotamia, the fact that the enemy had become so much more powerful cost the Romans, for evermore, huge and unprecedented sums, both in ordinary everyday defence and in the much larger expeditionary forces which were periodically needed to maintain and stabilize the position.

These were the largest armies which Rome ever mustered. In order to attain such a size, they had to be supplemented by troops from the northern frontiers. But whenever an emperor felt obliged to call such forces away from the Danube and the Rhine, the tribes beyond those rivers could take advantage of their withdrawal and confront the Romans with war upon two fronts at once.

Apart from two advanced bulges or bastions—the Agri Decumates beyond and between upper Rhine and upper Danube, and Dacia on the other side of the lower Danube—the principal northern boundary of the empire consisted of those two rivers.[32] Facing the easterly reaches of the border were independent Dacians, a people of Thracian origin, and tribes belonging to the large Iranian group of the Sarmatians—effective archers, and creators of the superb

45

animal art of the steppes which is particularly evident in this area. Beyond almost all other points on the frontier, as also in many regions within its limits, the inhabitants were Germans. These were to be found across the whole western length of the river barrier, from Aquincum (Budapest) to the mouth of the Rhine.

The principal gods of the Germans were concerned with war. Yet these peoples were also familiar with agriculture and stock-raising[33], and, although lacking in town-life and liable to internal dissensions, had worked out orderly systems of administration which gradually reached a certain size. Such governments were controlled by kings or groups of leaders, who were more or less dependent on the Assembly (*Thing*) of their tribe. Tacitus expressed the view that the freedom of the Germans was a deadlier enemy to Rome than the despotism of the Parthians. But this menace only became serious during the second century A.D., when the German tribes began to show themselves capable of co-ordinating their activities in larger confederations or coalitions. A good deal of gold came into their hands, partly from individuals who had served Rome, partly through cross-border trading relationships, and partly because the Romans liked their frontiers to be fringed by a *cordon sanitaire* of semi-dependent states which they were prepared, despite the unpopularity of this course in certain circles at home, to subsidize.

At first, the critical area for the Romans had been the Rhine boundary. In the second century A.D. the danger-point was the Danube, which now had a garrison of ten Roman legions compared with four on the Rhine. Restlessness across the river came to a head in the time of Marcus Aurelius, causing a series of events which permanently transformed the empire. For during a long period of relative stability, the numbers of the Germans had outgrown their partial simple agricultural techniques. They were land-hungry and wanted to abandon their marshy forest clearings for richer country within the frontier. This was the first time that German tribes had been covetous of Roman territory in order to settle there themselves. Furthermore, the frontier peoples were now under pressure from the other side. In the depths of the north, there were convulsive movements of population, and huge groups of tribes that had lived round the Baltic were on the trek towards the lower Danube frontiers where Sarmatians and free Dacians now dwelt.

When the storm first broke in *c.* A.D. 166, the initiative was taken by the Marcomanni of Bohemia (Czechoslovakia), who traded more extensively with the world of Rome than any of their compatriots, and were also more influenced by its social structure. In the protruding re-entrant between Danube and Tisza (now part of Hungary and Yugoslavia) which did not belong to Rome, a branch of the Sarmatians likewise moved to the attack.[34] This was a collusive general threat, and it was not unexpected; the onslaught had long been staved off by local Roman officials. But because of major fighting in the east the response of Rome was delayed for too long (p. 39).

The fighting in Marcus Aurelius' region was more serious than anything of the kind that had occurred before, and it continued, under the emperor's personal direction, for most of the remaining fourteen years of his life. The chronology of the campaigns is obscure, but they included two disasters which, according to one interpretation, both took place in the single year A.D. 170. In the first place, the Germans broke through into the upper Danubian provinces (Raetia, Noricum) and into the middle Danube area where flat land on the Roman side presented favourable ground for attackers. Crossing the Alps into Italy, they burnt the town of Opitergium (N.E. of Venice) and laid siege to Aquileia. Secondly, and perhaps almost simultaneously, a German tribe from the Carpathian region surged across the lower Danube and penetrated most of the Balkan peninsula very nearly as far as Athens, for they even plundered Eleusis.[35] Marcus' armies, incapacitated by plague brought back from the east, gradually and painfully regained control, in a long series of campaigns which created an almost desperate financial emergency.

Marcus now had two principal ideas for dealing with the situation. One was to admit large numbers of Germans into the empire as settlers. This would mean that pressure on the frontiers was diminished. The immigrants would also be able to cultivate land which, owing to the inadequacy of its own agricultural populations, was going to waste. And they would be available for recruitment into the army. This importation of northern tribesmen into the empire was not a new concept; Augustus may likewise have pacified a disturbed frontier by admitting 50,000 barbarians, and Nero seems to have settled twice that number. But from the time of Marcus the process became more systematic. The settlers, under special supervisory officials, ranked for many purposes as free men, but they were assigned to Roman proprietors or the leaseholders of imperial domains, and legally tied to their plots of land. The emperors who initiated arrangements of such kinds have been accused of barbarizing the empire. But these resettlements broke down racialism, and provided cultivators and soldiers whom the later empire needed in order to survive.

Marcus' other solution involved annexation. He intended to occupy the Danube–Tisza re-entrant and neighbouring territories and convert them into a new province of Sarmatia, thus shortening and strengthening the frontier, which would then rest upon the long line of the Carpathians. He also proposed to annex Bohemia, together with parts of Moravia and Slovakia, as a second new province called Marcomannia. This would have replaced a long section of the river boundary by the more defensible Sudeten mountains, in continuation of the Carpathian line. Such a move would also have prepared the way for additional future annexations making the total length of the frontier shorter still. With the same idea in mind, Augustus too had wanted to conquer Bohemia, as part of a plan to replace the Rhine–Danube frontier by a less elongated Elbe–Danube line which would have brought the most dangerous of the Germans into the empire.

Augustus had failed, and so did Marcus. His first endeavour to carry out the plan had to be postponed because of rebellion in the east (175),[36] and a second attempt was cut short by his death. Perhaps advised by the Bithynian Saoterus to whom these regions must have seemed alien and unattractive, Marcus' young son and successor Commodus, subject to various agreed conditions for peaceful German behaviour, abandoned the whole scheme. Pursuance of his father's policy might have transformed the entire future of central Europe by giving the empire more defensible frontiers and many able German cultivators and defenders; and Marcus showed his Romanizing intentions when he refused to allow a large group, on whose land he had designs, to emigrate northwards into territories beyond his reach (179).[37] On the other hand the conquests would have enormously increased the imperial burden of organization, development and defence. And so Commodus and his counsellors decided that annexation was impracticable. This decision was deplored by writers who hated the new emperor and liked aggression, but further annexations might well have brought more problems than they would have solved, and the expense was more than the imperial resources, already stretched to the uttermost, could afford.

However, conditions on the northern frontier remained unsettled, and during the next decades there was pressure from the free Dacians living beyond the lower Danube, who had been disturbed by Marcus' displacements of German tribes.[38]

Then, under Caracalla, a particularly serious danger came from the more westerly region of the Agri Decumates, in which upper Danube and upper Rhine are close to one another. Here, again as a result of Marcus' wars, various tribes and portions of tribes had coalesced into a new sort of formidably close-knit federation known as the Alamanni (Alle Männer), who have given their name to the French word for Germany today. After migrating westwards from Brandenburg under pressure from tribes in the heart of Europe, they now threatened the upper Danube–upper Rhine re-entrant. Caracalla, favouring the methods of treachery and encouraging trouble between one German tribe and another, defeated them on the river Main. Yet he also set a new fashion by liking the Germans. He wore their clothes (*Caracalla*, his nickname, means a German or Celtic cloak), and his murder was attributed, rightly or wrongly, to his preference for the German soldiers who were now playing an important part in the imperial armies.

Caracalla also conveyed extensive subsidies, in gold coin, to the German tribes across the frontiers. This policy, although it may well have been cheaper than fighting, was much criticized, and this criticism had its dangers. For when the young Severus Alexander, after weakening the frontier garrisons to provide reinforcements for the east, proceeded to Moguntiacum (Mainz) and tried to buy off German aggressors, his penalty for not striking a warlike figure was death at the hands of his own troops (235). His successor Maximinus I, himself a Danubian popular in certain circles beyond the frontiers, re-established peace along the Rhine and upper Danube. But his subsequent expeditions farther east, against the Sarmatians and Dacians, were immobilized by the civil wars that ended in his assassination (238).

The situation in this area, already productive of anxiety, now sharply deteriorated owing to the appearance of new German peoples more formidable than any that had been seen before. The dwellers beyond the lower Danube frontier had for some time been under increasing pressure from remoter areas beyond. For groups of tribes that lived round the Baltic had gradually been journeying towards the Danubian areas inhabited by Sarmatians and free Dacians; and so came the Goths. The long southward treks of this easternmost of the Teutonic peoples was to be celebrated throughout the ages in Germanic national sagas. During their migrations from Scandinavia in about the first century B.C. they had reached the lower reaches of the river Vistula, and at some date after *c*. A.D. 100 they started moving south-west.[39] Now, under pressure from Sarmatians in their rear, they were establishing themselves not far from the mouth of the Danube. During their travels and settlements in the Black Sea region they had acquired some Greco–Sarmatian culture and political cohesion, which they gradually transmitted to other Germans. Moreover, the Goths, though weak in tactics and siegecraft, were receptive to many Roman military techniques.[40]

In the 230s they began to burst across the lower Danubian frontier. Their first incursions may have occurred during the reign of Severus Alexander. At all events they crossed the river in 238, and were granted a subsidy by Rome. However, under Philip this was not or could not be paid any longer, and the angry Goths, tempted by Roman civil dissension and usurpation,[41] crossed the river again and surged forward as far as the key city of Marcianopolis (Provadiya, west of Varna), which barely managed to hold out against them (248). Philip's general Decius quelled invasions and mutinies with sufficient success to induce his troops to declare him emperor. But Decius' reconstruction of the Danube defences proved inadequate, for in Kniva the Goths had a leader of unprecedented calibre, whose large-scale strategy created the gravest perils the empire had yet undergone. Philippopolis (Plovdiv), far inside the empire, was captured by the Goths, and its population exterminated. Then, at Abrittus in the Dobrogea, the emperor himself fell to Kniva, probably with the aid of treachery from Gallus who became his successor (251).

And so in the north, as in the east, an enemy had appeared whose threat to the empire reduced all previous frontier activity, in retrospect, to something scarcely serious. These two menacing hostile forces on either flank took advantage of each other's activities; so that Rome was faced, for an indefinite period, with the gigantic expense and peril of a war on two fronts. For a time, this proved beyond any emperor's powers; and catastrophes on the Persian frontiers were matched by simultaneous unprecedented disasters at the hands of the Germans. They came in greater numbers, and at more numerous points, and with better organization, than ever before, and for a time they could not be withstood. While plague and internal strife raged in the empire, and the Persians overran the orient, the Goths, now joined by another east German people the Burgundians, plundered not only the Balkans but Asia Minor, as far south as Ephesus and as far east as the central plateau (253). Moreover the Goths, obtaining ships from the Greek cities on the Black Sea, embarked successfully on naval incursions which devastated important centres of civilization such as Chalcedon (Kadiköy). Moreover, ranging much farther afield, they even sacked Trapezus (Trabzon) on the Black Sea and Panticapaeum (Kerch) in the Crimea, with disastrous effects on future Roman agricultural supplies.[42]

Other northern tribes joined in the onslaught along the whole length of the frontier. Among them were the Franks, a formidable confederacy welded together from various small groups which population movements round the lower Elbe had propelled forward against the Rhine barrier. Repeatedly attacking in compact units of about 30,000 men each, Franks broke through the Roman defences and overran Gaul and Spain, destroying Tarraco (Tarragona) and raiding as far as the north African coast.

Since one man could not face both ways at once, the imperial armies were now divided between two commands, anticipating the later divisions between eastern and western empires.[43] Valerian assumed command against the Persians and his son Gallienus took charge of the west and north. Valerian perished, but Gallienus lived and fought on. Nevertheless, the pressure of invasions and the consequent breakaway of the western provinces under Postumus (p. 33) caused the frontier-line, at one important point, to be overrun by the Germans and evacuated by Rome. This was in the region of the Agri Decumates, linking upper Rhine and upper Danube. The abandoned area was never recovered, and the Rhine was henceforward the frontier from its mouth right down to Lake Constance (*c*. 259–60).[44] Although neither Gallienus nor Postumus were able to recapture this prong of potentially hostile territory, Postumus succeeded in keeping the Franks and Alamanni out of the rest of Gaul. Gallienus displayed more imaginative ideas. He appears to have authorized the Marcomanni of Bohemia to form a state, or part of one, on the Roman side of the frontier; and he even contracted some sort of a secondary marriage with the daughter of their chief (*c*. 260).

But soon Gallienus, now sole emperor, was faced with equally perilous German threats farther to the east. Utilizing the Heruli, recent arrivals in the Black Sea area, as their sailors, the Goths mustered unparalleled numbers of warriors and ships at the mouth of the Dniester (268). Greece and Asia Minor alike were yet again devastated. The course of events is obscure, largely because writers who disliked Gallienus preferred that credit should instead go to his successor. But it seems to have been Gallienus whom the invaders encountered as they were seeking to return home by the Balkan land-route; he cut off their retreat and won the bloodiest battle of the third century at Naissus (Niš), killing 50,000 of the enemy.[45] Thereupon the emperor reverted to the less traditional form of treatment, with which he had been experimenting earlier, by awarding the insignia of a Roman consul to the Herulian prince who had surrendered. But treachery behind the lines prevented the exploitation of Gallienus' victory, for he was stabbed to death by his own officers.

Yet a start had been made with the extraordinary effort by Rome which, against all likelihood, subjected the Germans to a series of overwhelming set-backs. When the Alamanni struck into Italy itself, Claudius II (268–70) crushed them at Lake Benacus (Garda), and then defeated the Goths in further engagements important enough to earn him the name of Gothicus.[46] Their expulsion from the empire was completed by Aurelian. Nevertheless other Germans were still pouring through the Brenner Pass into Italy. But they too, after winning an initial victory, were overwhelmed by Aurelian in two battles fought at Fanum Fortunae (Fano) and near Ticinum (Pavia) (271); and prisoners of war and their families were distributed among the owners of abandoned vineyards in Etruria. Farther east, however, Aurelian decided that the heavily infiltrated trans-Danubian province of Dacia was untenable, and he evacuated the whole region permanently (*c.* 271), thus shortening and strengthening the frontier.[47]

A few years later Probus had to meet a huge three-fold German invasion of Gaul (276–7). After dealing with it in spectacular fashion, he moved farther east to confront the Vandals, troublesome German settlers in eastern Hungary who had now invaded the Balkans. Probus revived on a massive scale the policy of settling northern barbarians on Roman territory. And yet, in spite of these concessions, and although the land-hunger of others was relieved by the Agri Decumates and Dacia which Rome had abandoned, the attacks of the Germans did not slacken for long. Tacitus (275–6) was faced with a new invasion of Asia Minor, and Maximian twice had to push back onslaughts upon Gaul. He crossed the Rhine, and, after victories won by his lieutenant Constantius I, was able to advance to the North Sea; a Frankish king was established as a bulwark between Rome and Germany (288). In the following decade Galerius was equally successful against both Marcomanni and Sarmatians, and then Constantine had to deal with Franks and Alamanni (306, 328). At the eastern end of the frontier, too, he built a stone wall from Cernavoda on the Danube to Tomis (Constanţa) on the Black Sea (replacing the former earth wall), and with the help of these fortifications the Goths, who had now become prominent again, were heavily defeated (334).

Constantine freely enrolled and promoted Germans, who henceforward provided most of his soldiers and generals (p. 62)—in this sense the German frontier menace had exercised a regenerative effect on Rome. He also continued the policy of importing tribesmen into the empire to farm depopulated areas. He won peace for a generation, but after 350, profiting by attempts of Roman civil war contestants to enlist their help, the Franks and Alamanni won permanent footholds on the Roman bank of the Rhine. Then the shattering defeat of Valens by the Goths (Visigoths) at Hadrianopolis (Edirne) irremediably threw open the Balkan provinces to their settlers.[48] From now on more and more German states in treaty relations with Rome established themselves within the frontiers. Indeed these barriers themselves rapidly became obliterated, and by the time Alaric the Visigoth, turning aside from the less vulnerable eastern empire, put Rome to the sack (410), the line had almost

53

ceased to exist. The German tribes were already beginning to form Europe's kingdoms of the future.

And yet, with only minor withdrawals, those frontiers had been astonishingly held for over a hundred and fifty years after the first terrible Gothic invasions and the destruction, chaos and defeat that they brought; and so the conditions were created by which the classical heritage, instead of collapsing in anarchy, could be conserved and handed on. Rather than enquiring why the Roman empire fell, commented Gibbon, we should feel surprised that it had endured so long. For example, in the continuous peril of the 250s and 260s, amid simultaneous catastrophes from uniquely powerful enemies upon two fronts, there seemed no probability that the world of Rome would survive. Yet it weathered the storm. The turning-point appears to have come in the last year of Gallienus, and then three Illyrian emperors, all commanders of genius, brought about a gradual process of recovery. This was the climax of Roman arms and stamina, and one of the outstanding military achievements of all time. Accordingly Gibbon's second observation, contrasting the fierce giants of the north with the pygmies who now peopled the Roman world, was wide of the mark. For the army leaders and soldiers of Rome, men of many races, confronted with problems far greater than those that had ever faced their predecessors, saved and prolonged the life of their empire with a vigour that was nearly superhuman.

Yet the price paid for so unlikely a reversal of fortune comprised incalculable losses of life and property and happiness, and the continual expenditure of vast sums of money. The money was needed because, to deal with these mighty problems, the army had to be reorganized and raised to dimensions which previous generations, living in less exacting times, had never conceived of as possible.

The Climax of the Roman Army

Since the first century B.C. the Roman army had been composed of two elements. The first of these was formed by the legions, each consisting of 5,000 foot soldiers and 120 horse. These men were all Roman citizens who normally joined up at the age of eighteen and served for twenty-five years. The second main component of the army was constituted by the *auxilia*, recruited from provincials who were not Roman citizens. These were organized in cavalry and infantry units either 500 or 1,000 strong. The emperor was also protected by his praetorian guard of some 5,000 picked citizen troops. During the reign of Augustus the number of legions was stabilized at twenty-eight, which the disaster of Varus in Germany (A.D. 9) diminished to twenty-five. After further fluctuations, Marcus Aurelius' creation of two new legions to reinforce the upper Danube frontier raised the total to thirty; and Septimius added three more. Throughout this period the auxiliary soldiers numbered about as many as the legionaries. Under Augustus, the entire strength of the army probably amounted to about 260,000. Under Septimius it reached a figure of more than 300,000.

Officers were now on the crest of the wave. Septimius gave them numerous privileges, and their military jobs provided openings to many careers. This was a new military aristocracy, a special caste which provided the empire with most of its senior administrators and indeed most of its emperors. And this *élite* was not static but always changing, since the new sort of army officers mostly rose from the ranks; it was Septimius' policy to promote more and more N.C.O.'s to be officers, many of them only slightly Romanized and with little education. Excavations at Dura show that the officers garrisoned there lived well, better than almost anyone else in the town. Nor is that surprising, since Septimius gave them more than fifty times the pay of a legionary.

At the beginning of the imperial epoch, many auxiliaries had originated from the northern parts of Gaul and Spain, while recruits for the legions came from the more Romanized southern regions of the same countries. Other legionaries, like most of the praetorian guardsmen, were from Italy, and particularly from its northern areas. But already before A.D. 100, although officers were still of Italian stock, provincials in the legions had come to outnumber Italians by four or five to one.

Originally legionaries and auxiliaries alike had been posted far from their homes. But there was a growing tendency for men of both categories to be recruited on the spot, and by the time of Marcus Aurelius most soldiers were serving in the countries of their origin. Men fought external enemies with increased determination when their own homes were at stake, and in any case it was only by local recruitment that a sufficient number could be found who would not desert. This decentralization created a greater danger of revolts and usurpations, but since enough soldiers could not be raised in any other way the risk of such usurpations had to be accepted.

Local recruitment had the further effect of gradually making soldiering hereditary. Egyptian lists of early imperial date show only two soldiers' children out of thirty-six new recruits, whereas in A.D. 168 there were twenty out of thirty-seven. Within the next century compulsion was employed to make sons of soldiers follow their fathers' careers.[49] Indeed, despite the incentive provided by local postings, almost all recruitment became compulsory. A document describing a levy in Asia Minor dates from the dynasty of Septimius,[50] but probably the system of coercion went back considerably further.

Moreover, by c. 200 the old differentiation of recruitment between legionaries and auxiliaries had disappeared or become nominal. When the whole Roman world was given the franchise by Caracalla the distinction was dead; its removal provided a useful, egalitarian uniformity, but made it harder to attract ambitious people into the military profession.

Since there were many legions in the east—eight on the frontier and four in other provinces[51]—local recruiting meant that a considerable proportion of all Roman legionaries were of eastern origin. But the Danube garrison was larger still; under the earlier emperors the Rhine and the Danube had been allotted seven legions each, but under Septimius their respective totals were four and twelve. Consequently, the predominant element in the Roman army came from the warlike populations of the Danubian provinces (p. 33).

External threats under Marcus had restored the army's sense of importance, and this applied to the key Danube legions most of all. Their massive concentration and racial unity made them a force which became the bulwark of the empire and the maker of its emperors. Three legions recruited by Septimius for service against Parthia are also likely, for the most part, to have consisted of men from the Danube countries. One of these legions, by a significant precedent, was transferred, when the Parthian war was over, to Albanum in the region of Rome itself. There had never before been a permanent legionary garrison in Italy, which was losing its superiority over the provinces. By the same token, Septimius had already made the traditionally Italian praetorian guard into a body drawn mainly from Danubian legionaries.

These policies were linked with a growing tendency to replace the earlier idea of an indeterminate, variable, invisible frontier protection zone by the doctrine of fixed and fortified barriers. Like the formidable walls which from the later second and particularly in the later third century were built round towns (including Rome itself),[52] these frontier defences were studded with numerous forts. The troops that manned them drew assistance, when necessary, from legions marching up from larger reserve camps in the second line. Forward and rear sectors alike were served by large, permanent and varied army workshops and arms factories and production centres.[53]

One result of this static arrangement was that military units were lodged within existing towns. Their quarters against the city-walls of Dura (c. 165), for example, were several times reconstructed and expanded. A second tendency was for fortresses and camps to develop into completely new towns, many of which still survive as cities. Originally such settlements were divided into a military section and a camp town for the civilian populations which collected to work and trade with the army, and sometimes for other native communities as well. Both the military and civilian accommodation was often improved and remodelled by imperial initiative. In a further attempt to make the army more attractive, Septimius granted legal recognition of the soldiers' associations with native women, who were often their compatriots.[54] Although regulations had not allowed men to marry while on active service, these unions had inevitably existed on a large scale; a good deal of earlier evidence is dramatically supplemented by the heaps of women's and children's shoes at the second-century Bar Hill fort on the Antonine Wall. Now, however, the concubines gained some sort of legal status, and so did their sons who were due to follow their fathers into the army.

To encourage this hereditary self-sufficiency, the garrisons were assigned land, in allotments large enough to help materially with supplies. This policy was also intended to reduce the army's costs, and at the same time, by turning its men into tillers of land, to remedy the dearth of agricultural labour. Consequently, soldiers took to farming as their principal peace-time activity.[55] They had other peaceful occupations as well—for instance, Marcus and other emperors placed them at the disposal of civilian builders. But it was Septimius Severus, above all, who made the military into peasants and farmers and owners of property. Papyri tell us the subjects about which they wrote home: their letters are about properties and purchases and servants and rents. Moreover, previous instructions forbidding enlisted men to engage in commerce had become obsolete, and there was a good deal of trade and speculation in the sale of army stores and workshop products.

Until the time of Diocletian at least, the pattern of defence varied according to the nature of the country. In north Africa, for example, there was collaboration between the army, the ex-soldiers settled in citizen colonies, and the manpower of imperial estates. The agricultural population of such estates was concentrated within fortified settlements disposed along the frontier in two sectors of depth. There in Africa, and behind the northern and eastern borders as well, the tenants of these *castella* were the backbone of defence.[56]

Service in the interests of imperial defence was also required from barbarian tribesmen living in frontier areas. Since Trajan's time there had been German and Sarmatian irregulars in the Rhine and Danube zones, and by 270, if not already by 245, whole groups of such Germans were promoted to form part of the regular army.[57] In Britain, too, entire tribes were pressed into the same task. The extensive use of barbarians as soldiers diluted the army's Roman character; but they fought well, and again their aid was indispensable.

Finally, and not least important, the Romans continued to make use of mercenaries hired from border kingdoms and puppet states. Conspicuous among these troops, especially in the third century A.D., were the mounted archers from Osrhoene and Palmyra. Many of these mercenary bowmen were utilized not only in their own regions but in theatres of war away from their homelands. The specialized local techniques of national units were valued highly.[58] Septimius extended their employment, and Caracalla multiplied light troops of this kind along the northern frontier.

Such mercenaries were among the few rapidly transferable elements in the Roman army of the day. But military disasters at the hands of the Germans under Marcus Aurelius, heralding even graver things to come, showed that the empire's static system of defence was inadequate to deal with recurrent emergencies. If a serious break-through occurred, and worse still if there were several break-throughs simultaneously, the protective zone was of inadequate depth. For, other than the small praetorian guard associated with the emperor's person, there was no central reserve that could come to the rescue. This had already been a failing in the parsimoniously financed army of Augustus, and now that the frontier situation was so much graver the deficiency was perilous. Marcus Aurelius formed temporary mobile field-forces comprising small detachments from several legions and auxiliary units. Septimius too, when he stationed a legion near Rome, may well have had in mind the idea of a reserve which could be dispatched to whatever sector of the defence line was in difficulties.

But a legion possessed much less mobility than mounted troops, and as the concept of a strategic reserve developed it was of cavalry that this formation came mainly to consist. Archers and javelin-men on horseback were useful, but what was really needed was heavy cavalry able to move against the similar units prominent in the armies of Parthians and Persians and Sarmatians. For the military strategies of those Iranian peoples had long been based on mailed horsemen (cataphracts) with metal helmets and long heavy lances and swords; and the idea was spreading to the east Germans who came under Sarmatian influence.[59] In the third century, the institutions of the Parthians taken over and improved by the Persian monarchy included their heavy cavalry, which was henceforward recruited from the lesser feudal nobles directly dependent upon the King of Kings (p. 42). The Romans had already employed a few cataphracts of their own as early as Hadrian (d. 138), but when they encountered the formidable Persian cavalry (c. 232–3) it was becoming clear that Rome, too, urgently needed to have more armoured horsemen.[60] Gallienus, threatened not only by all manner of external invaders but by the dissident western empire of Postumus, took the important step of creating a field army of cavalry (264–8), which was intended to serve simultaneously as a reserve and a mobile striking force. Its principal base was Mediolanum (Milan), located at a convenient distance from the frontiers and Rome alike. This strategic centre, rapidly becoming even more important than the capital, was joined to Aquileia, Verona and Ticinum (Pavia) in a new system of north Italian defence necessitated by the loss of the upper Rhine–upper Danube area (pp. 51–2). But the new plans differed from the old static protection because they were conceived in terms not only of fortresses but of the newly created cavalry army. This *élite* force consisted of squadrons (we do not know how many) which were mostly five hundred men strong. They included heavy Persian-style cavalry—looking like knights of the Middle Ages in their conical Iranian helmets, which the Germans later inherited; and an almost medieval concept of knighthood was to be seen in the hereditary gold ring granted to the sons of its centurions. Other elements in this army were Osrhoenian and Palmyrene mercenary archers on horseback, javelin-throwing Mauretanian riders, and a novel and valuable corps of mounted Dalmatians whose Illyrian origin guaranteed loyalty to Rome and leavened the exoticism of the other contingents.

This new arm of the services was celebrated by coins of Gallienus displaying the winged horse Pegasus, to whom a dedication is offered as the spirit of alertness (ALACRITATI). Other slogans speak of the courage of the cavalry (VIRTVS EQVITVM); and there are appeals to their loyalty (FIDEI EQVITVM). But this last point was where the arrangement proved vulnerable. Drawing upon the Greek models he favoured, Gallienus seems to have associated the high officers of the corps, who were mainly of Danubian origin, with certain other officers in a select club or staff college (*protectores*) stationed in the imperial camp and attached to his own person.[61] Yet the commanders of this formidable cavalry army, necessarily men of ability, were under great temptation to revolt. Indeed this temptation proved too strong for the very first commanders whom Gallienus appointed (p. 34). The first of them, Aureolus, before turning traitor, had demonstrated the worth of the new corps against a rebellion near the middle Danube.[62] The second commander, Aurelian, when he became the next emperor but one (270), employed his expert knowledge to operate light horse successfully against the massive mailed cavalry of Zenobia. Nevertheless, he also strengthened his own heavy cavalry on a large scale. A relief of a few decades later depicts these men in their scale-armour and Iranian head-gear, carrying Iranian standards emblazoned with gaping, hissing serpents.[63]

Diocletian (284–305) proceeded to a military reorganization of far-reaching variety and scope. Pursuing his predecessor's concern with mobile formations, he not only created a new barbarian mounted bodyguard (*scholae*), but made the field force into one of the two major parts into which the entire army was now divided. This *comitatus*, as the force was called, contained infantry, but it still remained particularly strong in cavalry. Diocletian is believed to have introduced some numerical reductions in the field army. Yet this is unlikely to have been less costly than before, since it was divided into four parts, all of which required their own supply units. For not only Diocletian himself but each of his three partners in the Tetrarchy of rulers was accompanied by a field corps of his own.

In addition to his innovations with regard to the mobile field army, Diocletian reverted to earlier preoccupations with frontier defence. He strengthened the fortifications along the frontiers, and their elaborate barriers were reconstructed on a uniform system throughout the empire. Uniform, too, were the state factories under military administration which made arms and materials for the defenders of these zones, and indeed for the entire Roman forces. The troops guarding the frontier areas were now constituted into the second main division of Diocletian's reorganized army, and the name of *limitanei*, earlier imprecise, was employed to describe this whole arm. Except in the Danube sector, they were not usually of the same calibre as the field force. Yet any deficiency in quality was henceforward to be compensated by numbers, for Diocletian, perhaps influenced by massive Persian mobilizations, decided that the principal solution to the problems of the day was that the Roman armed services should become enormously larger than they had ever been before. Whereas Septimius' army had totalled between 300,000 and 400,000 men, Diocletian's consisted of 500,000 or even more.[64] This huge quantity of soldiers was raised by more intensive methods of recruitment. Although Diocletian, like other emperors, was prepared to commute military service for payment, he seems to have been the first to institute regular, annual conscription, assessed on the same schedule as the land tax (p. 76). This was the main source of his citizen recruits. But he was also particularly eager to make use of the warlike tastes and varying specialist skills of barbarian tribesmen. The soldiers mobilized from this almost inexhaustible source of supply included upland Anatolians, who were to be the backbone of Byzantine armies; and many Germans.[65]

This German element in the army was greatly increased by Constantine. He appreciated their particular qualifications to deal with their hostile compatriots the other side of the border. High status was conferred upon German units, and corresponding favour accorded to German generals. Abolishing the time-honoured praetorian guard (which had fought on the enemy side when he captured Rome), Constantine replaced this by the largely German personal guard started by Diocletian. Many German soldiers were also incorporated into new units of cavalry and infantry. These, combined with detachments drawn from the frontiers, were drafted into the field army, which now constituted a central striking force and strategic reserve substantially larger than any that had existed before.[66] In Diocletian's time the praetorian prefects had often commanded in the field, but Constantine, in order to steer clear of the temptations to which powerful single commanders were liable, placed his field army under a pair of new officers, a Master of the Horse and a Master of the Foot. The frontier forces were less well paid and respected than the central mobile army, and this aroused criticism, but on the Danube border and elsewhere Constantine carried out a large-scale reorganization and reinforcement of garrisons. (He and Licinius, preparing for hostilities against one another, also strengthened their fleets, and it was at sea that the decisive clash came in 324.)

By the end of the fourth century the army was nearly twice as large as it had been two hundred years earlier, and more than twice as expensive because of the increase in horses, since their feed cost as much as a man's rations. While privileges were extended to the sons of ex-soldier frontiersmen, recruitment was enforced by severe penalties which caused widespread terror, especially in the more civilized provinces. The physical quality of soldiers improved—in earlier times their minimum height had been five feet or four feet eleven inches, whereas in A.D. 367 this requirement had risen to five feet five. Officers, too, being mostly professionals, were better than they had ever been before.

Since the crises of the third century there had been a gradual tendency to make greater use of mounted troops; yet events were to show that this had still not gone far enough. For the shattering defeat of Valens by the Visigoths at Hadrianopolis (378) was due to the superiority of the barbarian riders. Since reservoirs of manpower within the western empire were now failing, 40,000 barbarian confederates, who had been given lands within the empire, were mobilized by Theodosius to serve as Roman cavalry. This necessity was ominous in its political implications for the west, where confederate mercenaries of this kind soon became the only recorded units. From the middle years of the fifth century, the provincial forces were gradually disbanded, and disintegrated altogether; the western Roman armies had ceased to exist. In the east, on the other hand, the army and the state held together for another millennium. Cavalry was still the most important Byzantine arm, and remained the queen of battles.

The survival of this Byzantine state was due to the military achievements of the period between Marcus Aurelius and Constantine. During those hundred and seventy years the Roman forces had been obliged to face shocks and enemies and problems more lethal than any that had confronted earlier emperors. These menaces had made it necessary to reorganize the army completely and to expand it on a gigantic scale, and so it was able to overcome the crises of the mid-third century, and ward off the imminent dissolution of the empire until a still distant future. Already the army had lived through more than half a millennium of victorious activity; but these years of triumph over supreme emergency must be reckoned as the culmination of the Roman military achievement.

NOTES

1. Balbinus and Pupienus (238), Tacitus (275–6)
2. See Genealogical Tables at end of book
3. Pertinax, Didius Julianus
4. Macrinus (217–18), Florian (276)
5. Septimius Severus, Pescennius Niger, Clodius Albinus
6. In this book he is usually referred to as Septimius, for easy distinction from Severus Alexander and other emperors called Severus
7. Pacatianus (248–9), Ingenuus (258 or 259), Regalianus (259 or 260)
8. Spain and S. Gaul returned to central allegiance, perhaps under one of Postumus' successors (Marius, Victorinus, Tetricus)
9. Aelianus, Amandus. These "Bagaudae" continued to rebel down to the fifth century. Revolts under Probus: Proculus, Bonosus. Under Commodus: Maternus (Gaul and Spain), c. 186
10. Carausius was appointed to repel Saxons (spreading West from lower Elbe)

11. Iotapianus (*c.* 248–9), Uranius (Sulpicius) Antoninus II (*c.* 253–5), Macrianus and Quietus (260–2)

12. Uranius Antoninus I (time of Severus Alexander), Quartinus (235)

13. Another Roman protégé, the ruler of the Cimmerian Bosphorus, was also habitually called King of Kings

14. Neoplatonists from Rome assembled at Palmyra after the death of Gallienus

15. Cyzicus still coined for the central emperors

16. A. Alföldi. Zenobia's son was Vaballathus

17. *Acts of the Pagan Martyrs* (mostly late 2nd century A.D.). Massacre at Alexandria by Caracalla (215). Revolts: Mussius Aemilianus (261–2), then Memor, Firmus (after Zenobia—prolonged civil war), Domitius Domitianus (Diocletian)

18. There were also recurrent wars on the southern African frontier which reached its furthest extension under Caracalla. From Marcus, desert tribes encroached and even raided Spain. Mauretanian tribes rebelled under Severus Alexander, and they and Blemmyes from the Sudan (where there were powerful Roman client states) raided the empire under Diocletian and Maximian, who retracted the Egyptian frontier northwards

19. Macrinus, Severus Alexander, Gordian III

20. Seleucid military colony *c.* 300 B.C. Inscriptions in Greek, Latin, Pahlavi, Middle Persian, Safaitic, Palmyrene, Syriac and Aramaic

21. Dio LXXV, 3, 3. The garrison at Dura was enlarged at about this time (probably with Palmyrene troops) and served as a starting-point for expeditions

22. Although Septimius had also presented them with many skilled mechanics—who fled across the Tigris

23. Ruling as colleague or rival to his brother Vologeses V: ? also Artavasdes

24. On silver work and jewels Greek influences are gradually Iranized

25. *Sumer* II, Pt. 1, 1955, pp. 39–43 (A.D. 235–44)

26. Arsacid Pahlavi, Sassanian Middle Persian and Greek. In the "Kaaba of Zoroaster"

27. In the House of Frescoes the Persians are shown conquering the Romans or Palmyrenes or both

28. (? 253 ? 259 ? 260/1). Shapur set up the puppet emperor Mareades

29. Bishapur, Darabgird and Naksh-i-Rustam

30. Paikuli inscription: Narses' triumph, and acts of homage by Roman envoys and Asian vassal kings

31. Antioch and Damascus (also Edessa). Road of Diocletian: Sura, Palmyra, Damascus

32. The Forth–Clyde Antonine Wall in Britain had been broken through under Commodus, and after much of northern England had been overrun and Septimius and his sons fought personally in Scotland (201–11), Caracalla apparently withdrew all Roman garrisons to Hadrian's Wall (Tyne–Solway) and its forward zone. After Carausius' revolt Constantius I defeated Pictish invaders and, like Septimius, died at Eburacum (York) (306)

33. The early Middle Ages owed the "barbarians" cloisonné jewellery, felt-making, the ski, soap, butter, tubs and barrels, rye, oats, spelt and hops, fur-coats and trousers, and the heavy plough, stirrup and horseshoe

34. Jazyges
35. Costoboci
36. Avidius Cassius
37. Quadi (east of Marcomanni)
38. E.g. Carpi
39. The island of Gotland, the centre of Baltic trade, remained their link between Baltic and Black Sea
40. Dexipp. *fr.* 6, 10, 25, 27, 29
41. By Pacatianus
42. The wealthy trading kingdom of the Cimmerian Bosphorus was reduced to Gothic vassalage
43. Gallienus coin, Colonia Agrippina (*c.* 257): CVM EXER(*citu*) SVO
44. Cf. Niederbieber hoard: advanced line abandoned
45. Syncellus 717 ff., cf. *SHA. Gall. Duo* XIII, 9, Zon. XII, 24. Sometimes the victory is attributed to Claudius II Gothicus instead
46. Zos. I, 43, 2; 45, 1
47. Coins of Dacia had ended in 256. Aurelian formed a new province of this name on the Roman bank, with capital at Serdica (Sofia)
48. The Ostrogoths (Ukraine) had conquered widely under Hermanaric, but mostly fell under Hunnish rule
49. E.g. by Severus Alexander and Probus, and law of 313, *Cod. Theod.* VII, 22, 1
50. Keil-Premerstein, *Dritte Reise*, p. 87
51. 2 Palestine, 1 Egypt, 1 Arabia. Also 1 Spain, 1 North Africa
52. *Dig.* 50, 10, 6 (Marcus): emperor's permission needed. W. French group of city walls, e.g. Le Mans, 285–315. Huge gate-tower at Trier (Porta Nigra): cf. Deutz (*c.* 310). Rome's Wall of Aurelian—completed by Probus and improved by Maxentius
53. Veg. II, 11. E.g. Xanten, Ohrenbacher, Trennfurt, Carrawburgh
54. Herod. III, 8, 4–5. Septimius also introduced off-duty clubs for junior officers
55. Cf. sickles and scythes found at Pfünz, Weissenburg, Great Chesters
56. E.g. Sitifis; Kaua (Mauretania); Burgstall (Czechoslovakia); round Lake Balaton (Hungary); and in Thrace, Asia Minor, Syria
57. Aurelian formed auxiliary units of Vandals, Juthungi and Alamanni
58. Arr. *Tact.* XXXIII, 2
59. The Sarmatians influenced the Quadi; the Alani influenced the Goths. Similar influences helped to produce the armoured cavalry of China
60. The horseshoe was now in use in the east. Macrinus (217–18) equipped his infantry with long German two-edged sword and lance, against sudden cavalry attacks
61. Later extended to more junior officers; finally a sort of officer cadet force
62. Ingenuus: killed at Mursa
63. Arch of Galerius
64. Pace Joh. Lyd. (435, 266). Cavalry and infantry were now separated, and legions (now smaller) increased in number from 39 to 65
65. Galatians, Isaurians; Batavians, Tungrians
66. Under Constantine's sons an *élite* central group were known as *palatini*

3

The Cost of Survival

The Budget

The largest and most imperative of the Roman government's financial tasks was to meet the costs of this expanding army on which everything depended.

Under Augustus, the pay of a legionary soldier had amounted to 225 silver coins (*denarii*) each year. At the end of the first century A.D. Domitian had brought this figure up to 300. Septimius raised it again to 500,[1] and increased the pay of his reconstituted praetorian guard from 1,250 *denarii* to 1,700. His son Caracalla introduced a further 50 per cent pay rise, amounting to an annual charge on the exchequer of about seventy million *denarii*. Caracalla is reported to have said, "No one but myself ought to have money, and I must have it to give to the soldiers."[2] Yet the increases in army pay which resulted from this policy, comprising a five-fold multiplication of the expenditure of Augustus, must be related not only to the greater size of the army but to the rise in the cost of living that had occurred during the same two centuries on a scale at least as large as the augmentation of pay, and perhaps a good deal larger. That is to say, the soldiers of the second century A.D., before the pay rises of Septimius and Caracalla, had been poorly remunerated. This had been convenient for the government, which, except in emergencies, was able to afford its army. But it imposed a strain upon military loyalty and efficiency, and during the crises that followed, emperors felt that they could not take such risks.

However, their efforts to satisfy the troops by increases in wages rapidly became useless and irrelevant. For all this pay became little more than incidental pocket-money, owing to the total depreciation of the currency.

The empire had inherited from Augustus a magnificent coinage of a range never seen before. This included a gold piece (*aureus*) and the related silver *denarius*, both of which possessed a precious metal content worth as much, or very nearly as much, as the official valuations attached to the coins. The ancient public was convinced that the market value of a coin depended on the amount and worth of the metal it contained. Like people in our own century who were angry when first given bank-notes in exchange for their money, Romans and Greeks did not understand the token principle. In its issues of gold and silver, Rome had long paid defence to this attitude. With regard to base metal coinages, on the other hand, the government of the Republic had little by little induced the population to accept bronze small change which bore a token valuation exceeding the purchase price of its metal. When, however, that disparity between intrinsic and official worth became too glaringly noticeable, the Republican authorities had been obliged to discontinue even these bronze coinages, although many towns of the empire were allowed to maintain the lucrative issue of similar local token pieces on their own initiative. But then Augustus succeeded in reviving an official token currency of the Roman state. He did this by abandoning the discredited bronze in favour of two more attractive looking substances, yellow brass and red copper. Greatly overpriced, with a large margin of profit to the emperors, coinages in these metals soon circulated throughout Italy and all the western provinces.

Yet people throughout the empire remained unable to accept the notion of gold and silver coinages with a bullion content falling below their official valuation. Nevertheless, emperors soon began to infringe on this requirement in two ways. First, they made the coins in each metal lighter; and secondly, they adulterated the silver. These were both, in effect, disguised capital levies upon those who received the coinage. The former course could not be adopted very drastically since it was detectable, but debasement of the silver seemed an attractive solution. However, it raised a hazardous problem of confidence. For the debasement of *denarii* was resorted to in order that larger numbers should be issued; and the imperial administration was not aware—or, concentrating on current emergencies, did not care—that, if the quantity of coins was multiplied without a corresponding increase in the goods on the market, this would intensify the already existing tendency for prices to rise and the general standard of living to fall. In such circumstances it was inevitable that old, good coins would be hoarded, and the inferior new ones retariffed downwards—a process penalizing people with fixed cash incomes who had accepted the new pieces before retariffing, and inflicting losses on those who had lent large sums for fixed repayments.

And so the Roman government gradually moved into the danger area. It was tempting to issue debased silver coins which looked decent to begin with; it was also irresistibly tempting to multiply their numbers. When Trajan issued abundant *denarii* which were worth 85 per cent of their face value, irrevocable damage had perhaps not yet been done.[3] But other slow encroachments followed, and amid wars, earthquakes and plagues, the ethical code of Marcus Aurelius did not prevent his officials from depreciating the silver coinage by a further 6 per cent. By now the intrinsic value of the *denarius* was only three-quarters of its official value; and the situation soon grew worse when Septimius, needing more coins amid the stresses of civil war, again sharply debased the *denarius* (194–5) so that its contents now fell short of official valuation by 40 per cent.

This debasement had become too visible, and the issues too large, for public confidence to be retained, and the consequences soon became apparent.[4] An imperial decree found at Mylasa (Milâs) in Asia Minor indicates that illicit exchange-rates were flourishing, and forbids them on the ground that this wild speculation made it impossible for the citizens to secure the necessities of life (209–11).[5] However, almost immediately afterwards, Caracalla was impelled by his heavy military expenditure to issue an abundant silver coinage which was not only debased but of light weight also, this lightness being concealed by the issue of a new and larger denomination (named *antoninianus* after the emperor's official name). Its size and handsome appearance were meant to distract attention from the fact that its official value of two *denarii*[6] could not by any means be merited by weight. Meanwhile at Ephesus (Selçuk) the price of a loaf of bread had doubled in the course of a hundred years; and probably the pattern was universal. But the government's preoccupations were too pressing for these warning signs to be noted. Although it continued to protest its concern for the quality of the money,[7] the multiplication of ever more debased coins continued and gathered pace, until Gallienus, needing an immense number of coins to pay the army and unable to afford (or even find) the silver to put in them, issued *antoniniani* made almost entirely of bronze, with a thin surface coating of silver-wash. The real value of these *antoniniani* had sunk to 5 per cent of their pre-inflation worth. The commercial world, throughout the empire, rejected this currency; the psychological basis for any confidence at all had vanished. A papyrus tells us the sort of thing that happened. Faced, two years later, with a temporary ruler's coinage of this same depreciated character, Egyptian banks refused to accept it and closed their doors. They were ordered to open again, and told to "accept and exchange all coin except the absolutely spurious and counterfeit;"[8] but such injunctions were useless when the basis for voluntary acceptance had vanished. And meanwhile the gold coinage, formerly so stable, was providing no sort of a prop, and indeed, except as gifts for distribution to the army (p. 72), had almost ceased to exist. Because of the exhaustion and insecurity of the mines, it was inadequate in quantity, and its standard was so variable that the coins seem to have been bought and sold according to weight. Moreover, even this only happened rarely, because the inflation of base silver money sent almost every *aureus* out of the market into hoarders' chests.

The collapse of the silver coinage produced catastrophic effects during the decades following the death of Gallienus. In Egypt, for instance, papyri tell us that 30 litres of wheat cost seven-eighths of the Greek currency unit (*drachma*) during the second century; from twelve to twenty *drachmas* in the first half of the third century; and by the time of Diocletian the figure was as high as 120,000. Between the years 258 and 275, prices in many or most parts of the empire are likely to have risen by nearly 1,000 per cent. The result was untold misery. In particular, the wages and salaries of soldiers and other state employees were virtually eliminated.

Aurelian tried to deal with this situation by a monetary reform. But, like Caracalla's, it was only another debasement, in what was intended to be an attractive disguise. For Aurelian, too, coined a new piece containing no more than 5 per cent of silver but possessing reassuringly increased dimensions designed to soften the shock of its over-high official valuation, which was probably as high as five *denarii*.[9] Aurelian also tried to enforce acceptance of his new currency, and write off the past, by calling in old and better coins.

The rates which he paid for these demonetized issues proved unsatisfactory to their owners who, instead of handing them over to the government, buried immense quantities away. Aurelian's measures no doubt caused panic and hardship. But as a temporary palliative to galloping inflation they had some success, for prices seem to have remained reasonably steady for nearly twenty years.

Then, however, came a new spiral of inflation, and many of the steepest price increases of the whole half-century occurred between 290 and 300. Aurelian had not been able to revive a silver coinage, and the loss of Dacia's mines had meant that he could coin very little gold. But Diocletian made a determined endeavour to issue a stable coinage in all three metals of gold, silver and silvered bronze (*c.* 294/5). In the last-named alloy he produced larger and more generously silvered pieces than had appeared for years. These bore the same value marks, indicating five *denarii*, as had been seen on Aurelian's coins of half the size. This unusual idea of diminishing by 50 per cent the official values of his coins was a measure of deflation by which Diocletian hoped to bring down prices and stabilize them at a lower level. But the public instead hastened to turn this new currency into goods (which it was able to obtain at favourable rates) with the result that prices rose more sharply than ever. Nor was Diocletian's precious metal currency of much assistance. It is true that this included gold coinages (*c.* A.D. 286) of an exact standard such as had not been known in recent times and of a higher weight than before, as well as silver issues (*c.* 294) which, even if still rated above their intrinsic worth, were the best that had been minted officially for over a century.[10] Yet the gold and silver coins were not numerous enough to stabilize the situation. Although a tax on land had to be paid in these metals and cities were compelled to sell him bullion, Diocletian's stocks were still not sufficiently large for the issues to attain substantial dimensions.[11] The result was that they soon came to be virtually demonetized like their predecessors, changing hands at high artificial rates. Accordingly, they did nothing to stop the rise of prices, which continued with an ever-increasing momentum.

In 301–2 Diocletian made a further vigorous endeavour to check this avalanche. He now issued an edict fixing maximum prices for all goods and maximum wages for all workers, throughout the whole of the Roman empire.[12] This anticipation of modern Prices and Incomes Policies was based on the supposition that the increase of prices had been the fault not of the currency but of avarice among the combines and cartels of wicked profiteers. "The monstrous prices that human speech is incapable of describing", complained the rulers, "mean that in a single purchase a soldier is deprived of his bonus and salary, and that the contributions of the whole world to support the armies fall to the abominable profit of thieves." The government's overriding concern for the soldiery is apparent. Inflation or deflation being equally disastrous means of providing the army with its needs, it seemed that the only chance was to maintain stationary price levels; and these were enforced under the threat of execution. The new rates were all quoted in terms of Diocletian's reformed currency. Ceilings were fixed for over 900 commodities, ranging from pork sausages at 2 *denarii* a pound to cloaks of 1,500–10,000 *denarii* each. In the fragments that have come down to us, 41 maximum freight charges are recorded, and the salaries of 130 grades of labour. This edict, the most valuable document of all ancient economics, declares the official death of the world of free exchange and uncontrolled *laissez-faire* economic activity, and does so with an elaboration which was not seen again for another sixteen hundred years. And yet, even if it played a part in restoring a money economy (p. 77), the edict was a failure in its main task of limiting prices, because the authorities neither owned nor controlled the means of production and consumption, and proved unable to enforce the acceptance of their orders. The result was that goods disappeared from the market;[13] and inflation resumed its inexorable course. Diocletian's edict, accepting the spiral of recent years, had equated a pound of gold with no less that 50,000 *denarii*.[14] Yet in less than a decade after the edict the figure was already up to 120,000 or above, and by A.D. 324 it had risen to more than 300,000.[15] To base a price and wage structure on so rapidly depreciating a currency was hopeless, and Diocletian's novel attempt to create this structure on a comprehensive basis had failed.

Meanwhile, throughout all these years, the collapsing currency had been quite insufficient to meet the most urgent need of all, the payment and satisfaction of the soldiers. However much their regular pay was increased (p. 66), the low value of money still meant that it remained an inadequate pittance. Accordingly the emperors used two methods to supplement these annual sums.

First, it had long been customary to augment the pay of praetorians and legionaries by donatives. Originally shares of war-spoils, these were money gifts or bonuses handed over by emperors or left in their wills, in order to commemorate joyful events or anniversaries. In particular, each new imperial accession was the occasion of a donative. In the military crises of the second century these payments increased in size and frequency; and whereas donatives in the middle of reigns might make use of the contemporary debased coinage which was also employed for army pay, bonuses celebrating imperial accessions had to be paid in good, undebased gold coin.

Two transient emperors of the Civil War period after the murder of Commodus largely owed their downfall to refusal or inability to honour fully the promises regarding donatives that they had made at their accessions.[16] The lesson was learnt by Septimius, who increased these gifts to such an extent that they henceforward became a systematic purchase of military fidelity, glossed over by anniversary ceremonials intended to stimulate religious and patriotic emotions. At an earlier date the Praetorian guardsmen had received a good deal more money than the legionaries on these occasions,[17] but now, as the legions became the most significant element in the political scene, their donatives caught up with those of the guard. In a mutiny after the death of Gallienus, the soldiers were given twenty gold coins (*aurei*) apiece,[18] and the substantial gold medallions of the day often found their way into officers' hands.

During the civil wars after Diocletian's abdication, as on many other occasions, these donatives were a decisive military and political factor. Their multiplication by the emperors over the years indicated that the army had become predominant in the state, and that it had to be bound to themselves by personal links of gratitude. And yet, even though these donatives were no luxury but a necessity, the propaganda on the Roman government's coins, while loudly taking credit for every other kind of imperial generosity including free distributions to civilians, remained silent concerning these donatives for century after century. They were presumably regarded as nothing to boast about, because soldiers ought to have retained their famous, anxiously praised loyalty (FIDES MILITVM, FIDES EXERCITVVM) without such special measures.

The huge sums required to pay the donatives had to be obtained by increases in taxation. The land-tax and poll-tax, the direct contributions which fell upon provincials, did not seem the best medium for such exactions, because the collection of larger sums would have raised insuperable practical difficulties. Instead Caracall fastened upon a sort of extraordinary income-tax which was known as crown money. This had originally consisted of gold levied by Roman Republican generals from provinces and conquered peoples to make crowns for their Triumphs. From the time of Augustus onwards, many emperors accepted ostensibly voluntary presentations from the provinces and cities of the empire, though seldom from Italy. Marcus Aurelius, in spite of financial pressure, refused such gifts, or partially remitted them. Caracalla on the other hand, faced with even heavier military expenditure, made repeated demands for crown money, proclaiming fictitious victories which required celebration in this way.[19] He also doubled two of the traditional indirect taxes on Roman citizens, the death duty and tax on the liberation of slaves, and by making almost everyone into a citizen he greatly increased the number of payments (p. 111).[20] By the use of these stringent methods Caracalla became one of the few emperors who over-estimated rather than under-estimated his needs, since at his death a large credit balance remained in the treasury (217).

But the raising of all this money was of very little avail. Owing to the rapid rise in prices and depreciation of the currency, the sums needed for the army were far beyond what any taxes paid in money could provide. Besides, the system of taxation was too inflexible; fixed taxes fell unfairly and non-progressively on an agricultural economy, and the system was scarcely more satisfactory for the administration, since whether expenses were normal or exceptional the revenue remained the same. The government had no means of borrowing money. Faced with emergencies, Marcus Aurelius sold public property, Septimius, Caracalla and Maximinus I (235–8)—who earned the reputation of a grasping extortioner, confiscated personal possessions. Yet even if the proceeds from these more or less desperate measures provided just enough cash in difficult times, the multiplication of debased currency led to so rapid a rise in prices that the soldiers could not nearly subsist on pay and donatives alone (p. 69).

Accordingly the emperors had recourse, on a huge scale, to the

73

supplementation of these cash sums by free distributions of rations and clothing and the raw materials for arms.[21] These payments in kind, which came to be called the *annona militaris*, were placed on a systematic basis by Septimius and his successors. They are first heard of shortly before 200 in Egypt, where arrangements of this sort were then extended by Caracalla and Severus Alexander. Meanwhile, similar hand-outs to soldiers were beginning to be made with increasing frequency in other provinces also. As the quality of money deteriorated, and the treasury became more and more anxious to save metal, this quickly became the principal method of remunerating the army.

During the second century, rations, uniforms and arms had been issued against deductions from pay, but as the payments in kind gained in momentum they were all distributed free of charge. The civilian populations, who were compelled to hand over these supplies of foodstuffs and materials, were at first paid for them; and as late as the time of Severus Alexander, such cash transactions are still recorded.[22] But by that date what the authorities offered was nothing like large enough to correspond with increased prices. Moreover, it was now by no means universal practice to offer any payment at all. Forced deliveries for the army, without recompense, had already occurred during earlier emergencies, for example in A.D. 128. In the third century this practice became prevalent and indeed normal. To collect and deal out the goods, an elaborate organization was set up under the general instructions of the praetorian prefect as quartermaster-general of the army; and along the main highways there was a network of storage centres on which the armed forces received drafts for the products that they required. It may have been Septimius who enacted that each province was required to supply the troops stationed inside its borders with food.[23] The provinces in turn delegated the responsibility to landowners, who levied the required produce from their tenants. Leading officials of the cities were also ordered to raise extensive contributions, and papyri show towns and villages handing over their cows, calves, goats, hay and wine.

This requisitioning could be avoided, if one was rich enough, by the substitution of cash. Nevertheless, payments in kind were now virtually universal. It may seem strange that so huge an empire could not keep an army of between a quarter and half a million strong without supplementing ordinary taxation by these additional assessments reminiscent of a prehistoric non-monetary economy of kind. But money had become much less useful. And, in any case, the burden of supplying the army could only be met by some such radical and ruthless measures. For the Roman world was so technologically backward that the production of food, fabrics, arms and armour took a long time and was extremely costly; and so was their transportation. The receipts of taxes levied in cash did not provide the government with nearly enough to cover the cost of these operations. Consequently it had to supplement these cash receipts by raising contributions in kind, which enormously exceeded the monetary revenue in value, and constituted by far the most important tax in the empire and the principal means by which the army was maintained.

However, the army was not the only beneficiary from these exactions of goods: another was the ever-growing civil service. A further burden was the need to subsidize Italy. The decentralization of industry into the western provinces during the second century, due to a stagnant social structure, bad communications and rudimentary credit institutions, had increasingly turned the Italian homeland into a parasite, supported by the emperor's private estates and by taxation in cash and kind. Rome itself was in a privileged position of unproductive idleness. Its annual days of festival, enjoyed amid the amenities of sumptuous baths and other public buildings, numbered 130 in A.D. 150; two centuries later the figure had risen to 176. Over a hundred thousand of its citizens received free public distributions. These hand-outs were effected, under imperial direction, by numerous corporations (p. 82), and the authorities were proud that this generosity to civilians (unlike distributions to soldiers) should be commemorated on the coinage. Emperors levied payments in kind in order to collect enough corn to feed the entire Roman population. Under Constantine, these burdens of imported free gifts were duplicated at Constantinople, where 80,000 people received distributions of food. Further heavy burdens on the tax-payer were the imperial court, the public works administration and the official post, which was so formidably organized that mail could travel one hundred and twenty miles in a day.[24] Civilians who lived close to a postal station sometimes abandoned their settlements and moved away out of reach of its requisitions.

But the main demands came from the soldiers, and particularly from their inexhaustible need and appetite for the payments in kind which had become their main support. By introducing such arrangements Rome had at last succeeded, for the first time in its history, in setting up some sort of a permanent organization for the maintenance of the army. But the methods adopted caused widespread hardship to civilians. One of the main causes of distress was the unforeseeable irregularity of the demands that fell like thunderbolts upon the population. Accordingly, Diocletian felt it necessary to put an end to this unpredictable, arbitrary state of affairs. His need for large-scale supplies in kind was very great indeed; for his army was much larger than ever before, and the four courts of the tetrarchs had added an additional heavy expense. He therefore placed the whole levy of payments in kind on a systematic and regular basis. First, a novel method of assessment was worked out. Throughout the entire empire the agricultural land was divided into a number of units of measurement (*iuga*), reckoned to be of equal value to one another but calculated in various ways according to different crops and qualities and regions. Then the produce or materials required from every area were assessed in terms of a certain number of these *iuga*. Constantine added to the *iugum* a second sort of unit, the *caput* or head of agricultural population; Diocletian had apparently employed this method of reckoning to raise a tax in cash, but Constantine seems somehow to have equated and assimilated *capita* with *iuga*, employing both sorts of unit for the assessment of payments in kind.[25]

The government now had an unprecedentedly comprehensive method for estimating the quantity and nature of the goods which each area had to provide. But the main importance of the change was that these assessments were no longer suddenly announced at irregular intervals. Henceforward they were adjusted every year— and every year a new and revised announcement was publicly made. Even if people were no better off than they had been before, they at least knew what they must give. For the first time in history there was an annual budget.

In order to prepare for its compilation the praetorian prefects, whom Diocletian placed in charge of the system, were required each year to estimate the materials needed by the government in their territories. Over-estimates, which meant the wastage of perishable food stuffs, had to be avoided; so did under-estimates, which involved unpopular supplementary budgets. Having worked out their needs, the prefects calculated the amount of the levy in terms of *iuga* and *capita*. Next, before the beginning of the financial year, they circulated their requirements to the provinces, which had been increased in number so as to secure closer financial control. The provincial authorities then divided up these lump sums into assessments served on cities and institutions and individuals. In the interests of the greatest possible accuracy, a complete census of the empire was gradually carried out, region by region.

The census was only completed after Diocletian's death, but in Egypt, for example, the inauguration of the new arrangements had long since been announced by the country's governor, in terms which show the importance of the innovation (297).

> Our most providential emperors, Diocletian and Maximian, and the most noble Caesars Constantius and Galerius, having seen that the levies of the public taxes take place in such a way that some people get off lightly and some are overburdened, have determined to root out this most evil and pernicious practice in the interest of their provincials and to lay down a salutary rule whereby the levies shall be made. I have therefore publicly given notice how much has been assessed for each *arura* [⅔ acre] according to the quality of the land, and how much on each head of the peasants and from what age to what age, according to their published divine edict and the schedule annexed thereto, of which I have issued copies in this edict. So the provincials, seeing that they have received great benefits, must take care that they make their payment with all speed according to the divine regulation and do not wait to be compelled. All must fulfil their obligations with the greatest zeal, and if anyone be found doing otherwise after such great benefits he will be punished.[26]

The governor displays a certain anxiety about the likelihood of evasions, and indeed (in an economy unaccustomed to co-ordinated planning) this was one of the imperfections which accompanied the operation. There were others also. That the burden was primarily placed on agriculture was perhaps not so unjust as it might seem, since this produced a very large proportion of the empire's revenue (p. 86); but the rich were let off too lightly since, although subject to special requisitions,[27] they found it comparatively easy to obtain exemptions. Moreover, assessments varied greatly from place to place, and were often arbitrary and inequitable; there were obvious difficulties in striking a fair balance between units that were human and agricultural. Emperors tried to remedy these faults, but only with incomplete success, and censuses remained unrevised for many years. Moreover, the government, having all this administrative machinery under its control, was too easily tempted to raise its total requirements year by year. And yet, however fallible, crude and bleak the functioning of the scheme might be, it displayed a grand and sweeping homogeneity which meant that for the first time this major economic requirement of taxation had been clearly perceived as a whole and taken in hand on the necessary scale like a huge military operation. In the undeveloped fields of economics and public finance, this abandonment of tax-anarchy in favour of an annual budget was Rome's highest achievement.

The payments in goods, to which the annual budget was geared, so greatly overshadowed the cash economy that this seemed likely to disappear in favour of a more primitive economy of kind. And yet Diocletian's Edict of Prices, issued only a very few years after the initiation of his tax-reform (p. 70), was still expressed in terms of cash. Although the edict's main purpose of controlling prices failed, its adherence to cash values may ultimately have stimulated, or at least heralded, a surprising recovery of the money economy alongside the non-monetary economy which had threatened to wipe it out. The remnants of monetary arrangements had always persisted, and the framework had not been abandoned; some taxes were always paid in cash, soldiers and all other government employees still received cash payments, and wage-earning continued to offer some prospects of advancement. But now money was going to play a larger part again.

The denominations in which Diocletian's edict framed its price limits were the humble *denarii* which were the currency of the poor. But the next move towards reviving a money economy took place on the higher plane of the gold coinage. For in 312 Constantine introduced his new gold piece, the *solidus*, and enforced its acceptance by law. The coin was not, it is true, so heavy as Diocletian's *aureus*; Constantine evidently recognized the impracticability of such a standard, issuing his *solidi* not at 60 but at 72 to the pound. Yet the issue was successful. Even if people were reluctant to abandon the current practice of buying and selling their gold pieces by weight, it soon became established that these new coins were true and full-bodied and worth their face-value.

But the main reason for the success of the *solidi* was that Constantine before long began to issue them in far larger quantities than Diocletian had managed to coin. This was remarkable in view of the heavy drains on Constantine's resources. His new subsidization of the Christian clergy was expensive, and so was the foundation of Constantinople. Nevertheless, the emperor was able to find bullion for his coinage by four principal means. First, he collected two new taxes in precious metals.[28] Secondly, he insisted that rents from imperial estates should be paid in the same way. Thirdly, he acquired the substantial bullion reserves of his defeated rival Licinius.[29] And finally, at the end of his reign, he confiscated the treasures of some pagan temples (p. 304). All these stocks of gold made it possible to mint *solidi* in considerable numbers.[30] This, in its turn, meant that the relations between the two concurrent sorts of economic framework began to shift back to their former condition; the money economy gained ground again at the expense of its "natural" counterpart. Before long, the government started to commute certain payments in kind into payments in *solidi*, and this became a regular rule a century and a half later. Diocletian's annual budget relating to payment of goods had increasingly become a monetary budget, and the whole tendency of the Mediterranean world to revert to the barter-economy of ancient times had been arrested.

Yet this voluminous gold coinage was obviously more beneficial to the ruling class and officials, who wanted to be paid in cash, than to the poor who never set eyes on a gold coin. And meanwhile the inflation of the poor man's silvered bronze currency continued unchecked and attained extraordinary dimensions. The 300,000 *denarii* to the pound of A.D. 324 (4,250–4,500 to the *solidus*) had risen by A.D. 337 to nearly twenty million (275,000 to the *solidus*), and twenty years later the *denarii* which went to a pound amounted to more than three hundred and thirty million. The spiral went on rising to even more astronomical sums,[31] until the Byzantine emperor Anastasius I (493–518) inaugurated a coinage including large bronze coins of which people were prepared to accept the required quantity in exchange for *solidi*. The long epoch of insecure currencies was at last at an end. Stability, then, had not been finally attained until the end of the fifth century. But the decisive step was taken by Constantine, and the introduction of his *solidus* became a major landmark of economic history. The coin dominated the Middle Ages, and was one of the strengths of the Byzantine empire. *Solidi* retained their weight and purity intact until as late as 1070; and for more than a millennium they provided the basis of trade as far as Scotland, Scandinavia, Russia, Ethiopia and India.

The State takes over

The maintenance of the army by these taxes in cash and kind, levied amid damaging currency crises, caused misery on a gigantic scale. This was made worse by the staffs which proliferated in order to enforce the exactions. These special and military police, informers and secret agents were not new, but they were multiplied in number and placed on a systematic basis, thus adding a further substantial item to the expenses that the population had to meet. During the civil wars after Commodus' death military police officers became regular instead of exceptional phenomena,[32] and a complex network of local headquarters was established to provide them with bases for their operations. Spies, too, were everywhere. In implied contrast to the rapacious Maximinus I, a writer praises the emperor Philip, perhaps more hopefully than convincingly, for relieving the situation in which "many spies had gone round all the cities listening to what people were saying. All temperate and just liberty of speech was destroyed and everyone trembled at his own shadow."[33]

The large part played by the army in organizing these measures to guarantee its own supplies involved constant encroachment on the civil authorities, as a series of laws resisting the tendency bear witness. Military judges assumed a variety of tasks for which they were inadequately qualified.[34] Garrison officers, too, could make life bearable or unbearable as they chose; and ordinary soldiers (in addition to the army deserters who abounded) often became lawless and menacing, either through criminality or in order to obtain their quota of supplies. Pertinax (193) ordered them to stop oppressing civilians. The desperate condition of the persecuted populations emerges from their petitions to one emperor after another. These had also occurred earlier, but now there is a new urgency in appeals against oppression. The tenants on imperial estates in Lydia petitioned one of their rulers, probably Septimius, against military police agents and spies.[35] Villagers and property-owners at Scaptopare, near a health resort and seasonal fair (Kyustendil in Bulgaria), complain desperately of demands for unpaid lodging and food (238), threatening to run away and thus deprive the imperial treasury of their payments and services—"we have declared that our endurance is at an end".[36] Groups of tenants on imperial estates in Asia Minor make a number of similar complaints. The Aragueni of Phrygia, for example, write to Philip: "We are most atrociously victimized and squeezed by those whose duty it is to protect the people—officers, soldiers, city notables holding authority, and your own subordinate officials."[37] In Egypt, where soldiers are prosperous and peasants persecuted, requisitions inspire terror. "It is hard, even when justice is done to us, to accomplish our duties in full"—and the dishonest tricks of the oppressors make this quite impossible. The questions addressed to an oracle include: "Shall I be sold up? Am I to become a beggar? Shall I flee? Shall my flight come to an end?"[38]

This is a gloomy picture of violence and outrage. But in due course there was a change—not towards greater freedom but in the direction of more methodical regimentation. One of many forms of inexorable compulsion subjected the principal agents and operators of industry and trade. In spite of the disasters of the period and the economic decline of Italy (p. 75), commercial and industrial activity elsewhere presents a variable pattern in which deterioration in some regions and spheres was matched by improvements in others.[39] A large part of this business was in the hands of corporations or guilds (*collegia*). Such merchant and artisan associations of mutual help, each representing a profession, had, like clubs of other kinds, become familiar institutions in the later Greek world, and particularly under the Ptolemies of Egypt. The custom then extended to Italy, where, for example, there is record of a Sardinian guild of cooks at Falerii (*c.* 200 B.C.). In the late Roman Republic the corporations had been politically troublesome, but like so many other organizations they were legalized by Augustus so as to perform work of national importance (7 B.C.). For the same reason Claudius and other emperors gave the corporations tax concessions. But they were apparently abused, since Hadrian insisted that to be eligible for these advantages the corporation-member must devote the bulk of his capital to duties on behalf of the state; and Marcus Aurelius ruled that no one could be a member of more than one corporation.

Septimius, too, indicated that concessions were only claimable by guildsmen who contributed their own work on a personal basis. Yet this same emperor, as the jurists show, extended tax favours to such corporations as were able to help the government in its public services and requisitions, and their titles take the place of individual traders' names in state contracts. Traditionally the most important corporation had always been that of the shippers who carried corn and other public cargoes to Rome and the army's maritime bases, on vessels owned by themselves. Indeed, although corporations were by no means trade unions, the shippers at Arelate (Arles), who transported troops and supplies, even threatened to go on strike (201).[40] All over the empire this profession obtained a prominent share of Septimius' privileges. But he also laid special stress on the corporations which provided bread and meat for distribution in the heavily subsidized capital (p. 75).[41]

Septimius' idea of exploiting these institutions for what were regarded as essential tasks of the empire was rapidly carried forward during the years after his death. Severus Alexander increased the number of such organizations, and conferred special recognition upon those performing national service. A further step in the direction of state control was taken by Aurelian, who subordinated important corporations to his own direct orders. By the end of the third century these bodies, although they remained private and did not become completely nationalized, were subordinated to official direction and geared to fulfilling the government's policies. Members were tied to their jobs without the possibility of leaving them (except illegally), and similar obligations fell on all who by inheritance, dowry or gift had acquired land that was under a corporation's control.

Membership, it is true, was not made compulsory, at least in the eastern provinces, and not in the west until the end of the fourth century, when craftsmen had to be brought back to the towns from which they had migrated. Nevertheless, even by the time of Diocletian, a merchant could not prosper unless he was a guildsman. This closed shop system applied to every sort of trade and occupation, not only at Rome but in all communities of any size: to inn-keepers, fishmongers, potters, silversmiths and many others. The government was still susceptible to influence from the corporations, and particularly from ship-owners whose delegations extracted favourable rulings; but most legislation was repressive. Convicted criminals could be punished by assignment to a corporation. And we learn that bakers (presumably not alone in this) even had to choose their wives from the families of fellow guildsmen.

The corporations, as principal organs of trade, played a leading part in urban life. But the government, in its desire to establish the controls necessary to secure maximum payments in kind and cash, went beyond the corporations and tackled the cities themselves—the fundamental units of Greco-Roman civilization. During the second century A.D. leading men had become more and more unwilling to serve as town councillors. This was partly because of increasing interference by the central government. Emperors had started appointing representatives of their own to supervise the affairs of one city or several, and this sort of intervention made the work of councils seem trivial and tedious. But the most important reason for the unpopularity of council service was the expense it involved. In the first place there was a tradition that town councillors, and especially those elected to the annual chairmanships or joint chairmanships, must provide extravagant entertainments and buildings. Secondly, emperors came to rely heavily upon town councils for the collection of taxes.

The law had always provided that duly qualified citizens must perform appropriate services (*munera*), but this had not hitherto been enforced. Enforcement came under Septimius, whose army budget, swollen by wars, required that cities should keep up their payments in kind by extorting these from their populations. In order that the towns should thus operate as the central government's local agents with all possible efficiency, every qualified person who could not claim one of the meticulously specified legal exemptions was henceforward compelled to serve as a town councillor. Councils were still allowed to fill their own vacancies, but Septimius prescribed that every such body was to be directed by a steering committee of ten selected persons on whom the responsibility for collecting the necessary amounts of produce and materials would primarily rest. Provincial governors were charged with the task of ensuring the equitable distribution of public offices by a process of rotation according to age and rank. If requisitions proved inadequate, office-holders had to make up the short-fall out of their own pockets. Soon, therefore, we begin to hear of people giving up their properties so as to avoid having to take office[42]—and in Egypt at least, and no doubt elsewhere, such attempts at evasion were overtaken by punishment (c. 250).

The cities were rapidly losing their traditional freedom of action. But when the empire-wide financial crisis reached even more serious dimensions, the full opportunities for oppression lurking in the new arrangements became apparent. Maximinus I (235–38), himself a Danubian peasant, made ruthless inroads upon the property and persons of the urban middle class, who seemed to him a good deal less important than the soldiery. Thereafter these townsmen suffered grievously from the inflations, in which long-term mortgages and fixed rent charges on land were wiped out (p. 68). Another source of grave losses was the multiplication of large estates (p. 87), which more or less forcibly freed themselves from urban fiscal administration, depriving towns of the opportunity to pass on their burdens to the countryside. And meanwhile these hardships were punctuated by the holocausts of invasions and civil wars that afflicted the towns even worse than the countryside. Indeed, two of the greatest creations of Gallic urbanization, Lugdunum (Lyon) (197) and Augustodunum (Autun) (269), were destroyed. Aurelian's soldiers wanted to sack Tyana in Cappadocia, and he had to remind them: "The reason why we are fighting is to free these cities. Let us spare these men as our own people, and seek the spoil of barbarians instead."[43]

Yet almost at the moment when he was speaking, many eastern towns lost one of their most valued privileges, namely the right to issue their own bronze coinage; for this was now being exercised, by a very few surviving mints, for the last time. The legislative rights of the cities were also no more, and the whole tradition of municipal autonomy had been eroded to vanishing point. The town councils' main purpose was now to levy supplies for the central government, and to this end their membership, in about the time of Diocletian, became not only compulsory but the permanent duty of a hereditary caste. What people thought about these jobs is illustrated by the penalty imposed by Maxentius on a Christian; he condemned him to be a town councillor. Nevertheless, avoidance remained possible, for Constantine complained that the councils were left desolate.[44] One of the main reasons for such vacancies was a constant drain of council personnel into official jobs. Earlier emperors had likewise been unable to prevent this, and now there was an additional and abundant leakage because many councillors saw a new means of escape in admission to holy orders. Constantine tried to block the avenue by ruling that, while the poor should be maintained by the wealth of the churches, the rich ought to support the needs of this world.

However in spite of all these compulsions town life continued after a fashion, and sometimes without too much hardship. At Dura, for example, the cost of living remained fairly cheap. Important new cities appeared from time to time, notably Philip's foundation Philippopolis at his birthplace near Shahba in the Jebel Druze. The towns of Roman Africa were never more prosperous than between 175 and 240. Even after that, there was still a good deal of building as far afield and apart as Ostia, Britain and Egypt.[45] Moreover, Greek urban life, though some of its better manifestations had been driven underground, was hard to destroy, and would re-emerge later on. But it could never be the same again, and could never revive the self-sufficiency of earlier days. For meanwhile the urban middle class everywhere was almost taxed out of existence, or forced into the direct service of the emperor (p. 87).

This class had been the most typical institution of the ancient world, and was responsible for its major triumphs; it had also, under Roman rule, produced a regular supply of local loyalists or quislings prepared to collaborate with the central government. And yet any emperor who disliked the town-dwellers had his reasons. Leaving out of account their cultural dullness and unoriginality (which was not likely to worry a man like Maximinus I), they had for centuries lavished excessive sums on capital development and popular entertainment, and much of the imperial interference which had fallen upon them was due to their own extravagance and inefficiency. The rich townsmen, moreover, when not seeking popularity by adding unnecessary public buildings, spent their money on private luxuries or invested them in land; neither added to the wealth of the community. Moreover, some of the third-century emperors, with their peasant backgrounds, may have appreciated that the excessively urban nature of ancient civilization had set up a political and economic structure which disastrously divided the towns from the unprivileged countryside.

And yet this countryside, though it continued to be excluded from power, always remained the backbone of the Roman imperial economy. In an empire where foreign trade had never been important and was now further restricted by frontier hostilities and export bans, and where internal markets were limited to the very few people who could afford to buy any manufactured products whatever, the entire commerce and industry of all the cities together did not amount to more than 5 per cent of the revenue of the state— that is to say, of the payments in cash and kind required for the army and other services. The remaining 95 per cent had to be found from agriculture: principally wheat, with barley as the second most important cereal crop. And yet the cultivation of the land, in spite of these massive responsibilities, could not be improved very much, because a system founded on slaves[46] and tied tenants or serfs offered no incentives towards technological advance. Methods of cultivation and transport alike stagnated in conditions more primitive than those of the Middle Ages.[47]

And so the empire's output never rose much beyond bare subsistence level. During the third century agriculture, like commerce, does not, as has been sometimes supposed, show a uniform downward movement. Asia Minor was saved by its dependence on villages, and Britain, Aquitania, Syria, Palestine, north Africa and even disorderly Egypt had their agricultural successes. And yet a certain amount of soil must have gone out of use during the period. Factors contributing to this loss of cultivated areas included soil exhaustion and denudation, civil wars and invasions and plagues,[48] the failure and disappearance of cultivators ruined by heavy taxes, and the conscription of many more for the army and other services. The waste lands which thus came into being attracted the concern of a number of rulers.[49] Shrinkage of agricultural soil throughout the empire has been estimated at an average figure of 15 per cent. This was, for the most part, ground of inferior quality, and did not therefore represent the same percentual loss of production. Nevertheless, the diminution of land-use meant that those peasants who remained had a smaller area from which to raise their payments in kind.

Nor is it likely that the total population of the empire remained at its former figure of about seventy millions.[50] The devastations which caused land to go out of use raised the death-rate, and many country people were too poor to bring up their children. So the government's ever increasing demands for goods were levied not only from a smaller area, but also probably from a smaller population. But this was just the sort of factor likely to make emperors redouble their efforts to make their exactions as comprehensive as possible; and since the agricultural element in the imperial revenue was of such overwhelming importance, the conscriptions and compulsions imposed upon townsmen in cities and corporations were meticulously extended to the inhabitants of rural areas.

A great many of these, uprooted by the disorders of the third century, took refuge in the manorial estates which became one of the most prominent features of the age. Much the largest among such properties were those belonging to the crown. By his ownership of this vast and scattered complex of lands,[51] administered by an important ministry and contributing largely to the maintenance of parasitic Italy (p. 75), the emperor was far the greatest landowner in his empire. Furthermore he had become, by the third century, the greatest industrialist as well; for his mines, quarries and other industries, undertaken originally to support the needs of the estates themselves, had been expanded to dimensions which no other citizen, however wealthy, could begin to approach. In all these imperial activities, agricultural and industrial alike, forced labour was increasingly employed, and yet in order to stimulate recruitment the workers on imperial estates jealously tried to maintain their exemption from municipal burdens (p. 84).[52]

However, the emperor, although outstanding among landowners, was not alone in the field. For the concentration of peasants and other labourers on imperial land was increasingly mirrored on a smaller but still a very substantial scale in other estates. Indeed, during the third century A.D., these had replaced small-holdings as the dominant pattern of settlement and society. "The rich", said St. Cyprian, "add properties to properties and chase the poor from their borders. Their lands extend without limit or measure." The domains were controlled from huge country manors such as those which archaeologists have unearthed at Anthée (Namur), Cheragan (Toulouse), Brijuni Veliki (Brioni, Istria) and Fövenypuszta (Hungary). But there were also similar mansions and ranches in north Africa, Asia Minor, Babylonia, Palestine, Syria and south Russia. Some of these land-owners belonged to the old established

87

wealthy class, but on the whole this was a new aristocracy. The men who did well out of the authoritarian state regarded land as the only permanent investment for their gains. In Britain, as elsewhere, they lived at first in the towns, maintaining their estates as absentee landlords, but then during troubled times they withdrew to these country strongholds.

To the surrounding populations, the fortified manors were able to offer security. They provided a refuge to ruined freeholders, destitute urban workers and uprooted rustics, barbarians, vagabonds, deserters and slaves on the run. Without too many questions asked, these men became tenants (*coloni*) of the large proprietors and helped the slaves and imported barbarian settlers to cultivate their ranches.[53] Those who had a little land of their own placed it under the partial or complete control of their protectors, to whom they paid a fixed proportion of their crop.

These were self-contained great-house economies in which the central residence was surrounded by clusters of industrial as well as agricultural buildings.[54] The lords of the manor mobilized troops of tenants (*bucellarii*) who warded off disorderly plunderers—and tax collectors, both from the central administration and the cities, were kept at a distance too. But emperors could not do without the income which this new and powerful element in society was in a position to guarantee. Accordingly, the government came to an agreement with the landowners, in a fateful bargain and alliance. Their tax obligation was assessed at a fixed total, and they were authorized to raise this sum and whatever else they could from their tenants.

The texts of jurists reflect the rise of these self-sufficient feudal units. Emperors at first favoured legislation to protect the *coloni*, but before the third century was far advanced this considerate attitude had become subordinated to the need for funds. The instruments chosen to satisfy this need, the owners of the large estates, were excellently placed to cheat, not only the treasury, but also their own tenants, who rapidly deteriorated into serfs. Their wages were pegged down by the slave-labour with which they competed, and their helplessness laid them open to extortionate demands. Their fathers might have paid taxes amounting to one-third of their annual yield; they themselves probably paid as much as a half to their feudal boss. And the state, in collusion with these barons, decided that adequate extortions could only be maintained if tenants were forbidden to move from place to place. This process of fastening *coloni* to the soil had begun as early as the time of Hadrian. He deplored the practice,[55] and indeed even in the third century the law still left them free to go elsewhere. But a hundred years later they were officially tied to the land, and so were their descendants after them. In Europe, where there was always a source of potential new labourers from across the frontier, this subjection took some time to exercise full effects. It was more readily achieved in Greek lands, where hereditary service at a man's native place had been an institution of the monarchies that preceded Roman rule.

The emperor who completed the process of binding these tenants to estates was Diocletian, whose tax-assessments required that the rural populace should stay at work in the places where they were registered in the census. Thus landowners, as a reward for collaborating with the government, were relieved of their labour worries. Constantine confirmed that the attachment of tenants to manorial estates was legally binding, and he allowed landowners to cast into chains those suspected of planning to get away. Escape all too often meant vagabondage and beggary, but there were other loopholes and evasions as well, for the machinery for enforcement on the vast scale needed was lacking.[56] Moreover, in the Byzantine provinces ecclesiastical influence gradually secured mitigation of the law's full rigours, and after *c.* 600 eastern tenants became almost free. But the west, although it had been slower to adopt the system, did not relinquish it, and serfdom finally became the most characteristic of medieval institutions.

And so the government had imposed corporate and hereditary compulsion and liability upon the guilds, the cities and the tenants of great estates. Nor did compulsion stop there, for Diocletian and Constantine extended similar controls to government employees of every kind.[57] Soldiers, civil servants, miners; arms manufacturers, and workers in the state textile factories[58]; employees of the imperial police and postal service and mints and graveyards; all were under permanent and inherited obligations to remain at their jobs.

Except perhaps in the minds of a few lawyers, these gloomy results were not the expression of some theoretical *étatist* ideal. The authoritarian system was established because the Roman state would not be able to survive unless the army, confronted with vital tasks, received enormously increased payments in money and kind; and without this cumulation of Essential Work Orders and Restrictions on Engagement Orders, these contributions could not have been extracted from the population.[59]

Even if there was a merciful inability to bring into effect every coercion and prohibition which the emperors and jurists had thought out, this was a totalitarian state beyond anything which the ancient Assyrians or the Ptolemies of Egypt had contrived. The censor-ridden, standardizing police-administration advocated by Plato's *Laws* had arrived, and there seemed no possibility of its withering away. Aristotle regarded the state as originating in bare needs, and continuing in existence for the sake of the good life. But now, if the empire was to hang together, its bare needs were so great that the good life was enjoyed by very few. Even under earlier emperors, presiding over far more relaxed régimes, Tacitus had noted that liberty was the price that had to be paid for peace.[60] But he could have had no conception of the third and fourth centuries in which almost every trace of personal freedom was sacrificed to national survival. By these grim means, the empire regained its position against all its enemies, and endured. Many of its inhabitants at the time must have wondered if it was worth saving at the price.

If, on the other hand, these methods had not been adopted to hold the Roman world together, the classical heritage which it had taken over from ancient Greece could not have come down to us; and Christianity would have lacked the framework and civilized background which enabled it to expand.

NOTES

1. Commodus may have increased the sum to 375, but this is on the whole unlikely
2. Dio LXXVIII, 10, 4
3. There may have been a change in the relative values of gold and silver after his conquest of the Dacian gold-mines
4. The free Germans found good *denarii* hard to obtain, and turned increasingly to gold
5. *OGIS*. 515
6. Probably not $1\frac{1}{2}$ *denarii*, as has been suggested

7. MONETA AVGVSTI, AEQVITAS AVGVSTI, MONETA RESTITVTA (Severus Alexander)
8. P. Oxy. 1411 (Macrianus and Quietus)
9. Denomination-mark XX.I probably means: I *nummus*= 20 *sestertii* (5 *denarii*). The old brass and copper token coinage had ceased to exist
10. Gold pieces marked 60 to the pound, silver 96. Carausius had issued a good silver coinage in Britain
11. Mines were perhaps exhausted; cf. Cypr. *Ad Dem.* 1
12. Recently supplemented by fragment found at Sulmo (Sulmona)
13. Lact. *De Mort. Pers.* 7. In a papyrus a public official of Diocletian writes to a friend asking that all his money be laid out on goods regardless of price
14. The view that this is a mistake for 10,000 is probably wrong
15. P. Oxy. 1430. Perhaps the rise was not so extreme outside Egypt
16. Pertinax, Didius Julianus
17. Three times higher; more in second century
18. *SHA. Gall. Duo* 15, 1–2
19. Dio LXXVIII, 9, 2
20. Caracalla suppressed relatives' exemptions from death duties. The other principal indirect tax was the *portoria* (customs)
21. Rations were also found for armourers, animals and feed for the cavalry and postal service, foodstuffs for feeding the population of Rome, materials and labour for public works
22. *PSI.* 797
23. P. Ryl. 341
24. Chester Beatty Monographs No. 10, 1966 (Panopolis)
25. ? Or already Diocletian. Some regard *caput* as a unit of value (*unité de compte*) applicable to various standards. The tax was extended to non-agricultural populations in Italy and a few western provinces. Diocletian's operation had a dual rhythm, annual and quinquennial
26. P. Cairo Isid. 1 (tr. A. H. M. Jones)
27. P. Oxy. 2106
28. *follis* (*gleba senatoria*), tax on senators; *chrysargyron* (*collatio lustralis*) on traders
29. Maximinus II Daia and Licinius had made compulsory purchases of bullion from the cities
30. Constantine's silver coinage was not so abundant or successful as his gold, and before long lapsed
31. *Cod. Theod.* IV, 22
32. *frumentarii, stationarii, colletiones, eirenarchoi, diogmitai.* Centurions were especially prominent. Later, the church had its own legal and police officers
33. *Eis Bas.* 21 (62). Aristocrats' municipal police led revolution at Thysdrus (238) (for Gordianus I and II)
34. Lact. *De Mort. Pers.* 22
35. Keil-Premerstein, *Dritte Reise*, 9, 28, 55
36. *IGRR.* 1. 674; *Syll.*[3] 888
37. *OGIS.* 519
38. P. Oxy. 1490, 1469 (A.D. 298), 1477
39. Terra sigillata from Gaul, too, was for a time replaced by local wares from frontier cities (*c.* 200). Asia Minor still exported woollens, purples, linens; cf.

Egyptian textiles. Sea-transport, far cheaper than land-transport (*Edict of Diocletian*), was increasingly handled by a few Syrian and Jewish shippers. Against declines and obstacles (e.g. the ban on exports of military value to Parthia) and generally feeble technology can be set successes, e.g. the pure white glass made at Colonia Agrippina (Köln); water-wheel emplacements at Barbegal (Provence) turning out 8 times as much flour as neighbouring Arelate; perhaps production of first true steel, by means of improved bellows

40. *ILS*. 6987 (A.D. 201)

41. Eventually: bakers, carters, bargees, stevedores, tally clerks (corn-measurers), pork beef and mutton butchers, oil merchants, smiths

42. Mitteis, *Chrest*. 375, cf. P. Ryl. ii. 75 (2), *PSI*. 292

43. Petr. Patr. *fr*. 10, 4

44. *Cod. Theod*. I, 13

45. *Corp. Pap. Hermopolitanorum* (A.D. 250–75)

46. Slaves, very expensive in the first and second centuries A.D., then became much more numerous and cheaper amid disturbed conditions. Slaves were unknown in Egyptian agriculture, fairly common in Italy

47. An alternate year of fallow was normal, water-mills were rare, most corn was ground in hand-querns, cloth was woven on hand-looms, and the horse-collar had not yet been invented

48. Especially A.D. 167, spreading from Seleucia on the Tigris (? small-pox or exanthematous typhus or bubonic plague), and A.D. 250, from Ethiopia (lasting 13–15 years)

49. Marcus, Pertinax, Aurelian, Probus. Peasants and barbarians were brought in to work such lands in Africa, Italy, Greece, Gaul, Danube, etc.

50. A population decline has been argued from the hardships of the time and the sums paid for the manumission of slaves at Delphi. The birth-rate and death-rate was roughly equal to India *c*. 1900. Women lived for a shorter time than men, and townsmen than countrymen

51. Septimius distinguished between crown property and personal estate, built up by confiscations (later merged)

52. E.g. Marcus, Septimius

53. E.g. Preisigke, *Sammelb*. 4284 (A.D. 207). The process started first in second century A.D.

54. Anthée: foundries, breweries, bronze and enamelled articles, pottery, harness, leather work. Cheragan: 80 smaller buildings

55. *Dig*. 49.14

56. Constantine's ruling came to be limited to descendants of tenants originally registered on an estate. End of the fifth century: free tenants tied by a thirty-year prescription

57. Constantine extended Diocletian's compulsion of soldiers to officials

58. Under Diocletian and Constantine there were 17 in the west alone

59. A. H. M. Jones

60. Tac. *Hist*. I, 16; cf. *Dial. De Or*. 40, 41

4

The Emperor and His Agents

The Emperor

The later empire is often called the dominate as opposed to the principate of the early emperors. For the increased autocracy of the times, no longer concealed under the ingratiating Republican term of first citizen (*princeps*), was now brought out into the open in a new, undisguised presentation which may be symbolized by the title *dominus* or Lord. This form of address, used by slaves to their masters, was for a long time shunned by rulers who cared for public opinion. Gradually, however, it came to be applied to second-century monarchs in unofficial language and in the administrative terminology of the provinces. This practice was not at first followed by the central government, but Septimius was called Lord, or Our Lord, with greater frequency than his predecessors. It was characteristic of the third century to give official sanction to usages and titles that had hitherto been informal, and by the time of Severus Alexander the emperor was being called Lord on many inscriptions—though the *Historia Augusta*, at pains to emphasize his moderation, claims that he would not allow himself to be addressed in this way. But then Aurelian, at Serdica (Sofia) in his own home country, was described on a coin as 'born god and lord' (DEO ET DOMINO NATO). This remained exceptional; but the official coinage, habitually conservative about titles, extended the use of the word *dominus* to Diocletian and Maximian, though not until after their abdication (305). Licinius and Constantine, during their joint reign, seem to have been the first to bear the title officially.[1]

One of the Augustan fictions, then, had been dropped. But the dropping of slogans was never complete. Marcus Aurelius, while raising funds for his German wars, had declared that he himself

93

possessed nothing and was lodged by the state. This was a corollary of the Stoic view that a ruler was there to serve his subjects. The writings of Constantine, too, are full of references to his service and his mission. Throughout the period the two theories of autocracy and service co-existed, and were complementary to one another rather than contradictory. This parallel, simultaneous existence of two approaches to the imperial role was reflected by jurists. There was a longstanding tradition that the emperor was subject to the laws, and this interpretation continued to be expressed. But the situation was complicated by his role as creator of law (p. 103). The jurist Gaius, in the second century, had already recognized the full validity of imperial enactments, and in the Severan age Ulpian corroborated this.[2] Conservatives, such as the historian Dio Cassius, might express hopes that the senate would still legislate, but by the end of the second century its lawgiving activities were superseded, just as those of the national assembly had become obsolete two hundred years earlier.

Did the fact that the emperor had now become the one and only legislator mean that he himself was above the laws? His predecessors never had been, and emperors themselves continued to assert that they were bound by law. One of the outstanding jurists of the time, Paulus, takes the constitutionalist view that it is "befitting to the imperial majesty to live according to the laws from which the emperor himself seems to be exempt".[3] Ulpian, on the other hand, was conscious of cases in which the emperor's exemption was real and absolute.[4] Paulus' formula of constitutional monarchy may perhaps represent a reaction, under the correct young Severus Alexander, from the more autocratic version (departing from the principate of Augustus) that Ulpian had sponsored under Caracalla. But it was Ulpian's formulization which stood for the future in which it became possible to address a fourth century emperor as "the living law and superior to written laws". And this was generally acceptable, since anarchy and invasion had bred everywhere a passionate longing to be looked after by a superior being.

And yet, by a paradox, the only way in which the emperor could exercise this supremacy, and protect his people, was by a division of responsibility. The problems were too great for one man to deal with alone. Nor was it enough to delegate to the praetorian prefect the powers of a deputy (p. 105); he lacked the charisma, and was often rightly suspected of seeking to become emperor himself. For a spreading of the load which would not cause such anxieties it was necessary to turn to other members of the imperial family itself. From the time of Augustus onwards, sons and adoptive sons had been elevated to preferential status during the ruler's lifetime (p. 30). Marcus Aurelius and Lucius Verus reigned conjointly with equal rights and sometimes an informal territorial division (161–9), and then it was said that Caracalla and Geta, joint rulers as a result of the strong dynastic policy of their father Septimius, proposed to share out the empire by a geographical partition (211).[5] This is doubtful (and in any case Caracalla murdered Geta), but it represents the practice which soon developed as the best means of administering the empire, defending its frontiers, and keeping a closer watch on possible rivals and usurpers. Moreover, such measures could be commended by antiquarians—who were numerous in governing circles—through comparison with the ancient institution of the two consuls, serving together as colleagues. Later, it was with that antique practice in mind that the senate briefly and disastrously elevated two of its senior members, Balbinus and Pupienus, to joint imperial status, with the former to rule at home while the latter took the field against Maximinus I (238). This association was signalized on the coinage by untruthful references to "the Mutual Love of the Emperors". Then the hard-pressed Valerian divided the empire into two parts, taking the east himself, and giving the west to his son Gallienus (256). This was the first overt territorial division,[6] though it did not lessen the father's authority; the same was true when Carus left his son Carinus in charge of half the empire (282–3).

After Carus' death, Carinus divided the empire with his brother Numerian. But it remained for Diocletian to regularize the division, with himself remaining in the east and his fellow-Augustus Maximian in the west. Moreover, this was not a twofold but a fourfold division, with not only two Augusti but also in due course two Caesars (Constantius I Chlorus and Galerius)—each under one of the Augusti, and all four of them with a geographical region of their own. This situation was partly the product of necessity, for Maximian could not have lower rank than the British usurper Carausius against whom he or his subordinate was fighting (p. 34), and the two Caesars were likewise elevated under duress of outside events. But the arrangement was developed into a system which was intended to be permanent. This Tetrarchy multiplied authority, but did not divide it; in spite of the regional sub-divisions, the empire was still "an undivided patrimony".[7] The law of the one Augustus was the law of the other, and Caesars obeyed both Augusti, and legislation was in the name of all four.

After ruling for twenty-one years, Diocletian abdicated, though whether he did so by a long prearranged plan or owing to coercion and physical collapse will never be known. The simultaneous abdication of his colleague Maximian was reluctant and temporary, and the system of neat transitions and promotions, which had only held together owing to the force of Diocletian's personality, broke down. Within the next two decades Constantine managed to re-establish unity, and yet he too, looking into the future, finally thought it best to ordain partition among his three sons and another young kinsman. By the end of the fourth century the dichotomy between eastern and western empires was permanent, and in many respects the two halves were going their own ways.

All these measures of division, like the increasing autocracy which they accompanied, were directed towards a more efficient assertion of power against internal rivals and foreign enemies. Imperial propaganda does not refer to the former peril except in general, delicate, allusions to the Security of the Emperor. But there is continual stress on his role of conquering defender against the foreign foes who pressed remorselessly on every side. It was pre-eminently as conqueror of the barbarians that the publicity of the time liked to depict its ruler: and the inscriptions on the coinage pointed urgently to his military prestige. This emphasis becomes increasingly notable during the dangers which encompassed the empire under Marcus Aurelius. Forgetting the themes of domestic policy and religious myth which had figured largely on earlier issues, his coins proclaim him as supreme war-lord and warrior. From now on there is incessant concentration on this first and most imperative demand that the Roman people had to make—victorious leadership and prowess.

A statue of Hadrian had shown him with a recumbent captive beneath his feet,[8] and Septimius re-enacted in person the time-honoured practice of trampling down a fallen enemy with his horse.[9]

The theme developed to a feverish pitch under Constantine and his successors, who reiterate their victoriousness as perpetual conquerors of all races everywhere. And while the enemies who were crushed, in propaganda if not in fact, often included the Persians, these retaliated in the same vein, showing a probably fictitious scene of Shapur I trampling the Roman Gordian III (p. 43).[10]

The dangers and disasters of the mid-third century made people long to revere the saviour-qualities, if any, in the emperor. Gallic professors praising Maximian, Constantius I Chlorus and Constantine at Augusta Trevirorum repeat continually that these rulers have saved the world from catastrophe. Never has devotion been expressed in language so unrestrained; never has there been such intense hatred and fear of the barbarian foes. The man who could ward them off was surely the elect and companion of gods, and when Constantine made Christianity the state religion he, too, was seen to be in a special relation with his deity (pp. 224, 232).

This same aggrandisement of the emperor was reflected in imperial ceremonial, which developed into a formidable pattern not far removed in spirit from the customs which prevailed at the contemporary court of the Persian enemy.

A greeting ceremony for Caracalla had already shown the development of hierarchic etiquette,[11] and obeisance or kow-towing, of some more definite and subservient nature than hitherto, is taken for granted by third century writers.[12] The greeting (*salutatio*) received by earlier emperors was superseded by the prostration (*adoratio*) previously reserved for gods or kings. Elagabalus had already attempted to introduce prostration, but it remained for Diocletian to make *adoratio* a formal institution of the court. The move was part of a growing tendency, going back to various Greco-Roman and oriental traditions, to submerge respect for the emperor's personal qualities in a general reverence for the imperial office in the abstract. The obeisance to Diocletian worshipped the purple rather than himself. Such practices took permanent root; many features of his court and its behaviour and titles, formalizing earlier usages, led on to a thousand years of Constantinople, and to the ceremonials of Teutonic kingdoms.

Diocletian and his fellow-Augustus and their two Caesars were withdrawn from human contact, living in an awe-inspiring seclusion which was inaccessible to the security hazards of soldiery and disaffected subjects. The infrequent public appearances of the rulers, staged in imperial buildings designed for these occasions (p. 141), were spectacular epiphanies in gorgeous robes. Already for a century the dress of the emperors had been gaining in magnificence. From the time of Marcus Aurelius onwards the coins, and particularly the commemorative medallions which exploited less conservative aesthetic possibilities, increasingly concentrated on this aspect of autocratic grandeur. Gold embroidery as a permanent feature of the imperial mantle and tunic seems to date from Commodus,[13] and then, as the prejudice against emperors wearing military costume in Rome began to weaken, medallion portraits depict many a splendid variety of richly decorative shields, eagle sceptres, Olympian fringed cloaks (*aegis*) worn off-shoulder, and half-length representations of the imperial figure in god-like semi-nudity—just as, conversely, gods are now sometimes portrayed in the robes of emperors. A painting displays Septimius clad in a glorified variation of the costume worn at generals' Triumphs, and Severus Alexander's medallions show him decked out in a new elaboration of this triumphal guise.

During a brief interlude in the Severan dynasty (217–18), the emperor Macrinus appeared in public wearing brooches and a breastplate lavishly adorned with gold and precious gems, extravagances of which the Roman soldiery was said not to approve because they seemed more appropriate to barbarians and women.[14] The consular robes, too, were transformed into bejewelled splendour on coins of Gallus (251–3).[15] This sort of gala costume, richly embroidered with elaborate stitching, becomes ever more dazzling and stylized in a series of coin-portraits of Probus. Emperors now exhibit chain-mail of gaudy magnificence, and the laurel and oak wreaths traditional to Roman leaders are beginning to be replaced by diadems, which had always been understood to represent autocracy. A silver medallion of Gallienus seems to show such a diadem; Aurelian was said to have worn one, and a medallion of Numerian (283–4) displays a diadem with a star above the brow. Diocletian and his fellow-tetrarchs wear helmets studded with precious stones, and their grim features contrast strangely with the gold-hemmed gorgeousness of their robes. Then the heads of Licinius and Constantine are framed in a *nimbus* or halo which betokens the unearthly light streaming from their countenances, the outward expression of their inward divine illumination (p. 224). During the fourth century there is little to choose in hierarchic splendour between the Romans and their Sassanian enemies or "brothers", except that the Romans did not imitate the pleated ribbons, necklaces and ear-rings of the Persians, or their numismatic portrayal of monarchs each with his own distinctive crown. On the Roman side, no one was more fond of ostentation than Constantine, whose regal profusion of locks is adorned by diadems studded with pearls. Such glorious displays are the outer sign of the new Christian absolutism defined and described by Eusebius of Caesarea in Palestine (260–340) in his enthusiastic biography of Constantine. This pioneer ecclesiastical historian adapted the traditional Greek philosophies of kingship to Constantinian use, praising contemporary autocracy as the archetypal form of government which corresponded to God's monarchy and opposed the anarchic disorder of democratic equality.[16]

The emperor, encrusted with jewellery, had lost all personal characteristics except those expressible in the superlatives of veneration, and the statues which attempt to convey this grandeur had frozen into a supernatural immobility far removed from classical humanism (p. 130). Indeed during their public appearances the rulers themselves were as rigid and immobile as their statues. On the single occasion when Constantine's son Constantius II visited Rome (357), he moved through the city turning his eyes neither to the right nor the left. When the wheels of his carriage shook him, he did not even nod his head; and he never moved his hands. He seemed to onlookers like an effigy or simulacrum of a man.

The Government

The Roman senate had few powers other than nominal ones. But its six hundred members were very rich men. They also included the senior generals, whose support the emperor needed; and senators enjoyed great prestige among all classes.[17]

Originally they had all been Italians, and under Vespasian (A.D. 69–79) over 80 per cent were still of Italian origin. But Trajan (98–117), himself from Spain, admitted provincials as often as Italians; and soon after his death Italy provided not much more than half the senate's total strength, with Africans now becoming members alongside Gauls and Spaniards. During the latter part of the second century, in spite of Marcus' efforts to keep the senate racially pure,[18] there was a continuing shift of emphasis from westerners to Syrians and Asians and other orientals, who had provided only a small contribution until now.

Under Septimius and Caracalla these tendencies increased. Out of 479 of their senators whose origins are known, 204 were Italians, representing only just over 40 per cent of the total and including very few survivors of the 43 patrician families that had existed a century earlier. These Severan 479 also included 41 members from the western provinces, 72 from Africa, 5 from the Illyrian region, and 157 from the east.[19] Throughout the third century, Italian membership remained static at the same percentage, and the proportion of easterners stayed at a figure rather over 30 per cent.[20] But the proportion of westerners among provincial senators had declined from 70 per cent under Vespasian to 13.6 per cent at the end of the third century. The relatively uneducated Danubian populations, in spite of their immense contributions to the army and to the list of emperors, continued to provide only a few members to the senate.

The normal attitude of rulers to that body was a blend of conciliation and suspicion. The latter feeling showed itself in arrangements to keep certain key posts in the hands of non-senators. For example, although provincial governorships and military commands always went to members of the senate, Augustus had instead entrusted not only the governorship of the immensely rich new province of Egypt but the command of his praetorian guard to the knights or equestrian order (*equites*), the class of society based on property qualifications next below those of senators. During the second century the knights, who normally reached that rank by holding three officer posts in the army, often served as advisers attached to high senatorial officials and represented them as deputies.

Under the Severan dynasty this practice was extended to provincial governorships, which were kept vacant and occupied by knights in an acting capacity. Septimius, like some of his first century predecessors, was unfriendly to the senate, because so many of its members had supported his enemies in the civil wars; and its privileges must have seemed pointless in an age when there was a growing imperial civil service. Septimius eliminated the senators he disliked, and in their place drafted new members from among the knights. Many of these had reached knightly status from N.C.O. and private soldier rank.[21] Septimius further weakened the influence of senatorial traditionalism by selecting knights to occupy the recently established governorship of Mesopotamia, and the command of his newly mobilized legions.

This break-up of established patterns became clearly perceptible when the army created the first emperor who was not a senator but a knight, a lawyer from Mauretania named Macrinus (217–18). This was a severe shock to conservatives such as the Greek senator and historian Dio Cassius. Writing either just before or after Macrinus' reign,[22] Dio makes Augustus' adviser Maecenas, ostensibly debating against the more democratic Agrippa, advocate a stable, centralized, sharply graded society, opposed to change since this can only bring dislocation. Officials, believed Dio who was himself a Bithynian, should be taken from all parts of the empire, but only from the old-established citizens—a trained and *élite* ruling class which the emperor should take into partnership so as to prevent political interference by the proletariat.[23] The emperor, Maecenas is made to add, may regard consultation of the senate as a formality, but all the same he should not omit to seek its views, and he should guarantee the dignity and personal safety of senators.

Admirers of Severus Alexander (222–35), under whom Dio held high office, said that this emperor revived senatorial powers. But his apparent deference was due to weakness rather than liberalism, and in any case did not alter inexorable trends. Dio urged that senators should not be deprived of military commands, but the tendency in this direction was maintained.[24] Very soon knights are found as frontier commanders at Dura and in Tripolitania, and from the time of Gallienus, though he himself came from a distinguished senatorial family, military commands do not seem to have gone to any senators but were all held by knights. The senate now only provided the governors for ungarrisoned provinces and the occupants of certain administrative and judicial posts in Rome and Italy.[25] These developments formed part of a growing separation between civil government and military command. Each emperor wanted to give the big military appointments to experts—and experts who owed their positions to himself alone, and did not feel bound to any other loyalty.

Yet, though the senate no longer contained the most important officers and comprised few of the Danubians who dominated the military scene, its interests and those of the army were drawing together. The senate's membership included the great landowners who collaborated with the army to keep the peasants in tax-paying subjection. Besides, this was an age when symbolic and abstract values often seemed more important than reality, and, as the senate's power declined, military men venerated this ancient gathering more and more as the mirror of eternal Rome (p. 214). This was the spirit in which Diocletian, although he gave members little employment, repeated formal honours to the senate as an expression of the united commonwealth; and its Genius is portrayed on his monument in the Roman Forum.

The separation of the civil government from the military command was completed by Constantine. But by now, if not before, the old division between senators and knights was abolished altogether. In a senate of greatly enlarged dimensions[26]—duplicated before long at Constantinople—the two classes merged into a single grade of administrative officials and powerful landowners, of whom Constantine made abundant use. The old hierarchy had finally given way to a different and almost medieval system. Moreover, the same emperor sought to increase the number of his own devoted supporters by creating a new order of nobility, the Imperial Companions (*comites*). There had always been "friends of the emperor", enjoying privileges of personal association and etiquette; they were all senators until the time of Septimius, who had drawn them from the knights as well. But Constantine made these friends into official companions occupying the position at the emperor's pleasure or for life. They were divided into three grades, and selected members served on the imperial council.

That council, an inner advisory committee far closer to the emperor than the senate, originated from the traditional Roman practice by which an official of the Republic, in making a decision, was accustomed to choose a group of assessors or friends and take advice from them. Augustus had developed this Republican custom, and his councillors prepared the business of the senate. But the second century A.D. brought the council wider powers, because the emperors, being now practically the only source of law (p. 94), needed legislative advice: they also used their council as a judicial private court. Hadrian's council members already included a professional nucleus of experts, and by Severan times the policy-making departmental heads of the civil service were dominant in its deliberations, with the praetorian prefect as deputy chairman.

Septimius allowed his council considerable freedom, but his ill-tempered son Caracalla was impatient of advice. Nevertheless, as more and more branches of the government came under imperial control, this committee, with the approval even of Dio Cassius, reached the height of its influence, playing a dominant part in the transformation of the Roman world. The outstanding jurists of the day were now among its members (p. 105)—in Severus Alexander's council of seventy members they were twenty strong, the balance being provided by senators and civil servants. Their business had become so formalized that the written views of all members were now recorded. An emperor such as Maximinus I (235–8), whose autocratic tendencies were limited by his poor knowledge of Latin, depended on them to a considerable extent; though during the even tougher times that followed we do not hear a great deal about the institution.

Diocletian's council, however, was an influential advisory cabinet. Senior civil servants were prominent members, and Constantine's further reorganization of the body under the name of *consistorium* (because the members no longer sat but stood in the emperor's presence) was marked by the triumph of the civil service chiefs, who were subject only to the emperor in their exercise of judicial, executive and legislative control.

The imperial civil service originally consisted of slaves and freedmen, and eventually knights, from whom the emperor, in order to supplement the old Republican state machinery, had drawn his household staff and relatively small central secretariats and accountancy departments, and the financial staffs of his agents in the provinces. Second-century emperors and especially Septimius, who derived his major officials from Syria, Asia Minor and his native Africa, expanded this imperial bureaucracy, which now increasingly assumed the character of a separate organization. The chaotic period that followed, when few emperors were able to establish themselves firmly, gave the administrative machinery an independent strength of its own,[27] which rulers such as Gallienus, unwilling to make the senate a pillar of their regimes, gladly recognized.

Under Diocletian this autonomous civil service became enormous, absorbing a substantial part of the entire middle class of the empire. Diocletian needed a much more elaborate organization so as to levy the men and supplies necessary for this enlarged army (p. 76); indeed, in order to stress its subordination to the emperor, the governmental administration itself took on a military shape. And so the massive civil service pursued its bureaucratic, ill-paid, corrupt, and partly but not wholly inefficient career through the ensuing centuries,[28] becoming the essential element in the structure which held the Byzantine empire together.

A major change was also introduced in provincial administration. Diocletian, who had himself served as a governor, more than doubled the number of provinces, so that the men in charge of these relatively small areas, completely separated from military commands, should have little opportunity to revolt and should concentrate on jurisdiction and finance (p. 38). However, Diocletian also innovated by grouping these provinces, now a hundred in number, into thirteen major units or dioceses. These big territories, pointing the way to national groupings of the future, comprised the Orient (Syria, Mesopotamia, Palestine, Egypt), two dioceses in Asia Minor (Asiana and Pontica), three in the Balkans (Moesia, Thrace and Pannonia), one each in north and south Italy, Africa, Spain, north and south Gaul, and Britain.[29] The dioceses were for a time administered by governors-general (*vicarii*) under the praetorian prefects.[30] But in most areas, between the times of Diocletian and Constantine, governors-general faded out in favour of direct contact between prefects and provincial governors.

The praetorian prefects had originally been commanders of the emperor's personal bodyguard. In the early empire these functionaries, holding office singly or more often sharing their powers between two or occasionally three colleagues, had played vital parts in bringing emperors to the throne and keeping them there. Although this sort of crisis temporarily became more infrequent during the more stable second century, prefects continued to fulfil an increasingly important role as military deputies of the emperor, acting as his quartermasters-general and often performing the duties of chief of staff on campaigns.

Rulers had not interpreted the prefecture as anything like a vice-emperorship, preferring to keep exalted positions of that sort, if they were needed, within their own families. The first prefect given an opportunity to exploit such wider possibilities on an extensive scale was Perennis, who rose from being joint holder of the office under Marcus Aurelius to its sole occupancy under Commodus. Perennis fell (185), but his enhanced authority was soon afterwards inherited by the emperor's chamberlain, a Phrygian freedman called Cleander. The next prefect, Laetus, played a leading part in the murder of two emperors and was executed for suspected treachery by the next (193).[31] Septimius' African compatriot Plautianus reached giddy eminence by marrying his daughter to the emperor's son Caracalla, but his new son-in-law shortly afterwards arranged his downfall (205).

By now the prefects were deputy-chairmen of the imperial council. They were also given the function of raising the taxes in kind on which the army depended for its supplies, so that the prefecture, expanding far beyond its original functions, had become an all-important ministry of finance (pp. 74-5). Moreover, Septimius normally delegated to his prefects the hearing of appeals from provincial governors—which were particular frequently as a result of the civil wars—and entrusted them with Italian jurisdiction that standing jury-courts had undertaken before.[32] Because of this increasingly important legal aspect of the prefects' powers, there now followed a period during which the greatest jurists of the age, and perhaps of any age, served in the place (or as colleagues) of the generals who usually occupied the office. Papinian and Ulpian became praetorian prefects (p. 108), and the Roman government was in the hands of lawyers. But this phase, inaugurated by Septimius and continued by Caracalla, was not very successful owing to the difficulty experienced by lawyers in controlling the guardsmen, and after two decades prefects were army men again. Dio Cassius had been nervous that these officials would win too much power in the military sphere,[33] and indeed Gordian III, himself too young to lead the imperial forces, not only married the daughter of his prefect but entrusted him with the supreme wartime command (242).

Fortunately for him this official, Timesitheus, was not only an able general and administrator but a man of disinterested loyalty. It is doubtful if the same can be said of Philip, who succeeded first to the prefecture and then to the imperial throne. When Valerian and Gallienus divided the empire between them, each had his own prefect.

The praetorian prefect, like other military administrators, had always possessed a staff of officials and clerks seconded from the army, and under Diocletian, as part of a general militarization of the government, this infiltration by soldiers increased. By now the prefects, who were still two in number, had become grand viziers with a huge separate organization responsible for collecting the taxes in kind and cash. They also maintained the roads and postal service and arms factories, and supervised the administration of the provinces, first through their deputies and later direct.

But Constantine decided that such a concentration of powers in the hands of prefects was too large to be efficient or safe. From now on, although retaining many duties including the supply of the army's recruits, weapons and rations, they lost their functions of military command, which passed to the new Masters of the Horse and Foot. Moreover when Constantine, at the end of his reign, divided the empire among the younger generation, the praetorian prefecture was likewise split into separate offices at the disposal of each of the heirs apparent.[34]

The Climax of Roman Law

Roman Law is the supreme expression of Roman rational organization and order. Applying the laws as each instance arose, according to recorded precedents and with a keen eye for the practical needs and circumstances of daily life, the jurists gradually built a systematic structure, founded upon a blend of scientific thinking and common sense. They had come into existence in the remote past because the College of Priests, repositories of the sacred law, had disclosed its secrets to the general public. The consequent need for interpretation opened the way to secular jurists. But when secular courts were created it became established that legal rules could not be laid down by the arbitrary act of the public officials who presided over them. Accordingly expert jurists sat in their courts. These had to ask themselves what was implied in the ordinary or extraordinary informal acts and happenings of everyday life, and what the normal effects of these acts would be. The general recognition of such conclusions as valid and efficacious had been an early triumph of Roman Law. For half a millennium the central part of the jurists' work was the giving of legal opinions. They were not advocates, and their consequent detachment from the results raised their interpretations above partisanship to a universal significance. They were also engaged in literary and teaching activity, consisting of exposition on the basis of selected cases.

And so jurisprudence, defined as the knowledge of divine and human and of what is just and unjust,[35] developed steadily from at least 300 B.C. onwards. Its practitioners remained unofficial until Augustus permitted selected jurists to give opinions on his own authority, so that they became mouthpieces of the imperial régime. During the second century A.D., legislation ceased to be an activity of the senate, which gradually turned into a mere registry of laws communicated by the emperor.[36] But most of this imperial action was only legislative in a formal sense, consisting of answers to questions referred to the ruler for his decision. These answers were drafted for him by the jurists, who now ushered in the most creative and philosophical period of Roman Law. Salvius Julianus, an African of extraordinary talent, offered Hadrian a consolidated code when he was still under the age of thirty (129). Then Cervidius Scaevola advised one able emperor-lawyer, Marcus, and was the teacher of another, Septimius.[37]

In the latter's reign developed the second phase of this Golden Age of Roman Law. Although perhaps less creative than the previous phase, it witnessed the working out of existing principles over the entire field. The jurists who undertook this collection, criticism and interpretation of the classical heritage still spent most of their time advising officials; but they also displayed a Greek tendency (being mostly of eastern origin) to write down their transactions. These pronouncements, which came to be recognized as a source of law in themselves, are the most far-reaching of all Rome's contributions to posterity. They also provide one of the surest ways to a knowledge of the empire, revealing how rulers acted and considered themselves required to act—letting us into the secrets of the imperial machine, and of the imperial conscience as well.[38] The new urgency with which Septimius and his successors depended on the expert knowledge of the jurists is revealed by the appearance of their most eminent representatives as members of the emperor's council and, above all, as successive praetorian prefects (p. 105).

The first lawyer to hold the prefecture was Papinian, probably a Syrian by birth like Septimius' wife, and like Septimius himself a pupil of Cervidius Scaevola. Papinian became prefect in 203, but in 212 under Caracalla, either because of insufficient partisanship against the latter's murdered brother or owing to his own unpopularity as a non-military man, he was killed by the guard at the new emperor's instigation. Papinian wrote no comprehensive systematic treatise, but his voluminous collections and summaries of decisions have made him the most famous name in all Roman jurisprudence. Independent, unafraid of changing his mind, he produced solutions that are original, closely reasoned and of unequalled precision. A little more given to generalization than his contemporaries, he allowed full scope to equity, ethics and humanity. Papinian possessed a critical and judicial rather than a fertile mind, and his criticisms are deliberate, unprejudiced and moderate; he applied the law responsibly and with the surest instinct. There is elegance in the almost archaic, lapidary terseness of his style, which unerringly and without parade relates the facts to the legal principle involved, and brings out the essential point and only that.

In the fifth century Papinian was singled out as the decisive casting vote if authorities disagreed (A.D. 426). Nowadays much weight is also given to earlier jurists. And yet, with the possible exception of Hadrian's adviser Salvius Julianus, no one else can compete with him; though some would now add Ulpian.[39] That lawyer, who came from Tyre, wrote under Caracalla, became joint praetorian prefect in 222 under Severus Alexander, and after failing to master the guardsmen was murdered some years later. His enormous works, reflecting the contemporary civil service trend towards codification, were designed to cover the whole range of the law, so that reference to previous authorities would become unnecessary. Ulpian is reliable, businesslike and unaffected, writing with superlative clarity and ease (though also a certain bureaucratic guardedness), and displaying perfect mastery of his gigantic, complicated material.

Paulus was praetorian prefect at the same time as Ulpian; these last years of lawyer-prefects were full of trouble and mutiny, and the fact that the two men do not cite each other's works suggests that they had never been very amicable. Paulus' writings, the most voluminous of all, included a large number of systematic monographs, and an influential book (or compilation from a book) known as the *Opinions* (*Sententiae*).[40] The views and style of Paulus are so hard to disentangle from later interpolations that he has been subject to varied judgements, including accusations of being fanciful and doctrinaire. He was deficient in urbanity, and he had a taste for contradictions. And yet, while lacking Ulpian's exact clearness, Paulus seems to have excelled him in breadth of interest, independence, abstract reasoning power, and penetrating criticism of other jurists' opinions. But the aim of both of them was the same, and it was conceived in the spirit of late antiquity; to sum up and condense and clarify an enormous volume of earlier material into simple expositions of the whole legal system.[41]

The pursuance of this task was terminated in the middle of the third century by the increasing absolutism of emperors, the perilous instability of their governments, and the counter-attraction exercised upon able minds by the complexities of Christian theology. And so the age of the great jurists ended.[42] But imperial legislation continued on a massive scale. Diocletian, maintaining that "the worst of all sins is to upset things that have once been ordained and prescribed by our forefathers",[43] sought to suppress Greek and other non-Roman concepts and to spread Roman Law throughout his entire empire. Nearly 1,300 of his answers to judges' questions or to private petitions have survived. The same reign also witnessed the production of compilations, extending back to Hadrian's time, of the imperial rulings which were now the only source of law. These collections were utilized for generations as legal reference books and, despite their private character, were accepted as authoritative in the courts.[44]

Under Diocletian, then, the traditions of classical legal science were still preserved. But a new crudity became perceptible in the western emperor Valentinian III's Law of Citations (426), which laid down rules for the employment of classical juristic writings in court. The framers of the measure had a poor opinion of contemporary judges, and were not too able themselves; though their efforts at least allowed a careful barrister to tell his client the law. The Code of the eastern emperor Theodosius II (438), comprising an official collection of imperial statutes from the year 312, seems to have formed part of a general scheme for codifying legislation[45]; and together with Paulus' *Opinions* and Diocletian's collections, it passed into the Vulgar Law which summarized and simplified Roman Law for the barbarian west.

As the academic study of the subject continued to revive in the eastern empire, the jurists of past centuries were perpetuated in the code of Justinian I, which contains almost all that we know of Roman legal institutions (528–34).[46] This massive classification and commentary, which compressed a vast bulk of material into two volumes of manageable size, was undertaken by a commission of sixteen members, with a civil servant Tribonian usually in the chair; the commissioners were directed to apply considerations of humanity, common sense and public utility. The main part of their task, the compilation of the *Digest*, was a monument to the Severan jurists, for more than half its contents are versions – partially interpolated and modified – of the writings of Papinian, Ulpian and Paulus.[47] Ulpian alone provided 2,462 extracts, amounting to one-third of the entire collection.

Through this preservation of their work in the *Digest*, the lawyer-prefects of Septimius and his successors have exercised more far-reaching influence upon the world than any other Latin writers, without excepting even Virgil, Cicero or Ovid. For when Justinian's Code was rediscovered in twelfth-century Italy and utilized by Irnerius for his teaching at Bologna, it became the principal support of popes and emperors and men of affairs, and a major factor in the intellectual reawakening of Europe: the universalist dreams of Caracalla and Diocletian had almost been fulfilled after a thousand years' delay. The writings of the Severan jurists, embodied in the *Digest*, were now the *lingua franca* of the law, and these abundant practical solutions and clear and rational distinctions fascinated the most gifted men of the day. And so the legal methods and conclusions of Septimius' time became patterns for future ages. Until a century ago, they still dominated large areas. Even today, as in the past two millennia, they still provide, through direct and indirect descendants, much of the method and framework by which the law adapts itself to successive generations and forms of government.

The jurists of the second, third and fourth centuries respected human rights in so far as these did not conflict with the overriding needs of the state. Marcus Aurelius gave women more of a legal existence than they had enjoyed before, and both he and Septimius protected the interests of minors and slaves. The latter, it is true, were still chattels, and slavery was recognized to be part of international custom, but some lawyers now asserted that it was contrary to nature.[48]

Where politics and taxation were not involved, the jurists, sitting as prefects or as judges in the prefects' courts or as advisory experts on the emperor's council, did what they could to maintain the fundamental institutions of Roman Law—the family, private property and the sanctity of contracts—and even modified them in humane directions compatible with a new sensitiveness for human suffering (p. 119). Consequently, in spite of the severity of his régime, Septimius showed humanitarianism in his laws against abortion, measures protecting wives against the loss of their dowries, grants of privileges to large families and destitute children,[49] and a general tendency to ensure that people suffered less for the sins of their fathers. Loan-banks were established for the purchase of land, and wider autonomy was given to provincial governors, so as to enable them not only to meet emergencies but to protect the weak and poor against their more powerful neighbours and the soldiery (p. 81).[50] Later emperors continued to legislate in similar vein.[51] Thus the autocracy which the lawyers were now helping to create was not only centralized but showed a marked increase in standardization and equalization. These processes had already become perceptible under Marcus Aurelius, whose policy mirrored the praise of equal law and rights which he expresses in his *Meditations*.[52] Dio Cassius, too, speaking through the voice of Maecenas, advocated a general ironing out of distinctions.[53]

These views provided appropriate theoretical façades, but the real purpose of the levelling was the elimination of any possible mutinous tendencies and discontents which might prevent the maximum exploitation of all classes to serve the state and pay its enormous taxes. A fiscal aim is again expressly attributed by Dio Cassius to

Caracalla's enactment known as the Constitutio Antoniniana (212/13).[54] This gave the entire population of the empire, apart from slaves and a few other exceptions,[55] the status of Roman citizens which had hitherto been restricted to Italians and to an élite and privileged minority of provincials. Caracalla's measure is not even mentioned on the coins, which mirror many far less significant events. The slightness of the measure's impact is in accordance with its position as a single, final step in a long and gradual process of development, already evident in the words of the jurists and the mind of Marcus Aurelius. The Constitutio struck a democratic note, which harmonized with Caracalla's vast Alexander-like conceptions, and the increasingly wide diffusion of education (p. 156).

Yet, like moves to erode Italy's privileged status, the effect was to equalize people not upwards but downwards. For henceforward death duties and taxes on the liberation of slaves, to which the older category of citizens had been liable, were payable not only by them but by the multitudinous new citizens as well[56]; and the rate of the death duties was doubled (p. 73). However, this fiscal motive was duly covered over by an appeal to religious sentiment. The Constitutio was represented by Caracalla as a thanksgiving for the liquidation of his allegedly treacherous brother Geta; and it also helped to associate his subjects more closely with Rome and the traditional gods.

Since the abolition of any distinction between citizens and non-citizens and between Italy and the provinces tended to replace separate local systems by Roman law,[57] there could scarcely, it would seem, be any discrimination between one free person and another in the courts. The actual situation, however, was different. So far from creating such equality, the merger of citizens and non-citizens occurred at a time when legal dissimilarities were becoming crystallized on another basis. For the old territorial and civic differences were now replaced by a social distinction between two main groups to whom the law gave entirely separate treatment. The superior class (*honestiores*) included land owners, officers, civil servants, town councillors and eventually priests. Everyone else belonged to the lower class (*humiliores*), which possessed inferior legal rights and incurred heavier penalties in the courts. Although now

Roman citizens, these people were liable to flogging, torture and summary execution, which only non-citizens had suffered before. Indeed their punishments were practically those of slaves,[58] and that is just what many "free" tenants came to be called. Moreover, the right of appeal to the emperor, after only a preliminary enquiry or none at all, was now reserved for the *honestiores*;[59] and, although they too had their oppressive compulsory services spelt out for them by the jurists,[60] the worst thing that could happen to them was to be deprived of that rank.

This differentiation was not entirely novel; except when suspicious emperors took a particular dislike to senators, the administration of Roman law had always favoured the upper class. Already in the second century a distinction between two classes had existed on an unofficial basis; and next came an age in which titles of rank were increasingly employed, gradually ceasing to be informal and assuming official shape. Such was the hierarchic background against which Severan jurists gave their authoritative stamp to the barrier between *honestiores* and *humiliores*. However frequent the attempts to soften this situation by humanitarian legislation (p. 111), far more numerous measures, often prompted by landowning interests, were aimed at keeping the poor in their dreary and laborious place. Accordingly in times of crisis, despite every effort to whip up enthusiasm, their response to patriotic appeals was sometimes sluggish.

The laws of Diocletian and Constantine blend humaneness with disagreeable threats. In contrast to the penal savagery of much of his legislation, Diocletian's Edict on Prices was specifically designed to assist the common soldier, and indeed sought to help poor people in general by framing its provisions in terms of their humble base-metal monetary denominations. In the same spirit Constantine put an end to many harmful conflicts of law, and his legal reforms, inspired by Christianity, prohibited brutal penalties, tried (though ineffectively) to limit gladiatorial shows, and eased the position of women, children, debt-ridden farmers, prisoners and slaves.[61] Yet he allowed judicial torture as a means of finding out the truth and confirming guilt, and the punishments laid down are ferocious.

The laws denounce and justify with a strident and menacing plaintiveness, repeating the same prohibitions for decade after decade. This was because warnings were laxly enforced, indeed often virtually ignored. The gears turned, but did not mesh.[62] Septimius and many others penalized corruption,[63] but the "selling of smoke", *fumum vendere*—graft and patronage—poisoned the whole government, and especially the courts of law. Criminal justice was not only dishonest but brutal and arbitrary. The law courts of the later empire, despite improvements by Diocletian, remained labyrinthine, costly and slow-moving. They were burdened by many obscure and expensive conflicts of jurisdiction; and the judges, whose tenure was too short, were liable to intimidation, and became more and more ignorant as the empire went on. And yet this inefficiency proved not too bad a thing for the mass of the people, because it was better to escape the laws, which were so often tyrannical, than to have them all enforced. This was a distasteful and heavy-handed form of government, but it was not efficient enough to keep everyone miserable for the whole of the time.

Such, then, was the epoch which began, under Septimius and his successors, with jurists who were among the greatest of all time, and have certainly been exceeded by no others in their effect on the world to come. This influence attained its zenith in centuries that still lay a long way ahead, and it contributed greatly to the future of Europe. In their own day the enormous talents of these men probably caused more unhappiness than happiness, since their labours were directed not only towards humane legislation but also, and in greater degree, to the tax-extortion and regimentation which were regarded as necessary for the upkeep of the army and salvation of the state. Yet formidable though such efforts were, they did not have as evil or as universal results as might have been feared, since the inadequacies of the enforcement agencies enabled many people to disregard what the jurists had so brilliantly and painstakingly thought out for their repression.

NOTES

1. Also Licinius' short-lived junior Augustus, Martinianus (324)
2. Ulp. *Dig.* I, 4, 1; cf. Gaius I, 5
3. Paul. *Sent.* V, 12, 9a, cf. IV, 5,3; *Dig.* XXII, 23, V, 28, 2; *Cod. Just.* VI, 23, 3
4. Ulp. *Dig.* I, 3, 1
5. Herod. IV, 3, 4ff.
6. It had been foreshadowed by a separate eastern administration under Philip
7. *Pan. Lat.* XI, 6, 3
8. Istanbul

9. *SHA. Sev.* XI, 8; cf. *II Kings*, IX, 33
10. Bishapur
11. *Cod. Just.* IX, 51, 1
12. Dio, Herod., and *Eis Bas.*
13. Dio LXXIII, 17, 3, Herod. I, 14, 8
14. Herod. V, 2, 4–5
15. *toga picta, tunica palmata*
16. Eus. *V. Const.* 3
17. From about the time of Marcus they were called *viri clarissimi* (the knights being *viri egregii*)
18. Marcus made marriages between senators and freedwomen illegal, *Dig.* XXIII, 2, 16
19. Africans had been becoming increasingly prominent but Septimius did not markedly favour them. Caracalla admitted the first Alexandrian
20. Elagabalus–Severus Alexander (out of 238): 113, 17, 33, 3, 72. Rest of third century (out of 265): 116, 23, 34, 6, 86
21. The sons of centurions also had equestrian rank
22. Either under Caracalla or Severus Alexander
23. Dio LII, 14, 5
24. The significance of Victor *Caes.* 33, 34, is disputed
25. Only Africa, Sicily, Achaia and the Italian provinces
26. 2000 by A.D. 350. A century later, two of the three grades of senators were excused attendance at the capital
27. Cf. the Byzantine empire, in which when there was a bad ruler the civil service worked on under its own momentum
28. Constantine introduced several new ministerial posts
29. Spain included Mauretania Tingitana; Southern Italy included Sardinia, Corsica, Sicily; Northern Italy included the Alpine provinces. Constantine split Moesia into two, and Valens separated Egypt–Libya from the Orient
30. There had been extraordinary deputy prefects before
31. Commodus, Pertinax; Didius Julianus
32. There was no appeal from the praetorian prefect. In Rome, this jurisdiction was transferred to the prefect of the city
33. Tullius Crispinus had commanded for Didius Julianus, the nominee of the praetorians (193)
34. Constantine's greatest prefect was Ablabius, a Christian whose father was a provincial official in Crete
35. *Dig.* I, 1, 10
36. Ulpian archaistically asserted the legislative power of the senate
37. The emperor Macrinus (217–18) was also a lawyer, and had become praetorian prefect as such
38. H. Mattingly
39. Ulpian and Paulus freely added annotations to Papinian, rejected by Constantine as distortions
40. Paul. *Sent.* (not dealt with in *Dig.*) was given special authority by Constantine. One scholar has seen six layers in it; others deny Paulus' authorship
41. W. Kunkel

42. The last was Modestinus (Gordian III, of whom there are 300 rescripts)
43. *Coll. Lib. Iur. Anteiust.*, ed. Krueger, iii, 1890, 187f.
44. *Codex Gregorianus* (291, *constitutiones* Hadrian-Diocletian) and *Hermogenianus* (probably 294, almost wholly Diocletian). Both known from later citations
45. In *c.* 300 the *volumen* had been replaced by the *codex*, and legal works reproduced in the new form became canonical
46. Except Gaius' *Institutes*
47. The alterations (highly controversial) are often badly executed shortenings by compilers, frequently long before Justinian. *Digest* (50 books with 432 titles) was drawn from 2000 works. The other components are the *Codex* (imperial statutes), *Institutes* (elementary) and *Novellae* (new laws)
48. Florentinus, *Dig.* I, 5, 4 (end second or early third century). The slave was still a chattel in Ulpian and Paulus, though Ulpian declared all men equal by natural law
49. Dig. XXXV, 2, 89. Septimius distributed free medicine to the sick under Galen's supervision, *De Antidot.* I, 3, *De Theriac.* I, 2
50. Ulp. *Dig.* I, 18, 6, 2
51. E.g. Philip, Valerian, Carus
52. M. Aur. *Med.* I, 14
53. Dio LII, 19, 6
54. Dio LXXVIII, 9, 4f.
55. Exceptions: *dediticii* (P. Giess. 40), much disputed = ? freedmen with criminal records, persons belonging to no communal organization, former enemies (barbarian settlers or soldiers)?
56. But new citizens were favoured at expense of old (Dmeir; *Syria*, XXIII, 1942/3, pp. 173 ff.)
57. Though substitution for local law was not immediate or complete, and Ulpian and Paulus concede force of law to local customs
58. Aem. Macer, *Dig.* XLVIII, 19, 10 pr. Already in the second century governors sometimes condemned and executed Roman citizens without appeal
59. *Dig.* XLIX, 1, 25, P. Oxy. 2104. *Humiliores* could still appeal, but only after sentence
60. E.g. *Dig.* L, 4: classification of services to state
61. He prohibited married men from keeping concubines
62. R. MacMullen
63. *Dig.* I, 16, 6, 3; cf. the concern of Constantine. Latitude of appeal was excessive

PART III

Artists, Architects, Novelists, Philosophers

5

Imperial Artists and Architects

The Climax of Imperial Sculpture

The outstanding sculptural achievements of the second century A.D. were imperial reliefs; the supreme masterpieces of the third century were imperial portraits.

The characteristically Roman method of depicting the emperor's achievements upon a relief had already found important expression in Augustus' Altar of Peace, the Arch of Titus, and Trajan's Column. The Column of Marcus Aurelius, completed after his death (?*c.* 190–5) to celebrate his German victories, resembles its Trajanic forerunner in that its pictures narrate a story of war which winds spirally upwards in successive scenes. Yet the Column of Marcus has entered a new and more sensitive world. For its sculptors are not content with Trajan's extrovert record; instead they tell a tale of humanity and pathos. Now that the wars of Rome have become a much more serious matter, they are seen no longer as an ordinary busy activity but as a grim and sordid necessity of burnings and executions. There is a deeper feeling for sufferings and deaths, and especially for those of the barbarians, who are no longer just untutored enemies—as they were on Trajan's monument—but anguished human beings. This is a world of fear and horror. It is also full of the supernatural, given haunting shape in the half-personalized Miracle of Rain which was believed to have saved the imperial troops (p. 246). There is a novel artistic spirit too, and an emotional striving for essentiality and effect which banishes all illustrative detail in the interests of centralization. The deeply incised and undercut designs leap out from an abstract, shadowy space, and the emperor, now a size larger than the companions who attend him like disciples, turns not to them but to the people who are studying the column.

The reliefs of the Arch of Septimius Severus at Rome (203) are worse preserved than those of the Column of Marcus, but not entirely different in character. Yet there has already been a development, for the figures are more squat, and an intricate division between scenes, shown in a bird's eye perspective, conveys the impression of a textile surface. Probably this sort of pattern was inspired by popular paintings, now vanished, such as those which Septimius exhibited at his Parthian Triumph.[1] His arch at Lepcis Magna (c. 203) has a panel depicting a siege with the same map-like, spatial narrative convention. But another scene on the Lepcis monument, showing the ruler in his chariot, introduces a novel and almost medieval technique, two-dimensional rather than plastic, that concentrates upon rhythmical repetitive symmetry and rigid frontality.

The principle of symmetry, which increasingly gains artistic favour from now on, had already been favoured by certain Roman medallions. A century later this type of balanced composition had become as normal on Roman coinage as the schematic fire-altars on coins of Sassanian Persia. Some of the artists of the Lepcis arch have been traced to a long-lived school of sculpture at Aphrodisias (Kehre) in Asia Minor. But the emphatically frontal presentation of the imperial figure, which recurs on the small Gate of the Silversmiths at Rome (204), comes from a good deal farther east than Aphrodisias, being typical of the fringe regions between the Roman and Parthian empires. Frontality had, it is true, been seen before on Greek and Roman reliefs and coins, but this stiff hieratic posture recalls saviour-gods at Palmyra in the Syrian desert, and Dura and Hatra in Mesopotamia.[2] Many centuries earlier there had already been frontal portraiture in western Persian lands.[3] A contemporary analogy seems to have been the Greco-Buddhist art of northern India. This is very close to Palmyrene work, and may have come eastwards by sea via the Persian Gulf.[4] Parthian and Persian kings, too, are occasionally shown facing the spectator, like potent talismanic images.[5]

The chariot on the arch of Lepcis is partly frontal and partly in profile, but coinage shows how these chariot scenes rapidly assumed a complete heraldic frontality, first in the eastern provinces and then later at Rome.[6] When the Lepcis relief shows the central, frontal Septimius among other figures, he—even more emphatically than Marcus Aurelius on his column—is united not with them but with the reverential spectators, at whom he is gazing as the Boddhisatva gazed at his worshippers. This is an onslaught upon the emotions rather than an approach to the mind, a spiritual revolution that led to the frontal, symmetrical mosaics of the Byzantine age.

During the hundred years after Septimius' Arch at Lepcis, the principal masterpieces of historical relief were achieved not at Rome but among the Sassanian Persians. The massive reliefs of the middle and later third centuries commemorating their victories improve upon the precedents which Parthia had handed down from the ancient Assyrian and Babylonian empires, but were still not motion-pictures, like those of the Romans, since they concentrate instead upon symbolic scenes which convey the quintessence of triumph.[7] There are also occult implications, for the representation of a victory magically enhanced the glory of the prince.

But until the very end of the third century this imposing series of reliefs was not paralleled by any further exploration of the same medium at Rome. In a culture which still retained certain human-istic values, the new methods, with their frontal, symmetrical em-phasis, did not lend themselves to the old narrative expositions of human beings and their deeds. Yet relief design was still very active in the Roman empire. There was admirable silver-work, more or less naturalistic in style.[8] There were also reliefs on innumerable sarcophagi (p. 242), and upon this more restricted scale artists in sympathy with official ideas perpetuated the tradition of the large historical relief by utilizing the medium to glorify the imperial dead. At least two types of theme were employed for such purposes. One of them was the scene which incorporated philosophers and sages, representing a Hellenic thread in the spiritual and artistic move-ments of the day (p. 127); a sarcophagus of this kind is topped by a three-dimensional reclining figure that may represent the transient emperor Balbinus (238).[9] Other sarcophagi seem to show rulers, or their illustrious kinsmen, upon their reliefs, and particularly in the middle of elaborate, contorted battle scenes,[10] paralleled by almost equally intricate intertwinings of figures on coins and medallions.

These battles represent the annihilation of death and evil by the victorious dead. In scanning their unplastic carpet-like textures, the eye fastens on the central horseman, who emerges from congested planes of tormented combatants in grandiose, superhuman serenity. The Ludovisi sarcophagus, in which the genre reaches its height, shows a central imperial personage who has been identified (without certainty) as Hostilianus (d. 251) the younger son of Decius.[11] The technique of the sculptural relief is still being used for official or quasi-official publicity; although, like the portraits of the day, it is publicity of equivocal value, redolent of an age of brutality and pain (p. 126).

The historical relief proper, according to the tradition of the Arch of Titus and the Columns of Trajan and Marcus, was revived by the arch which Galerius erected at Thessalonica (Salonica) in celebration of his Persian victories (296)—and in knowledge of the reliefs the Persians themselves had recently been making. The small-scale figures of Galerius' Arch, abandoning space and perspective, recall sarcophagi. Two main types of composition are employed; one is a lively movement in a single direction, and the other is static and hieratic, displaying immobile figures that confront the outside world in the tradition already suggested by a few works under Septimius a century earlier. The four rulers appear in an 'epiphany', much larger than their audience, and Galerius, addressing his troops, surmounts the whole pyramidal composition, and symbolizes the imperial control which reflects a divine eternal harmony.

The flat, stocky and unnatural shapes of these figures are reproduced with further distortions upon the arch which Constantine commissioned in order to commemorate his victory over Maxentius (312). These laterally moving compositions, more stylized than those of the Arch of Galerius, resemble the lines of uniform figures in third and fourth century wall-paintings,[12] and point forward to Byzantine mosaics at Ravenna.[13] The scenes of Constantine addressing and distributing largess to his troops again employ a rigidly symmetrical, centralized method. The emperor himself is the central figure, unmoving and yet the sole creator of action. His subjects, who provide the framework of this glory, are massed lines of undistinguishable figures, like the immobilized, subjugated corporations and labour-gangs of the time (pp. 88ff.).

Contemporary artists were not incapable of classical naturalism when a touch of this was wanted. For example the heads of Constantine and his colleague Licinius on the arch are fine examples of the transitional phase before schematization was complete (p. 129.) But in the same way as other portrait-sculptors were rejecting this humanistic element, so also the designers of the mass-scenes on the arch are instead inspired by an ancient, crude and forceful popular art. This had always lived on in the provinces and the cultural underground, and now for the first time, during an age when emperors were of provincial and peasant origin, it had welled up to dominate a principal imperial frieze. Constantine dispensed grants of tax-immunity to encourage the sculptors, painters and mosaicists who put the artistic themes of his age into effect.[14] Their broad, coarse renderings in a sort of woodcut style seem, by classical standards, deficient in technical skill. But those standards are no longer applicable. Just as there was now no objection to introducing old imperial reliefs, of an entirely different style, alongside the new ones on Constantine's Arch, and just as his architects were so neglectful of the traditional harmonies that they imported a variety of old, ready-made capitals for their new churches, so too these artists, pseudo-primitives rather than primitives, rejected classical delicacies, idealisms and realisms as irrelevant. They were representing not human beings but major imperial and spiritual movements in which the individual mortal frame possessed trifling significance except as a tiny component of the massive automaton.

In the evolution of the imperial portrait between Marcus Aurelius and Constantine a similar series of developments occurs, but with richer, more varied and more sensational results. For portrait sculpture, within the space of only a few years, passed through a series of artistic changes scarcely less far-reaching than those which transformed French painting in the nineteenth and early twentieth centuries.

There were still many private portrait-busts of the utmost skill,[15] but the distinction of the age lies in its imperial portraits, which echo with incomparable brilliance the successive individual or official personalities of the emperors and their families. In times of stress, when new rulers needed to assert themselves quickly, their features had to be made familiar to the people with all possible rapidity, in every main square and public building throughout the empire. Elagabalus sent Rome a portrait of himself as high priest in advance of his own arrival,[16] and emperors employed also the most distinguished professional sculptors of the day. For the same reason careful attention was dedicated to coin-portraits (which often enable us to identify the busts), since their superior mobility gave them an even wider circulation. A *coup d'état* was habitually accompanied by a monetary issue, to serve as army wages and donatives; so that there were pretenders whose coins, even after the briefest of reigns, are still not too rare today.[17] Much more limited than these pieces in circulation, but often equal in artistic excellence and variety to the finest sculptural achievements, are the portrayals of imperial personages on the commemorative medallions, bronze in the second century and mainly gold from the mid-third century onwards, which were distributed by the emperors to officers and other favoured persons.

Marble portrait busts of the second century A.D. show the increasingly free use of a drill in order to produce contrasts of highlights and shadows, which exercise their maximum effect, not in the dimness of a modern museum, but under the strong Mediterranean sun for which they were designed. The portraiture of Marcus Aurelius, in which these tendencies are well developed, is more significant than most of his better known, blanker portraits suggest.[18] His pensive Hellenic idealism sometimes verges upon a spirituality traceable to slightly earlier portrait-styles in Asia Minor and Greece; a recently discovered gold head believed to represent him reminded its first viewers of "a saint in church". Certain of his other heads show how classicism was moving towards the more stereotyped symbolic formulas of late antiquity. But there were generally several different styles in operation at the same time, and artists depicting Marcus' colleague Lucius Verus and son Commodus often preferred various amusing mannered or baroque treatments, concentrating on polished satiny surfaces which show a new sensuous appreciation for the texture of flesh.

Septimius, in order to conceal the advent of grimmer times, reverted to propaganda recalling the Golden Age of the Antonines, whom he claimed as his ancestors in spirit and by adoption. Consequently, the naturalistic bearded heads on his medallions continue the richly elaborate technique of the previous generation. His portrait busts, too, go back to Marcus and Verus, but with certain technical and psychological changes. Volumes are more solid, the lavish hair with the curls of the god Serapis is closely integrated with the skull (p. 290), and in anticipation of future styles the eyes (incised since early in the second century) are sometimes raised to heaven, gazing up with exalted emotion to the gods who were the emperor's companions (p. 223).[19] The coins, for their part, occasionally show schematic, linear methods of depiction which likewise point towards the future. Meanwhile the portrait-busts of the Syrian ladies of Septimius' house display a new, subtle and confident sensibility which reflects their strong, un-Roman characters and political and intellectual power. Picturesque coiffures help to form sinuous or geometric patterns of line and form. The disturbing turn of these heads and eyes reinforces the suggestion, apparent in some of the heads of Septimius, that the spirit, a mere alien sojourner in the human frame, can be detected behind and beyond its features: self-contained and self-centred humanism is coming to an end.[20]

Among the most remarkable portraits of the age are the nervous, scowling, Alexander-emulating busts of Caracalla, with restless head and wrinkled brow: an outstanding example of the baroque portraitist's new kind of face, stamped by destiny, excitement and violence. This is no longer a philosopher on the throne; although his official name was Marcus Aurelius Antoninus, Caracalla's harsh violence has abandoned the Antonine synthesis in favour of a more excitable and defiant self-assertion. Hellenic locks, too, have been replaced by short neat curls, which eastern local coinages also now begin to show in stylized patterns.[21] A marble bust, which may represent Caracalla's murdered brother Geta, makes this hair-style into a close-cropped skull-cap, symbolizing military puritanism against Hellenic culture,[22] according to a convention which became widely accepted in the years ahead. Roman coins (217–18), and then portrait-busts of Severus Alexander and particularly Maximinus I (235–8), sketch this sheath-like hair and beard with light, rapid pointillist strokes of the chisel,[23] drawing upon the illusionistic techniques of painting with the aid of tints to flesh and hair which have now vanished.

Naturalistic and schematic tendencies are now balanced one against the other, and it is just this balance and tension that gives the portraits of this age their claim to be the most remarkable (as well as the most accessible to modern taste?) that Rome ever produced. A single solid line is sometimes used for the eyebrows, drawing attention to the upturned eye beneath the heavy eyelid. The Severan tendency to stress the eyes is enhanced, for in this spiritual age they seemed the mirrors of the soul (cf. p. 164), and the region about them fascinated portrait-painters for its character-revealing properties. But nothing must distract attention from the rolling intensity of the eyes themselves, emphasized by sharply outlined pupils and deeply drilled iris. Rolling sideways as well as upwards, the glance is phosphorescent with the inner life and light of that divine ecstasy which philosophers and religious writers were trying to describe.[24]

Yet this inner man, on whom the sculptor so ardently concentrates, is not yet by any means spiritualized to the point of glassy immobility. On the contrary, this close examination shows him to be a prey to appalling uneasiness, doubt and distrust. Such representations reach a climax in the 240s and early 250s under Philip, Decius and Gallus. Their portraits, like those on the coinage, are overwhelmingly expressive of this age of emergency. The strange thing is that the rulers should have wanted to be represented like this—rather as the Spanish royal family were content to be shown as imbeciles in Goya's paintings. These Roman crisis-emperors were not stupid, but they look desperately worried, and portrait-sculptors and artists of outstanding gifts, unfortunately anonymous, were brought in to display these worries with incomparable skill. They made it very clear that the emperors shared the distresses of their subjects, and carried the cares of the world upon their shoulders. But it almost appeared, from these masterpieces, that the burden was too great for them: as indeed it was. Either the talent of outstanding artists ran away with them and overcame the requirements of publicity, or this corresponded with the image of the ruler that the imperial chancery thought was needed—embodying all the anxieties of the times, needing the people's help; with an added trace of desperate *condottiere* defiance, and just a touch of scepticism about the total possibilities of this material life.

The climax of this style appears in a superb portrait of Philip the Arab (244–9)—a new aggressive, barbarian type who has nevertheless risen to the traditional dignity of his imperial office. His personality is revealed in one highly-charged moment; this is the zenith of the traditional Roman artistic endeavour to hold on to what is personal and characteristic by a sudden transitory, impressionistic snapshot glimpse. Yet the method is no longer a loving delineation of realistic detail but a single, simplifying strike and sweep. That, in an otherwise all too human portrait, is the contribution made by the schematic tendency of this age. The central motif is a lowering of brows, accompanied by contractions of the mouth and forehead muscles. Philip's mobile features, the expressions flickering over his face, are eloquent of suspicion and repressed turbulence.[25] This was the age of Plotinus, who, seeing art as an outcome of material evil (p. 191), spoke of its need to illuminate the body by the soul,[26] and declared that the ugliness of a living being is more beautiful than the beauty of a statue.

Similar disturbances are expressed by a violently asymmetrical, anxiously gazing Decius, and by the grotesquely tormented brow of his successor Gallus.[27] Even stronger, now, above the eyes and beside the nose and mouth, are the furrows that declare extreme strain. And yet there are already signs of this intense gaze becoming more stationary. A slight stiffening of features, and hardening of anatomy, and simplifying of lines, have already begun to remodel and distort the face into inorganic forms which correspond not to the human shape but to deeper movements within its soul and the universe. Whatever these men feel, and they feel strongly, is on the way to becoming a generalized rather than an individual feeling.

These tendencies were to return in extreme forms later on, but the development is not continuous; the history of imperial portraiture is no straight line but an oscillation of alternating phases and fashions. For at the height of the military and economic crises and artistic movements resulting from them, Gallienus turned back from the harrowing delineations of his predecessors and caused his sculptural and numismatic portraits to be executed in a pronouncedly classical, Hellenic style, reminiscent at first of Augustus and then more particularly of Greek monarchs and Hadrian who had favoured their tastes.[28] This classicism, which was to continue alongside newer trends in the Byzantine empire, showed even more durable powers of survival than the various provincial, proletarian and archaic elements that might temporarily assume greater emphasis (p. 123). Sometimes classical factors are an unconscious contribution—the ordinary tools and traditions of the trade— but the plastic Hellenism of these portraits of Gallienus, with their softened, slightly bearded features and flashing gaze of pride, is deliberate. And yet the revival, like all valuable revivals, was not a complete one; these portraits were not as old-fashioned as they might seem. The underlying forms show new rigidities, facial features are only surface-deep. The tension of humanity and transcendence, of nature and schematism, has reached a brief precarious equilibrium. Momentary dispositions and moods still receive attention, but the inner quest for invisible reality is on the point of beginning to over-shadow them. A new world order is not far off.

Gallienus' partial reversion to classicism corresponded to his personal Hellenizing tastes. Like Augustus and Hadrian, he had been initiated into the Mysteries of Demeter at Eleusis (p. 240). And yet this personal element is not the whole explanation. For there was also a strong contemporary vogue for the spiritualized, inspiring portraits of philosophers and holy men. These heads, often identified (inconclusively) with their most distinguished contemporary representative, Gallienus' friend Plotinus, infuse a new ascetic sanc-tity into the ancient idealistic tradition of depicting philosophers.[29] So the Hellenizing tendencies of the 260s extended beyond Gallienus himself. Furthermore, the most Hellenic and classical of all the portraits of the age are those not of Gallienus but of his hostile contemporary Postumus, ruling in the western provinces.[30] These heads appear on his gold pieces, while other coins of Postumus innovate by remarkable near-frontal portraits recalling the strong trend towards similar poses in sculptural reliefs (p. 120). Frontal coin-portraits have a few Greek and Roman precedents, but frontality had long been a common near-eastern phenomenon, and there is special relevance in the coinage of Parthian and Persian kings.[31] For although the treatment of Postumus' head is naturalis-tic, its posture, like theirs, brings the ruler before his subjects in the manner of an oriental god, and the way is cleared for the future hieratic, immobile frontality of coin-portraits in the early fourth century and the Byzantine empire that was to follow.

From now on there was no single, unified official art of portrait-sculpture, but a great autonomy among regional schools. For ex-ample, a distinctive series of heads produced at Aquileia includes a bronze bust of Claudius II Gothicus which, in so far as it shows any classicism at all, is Roman and not Greek, for the Hellenic revival was not pursued by the successors of Gallienus at Rome. Slowly but steadily schematic elements grew, with exclusive stress on the eyes and other features which determine the spiritual expression. This spirituality was still enlivened with contrasting realistic touches in a provoking, strongly shaped portrait of Carinus (283–4).[32] His gaze waits for a message from distant regions; and yet it also reflects his own subtle individuality. The face is a receptacle, a prison, from which the spirit looks outwards, searching "nervously, uneasily for some meaning beyond a world that lives by the sword".[33] But the relationship of soul and body is no longer a union or blend; it is a contradiction. The aesthetic components that make up a portrait have become disjointed, and cry out for a new synthesis.

And so, rather as nineteenth-century impressionism was superseded by the structural solidity of Cézanne, the impressionistic realism of the third century now gave place to more massive, simplified and permanent lines. But here the comparison ends, for the artistic changes of *c.* A.D. 300 displayed none of the attention to nature which Cézanne united with his search for form. Or rather, the analogy of Van Gogh, or even of the cubists, may be substituted for Cézanne. For this was no longer the realism of nature, but an attempt to depict the hidden, eternal reality of the inner world: the art of Diocletian, Licinius and Constantine is the supra-realism of magic.

Cubist conceptions, which the structure of Carinus' head had already begun to approach, took command of the portraiture of Diocletian and his three fellow-rulers and their immediate successors. Even more than in contemporary reliefs, the upsurging of subterranean, proletarian, peasant, provincial art-forms, and their mingling with the new ideas of the day, contributed to an artistic revolution, comparable with the changes taking place in political and social life. While art of a more traditional kind sporadically continued, and in the west still attained important results as late as the joint reign of Constantine and Licinius (310–24),[34] many coins of Diocletian's reformed currency (*c.* 294) and contemporary medallions already displayed a style of incised, harsh angularity and dry linear flatness, strongly advancing and emphasizing tendencies already apparent for many years on issues of the eastern provinces (p. 125). But above all, these coins show square, cropped, neckless portraits alien to all classical humanism and emphatic in their brutal rejection of any mortal weakness or refinement.

Meanwhile portrait-sculptors were producing similar and even more peculiar results. The new style was an oriental one, for, just as the most radical coin-heads are those of Syrian Antioch, the two most extreme sculptural examples, both perhaps identifiable with Licinius, come from Egypt.[35] The same deliberate rejection of traditional Greco-Roman values is shown in an even more startling form by two groups of full-length figures of embracing Augustuses and Caesars in military uniform.[36] These representations are un-realistic and stylized and symmetrically balanced, and the rulers are indistinguishable one from another; this total sameness is pointed out and praised by contemporary flattery as a feature of their eternal unanimous concord.[37] Carrying to ultimate lengths the block-like, squat deformity of contemporary relief-work, the smouldering, menacing blankness of these nightmarish facial masks is a product not of technical failure and decadence (seen in such art by Gibbon) but of the sculptors' new and unclassical, indeed anti-classical, interpretation of their peasant emperors and of life itself (p. 123).

By the time Constantine had become sole emperor (324), the old plastic language, especially in the east but also to a considerable extent in the west, had largely been jettisoned. Man and nature were reduced to a code which needed to be read. Life had stiffened into impersonality; and people are no longer individuals. But they are not yet entirely abstractions. That final and total spiritualization was the work of Constantine. From now on the magnified faces of emperors stare immobile, with eyes surrealistically enlarged, into a distant world we cannot see[38]—just as Constantius II moved not a feature when he proceeded through the streets of Rome (p. 99). These heads, built up with a minimum of detail into a system of concentric arches including the arching brows that stress the steady gaze, are cult objects like the colossal statues of Persian monarchs,[39] and Christian icons of the future. The effigies of Constantine and his successors were idols animated with divine presence, in contrast to the demons believed to inhabit pagan images.[40] The disturbing formulas of Diocletian and Licinius have given way to the unap-proachable gravity of this hypnotic gaze into unending space. Such was the "divine face", the "sacred countenance", in which the artist of the Christian epoch saw a mirror reflecting the eternal order.

He, like his master, has not wholly forgotten the tranquil orderliness of the empire of Augustus of which they were both still the heirs.[41] But he had only remembered the Augustan portrait in order to recast it in the idiom of a new world. That world, with its assurance of human inadequacy, had erected serene immutability and transcendence into the merits that were praised in emperors.[42] But these were also qualities which inevitably brought the specific Roman art of portrait-sculpture to an end. Rulers now only needed a two-dimensional art to express the aims of themselves and their church, and this new artistic style, which had reached its decisive stage under Constantine, remained to inspire the mosaics and other arts of the Byzantine empire.

Cities and Palaces of the Later Empire

This story of portraiture has shown a combination of influences deriving from many parts of the Greco-Roman world. During the whole of the period the provinces had been gaining in importance at the expense of Italy; while Rome itself, even more heavily subsidized than the rest of the peninsula (p. 75), had become—in all but its immense monuments and no less immense prestige—no more than one among a number of capitals.

This transformation is clearly mirrored in the development of the imperial mints which provided coinage for the army and the empire. In the second century A.D., with the exception of issues at Alexandria and certain other cities striking Greek denominations, the official currency, even if partly (for convenience's sake) coined in the provinces, depended upon the Roman mint for its central administration, design and style. But from the time of the civil wars of 193–7 it becomes possible to detect the operations and distinct designs of separate official mints for gold and silver money in various parts of the empire.[43] As the third century proceeded, fresh mints for gold and base metal sprang up temporarily as generals grasped at the purple. Moreover, the central emperors, too, now used widely dispersed official mints which become more and more clearly distinguishable, and sometimes identifiable with a particular town.[44] Then, from the reign of Gallienus and increasingly under Aurelian, imperial coins begin to bear mint-marks explicitly indicating the city of their origin.[45] These appear regularly on the vast, homogeneous coinages of Diocletian and his colleagues, whose centralization of control could only be effectively undertaken by decentralizing manufacture.[46]

By that time, it was nothing new for emperors to find Rome inconvenient as a base for their government, which was so largely based on military needs. Many rulers had spent years near the northern and eastern frontiers. For example, Sirmium (Sremska Mitrovica), the most important strategic centre in the Danubian area, became for considerable periods the headquarters of Marcus Aurelius, Maximinus I and other emperors. When Valerian found it necessary to divide the government of the empire with his son Gallienus, Antioch became a duplicate imperial capital; and after Valerian was dead, military threats to northern Italy made Gallienus treat Mediolanum rather than Rome as his residence.

When Diocletian and Maximian again divided the empire between east and west, they were assisted by two Caesars, so that there were now four capitals. In the west, Maximian lived at Mediolanum and his Caesar, Constantius I Chlorus, at Augusta Trevirorum (Trier). In the east, the second Caesar Galerius dwelt at Thessalonica (Salonica), a strategic rear headquarters to Sirmium and the vital Danube command. But the senior capital was the place where Diocletian had been nominated to the throne and where he also chose to reside, Nicomedia on the Sea of Marmara. Nicomedia possessed a good harbour (the Turkish naval port of Izmit today), and was strategically situated out of danger of invasion but on the main line of communication between the Danube provinces and the eastern frontier (Danube—Morava—Maritza—Asia Minor—Antioch—Euphrates). This was the sort of consideration which now weighed heavily in the choice of a capital, and Constantine, after living at Augusta Trevirorum (Trier), Arelate (Arles) and Ticinum (Pavia), settled successively at two important cities of his native Balkans which were situated on the main strategic route, first Sirmium (c. 317) and then Serdica (Sofia). "Serdica", he said, "is my Rome".[47]

But the necessities of imperial defence would best be served by a headquarters situated at the point where the road between Danube and Euphrates is crossed by the maritime passage linking the Mediterranean and the Black Sea. The two lines meet in the narrows at the Hellespont (Dardanelles) and the Bosphorus. Near the former point, Constantine was reported to have begun building at Troy.[48] But he preferred the Bosphorus, and rebuilt its ancient city of Byzantium as Constantinople (324–30). This site, near to which his fleet had just won a decisive victory over Licinius, possessed the majestic harbour of the Golden Horn. The place was also fortifiable by land and sea (as it had shown in a long resistance to Septimius Severus) and possessed easy accessibility, again by land and sea alike, to the all-important industrial and cultural centres of Asia Minor and Syria, and to the corn of Egypt which was needed to maintain a large population.[49] Byzantium, it is true, had no Christian tradition; moreover, the initial foundation rites of Constantine's city were pagan and the Sun-god played a central part in them (p. 233). Nevertheless, the new foundation could be bent to the imperial will and made Christian with greater ease than incurably pagan Rome (p. 310). Constantine may not have announced immediately that the new city he had created was to become his sole imperial residence, or that it should be called the New or Second Rome.[50] However, like its antique model, it was given a Forum and a senate of its own, and its population received free distributions from the corn-fleet which had previously served the more ancient capital. In c. 330 there were special coinages honouring CONSTANTINOPOLIS; but they were paralleled by issues celebrating the City of Rome. For the emperor was proceeding carefully. Rome lost none of its privileges, and at first Constantinople ranked as its inferior, with its senators taking a lower precedence than those of the ancient capital. Nevertheless, it was Constantine's intention to make Constantinople his single headquarters.

And so the scene was set for the Middle Ages. The western empire went under, but the eastern Byzantine empire survived because of its lesser vulnerability, bigger population, more efficient government, and larger and more equitably distributed economic resources. Constantinople was not only the capital of that empire but, until its capture by the Latins (1204–61), the most important place in Europe, the representative of the Mediterranean great city in a new age. Then, after nearly two more centuries of Byzantine rule, it again achieved extraordinary magnificence and prosperity when the Ottoman Turks made it their capital (1453). By the sixteenth century, Istanbul was once more the centre of an empire without equal in the west. The city founded by Constantine has rivalled Rome as a political, spiritual and artistic leader of the world.

In spite of almost perpetual financial crisis, imperial prestige required that imperial buildings should be bestowed upon these cities with unprecedented lavishness. At Rome in particular, despite its waning political and economic significance, public buildings occupied a far greater proportion of space than in any modern city, and their creation and adornment formed an important part of official policy. The Severan dynasty was the last to change the face of Rome extensively. Septimius constructed a fanciful magic castle of fountains on the Palatine Hill, the Septizodium (203). His own statue appeared as the Sun-god, whose role in official paganism was growing (p. 228). It stood among the Seven Planets of astrology, which had also figured prominently in the Pantheon constructed at Rome by Augustus and refounded by Hadrian. But whereas that had been the most splendid hitherto of all domed designs, the Septizodium stood for the more antique tradition of verticals and horizontals. Although it was finally demolished in 1588–9, its elegant cumulation of three tiers of porticoes, one upon another, is to be seen from Renaissance illustrations.[51] The style is reminiscent of similar buildings, perhaps of Asian inspiration, in Septimius' north African homeland,[52] and the ornamental façade of the Septizodium was orientated not towards the Forum but to the emperor's fellow-Africans arriving at Rome by the Appian Way.[53]

The orthodox Greek rectangular temple, which had been magnified by the Romans to novel dimensions, attained spectacular elaboration and size in the centre of Sun-worship at Heliopolis (Baalbek, Lebanon). There, upon the artificial vaulted terrace of the Sanctuary with its superb religious adaptation of Forum-like axial planning, a huge shrine of Jupiter and the Sun was joined in the later second century A.D. by another grandiose temple which is the best preserved of any in the Roman world. It was probably dedicated to Dionysus-Bacchus, and its platform served as a stage for performances of his Mysteries (p. 241). But the crypt, below the flights of stairs leading to this altar platform, foreshadows a Christian church (p. 145), and the colossal fluted pilasters, rising above not one but two tiers of niches in strongly plastic chiaroscuro, echo the painted scenes of theatres in a three-dimensional form which pointed the way to favourite Renaissance designs.[54]

The splendour of this temple at Heliopolis was equalled or exceeded by the shrine erected by Elagabalus at Rome for his native Sun fetish, whom he raised to supremacy over the other gods (p. 229). This enormous building on the Palatine, now vanished, was renamed after the more traditional Jupiter the Avenger by Elagabalus' cousin and successor Severus Alexander, whose medallions display its six-column façade surrounded by porticoes and approached by a monumental gateway and flight of steps. Emperors continued to be interested in the planning of towns and colonnaded parks,[55] but the age of colossal Roman temples adapting the Greek horizontal-vertical tradition practically came to a close with Aurelian's Temple of the Sun in the Campus Martius, which seems from a drawing by Palladio to have been built in a gigantic rectangular enclosure (approached by two courts) reminiscent of Baalbek.

However, the major architectural effort of the time was lavished on other kinds of building. Conspicuous among these were public Baths. These magnificent structures, of which there were finally eleven at pampered Rome, nine at Constantinople, and further examples in almost all the cities of the empire, displayed much ingenious variety of function, being designed not only for luxurious bathing but for all the activities of an elaborate community centre in which many people of the time spent a substantial part of their day. All the features of the thermal complexes built at Rome by Agrippa, Titus and especially Trajan, with a new elaboration of terraces and ceilings and vaults, were incorporated in the Baths of Caracalla. Begun by Septimius (206), inaugurated by Caracalla, and completed by his successors, this outsize building, or rather group of buildings, has lost its sumptuous decoration; but the ground-plan and part of the massive brick-faced concrete framework are still to be seen. The external elevation must to some extent have lacked unity and logical coherence, though the architect was feeling his way towards a new aesthetic of functionalism based on a three-dimensional play of thrust and counter-thrust. But such ideas were still much more evident in the interior. These halls are so large that man vanishes—for all its human purpose this is the architecture not of humanism but of a new age in which the individual is one of a mass. The main building (750 by 380 feet), flanked by an elaborate enclosure with garden, open-air gymnasium, works of art and every other amenity, could probably accommodate as many as 1,600 bathers at the same time. There was a circular domed hot room, measuring 115 feet across; its ruined apse is still visible. But the central feature of the Baths of Caracalla was a great cross-vaulted hall, measuring 185 by 79 feet and including a swimming pool. The load of the concrete intersecting vaults, with their increased span and assurance, was carried not on a row of columns but on only four enormous piers (in which the classical columns have become non-functional), so that the building is a prototype of medieval cathedrals with their vaulted naves.

Vaults and domes and semi-domes and apses, based on the revolutionary and gradually improved technique of light-weight thrustless concrete, were the peculiar achievement of Roman architecture, and they attained full expression in the great halls of the Baths.[56] Such buildings erected by later third-century emperors, if enough of them had survived, would have illustrated this theme further.[57] They would also have demonstrated the increasingly skilful employment of exterior brick facings (without marble or stucco veneers), still to be seen at Philip's Baths and Theatre at Philippopolis in Trachonitis and in private houses at Ostia.[58] A semi-dome in the cold room of the Hunting Baths at Lepcis Magna, of third- or early fourth-century date, shows how this sort of surface enabled mosaics, of which the most substantial examples had hitherto appeared upon floors, to be used also for the decoration of curved upper surfaces, where they were to provide the Byzantine empire with its major religious works of art (pp. 12, 140).[59]

The Baths which Diocletian and Maximian built on the ruins of a great fire (283) seem to have been nearly twice as large as those of Caracalla. In what remains of the central hall, vaults spring from a horizontal entablature which projects from eight huge granite monoliths.[60] Augusta Trevirorum (Trier) was the capital of the westernmost of Diocletian's co-rulers, Constantius I Chlorus, but it may have been the latter's son Constantine who completed its Imperial Baths. In a ground plan combining unity with movement, the three arched apses of the hot room created an interior of unusual spatial effects, and at the same time added variety to the plastic form of the exterior which now becomes an organic artistic achievement in its own right. A new feature of recessed window-frames anticipates the

forms of medieval gateways; and indeed the whole powerful interpretation of architectural masses exercised its influence on later
ecclesiastical design.

The Senate-house (Curia) erected by Diocletian beside the Roman
Forum adapted many of these ideas to a building which instead of belonging to a large complex of Baths stood by itself. This is a lofty,
austere, box-like simplification, a structure reduced to a shell or
enclosure of broad planes and lines varied by niches. The large
blank façade, crowned by a simple gable, is broken only by the
doorway and three large windows near the roof.

The masterpiece of the age was the Basilica Nova nearby. Again
free-standing, this building, which is about the size of the Cathedral
of Notre Dame at Paris (265 by 195 feet), was mainly constructed by
Maxentius but altered by Constantine, who changed the orientation
from the long to short sides. Reminiscent of a Sassanian throne-room,
the Basilica Nova was based on the bold technical and aesthetic idea
of extracting and isolating *en bloc* the central cross-vaulted hall
familiar in Baths, and making this into an independent structure.
Until recent experiments such as Diocletian's Senate-house, free-
standing halls, notably market-basilicas—social, judicial and commercial meeting places associated with a Forum—had normally been
rectangular buildings with colonnaded aisles and flat roofs.[61] They
had sometimes terminated in apses, and their naves had possessed
windowed upper stages extending above the roofs of the adjacent
aisles. The vast, vaulted Basilica Nova shares these features; but
under the influence of the designs of Baths they are transformed. The
114-foot-high nave, with a daring application of intersecting groin-
vaults (which had occasionally appeared at Rome for four centuries
past) is illuminated in its upper reaches by a new kind of lighting.
This was effected by huge half-circular Romanesque-looking
windows, one for each bay, creating a rhythmical relation of window
to massive, medieval wall. There were only three bays, separated by
huge internal supports which arches (across the barrel vaults of the
aisles) linked to piers projecting from the side-walls. This exercise in
the maximum dematerialization of space can still be imaginatively
reconstructed from the three soaring spans of nave and aisles that
remain, leading to the northern apse added by Constantine.

The talent for supremely managed immensity reached its zenith in the imperial palaces which provided the epoch with its principal architectural splendours. Earlier emperors had developed the conception of a palace-city in a park, but their successors may also have been stimulated to their ever more imposing construction by the example of the Parthians and Sassanian Persians (p. 41); who in turn owed the lay-out of their palaces, as well as of circular camp-cities such as Ardashir I's Firuzabad and reconstructed Seleucia on the Tigris, to their own Assyrian and Babylonian forerunners. The Versailles of Shapur I (? 239–70) was at Bishapur in Fars, a quadrilateral design in the Greek style adorned with carpet-like floor mosaics combining Iranian and western trends.[62] But Shapur also built another imposing palace (Taq-e-Kesra) at his capital of Ctesiphon on the Tigris. Its surviving 83-foot-wide elliptical barrel-vault dispenses with supporting arches. Employing brick in Mesopotamia and Persia, and rough-hewn stone and quick-setting gypsum mortar on the plateau, the Sassanians equalled or exceeded contemporary Rome in the structural and artistic boldness of their vaults, cupolas and enormous side-chapels. On the other hand, the limitations of their art and government alike were shown by the monotonous recurrences of bloodthirsty warfare on the stucco and fresco decoration of these vast buildings. More significant is the architectural ornamentation of Ctesiphon, for the over-all simplicity of its design is modified by non-functional pattern-making rows of recessed blind arcades. This was one of many elements freely adapted from Greco-Roman lands, and due before long to appear in them again (p. 121).

The first Roman imperial residences of similar type may well be datable to the time of Valerian and Gallienus, though the discovery of their palaces remains the task of excavators of the future. Valerian perhaps began, and Gallienus developed, a camp-headquarters of palatial style at Syrian Antioch, precariously situated at the hub of the eastern defence-system. The equal significance of Mediolanum in the western frontier zone was probably signalized by similar constructions under Gallienus. Mediolanum looked outwards to the dissident, competing empire of Postumus (p. 33), who likewise developed a complex of imperial buildings, subsequently demolished, at his capital of Augusta Trevirorum on the Moselle.

But it was not until Diocletian divided up the empire with three colleagues that palaces were built at these and other centres on a truly massive and extravagant scale. At Antioch, the base for Galerius' eastern victory and the place of his Triumph, his senior colleague Diocletian designed a new city in something like the circular Persian style (p. 138), though its intersecting streets conformed with Roman military fashion. An insatiable builder, Diocletian endowed this renovated and expanded Antioch with granaries, two temples, several Baths, arms factories and a reconstructed stadium. He also completed and expanded the palace that had been started by Valerian or Gallienus.[63] Palmyra, restored from its destruction after Zenobia (p. 37), was another eastern city which received from Diocletian not only extensive military buildings but a palace (or temple). This, with a Hall of Audience or throne-room (?) at its central point, stood upon a lofty built-up terrace above symmetrical, camp-like constructions situated on a steeply rising terrain. And yet Diocletian himself lived at neither of those eastern cities, but at Nicomedia (Izmit), on which he bestowed new buildings that have not survived but were planned on a scale intended to rival Rome itself.

His co-rulers lived at Mediolanum, Thessalonica and Augusta Trevirorum (p. 132). At Mediolanum, an important cultural and artistic centre, Maximian is likely to have built a splendid palace. At Thessalonica, recent excavations have revealed something of the residence of the Caesar Galerius. This, including a large octagonal hall, lay to the west of a processional street linking the sea with other new buildings. The massive complex included a hippodrome, theatre and colonnades, and the present circular church of St George was almost certainly Galerius' mausoleum (cf. p. 107). But the best idea of a tetrarch's court (and the finest collection of Roman buildings north of the Alps) is to be found at Augusta Trevirorum, where Constantius I developed his capital on the site of the residence of Postumus; the city-gate (Porta Nigra) is almost a castle in itself. Constantius' palace occupied the whole north-eastern part of the city. The so-called "Basilica", a building 280 feet in length and 100 feet in height which originally dates from c. A.D. 300 and was probably completed by Constantine, has now been recognized as the Hall of Audience or throne-room of the palace (above) corresponding to Diocletian's at Palmyra. The spacious, timber-roofed hall at Augusta Trevirorum has the aisle-less box-like simplicity of

Diocletian's slightly earlier Senate-house at Rome; the classical orders only survive as niche-frames, on either side of the raised semi-circular apse. This, at the short north end of the hall, is divided from the nave by a chancel arch anticipatory of Christian churches. The thick, concrete walls are lit by two storeys of rounded windows. As in the Roman Basilica Nova, these dramatic internal effects are echoed and equalled by a novel grandeur of external design, in which the outer walls are strengthened and diversified by massive arcade-like projections which rise above both tiers of windows, transforming the surface into an articulated, vertical unity of light and shade.[64]

Portions of figured frescoes recently discovered in the imperial palace of Augusta Trevirorum show that the heavily ornate ceiling was painted with imitation coffering, of which the eight surviving panels represent Cupids, and women handling jewels. These fragments serve as a reminder that the well-known catacomb pictures of this and earlier periods were accompanied by a long and diverse series of pagan counterparts, usually more technically skilful than the Christian paintings but not often so emotionally convincing (p. 275).[65]

Another outstanding art which reached its decorative culmination during the third and fourth centuries A.D. was that of the pavement-mosaic, which was still more frequent than mosaics on vaults and walls (p. 136).[66] In general, "carpet" designs extending all over the floor increasingly superseded the rug, mat or panel conception. Nowhere are these mosaics more spectacular than in the large palace discovered not long ago at Piazza Armerina near Henna in Sicily. Excavation has disclosed 42 polychrome pavements comprising 30 million pieces of mosaic spread over 3,500 square yards. Although most of the designs deal monotonously with the royal and imperial sports of hunting and the massacres of animals which accompanied them,[67] the decorative possibilities of this medium are explored through contrasts between lively, precise, naturalistic, narrative details and a rival tendency towards schematic distortion of natural shapes.

Oblivious of nature in the spirit of Hadrian's villa at Tibur (Tivoli) and late Roman houses at Ostia,[68] the conglomeration of Piazza Armerina reveals an inorganic, twisting, triple-lobed design full of surprises and restless convolutions, worked out with a "persistent deviousness, eternal changing of direction, and hiding of the goal". The mosaic portrait of the lord of the palace, in his purple-ornamented tunic and long grey trousers, has a good deal in common with coins and statues of Diocletian and Maximian and their colleagues, and when these two Augusti both abdicated in 305 this may have been one of the mansions to which Maximian reluctantly, and as it turned out by no means finally, agreed to retire—though his main abode was in Lucania.[69]

Whether or not that was the purpose of Piazza Armerina, Maximian's senior colleague Diocletian abdicated once and for all, and went to live at Salonae (Split) in Dalmatia; and his residence there has survived on a far more impressive scale than any other. This was the project, supported by the appalling taxation of the time, upon which Diocletian spent the years of his retirement, outdoing the numerous palaces of his predecessors and younger colleagues and Persian rivals. This blend of civil and military architecture, much more compact than Piazza Armerina, amalgamated the public rooms of a palace, the residential quarters of a great Dalmatian villa or a commander-in-chief's house,[70] and an inward-looking impregnable fortress, guarded by a wall that was studded by square and polygonal towers.[71] Central to this ruthlessly axial plan is a main avenue which leads through the palace city up to the focal Hall of Audience. Beyond a colonnaded courtyard (*atrium*), the main surviving feature of this throne-room is its three-bayed columnar façade, crowned by a gabled Pediment of Glorification. Over the middle columns curves an arch, beneath which, as if framed by the vault of heaven, Diocletian made his appearances and received homage like a divine effigy.[72] Behind the courtyard was a domed circular vestibule with four small apses, and behind that again the shrine-like Hall of Audience itself, where the retired, revered emperor sat, jewelled and haloed, beneath a columned canopy.

On either side of the courtyard approaching these buildings stand arcades of which the arches are not surmounted by horizontals but spring straight from the Corinthian columns in an energetic, unclassical fashion, which had occasionally been seen since Augustan times[73] but was now fully exploited in the form which was to lead to the main architectural styles of later Europe. Another forward-looking type of colonnade appears on Salonae's richly decorated

Golden Gate, which has a row of seven dummy arches like those at Shapur's Ctesiphon (p. 138). This gate, once flanked by towers, stands at the far north end of the processional avenue which leads through the town to the Hall of Audience at its opposite extremity.[74] The south face of the Hall looked directly upon the sea, and here, between two square towers, the wall is broken by a gallery with a loggia at each end and in the centre. The gallery has forty-two arched windows; between them are engaged columns which rest upon blocks (corbels) projecting from the wall, a motif that was still a rarity.[75]

In the middle of the whole rectangular complex, the courtyard leading up to the Hall of Audience was flanked on one side by almost the last recognizable Roman temple[76]—and on the other by the building which was to contain Diocletian's tomb.

This mausoleum illustrates a fertile contemporary trend towards domed constructions. There were many Greco-Italian precedents for such buildings, including Etruscan funeral monuments, round temples[76] and large thermal halls, such as the circular hot room of Caracalla's Baths (p. 136). Recent examples had shown growing expertise in dealing with a problem beyond the range of earlier Greek architects. That consisted in placing a dome over a building which was square or polygonal. During the second century A.D. there were attempts to unite these two shapes by means of triangular concave sections (pendentives) joining the curved base of the dome to the angles of the walls.[77] The problem approached its final solution in a marble pendentive from Septimius' four-way arch at Lepcis Magna, and in two small domed octagonal halls (externally square) on the periphery of the Roman Baths of Caracalla.

A highly sophisticated specimen of these centralized buildings, straining the classical Orders as far as they would go, is the small so-called "Temple of Venus" at Heliopolis (Baalbek), perhaps built in the second and rebuilt in the third century A.D. This elegant baroque shrine, aptly imitated by Borromini,[78] is round, but the circle is broken by five concave niched recessions between columns. Although most third-century Roman buildings have vanished, coins and medallions show a number of unknown centralized temples,[79] and a diversity of ribbed or plain vaults and curves is detectable from the scanty remains of various edifices in Rome and its suburbs. At Salonae, the vestibule of Diocletian's palace is domed and circular, but the dome of his mausoleum nearby is internally circular while presenting a façade and external colonnade which are both octagonal. Inside, there are eight deep wall-niches alternately rectangular and curved.

The Middle Ages are announced by the crypts which now appear not only in an occasional temple of longitudinal shape (p. 134) but also in these centralized buildings, notably the circular Diocletianic "Tomb of the Gordiani" at Rome.[80] Its walls are pierced with rounded openings for the admission of light. A small ten-sided Roman structure of the same epoch, with another fictitious name ("Temple of Minerva Medica"), again possesses large rounded windows in each of its sides. This building has not only four closed apses, which are a familiar feature of the period, but also five recesses which open up the interior through curving columnar arcades that perforate and dematerialize the outer walls in a fashion not apparently seen again until the mid-fifth century.

When these circular or centrally planned edifices were mausoleums, they were the immediate ancestors of Christian buildings commemorating martyrs and serving as burial-places and baptisteries and churches.[81] Owing to the increased connection of religious services with martyrs and holy sites, Constantine joined this type of building onto rectangular churches or basilicas (p. 145): when, later, the two formulas were completely integrated, the result was Justinian's Santa Sophia. At Constantine's Grotto of the Nativity at Bethlehem, excavations have shown that an octagon was attached to the east end of a rectangular church hall, and the original Church of the Holy Sepulchre at Jerusalem (Golgotha) (328–36) had a circular martyr's shrine (upon the site of a Jewish tomb chamber) in the middle of an apsed basilica. His new capital of Constantinople (p. 133) did not at once become a major architectural centre, but Constantine built its first church of the Holy Apostles to combine in novel fashion the functions of his own mausoleum and a Martyrium of the Apostles.[82] This was a cross-shaped structure, and under the central drum, surmounted by a conical roof, were placed for a time the remains of the emperor, who was venerated as the thirteenth of the Disciples.

These churches have now vanished, and so has another important centralized building which Constantine constructed at Antioch.

Here, next to the imperial palace on the Orontes island in the centre of the city, he began and nearly completed the magnificent Golden Octagon, dedicated to Harmony, the divine power that unites Universe, Church and Empire (327–41). Descriptions and a sketch on a floor mosaic suggest that the gilded wooden roof was either pyramidal or, perhaps from the outset, a dome,[83] and that this central area was surrounded by a colonnaded aisle in two storeys. The Golden Octagon was not a cathedral or a martyr's shrine but a palace church, and the ancestor of similar octagonal, galleried palace chapels built by Justinian at Constantinople and by Charlemagne at Aachen.[84]

These and many other buildings of Constantine were the products of an architectural revolution (c. A.D. 315), proceeding from the religious revolution which had made Christianity supreme (p. 302) and accompanied by official encouragement to engineers and architects.[85] The round or polygonal churches provided one result of these new developments, but their principal manifestation was the new Christian basilica. These successors of humble house-churches[86] were oblong longitudinal buildings—often entered from a large external courtyard—containing side-aisles separated from the nave by arched colonnades. Above these colonnades, since the nave was higher than the aisles, came brick walls standing directly on the arches, and usually pierced by windows. Beyond the chancel arch was an apse, rising behind the canopied altar and containing the bishop's throne (*cathedra*). The main part of these basilicas, however, was not vaulted; they had wooden roofs, open or concealed by a flat ceiling. The great Roman cross-vaults seemed too earthly and reminiscent of pagan buildings, and they would have slowed down the single irresistible tide of nave and aisles which drew the eye towards the altar and the apse.

These resplendent buildings, which set so historic a pattern for the future, owed their structure and window arrangement to the colonnaded pagan basilica which had served as market, court and meeting place—with a tribunal where the bishop's seat was now. And yet the strong axial direction of the churches towards their altar was quite different from the passive orientation of the pagan building. The Christian basilica, with its internal colonnades, has been described as a Greek temple turned inside out.[87] But one of its immediate models was provided by the Halls of Audience in recently constructed palace-cities such as Augusta Trevirorum and Salonae. Just as the elaborate palace ceremonial was incorporated into Christian liturgy (p. 302), so too the Christian altar beneath its canopy was like an emperor's throne, and the triumphal chancel-arch echoed the gable of imperial glorification upon the Hall of Audience. The courtyard of the Christian churches, too, once had its forerunner and counterpart outside the Basilica Nova of Maxentius (p. 137). And from there the imposing doors of the Christian basilica disclosed a dignified, visionary, spiritualized interior which interpreted the mysteries of heaven while remaining mindful of the disciplined Roman past. Many of Constantine's basilicas were entered from the west, so that the rising sun fell on a celebrant as he stood before the altar facing his congregation. For the space-creating essence of the revelation is incorporeal and insubstantial Light: there is holy penumbra below, but radiant luminosity bathes the building and its worshippers from above.

Constantine's dramatic basilicas, erected in many parts of the empire, abounded in this light and colour, enhanced by gilding and other precious decoration. Yet there is nothing to be seen of his major monuments today. Some have disappeared, but most became so famous that new churches were subsequently erected on the same sites. This, for example, was the fate of the wide, double-aisled church of Holy Wisdom (Santa Sophia) he began at the new Constantinople; it was replaced by Justinian's building. Constantine's Lateran Church, the cathedral of Rome, has likewise been supplanted by a series of successors. This Basilica Constantiniana, dedicated at first to our Saviour,[88] was laid out shortly after the donation of the neighbouring palace to the recently recognized pope and bishop (c. A.D. 313). The church had a nave flanked not by a single side-aisle on either side but by a pair. These, adjoined at the east end by small wings or sacristies like miniature transepts, were supported by rows of huge columns of yellow and red marble, and speckled green on the outside rows. The building terminated in a lofty projecting apse, with a huge screen of silver (adorned by solid silver statues) extending across its entrance. "The congregation saw Christ the Teacher seated and flanked by his apostles, while the clergy were faced by a Christ Resurrected, enthroned between four angels. Like the emperor, then, Christ revealed himself under the upswept lintel in different but complementary aspects to the people and high officials of his court.''[89]

Then, near Nero's Vatican Circus, Constantine built the Basilica of St. Peter (c. 333?–37). This church, before its replacement in the sixteenth century, resembled the Lateran in possessing resplendent, colourful decorations, and two aisles on each flank of its long, tall nave. But between these and the apse to which they led there was a massive transept extending on either side, filled with the light from sixteen great windows in contrast with the darkness of the aisles. This is a novel response to the cult of martyrs which led Constantine, elsewhere, to blend longitudinal basilicas with centralized shrines (p. 143). For the church stood on the site which had long been believed to be the burial place of St. Peter (p. 295). Since the crowds who came to venerate the martyr were too great to be accommodated in any less spectacular way, Constantine erected this spacious transverse annex—a covered cemetery or catacomb moved above ground, and merged with the largest building and holiest sanctuary in the western church. Because of this exceptional purpose, the architectural feature of a continuous transept was at first rarely copied elsewhere,[90] until the architects of Charlemagne brought it into more extensive use.

NOTES

1. Herod. III, 9, 12
2. E.g. temple of Palmyrene gods at Dura (A.D. 85), statue of king Uthal from Hatra (Mosul Mus., second century A.D.)
3. E.g. Luristan bronzes, 8th–7th centuries B.C.
4. Gandhara, Surkh Kotal, Mathura, Bharhut, Sanchi. ? Via Hellenized Bactria
5. E.g. Shapur I (Indian triumph), Bahram II (frontally enthroned), coins of Ardashir, and a governor at Dokhtar-e-Nushirvan (painting)
6. Septimius (Mandela), Caracalla (Tarsus), Severus Alexander and Gordian III (medallions). Wholly stylized: Aurelian, Probus; cf. *opus sectile* mosaic from fourth century, Basilica of Junius Bassus (Rome, Pal. del Drago)
7. Climax in bas-relief of Bahram I, Bishapur (c. 273–6).
8. E.g. the extensive treasure from Chaourse (Aisne), in the Hellenizing style of Gallienus and Postumus
9. From the Catacomb of Praetextatus. The figure on the Acilia sarcophagus is probably not Gordian III but of c. 250–60
10. Early battle sarcophagus: Portonaccio (c. 190–200). Crowded coin and medallion designs: from Caracalla, and e.g. VICTORIA GERMANICA of Maximinus I

11. Or Timesitheus, Volusianus (son of Gallus), Claudius II Gothicus?

12. E.g. House of Palace Heralds, Via dei Cerchi, Rome

13. E.g. S. Apollinare Nuovo

14. Diocletian had included sculptors, painters and mosaicists among the ranks of superior craftsmen

15. Particularly significant: young woman (Kansas City, W. Rockhill Nelson Gall., c. A.D. 175); *cosmetai* from Athens; old woman (Tripoli, Castello Mus.); philosophers' busts; Christ-like Athens head probably Gallienic; Miletopolis head (Berlin, c. 260–70); bronze (Allard Pierson Mus., ? Gallienic); stylized Ostia head (c. 280); sarcophagus portraits (Acilia, Balbinus, local styles at Noviomagus (peasant), Palmyra, Petra, Hatra

16. Herod. X, 5

17. E.g. Postumus' successor Marius

18. E.g. from Gerasa (Domin. Mon., Jerusalem), Ostia (Indiana Univ., Blooming-ton). "Saint in church": Plotinoupolis (Didymoteichos, Thrace)

19. Raised eyeballs and lofty hair style already in portraits of Marcus (c. 169). Septimius wears the forelocks of the Egyptian god Serapis.

20. E.g. Cincinnati Art Museum (? Didia Clara (193), d. of Didius Julianus, or probably Julia Domna)

21. E.g. at Prusias ad Hypium; cf. Severus Alexander, Edessa

22. Venice (Mus. Arch.); cf. Philostr. *V. Apol.* VIII, 7

23. E.g. coins of Diadumenianus (son of Macrinus); Severus Alexander, Apollonia Salbace. Cropped hair with long Antonine beard: Pupienus (Vatican, Braccio Nuovo)

24. Mirror of soul: Polemo in Förster, *Script. Physiogn.* I, 106–20. Portraits: Plut. *Alex.* 1. Rolling eyes: Via dell' Impero head (Mus. Nuov. Cap., c. 240),? Otacilia Severa wife of Philip (Walters Art Gall.). Icon-like wide eyes: Caracalla, coins of Hierapolis

25. Vatican (Braccio Nuovo). Cf. H. P. L'Orange. The realistic detail harks back to the late Republic

26. Plot. *Enn.* I, 6, 1; cf. Philostr. *V. Apol.* VI, 19, P.l *NH.* XXXV, 98

27. Decius: Oslo (private collection). Gallus: Florence, New York

28. Cf. also cameos, e.g. his wife Salonina. Not echoed by painting or architecture

29. "Plotinus" (Ostia, Vatican): Acilia sarcophagus (Rome, Mus. Naz., c. 260–70); Manisa (Sardis, c. 260–84); figures on Lateran sarcophagus, then Christians

30. Cf. lapis lazuli (Brit. Mus.), perhaps of Laelianus (c. 268)

31. E.g. Mithridates III (57–54 B.C.), Ardashir I, Roman *imagines clipeatae* (coins of Augustus, Tiberius), medallion of Commodus; cf. classical Greek frontal coin-portraits of goddesses

32. Rome (Mus. Conserv.), cf. Probus (Mus. Cap.)

33. G. M. A. Hanfmann

34. E.g. colossal Nicomedia head and early coins of Diocletian, bronze Belgrade head of Constantine, excellent Constantinian female portraits, earliest ivory diptychs

35. From Athribis (Cairo, red porphyry), and Alexandria (? or Maximinus II). Cf. Palmyrene work

36. Venice (outside St. Mark's), Vatican, chalcedony cameo of Diocletian and Maximian (Dumbarton Oaks Coll., Washington), and medallions of Licinius, etc.

37. Mam. *Genethl. Max.* II, *Pan. Lat.* 9

38. Constantine (probably): Rome, Mus. Conserv. Uncertain successor: Barletta head

39. E.g. Shapur I (in pillar of stone), near Bishapur

40. *Acta SS. Abramii et Mariae*, *Acta Sanctorum*, II, p. 933

41. Cf. Constantine Statue in Vatican, with Augustan traditional gesture of command

42. Synes. *De Regno* 6 (10)

43. Mints of Severan dynasty: Rome, Laodicea ad Mare (later Antioch), Emesa or Samosata, Nicomedia. Bronze city-coinages and a few provincial issues were minted until latter half of third century

44. Mints of central emperors 238–84: Rome, Mediolanum, Verona or Aquileia (?), Viminacium (?), Colonia Agrippinensis (?), Arelate, Siscia, Antioch, Cyzicus, Ephesus (?), Samosata (?), Serdica, Tripolis, Ticinum, Lugdunum (?) and Augusta Trevirorum (?) The last two and Moguntiacum and Bonna (?) were mints of Postumus and his successors

45. Colonia Agrippinensis, Lugdunum, Arelate, Siscia

46. New mints were Nicomedia, Heraclea (Perinthus), Thessalonica, Carthage, Londinium; Ostia under Maxentius; Sirmium and Constantinopolis under Constantine

47. *FHG.* IV, 199

48. Zos. II, 30, 1; but cf. earlier rumours for Julius Caesar. Constantine was also believed to have considered Thessalonica and his own birth-place Naissus (Niš)

49. From 332 this was set aside for Constantinople, with Africa to supply Rome

50. Socr. I, 16. Septimius had begun an extensive reconstruction of the city

51. Botticelli in Sistine Chapel (Vatican)

52. Lambaesis, Sabratha (stage), Lepcis Magna

53. *SHA. Sev.* XXIV, 3. "Septizodium" rather than "Septizonium"

54. Michelangelo (Capitoline palaces), Palladio (Loggia del Capitanio, Vicenza)

55. E.g. colonnaded park of Gordian III (Pincian–Campus Martius)

56. In the hot room of Caracalla's Baths hollow pots were inserted in the dome to reduce weight

57. E.g. Baths of Severus Alexander (reconstruction of Agrippa's), Decius, Gordian III (Volubilis)

58. E.g. brick arches of House of Cupid and Psyche

59. Earlier mosaics on vaults, etc.: Hadrianic niche at Baths of Seven Sages, Ostia; late second century niche from Ostia (Lateran). On walls: Pompeii, Herculaneum

60. S. Maria degli Angeli, though a large church, is a reconstruction of only about half of this hall

61. E.g. Shaqqa, Hauran (late second century); unusual stone roof

62. Louvre and Teheran Mus.

63. Liban. *Or.* XI, 203–7; cf. on Arch of Galerius at Thessalonica. Camp-plan also at Philippopolis (in Jebel Druze)

64. Marble and mosaic coverings, atrium and flanking colonnades have disappeared

65. Severan dynasty (violet, white are dominant): Houses in Via dei Cerchi and below SS. Giovanni e Paolo, Rome, and Baths of Seven Sages and Pharos, Ostia. Dura. c. 250–80 (red, orange, green; broken, asymmetric): Caseggiato degli Aurighe, etc. Carterius made a memory likeness of Plotinus (Porph.). End third century (important figured scenes): Tomb of Trebius, Via Latina; House of Nymphaeum, Ostia. New fashion of imitating marble. Constantine and after (blue, yellow): Via Livenza; Barberini Roma; Durostorum (Silistra). "Neo-Attic": mainly at Alexandria. Egyptian mummy portraits continue.

66. E.g. Antioch (first to sixth centuries, influenced Sassanians), Edessa, Zliten (c. 200), Lepcis Magna (transition to larger stones), Thysdrus hippodrome (blend of visual and explanatory space), Britain, Ostia (ships in Severan Piazzale delle Corporazioni)

67. Exceptions: group of classicizing girl athletes in bikinis

68. E.g. House of Dioscuri

69. But other prefer a middle or late fourth-century or even fifth-century date

70. Cf. Palace of Dux Ripae, Dura (early third century)

71. Inward-looking houses (cf. later Arabs) also at contemporary Ostia: House of the Round Temple

72. *Pan. Lat.* X. 3

73. E.g. House of Fortune, Pompeii; Villa of Hadrian, Tibur; Severan Forum at Lepcis Magna

74. Unlike Palmyra, where the Hall (?) was the central point of the design

75. Cf. columns on Golden Gate, now vanished. Corbels are also found at the Thermopolium at Ostia. Compare other columnar experiments at Ostia: Houses of Cupid and Psyche, Fortuna Annonaria

76. E.g. Pantheon; cf. centralized temples of Romano–Celtic type at Perigueux, Silchester, Caerwent

77. E.g. second-century tomb, Via Nomentana, Rome; and Philadelphia (Kasr-el-Nueijis, Amman), Gerasa, Petra, Sebaste. Squinch (arch[es] in angles instead of pendentive): ? Firuzabad

78. S. Ivo della Sapienza, Rome (Lantern)

79. E.g. Gordian III (Victory "Hoplophoros"), Gallus and Volusianus (Juno Martialis). Cf. domed, square Parthian building shown on Arch of Septimius

80. Cf. T. Telesphorus (Asclepieum, Pergamum, second century): Tor de' Schiavi sepulchre, Via Praenestina

81. E.g. cruciform martyria (Bin Bir Kilise); rock-cut tombs and centralized churches. Best surviving example, probably c. 350: Mausoleum of Constantia at Rome (S. Costanza), perhaps imitated from Church of Holy Sepulchre at Jerusalem (Golgotha) (dome set on masonry drum as in Byzantine churches)

82. The attribution of the church to Constantius II is less probable. It was replaced by Justinian. Constantine may also have laid out the octagonal Lateran baptistery

83. Eus. *V. Const.* III, 50, etc.

84. SS. Sergius and Bacchus; Palatine Chapel, Aachen; cf. also round cathedrals at Bostra and Gerasa

85. *Mechanici* and *geometrae* (surveyors) came above architects. Constantine gave immunities and scholarships and insisted on a liberal education.
86. Pre-Constantinian "house-churches" have been identified at Dura and Lullingstone
87. In a third-century temple at Rusucurru (Tigzirt, north Africa) a solid internal wall without architrave had risen straight from columns as in Christian basilicas
88. Later to St. John the Baptist and St. John the Evangelist. It has recently been questioned whether the Lateran was the Pope's cathedral. Tyre, Orléansville and Aquileia provide other early examples of basilicas
89. R. Krautheimer
90. S. Paolo fuori le Mura (385), Manaštirine (Dalmatia) (*c.* 400); S. Denis (775), Centula (S. Riquier) (791–9), Fulda (802)

6

The Culture of the Novel

Education

Youths with a knowledge of Latin or Greek, who wanted to prepare
themselves for the professions, could go to one of the principal centres
of higher learning, staffed by groups of lecturers paid by the state
or the municipality. These centres included Rome, Athens, Alexandria, Berytus (Beirut), Antioch and Carthage, and in the fourth
century Constantinople, Augustodunum (Autun) and Augusta
Trevirorum (Trier).

Attempts were made by emperors to encourage recruitment to
these university institutions. Commodus, like Antoninus Pius before
him, increased the exemptions and privileges of their teachers.
Caracalla, though personally averse to learning and learned people,
extended similar exemptions to students.[1] Then Severus Alexander
improved professorial salaries, and further measures on behalf of
these staffs were taken by successive Illyrian rulers, themselves of
extremely scrappy education, namely Diocletian and Constantius I
Chlorus; the latter's son Constantine continued with this policy,
deliberately seeking to combat anti-intellectual trends.[2]

Yet this officially favoured instruction at advanced levels was reserved for men: women had to be content with secondary or private
tuition. Higher education was also limited to members of the upper
and upper-middle classes, and intended particularly for the sons of
senators and knights. Dio Cassius cites Maecenas as expressing
explicit approval of this restriction (p. 101). He was evidently of the
same opinion himself—and throughout antiquity that is where
matters rested.

The principal subject of these courses was rhetoric or classical literature. Public lecturers of the concert-orator type attained fame and wealth by oratorical fireworks based on flamboyant adaptations of the antique models. The poetry of the entire period, though abundant, is almost all depressingly derivative. With little change throughout the centuries, the old-fashioned, verbal, pedantic classical education continued to reign paramount, full of quotations and empty of new interpretations or ideas. The system went on producing cultivated gentlemen with a gift for verbal felicity but few constructive plans for combating contemporary emergencies and no valid alternatives to fashionable, irrational solutions and salvations. For this system, valuing superficial expression above substance or originality, imported its pervasive barrenness into the court, the civil service and the administration of every province.

The position of grammar and rhetoric alike was strengthened, early in the period, by the publication of uniquely authoritative studies. The most influential of all grammarians and historians of grammar was Apollonius "the Crabbed", an Alexandrian of the mid-second century A.D. who specialized in settling syntactic details according to considerations of principle.[3] Then, in Marcus Aurelius' Rome, Apollonius' son Herodian was the author of immense, learned works on grammar and accentuation, which, like the works of his father, were minutely studied throughout the Byzantine epoch.

The position of rhetoric was similarly reinforced by the subject's leading theoretician of the whole imperial age, Hermogenes "the Polisher" of Tarsus in Cilicia (c. 175). His massive attempt to reduce the study of literary style to a fixed system was as influential as the writings of the grammarians; and this, too, perpetuated sterile scholastic standards for hundreds of years. Slightly later in date was another author, not now identifiable, who wrote a varied handbook of precepts relating to the ever-fashionable and job-winning occupation of oratory.[4]

Higher education, however, was also concerned with subjects other than rhetoric and grammar. One of these was philosophy. Marcus Aurelius' preference of philosophy to rhetoric as being of more practical use caused great disappointment to his tutor Fronto. Marcus founded four Chairs of philosophy at Athens, and was an outstanding practitioner of the subject himself. Alexandria also possessed highly distinguished teachers of the subject, who contributed both to the new, learned expositions of Christianity and to the achievement of Plotinus.

Another flourishing topic of higher education, in an age which appreciated training for careers, was Roman Law, of which the leading centre, founded by A.D. 200 and probably earlier, was at Berytus (Beirut).[5] From the days of the outstanding Severan jurists, and especially after Caracalla's extension of Roman Law by his grant of universal citizenship, Berytus continued to prosper (pp. 107 ff.). In pursuance of his attempt to Latinize the east and its laws, Diocletian endowed the school with scholarships, and, in spite of Syria's distinction as a nucleus of Greek culture, instruction continued to be given in Latin until c. 400. Berytus was also unusual among university centres in that its courses were based on prescribed books—and followed a fixed duration, usually lasting four years, to which a fifth was sometimes added.

Mathematics were taught at Alexandria, and astronomy at Sidon. But the history of science during the period was uninspiring. The astonomer and geographer Ptolemy of Alexandria (d. c. 170?), although not a figure of first-rate calibre, had attained new results in mathematical geography, and his encyclopaedic achievement was comprehensive and enormously influential. Now, there was no one to compare with him. Greek science had always disregarded attainable minor discoveries in favour of unattainable major ones, tending to see physics as philosophy and not mechanics; and now men no longer probed into the secrets of nature at all, but regarded it as the agent of wonders. "Greek rationalism spent itself like a fire which dies for want of fuel."[6] Understanding, aptitude and experiment alike showed little or no progress. Theories and hypotheses and concepts of the universe were still analysed from logical and mathematical viewpoints,[7] but factual discoveries faded out. Severus Alexander is recorded to have taken notice of scientific education. But no significant result emerged from any such methods of encouragement, except in the field of architecture where practical assistance given to members of the profession by Diocletian and Constantine bore impressive fruits (pp. 138ff). The backwardness of industrial and particularly agricultural technology was disastrous to the empire (p. 86).

The centres of medical instruction were Alexandria, Syrian cities such as Apamea and Laodicea, and a number of important schools in Asia Minor.[8] Galen (*c.* 130–99) was educated at one of these Asian centres, his home town Pergamum. Rising from the job of a doctor of gladiators, he enjoyed the successive favour of Marcus Aurelius, Commodus, and Septimius' wife Julia Domna. He also wrote books covering every specialist field. What survives is not by any means his complete work, yet it fills twenty quarto volumes.

Galen is an assured biologist, emphasizing anatomy and recognizing the unity of the organism. The approach he urged was not only scientific but broad, conveying the firm principle that the best doctor is a good philosopher—the man who loves the truth, laboriously studies the ancients, and is not afraid to apply his own tests. A medical student, he says,

> must become possessed with an ardent love for truth, like one inspired. Neither day nor night may he cease to urge and strain himself in order to learn thoroughly all that has been said by the most illustrious of the ancients. And when he has learnt this, then for a prolonged period he must test and prove it, observe what part is in agreement, and what in disagreement with obvious facts; thus he will choose this and turn away from that. To such a person my hope has been that my treatise would prove of the very greatest assistance. Still, such people may be expected to be quite few in number, while, as for the others, this book will be as superfluous to them as a tale told to an ass.[9]

The same somewhat impatient conceit is expressed in Galen's sharp language about his Roman colleagues. His own capacity to respect, digest and assimilate tradition—a characteristic feature of late antiquity, seen also in the great jurists of the same epoch—were what made him so valuable for future generations, because it enabled him to transmit all the best work of past Greek medical schools. Yet there were also other qualities in Galen, equally appreciated by subsequent ages, which proved more dangerous to science. First, he believed that the purposes served by all parts of the body, which require them to be constructed as they are, could be discovered, and that he himself could discover them. He explored all these purposes and considered that it was impossible to imagine any better arrangement, citing Aristotle's principle that nature makes nothing in vain.[10] And Galen was a pioneer believer that the existence of the divine, creative deity can be argued from the existence and perfect beauty of what has been created. Convinced that the human body is the divinely fashioned instrument of the soul, he saw the praiseful worship of the divinity as the particular sphere of anatomical study, and believed that if this were pursued with the same earnestness as the famous religions it would exceed them in its comprehensive and effective revelations of the divine mystery and power. And so, although Galen was himself as critical of Christianity as of pagan philosophical schools, his doctrines, translated from the Arabic, became immensely popular in the medieval west. Schoolmen liked his apparently logical attitude, and Thomas Linacre was still propounding him in 1523; his conclusions determined medical thought for nearly a millennium and a half.

But that lay in the future. The immediate result of his attitude was to accelerate the decline of the scientific approach. During the centuries that now followed nobody else tried to repeat Galen's exploration of the purposes served by the parts of the body. This was partly because no successor could improve on his massive labours, but chiefly because the problems of physiology seemed to need no further experimentation; he had already solved them, and had done so in accordance with a theory of the godhead (and its purpose) which could not be tampered with. And so his method 'carried the implication of the worthlessness of research . . . the world was worth exploring only to verify the hypothesis. On his death, silence descends like a curtain; the classical period of the subject is over and the Dark Ages have begun.'[11]

The advent of Christianity, which made theology the subject of lively intellectual achievements, did not perform the same service for scientific inquiry. 'For wherein', as St. Ambrose asked, 'does this assist our salvation?'

And yet the narrow and largely barren slopes of higher learning rested upon a broad base of school education. This instruction was provided in for both sexes. First, there was the elementary school, always private, the teacher living on the fees of his pupils. Upper and middle class children did not go to these schools, but were taught at home, and then went on (unlike their poorer contemporaries) to one of the instructors in grammar who existed in all towns of any size. Some of these pupils subsequently entered courses given by the teachers of rhetoric to be found in provincial capitals and other cities of comparable importance. These schoolmasters, and their colleagues who taught grammar, were either paid salaries or lived on fees as freelances. Their earnings were fixed by Diocletian at between four and five times those of elementary teachers; their training was expensive and they ranked among men of property.

Yet this secondary teaching, like most instruction at university level, was limited in subject-matter. Theoretically, there was a general training in grammar, rhetoric, dialectic, arithmetic, geometry, music and astronomy, the seven liberal arts of medieval fame.[12] But in fact, mathematics were almost completely ousted, music also dropped out, and very little was taught except grammar and rhetoric. This was an exclusively linguistic and literary curriculum, based on a syllabus consisting of commentaries upon a restricted range of classical authors.

However, during the hundred and fifty years between Marcus Aurelius and Constantine this education, such as it was, reached considerably larger numbers of people than ever before, in keeping with a general tendency towards egalitarianism (p. 111). Egyptian papyri show that, although illiteracy existed, school education, both for boys and for girls, was widespread. From the time of Severus Alexander town and village teachers are recorded as a class. We have papyrus text-books for schools, giving practical exercises in the forms of words.[13] There are also bilingual manuals of early third century date, inaugurating the practical phrase-book of modern times. These works insist on student-teaching and the use of black-boards, and pay careful attention to the individual pupil's ability, age, knowledge, temperament and interests.[14] A little Latin work of moral admonitions in couplets, the *Sayings of Cato*, became a medieval text-book second only to Virgil in the fascination it inspired.[15] Such were the teaching aids which supported this primary and secondary education throughout the empire. Moreover, in an indirect fashion and at a low level, the great-house economy of the age played some part in the diffusion of culture (p. 88).

As might be expected, the progress of education was not evenly distributed. At the end of the third century, for example, Egypt was showing signs of educational weakening. But in Gaul, on the other hand, teaching centres multiplied—and were perhaps doubled by Constantius I Chlorus.[16]

Yet this wider diffusion of education still did not affect a large percentage of the population. For its media were Greek and Latin. These were the principal written languages of the Roman world, and the sole tongues capable of conveying this literary, classical training. But they were only spoken by a minority of the populations of the empire, which, being mainly agricultural, contained elements untouched by the culture of Greece or Rome. Such, for example, were the people who still spoke Celtic, Punic, Berber, Coptic, Syriac, Aramaic, Illyrian (Albanian), Thracian or one of the many tongues of Asia Minor. Nevertheless, the total proportion of Greek and Latin speakers throughout the empire probably increased during the period, because of the expansion of schooling.

The growth of instruction in Greek and Latin also developed native and national patriotisms. That may seem paradoxical, since the spread of native literatures such as Syriac and Aramaic was likewise one of the principal causes of this kind of development. However, the spread of Greek and Latin had a similar effect since, as in modern times, introduction to the conqueror's culture gave articulate expression to feelings directed against him. In the east, particularly, the spread of Greek produced all manner of hate-literatures against the Greek agents of Rome, as well as against the Romans themselves (p. 38). By a somewhat similar process the Romanization of Gaul during the second and third centuries gave its people the civilization and self-consciousness which inspired a marked revival of non-Roman cults, some of which, dating back to Celtic origins before Rome ever arrived, now spread beyond their homeland. In the time of Commodus, these deities even obtained official sanction, under Roman guise, in the shrines of the imperial armies.[17]

Between Latin and Greek the linguistic cleavage was now growing sharper. Men of high education like Marcus Aurelius could still be bilingual, and Severus Alexander was brought up as a "Greek and Roman", but this became increasingly unusual. An age which needed bilingual text-books also required official concessions regarding the use of languages. When Caracalla conducted a trial at Antioch, its title and sentence were written down in Latin, but all the rest—including the emperor's words—appeared in Greek.[18] Moreover, although Latin remained the language of the law, Severus Alexander allowed Roman citizens to make Greek wills. Diocletian, a Balkan peasant who continued the levelling-down of

Italy and established his capital at Nicomedia in the Greek east, was nevertheless determined to make Latin the exclusive governmental language (p. 109). He sent Roman grammarians and rhetoricians to the east, and even in Egypt Latin became the judicial tongue. But any progress in this direction was only temporary, and within another century (to the pecuniary advantage of translators and adapters) the linguistic barrier between east and west was already substantial. The opportunity, or visionary ideal, of creating cultural and religious unity had gone for ever, with immense consequences for the Mediterranean world.

Diocletian's attempt had been a hopeless one, for the previous hundred and fifty years, in every field except the law, had revealed an extreme scarcity of Latin writings of any importance whatever, from the viewpoint of substance or of style. Apart from one small poem, only Apuleius and Tertullian provide surviving exceptions; and they both came from the flourishing culture of Roman Africa (p. 160). Stylistically, the Greek work too is almost all of a low standard, and indeed there is an immense bulk of Greek writings that are worthless in every other respect as well. And yet the age also produced writers of immense significance—and, whether their race was Greek or eastern or (less often) Roman, nearly all but the jurists wrote in Greek. Even Marcus Aurelius, a Roman emperor of Romano-Spanish family, chose that language for his private *Meditations*; and so did the Egyptian Plotinus for his philosophy. Juvenal complained that the river Orontes had flowed into the Tiber, but more momentous than this racial conglomeration was the almost total supremacy, on the highest cultural planes, of the lingua franca provided by Greece. The African St. Augustine and his contemporaries would later rescue Latin for the Middle Ages, but between the second century and the fourth, except in the single field of law, it was men writing in Greek who create and express and define the climax of ancient Rome.

The greatest of them dwelt on peaks which even the outstanding thinkers of classical Greece had seldom, if ever, attained. Below them was a more widely disseminated literacy than there had ever been before. But this lay an enormously long way beneath their level, for higher education in its most typical aspects had failed, and its most rarefied manifestations, such as the philosophy of Plotinus, were far beyond the reach of this new public. Theirs was a middle-brow civilization, and its characteristic form of literature was the romantic novel.

The Best Romantic Novels

The novel, which was thus the typical manifestation of the culture of the time, included masterpieces. Outstanding among them was the isolated Latin work of extraordinary distinction written by Apuleius from Madaurus (Mdaourouch) in north Africa, who flourished in the time of Marcus Aurelius. The last and most peculiar of the Latin stylists, Apuleius was a great deal more than a mere middle-brow writer of romances; and his many interests form a valuable key to the period.

Novelist, poet, popular philosopher, rhetorical lecturer and man of religion, Apuleius was taken to court to answer the charge of addiction to magic, which was one of the principal concerns of the age (p. 246). His startlingly flamboyant, mesmerically ornate defence, a mixture of wild rhetoric and skilful argument, presumably secured his acquittal, but later St. Augustine was by no means sure that the accusation had been untrue[19]; and he felt obliged to warn his readers against people who, more than two centuries after the death of Apuleius, estimated him above Jesus Christ.

Magic is the main theme of Apuleius' novel the *Metamorphoses* (*Golden Ass*). The hero, Lucius, is turned into a donkey because he is excessively curious about the black art. Tales of sorcery and ribaldry contribute a great deal to the pulsing life and fantasy of this unparalleled book. Apuleius' strongly marked, off-beat sense of humour suggests that the whole work may be a satirical mockery of magic and superstition. Yet, if so, he is at least half serious and believing. In religion, despite frequent plunges into obscenity—and jokes about the petty and bourgeois Olympians—he is a determined adept, prepared for anything. "In Greece I took part in very many initiations. I keep carefully certain symbols and memorials of them handed to me by priests. ... I learned worship upon worship, rites beyond number, a great variety of ceremonies, in my zeal for truth and my dutifulness to the gods."[20]

To one of these faiths Apuleius had attached himself with passion. For the description of his encounter with the saviour-goddess Isis is a vivid indication that the cults of the middle and later empire were not artificial survivals but heartfelt realities (p. 241). There is also a spiritual undercurrent in the most famous and longest of the many self-contained stories that appear in the work,[21] the fairy-tale of *Cupid and Psyche* that has echoed round the world. Although this provides some of the most glorious entertainment in ancient literature, it is different from the ribald, hair-raising horror stories which liberally bestrew the rest of the book, because it echoes, at a distance yet with deliberation, the absorbing contemporary theme of the progress of the Soul (*psyche*), and its quest through carnal adventures for the ultimate attainment of happiness and peace (p. 242).[22] This, then, is escape literature of several kinds at the same time. It is full of the magic which was one of the chief means of liberation from the evils of this world. It tells allegorically how the Soul achieves this escape, and it provides a series of gorgeous enchantments which proved irresistible to Raphael and Elizabethan and Jacobean writers.

Apuleius' luxuriant Latin is far removed already from Cicero, and almost half-way to the tongues of modern Europe. The writer apologises, not very sincerely, for the rude and exotic Latinity which he, a poor Grecian, had picked up at Rome.[23] But his Latin was far the most accomplished of the age. The writer's native Africa, with its flourishing, emperor-producing culture, now possessed almost a monopoly of first-class Latin, and more was to come from Tertullian. Apuleius, who probably died some time towards the end of Marcus Aurelius' reign, may have written his *Metamorphoses* at the end of his life when Marcus was compiling his singularly different *Meditations*.

With its sparkling, cutting edge and unsentimental approach, this masterpiece of Apuleius is quite distinct from other ancient novels, which (except for Petronius' earlier *Satyricon*) are in Greek and belong to the eastern regions of the empire. Yet there was also a Greek novel on this same theme of a man turned into a donkey, *Lucius or the Ass*, by an unknown Lucius of Patrae.[24] That work, of which an excerpt or summary survives, may have provided Apuleius with his subject, though as often in ancient literature borrowings of such a kind do not lessen the extreme individuality of his treatment.

The Greek novel, of which Lucius of Patrae was a representative, had an extremely complicated literary pedigree. Everything was, indirectly, grist to the mill—the *Iliad* and many tales of Troy, the

Odyssey and all the travellers' tales that flowed from it, history and historical fiction from Herodotus to the *Alexander Romance*, devices and narrative speeches of tragic dramatists (and particularly love-themes of Euripides), myths of Plato, stock speeches and incidents of rhetoricians, characters and plots from Menander's Athenian New Comedy, erotic story-telling by elegiac poets, adventures and dialogues in mime and satire, the frivolous excitements of novella and short story, and many a national or religious eastern theme. Egypt played a particularly important part, and the earliest piece of Greek prose fiction (partly a love story), the *Dream of Nectanebus*, is translated from Egyptian.

Discoveries of Egyptian papyri have shown that the Greek novel which emerged as a blend of these various types of literature developed much earlier than had been thought. The oldest original example known at first-hand is the Ninus Romance, from which passages have survived in papyri.[25] The hero and heroine, oriental as in much popular anonymous fiction, are Semiramis and Ninus who was traditionally the first king of Assyria.[26] One fragment shows him about the fight against the Armenians; the other describes how, in the desire of the two lovers to be united, Ninus appeals to the girl's mother, and Semiramis to his. The love-motif is already established, and other keynotes of future novels are apparent in the king's determined pre-marital sexual continence and the bashfulness of the maiden. Known texts seem to belong to the first century A.D., but a resemblance between their contents and Greek works of history and pseudo-history suggests that the Ninus romance may originally have been written two if not three hundred years before that; and considerations of language point to the same conclusion.

Further papyrus discoveries have now confirmed that the Greek novel had reached maturity several centuries before the dates to which its main evolution was hitherto ascribed. For example *Chaereas and Callirhoe*, by Charito of Aphrodisias in south-western Asia Minor, cannot be of the Byzantine age, as had been believed, since papyri are earlier than A.D. 200.[27] The story, written in eight "books", is based on the Athenian expedition against Syracuse in the fifth century B.C. Hermocrates, who commanded the Syracusan forces, has according to the novel a beautiful daughter Callirhoe, loved at first sight by Chaereas the son of a political opponent.

There are the usual intrigues, suspicions, perils and robbers, and the heroine (as often) is mistakenly believed to be dead. But finally Fortune, the supreme goddess of later Greek times who is made by such writers to account for all their more excessive implausibilities, brings the loving pair together; and Aphrodite (Venus) also plays her part. When the writer promises in his final section that "in this book you shall find not brigandage and slavery and trial at law, fighting and heroism, war and capture, but honourable lives and lawful wedlock", he must be referring only to that concluding portion of his work; because elsewhere such features are present in abundance. Drama runs high—Charito himself says the trial-scene will surpass the stage—and so does chivalry; Dionysius of Syracuse, paying court to Callirhoe who has been sold to him as a slave, shows courteous restraint. Constance and chastity defeat all encroachments. There are quotations from Homer and the Athenian New Comedy, but the plot goes ahead without too many irrelevancies, and Charito's lucid style was much admired by the Renaissance. He could be as early as *c*. A.D. 100, or earlier.

Another author who belongs to the novel's rise to full development was Xenophon of Ephesus. His *Ephesiaca*, written in a form reminiscent of his fellow-Asian Charito, contains a reference to an event of Trajan's reign (98–117), and this romance almost certainly belongs to the second century A.D. Xenophon has got away from the persistent tradition that novels should be, however remotely, based on historical fact. Habrocomes loves and marries Anthea, but the oracle of Apollo of Colophon, which was still famous and active, warns them of perils ahead (p. 248). To frustrate these hazards the relatives of the young couple send them on a journey, but they encounter gales, shipwrecks, bandits, separations, and attempts on the virtue of Anthea. All these hazards are overcome. "I have escaped", she triumphantly records, "the threats of brigands, the plots of pirates, the outrages of brothel-keepers, and chains, and pits, and beams, and poisons, and burials—but you now, Habrocomes, have you abided chaste?" Yes, he has.

The *Ephesiaca* is relatively short, at least in its present form which is disjointed and may be an abridgement. The plot is concisely packed with incident. "Once more pirates and sea! Once more I am captive!" understandably sighs Anthea. And yet the author, a man of some taste but no great literary learning, prefers simplicity to rhetoric. However, he adds a clever, macabre, and bitter-sweet story within a story,[28] and a quasi-mystical insistence that material sacrifices to the purity of love will mean a happy life in the hereafter —which was the main concern of the times.[29]

Then comes a rich crop of novels dating from the times of Marcus Aurelius, Commodus and the dynasty of Septimius. These were not, as had been believed, the first important examples of the genre, but represent its mature output, brought to a new level of achievement (and no doubt read with increased appreciation) owing to the spreading, if somewhat low-level, secondary education of the age. Iamblichus, a Syrian like the later philosopher of the same name, was once thought of as the first of these writers; but he is now seen to be an heir of the prolonged earlier tradition that has been described. His romance, the *Babylonica*, is dateable from its reference to an Armenian king restored by the Romans in 165; and there seems to be a suggestion that Marcus Aurelius (d. 180) is still alive. The original work itself is lost, but a Byzantine summary has survived. Retreating from Xenophon's attempt to eliminate the pseudo-historical framework, Iamblichus set his scenario in ancient Mesopotamia, where Garmus, the cruel king of Babylon, casts a covetous eye upon Sinonis, wife of Rhodanes. The usual shipwrecks are lacking, but instead there is no shortage of persecutions, phantoms, sorcerers and mistaken identities. Iamblichus marshals a large cast whose adventures, though skilfully interwoven with the main plot, even exceed earlier novels in improbability.

Leucippe and Clitophon by Achilles Tatius was formerly ascribed to the fifth century A.D., but a papyrus has revealed that any such attribution is more than three hundred years too late.[30] A storm at sea, one of a series of melodramatic happenings presented in breathless succession, delivers the young lovers into the hands of Egyptian pirates. For Achilles Tatius was not a native of Asia Minor or Syria like his predecessors but an Alexandrian, and although wanton Fortune for the most part prevails in his work, the Egyptian god Serapis, who was greatly favoured by Septimius Severus, also fulfils a prominent role. We are back again in pure fiction, but with a spicy twist. True, there are the usual disasters, and time after time Clitophon can scarcely believe that his beloved is still alive. Indeed, she is apparently killed—not once but three times! This sort of exaggeration, of which there is a good deal, rather suggests that Achilles Tatius is making fun of such hackneyed themes. On one of the occasions when Leucippe seemed to meet her end she was thought to have been stabbed, by a servant of her bandit captors. Her intestines were even observed to gush out. Indeed they were removed and placed on an altar for sacrifice. But fortunately this was all an act staged by her friends to save her life from these robbers; the damage was inflicted not upon herself but upon a sheepskin secretly attached to her body, and the dagger had springs which prevented it from penetrating any deeper.[31]

Another unfamiliar touch indicates that the hero Clitophon, in the absence of Leucippe, goes to bed with another woman. Admittedly this was under *force majeure* (rather in the tradition of Odysseus), but in other novels only secondary characters had succumbed to illicit lovemaking in any circumstances whatever. In *Leucippe and Clitophon*, on the other hand, there is a new ironic tolerance of human frailty, implying criticism of his fellow novelists' standards of impregnable sexual restraint.

Achilles Tatius is particularly interested in love, which, in pursuance of a current Platonic fashion, he compared with religious Mysteries (p. 195). But he improves on preceding novelists by not remaining content with the comparatively uninteresting phenomenon of love at first sight. Instead he dwells on the gradual stages of courtship and the art by which it progresses. He is also articulately aware of the wild erotic urge, and the restless agitations and psychological disturbances it brings in its train. Clitophon is told by a cousin:

> Some lovers have to be content with a mere look at their sweetheart, so well guarded is she, and think themselves very lucky if they can obtain this pleasure of the eye; others are more fortunate, if they can but get a word with her. But you—you are constantly seeing her and hearing her; you eat with her and drink with her: and yet, with all this good fortune, you grumble. Let me tell you that you are ungrateful for this gift that Love has made you. You do not know what it is to be able to see the one you love. When the eyes meet one another they receive the impression of the body as in a mirror, and this emanation of beauty, which penetrates down into the soul through the eyes, effects a kind of union however the bodies are sundered, a new kind of bodily embrace.[32]

Towards the sufferings of love, like other sufferings, Achilles Tatius is unusually sympathetic.

Centuries later, the Byzantines (like people in Elizabethan England) keenly read Achilles Tatius; and one of their leading ecclesiastical scholars, Photius, detected indecency in the work, which does indeed like most of these novels reveal an occasional prurience, though there is the usual impeccably moral conclusion. Photius is more surprising when he praises this author for the clarity of his style. Although the story, for all its exuberance, is told lucidly enough, with its characters more human than hitherto, the language is artificial—or sometimes artificially simple—to a remarkable and even ridiculous degree. Free indulgence in the inquisitive encyclopaedic credulity which flourished in this epoch leads Achilles Tatius to digressions and set-pieces on a vast variety of subjects. They hold up the action of the novel, to which they are irrelevant. But readers of the time were entranced by the exotic mysteries and science-fictions of far-off lands to which Achilles Tatius particularly often devotes his wide-ranging curiosity.

> I myself have seen some of these miraculous phenomena . . . In Libya there is a lake which may be compared to the soil of India: the Libyan maidens know its secret, that its water contains a store of wealth; this is preserved below as in a treasury, being intermingled with the mud of the lake, which is a very spring of gold. So they smear with pitch the end of a pole and thrust it down beneath the water. Thus they open its concealed store-house, the pole being with respect to the gold what the hook is to a fish, for it does the fishing, while the pitch acts as bait; since all the gold which touches it (and nothing else) sticks to it and thus the pitch draws its capture to the land. That is the manner of the gold fisheries in this Libyan stream.[33]

And then the marvels of India, which were so fascinating to Greeks and Romans of this age (p. 236), include the healing fragrance of the elephant's breath when it has been feeding on the leaf of the black rose.

> I once saw an extraordinary sight. There was a Greek who had put his head right into the middle of an elephant's jaws. It kept its mouth open and breathed upon him as he remained in that position. I was surprised at both, the audacity of the man and the amiability of the elephant; but the man told me that he had in fact given the animal a fee for it, because the beast's breath was only less sweet than the scents of India, and a sovereign remedy for headache. The elephant knows that he possesses this power of healing, and will not open his mouth for nothing; he is one of those rascally doctors that insist on having their fee first. When you give it him, he graciously consents, stretches open his jaws, and keeps them agape as long as the man desires; he knows that he has let out on hire the sweetness of his breath.[39]

Achilles Tatius is not entirely serious. And his contemporary Lucian, looking round for things to laugh at, devotes his *True Stories*— model for Rabelais, Swift, Voltaire—to making fun of this sort of scientific observation quite openly (p. 246).

> Sure enough, just before sunset twenty more pirates suddenly darted out at us from an apparently uninhabited island. They were mounted on large dolphins, which neighed like horses as they bounded across the waves. The pirates quickly surrounded our ship and started pelting us at close range with dried squids and crabs' eyes, but as soon as we let fly with our arrows and javelins so many of them were wounded that the whole lot turned tail and fled back to the island. About midnight, when the sea was very calm, we inadvertently ran aground on a halcyon's nest. It was nearly seven miles in circumference, and the bird that was sitting on it was not much smaller. We interrupted her in the process of incubating her eggs, and she flew up into the air with a melancholy cry, creating such a draught with her wings that she practically sank our ship. As soon as it was light we disembarked and went for a walk round the nest, which consisted of a vast number of trees plaited together to form a sort of raft. On it were five hundred eggs, each about the size of a barrel, from which impatient chirpings could already be heard.[35]

Daphnis and Chloe, written by Longus of Lesbos, is probably a little later than Achilles Tatius and Lucian; comparisons based on the symmetry and other devices of the style suggests a date early in the third century. Longus' hero and heroine, like many real children in the ancient world, were exposed by their father and mother at birth. But they were found and adopted by foster-parents, whose goats and sheep they tended together throughout their childhood. The usual themes of piracy, war, unwelcome suitors and kidnappers are introduced, but with a difference; for here they rank as secondary mishaps, intruding in incidental fashion upon a setting that is bucolic and idyllic. The boy and girl are in love with each other, but they do not know what this means or what to do about it. Daphnis is taught the necessary methods by an older woman—in pursuance of Achilles Tatius' suggestion that the hero's chastity need not be absolute—and finally he and his beloved marry, after they have been reunited with their parents who turn out to be rich citizens of Mitylene.

Daphnis and Chloe is the only surviving pastoral prose romance from the ancient world; one manuscript calls it "The Pastorals of Lesbos". There was, at this time, a lively literary interest in Theocritus who, living at another Aegean island, Cos, had founded pastoral poetry half a millennium earlier. His poems had built a fantasy of rural life for city-dwellers, and Virgil's *Eclogues* (*c.* 37 B.C.) imbued this sophisticated mood with a subtle nostalgic elegance. Longus, like them, is fond of the country, in a way that no rustic ever was; and he advertises such artificiality at once by describing his scene as the literary pendant of a painted picture. This elaborate Arcadian background, only briefly disturbed by the hazards required in a novel, provides unusual unity of place—it is a sort of laboratory in which, while nothing changes but the seasons, the unspoiled hero and heroine can be observed away from the world, watched by Pan with his pipes and the nymphs of woods and meadows, rustic deities who preside over this Golden Age in which Daphnis and Chloe lived and loved.

> Their amusements were of a childish and pastoral kind. Chloe would go hunting asphodel stalks, of which she wove traps for grasshoppers, neglecting her flock the while. Daphnis cut slender reeds, perforated the intervals between the joints, fitted them together with soft wax, and then practised piping till nightfall. Sometimes they shared their milk and wine, and made a common meal of the provisions they brought from home. Sooner would one see the flocks of sheep or goats separated from one another than Daphnis and Chloe apart.[36]

Yet there is a certain ironic tang, which lessens the danger of insipidity, in Longus' balance between the simple day's work and life in the town. This is not quite a flat contrast between good and bad; the two worlds can be reconciled if wisdom is applied to the task. And in any case the country is a rococo Arcadia, a gracious ideal but in plain reality something of a joke. Yet in the end it is to this nonexistent rustic life that Daphnis and Chloe return for their wedding, because they could not endure their visit to the city. "Even the goats grazed nearby, as if they too shared in the festivities. To the city folk this was not very agreeable, but Daphnis called the bucks by name, and gave them green leaves to eat, and held them by the horns and kissed them."[37]

But the translator of Cromwellian times who called this "a most sweet and pleasant romance for young ladies"[38] should have added that Longus was mocking gently at the conventions of his own story. His romance, ripening in the tranquil seclusion of true love's spring time, is not naïve but sophisticatedly naïve, wavering between naturalism and frivolity; its detailed account of the pair being so simple that they do not know how to make love is written and intended in a lascivious way. Furthermore there is a religious or philosophical undercurrent. Just as Plotinus called Plato's Love (Eros) the essence of mystic union, so Longus, at a lower level, sees him as the supreme Dionysiac motive-power of events, the prime cosmic force whose strength is demonstrated both by nature and by the experience of the lovers.[39] The old Philetas tells them:

> If I have not grown these grey hairs in vain, you, my children, are consecrated to Eros, and Eros has care of you. He possesses greater power than Zeus himself. ... He rules the elements, he rules the stars, he rules his fellow deities; your power over your goats and sheep is not as great. All flowers are the work of Eros, all these plants are his handiwork; it is through him that rivers flow and breezes blow.[40]

Longus is an elegant, studied stylist, vivid and concise. Unintentional outrages to common sense are avoided, sentiment rings true, bold realism is not lacking, and the plot, which could have been monotonous, is an intriguing blend of seriousness and levity. *Daphnis and Chloe* is a minor masterpiece. To the later world, it often seemed a major one. Medieval monks read the book surreptitiously—one manuscript is of a miniature size suitable for rapid concealment, and begins and ends with religious texts which hide the romance sandwiched between them. A Byzantine philosopher-historian found it necessary to advise monastic novices to start their reading with "the more serious works of the great age" instead of Longus or Achilles Tatius, who were evidently much more popular.[41]

Daphnis and Chloe also exerted great influence upon the medieval pastoral tradition. But it was the writers and particularly the courtiers of the sixteenth century who most of all welcomed this gay combination of artificial rusticity and incident as an inexhaustible source for their own poetry and fiction. Jorge de Montemayor's *Diana* (*c.* 1559) is a Spanish *Daphnis and Chloe* (via the Italian) with more adventure and less psychology, and Sir Philip Sidney's *Arcadia* likewise owes much to Longus. There were French and English translations, and a Greek first edition at Florence in 1598.[42] Rousseau and Goethe were admirers of the work, and Rousseau's friend Bernardin de St. Pierre adapted Longus' analysis of friendship ripening into love for his best-seller *Paul et Virginie* (1787).

Some people have regarded *Daphnis and Chloe* as the most successful of the Greek novels. Others prefer another book of about the same date or a little later, the *Aethiopica*. Its author, Heliodorus, came from Emesa (Homs) in Syria. This was also the home of Severus Alexander's mother, and it was perhaps in his reign that the book was written; for Heliodorus seems to have known Philostratus' *Life of Apollonius of Tyana* (*c.* 217–18, p. 235) and he mentions armoured Persian cavalry, which the Romans encountered in *c.* 232–3. Yet the work might not be so late as that.

The courageous, beautiful and gifted hero and heroine are Theagenes and Chariclea, after whom the work is sometimes named. Chariclea was exposed in infancy by her mother, the queen of Ethiopia. Rescued by a Greek priest, the girl grew up in Delphi, where she and Theagenes fell in love. In the company of Calasiris, an Egyptian sage whom the queen had sent to search for her daughter, they both set out for the far-off lands where the oracle had declared that happiness would be theirs. After various adventures they reach the coast of Egypt as captives of a pirate band. Separated and then reunited, they finally come to Meroe as prisoners of the Ethiopians whose capital this is. Just in time to save them from the fate of sacrificial victims, their parents recognize them. Their marriage receives the royal blessing, and priesthoods are bestowed upon them both.

The beginning of the *Aethiopica* is one of the sensations of Greek literature. Like the *Odyssey*, the book plunges straight into the middle of its adventurous theme. While all identities and intentions are still unknown, we rush through strange events and hazards producing repercussions which spread out both backwards and forwards into time and transform the lives of the hero and heroine.

The cheerful smile of day was just appearing, as the rays of the sun began to light up the mountain tops, when some men armed like brigands peered over the ridge that stretches alongside the outlets of the Nile and that mouth of the river which is named after Hercules. They halted there for a little while, scanning with their eyes the sea that lay below them; and when they had cast their first glances over the ocean and found no craft upon it and no promise there of pirates' plunder, they bent their gaze down upon the shore nearby. And what it showed was this: a merchant ship was moored there by her stern cables, bereft of her ship's company but fully laden; so much could be inferred even at a distance, for her burthen brought the water as high as the third waling-piece of her timbers. The shore was thickly strewn with newly slain bodies, some quite lifeless, and others half dead whose limbs were still a-quiver, thus indicating that the conflict had only just ceased.

That it had been no regular engagement was betokened by what was visible. For there lay mingled the pitiful remnants of a feast that had come to no happy conclusion. There were tables still laden with their victuals; some others, overturned on the ground, were held in the grasp of those of the vanquished who had used them as armour in the struggle—for it had been a fight on the spur of the moment—and underneath others were men who had crept there in the hope of concealment. Wine-bowls were upset, and some were slipping from the hands of their holders—either drinkers or those who had taken them up to use as missiles instead of a stone. Here lay a man wounded with an axe, there one struck by a stone that the shingle had provided on the spot, another mangled by a piece of timber and another burnt to death by a firebrand; but most had fallen victims to darts and arrows. The conquest was clear as day, but the spoils were unseized; while the vessel, deserted and void of men, yet held its cargo intact, as though protected by a strong guard, and it rocked gently at its moorings as in a time of peace. . . .

When they had advanced to a little way short of the ship and the fallen, they came upon a sight more unaccountable than what they had seen before. A young girl was seated on a rock, so inconceivably beautiful as to convince one that she was a goddess. Though sorely anguished by her present plight, she yet breathed forth a high and noble spirit. Her head was crowned with laurel; a quiver was slung over her shoulder; and her left arm was propped upon her bow, beyond which the hand hung negligently down. The elbow of her other arm she supported on her right thigh, while on its palm she rested her cheek; and with downcast eyes she held her head still, gazing intently on a prostrate youth. He, cruelly wounded, seemed to be faintly awakening as from a deep slumber that was well-nigh death. . . . She sprang up from the rock; the men on the mountain, struck with wonder and alarm by the sight as though by some fiery blast, cowered under bushes, for she seemed to them to be something greater and more divine when she stood erect. Her arrows rattled with her sudden movement. The inwoven gold of her dress glistened in the beams of the sun, and her hair, tossing below the wreath like the tresses of a bacchante, flowed widespread over her back.[43]

Curiosity has indeed been aroused, and tension is high. Heliodorus excels at constructing a plot, and the conventional motifs of oracles, oaths, letters, soliloquies, meditated suicides and apparent deaths are given epic and dramatic treatment in a style loaded with bright narrative and laced with a sparse but brisk humour. There is a steady and rapid progression of vigorous episodes, backed by cleverly depicted subsidiary characters and stories. These secondary themes are, for the most part, sufficiently relevant not to hold up the main narrative too much.

But Heliodorus is also abreast of the contemporary mode in his liberal infusions of imaginative geography and ethnology.

> The whole region is named by the Egyptians "Herdsmen's Home"; it is a low-lying tract which receives certain overflows of the Nile so as to form a lake which is of immense depth at its centre but dwindles towards its edges into a swamp. What shores are to seas, swamps are to lakes. Here it is that Egyptians of the bandit kind have their city. One man has built himself a cabin on a patch of land that may lie above the water level. Another makes his dwelling in a boat which serves at once for transport and for habitation; upon this the women spin their wool, and also bring forth their children. When a child is born, it is reared at first on its mother's milk, but thereafter on the fish taken from the lagoon and broiled in the sun. When they observe the child attempting to crawl, they fasten a thong to its ankles which allows it to move to the limits of the boat or the hut, thus singularly making the tethering of their feet serve instead of leading them by the hand. Hence many a herdsman has been born on the lagoon, and reared in this manner, and so come to regard the lagoon as his homeland; and it fully serves as a strong bastion for brigands.[44]

Although the novelist is Syrian, his eastern patriotism is enlarged to include Egypt. The wise Calasiris asserts that Homer was a fellow-Egyptian, just as the *Alexander Romance* made the same claim for Alexander the Great.[45] The descendants of the proud peoples whom he had conquered on the periphery of the Hellenic world consoled their self-esteem by fiction displaying a national, religious emphasis. Heliodorus also extends this sympathetic attention to Ethiopia. Nevertheless Chariclea, in spite of her coloured parentage, is white; and the Greeks are superior to non-Greeks. The book is written for the people, pervading the Roman empire of the day, who were Greek not by birth but by language and partially by culture. And there is perhaps the additional purpose of showing them that their more Hellenic neighbours, for all their superior airs, could be successfully emulated.

Achilles Tatius had been good at writing about love; so is Heliodorus, and he too contributes a special treatment of his own. The innovation in the *Aethiopica* is the energetic and resourceful companionship provided by Chariclea to her lover. In many crises it is she who takes the lead and is a more inventive thinker than the brave but easily discouraged Theagenes. Later, the book was sometimes called just *Chariclea*; for here is a woman, almost for the first time in literature, assuming her proper station as the friend and companion of man. In view, however, of her ferocious chastity, which is no longer a literary pose but an urgent inner commandment characteristic of a powerfully ascetic era (p. 181), it seems strange that Montaigne saw her as "peradventure a little too curiously and wantonly tricked, and too amorous for an ecclesiastical and sacerdotal daughter". But what, no doubt, surprised him was the uninhibited nature of her loyalty and love for Theagenes. She is lavish with outbursts of emotion, which are expressed not so much by psychological description as by the recording of vigorous and excitable facial expressions, gestures and movements. No runner in a race could want a more enthusiastic partisan than Theagenes possessed in his beloved.

> Chariclea's excitement knew no bounds; and I, who had been observing her for some time, saw continual changes occurring in her demeanour. When, for all to hear, the herald had proclaimed the names of the entrants for the race, calling out "Ormenus of Arcadia and Theagenes of Thessaly", and when the cord was let fall and the race was started at a speed which almost defeated the quickest vision, then the young girl was no longer able to keep still: her legs quivered, her feet danced, as if, to my thinking, her soul were floating away with Theagenes and were zealously supporting him in the race.[46]

Indeed, Chariclea's reactions to the temporary disappearance of her lover are so violently tearful that they invite and receive rebuke.

> When he saw her dishevelled hair, her dress all tattered on her bosom, and her eyes still swollen and showing traces of the frenzy that held her before she fell asleep, Calasiris understood the cause. He led her back to the bed, seated her and put a cloak about her. Having her thus more suitably attired, he asked: "What is this, Chariclea? Why such excessive, such immoderate dismay? Why this senseless subjection to circumstances? . . . Be considerate of us, my child; be considerate, if not of yourself yet at least of Theagenes, to whom only life with you is desirable, and existence has value only if you survive." Chariclea blushed as she heard these words. . . .[47]

Another profound concern of Heliodorus was to show the divine guidance behind this love. Reflecting upon the world's infinitely varied activities and interacting events, he does not attribute all of them to Fortune but explains many others, through the mouth of a priest or prophet, as the work of Providence and divine justice. For the *Aethiopica* is much concerned with philosophy and religion. Like contemporaries whose work he seems to know, Heliodorus wants to simplify and unify myths and cults, and reunite them with their eastern origins. In particular, he reveals a lofty conception of the Sun-god, felt to be universal and identified with Apollo (p. 226). He himself was connected by heredity, as by name, with the Emesan Sun-cult from whose priestly family the emperors of the time were descended (p. 229), and Sun-worship is therefore prominent in the *Aethiopica*.

Indeed, Heliodorus provides the most conspicuous example of a religious preoccupation which is apparent in almost all the novels.[48] Despite every incidental set-back, the gods are helping and guarding their special charges. Each writer tends to have a favourite god or gods of his own, and the general theme of attaining fulfilment through initiatory ordeals, described with almost formulaic uniformity, possessed obvious analogies to the ceremonials of salvation prescribed by the Mystery faiths (p. 240). Like the audiences of medieval miracle plays we must put aside the modern idea that religion and entertainment are incompatible.

Byzantine tradition retrospectively turned both Heliodorus and Achilles Tatius into Christian bishops, in order to make their novels respectable reading for monks, who were so fond of this sort of literature. They justified the taste by interpreting each amorous intrigue as a moral lesson. These lessons were then incorporated in similar Christian romances with heroes and heroines who were terrorized by hazards imposed by the demon of sensuality, and took refuge in penitence and asceticism.[49]

Tasso praises the skilful suspense of the *Aethiopica* and its gradual clearing up of perplexities. He and Cervantes show how much the sixteenth century loved Chariclea. So do paintings by Raphael, for these novels excelled in visual appeal. A French translation of Heliodorus by Amyot (1547) ran into ten editions during the latter half of the sixteenth century, and Underdown's English version was reprinted four times within fifty years after its first publication (1587).[50] Racine loved the *Aethiopica*. Although forbidden to read it as a fifteen-year-old boy at Port Royal, he learnt the novel by heart and it affected him deeply and awoke many echoes in his own plays.

Because of its complex and diversified contents and origins (p. 161), this fictional literature was not given any specific name by the ancients themselves; there is no Greek or Latin term for "novels" or "romances", and in Byzantine times they were still classified under drama or comedy.

For quite different reasons, some modern critics refuse to allow the word "novel" to be applied to the writings of Heliodorus and the rest, reserving this term for works more concerned with character and motive, and preferring that these stories of incident—as they consider the Greek books to be—should be called romances instead. This is, perhaps, an untenable distinction, but there is a difference between high-brow novels requiring some mental effort and middle-brow novels involving little or nothing except the plain task of following the plot, which may be variegated, perhaps, by a modicum of cultural or religious themes and allusions. The greater part of the remaining Greek and Latin writings that have come down to us—the most notable exception is the comedy of Plautus—is aimed at men whose traditional higher education had equipped them for intellectual exercise; it may therefore, whatever its defects, be classified as mainly high-brow. Readers of the novels, on the other hand, were the middle-brow products of a widespread secondary education system which did not aspire to university standards. Similar romantic novels, "missing the advantage of the dry light of academic judgment",[51] have been composed and enjoyed at many other epochs also, influenced by the ancient writers sometimes not at all, sometimes indirectly, and often directly, Such were the intricate webs, full of "feyned nowhere acts", popular in the Elizabethan age which found them more realistic than the tales of chivalry that were at last going out of fashion. The formula was fresh and childish, the sentimentality cloying, and as in ancient times a few acceptable references of an erudite character were inserted for the sake of impressiveness and uplift.

And then again Pierre Huet of Caen (1670) and Dr. Samuel Johnson define the same type of literature in terms which apply very nearly as well to Heliodorus as to their own contemporaries. Walter Scott admitted that as a young man his addiction to light reading of this kind was so persistent that it amounted to a dissipation. Thereafter, his own conspicuous achievements in the ancient genre of historical romance brilliantly fulfilled Coleridge's criterion of this sort of writing, "to amuse without requiring any effort of thought, and without exciting any deep emotion". In the present century this same middlebrow novel (rarely composed with Scott's artistry) has been called a morally and intellectually betwixt and between mixture of geniality and sentiment, stuck together with a sticky slime of calves'-foot jelly—not therefore literature, but interesting for its choice and handling of material, and useful for "keeping the lower levels posted with what is stirring higher up"; more decent than high-brow stuff, or more conventionally so[52]; but selling better, at least until television came along.

"My pictures of life," said Gene Stratton Porter, "are sentimental and idealized. They are! And I glory in them!" So might have spoken, though likewise without total solemnity, Achilles Tatius or Longus or Heliodorus. For the kind of writing that culminated in their work was the only literary form (other than those directly sponsored by religions) extensively developed during the period that is the subject of the present book. Such fiction flourished because it supplied lively entertainment with just a little, but not too much, intellectual or pseudo-intellectual and religious stimulus, and because the hero's and heroine's unassailable chastity, a new dominant motif in western literature, gave the illusion of edification. An exciting flavour of sensuality is added, and yet everything still remains full of fine, pure feeling. This is a literature for the young— or the immature wishing they were young—to whom everything is black and white.

But above all novels were read because their dream-dramas, although not wholly escapist seeing that they look honestly (if symbolically) at the hazards of the world, were nevertheless a relief from the tedious and anxious realities of daily life. Fantasy-fiction is the typical nourishment of people whose normal impulses are starved of the means of expression. The politics of the Greco-Roman world were unpleasant, and in any case out of reach. A much more agreeable, accessible and flattering wish-fulfilment was to be found in imaginative identification with the young lovers in these novels. In an age, moreover, when very nasty things could happen, these appalling ordeals gave the vicarious thrill which attracts harmless people to stories of crime and murder today. Besides, there was always the assurance of a respectable, matrimonial happy ending. A vital psychological part was played in the Roman empire by the Greek middle-class middle-brow fiction—infinitely far removed from the classic Greece of marble ruins—which provided in skilful fantasy the happiness real life failed to offer.

1. *Frag. Vat.* 204; cf. Dio LXXVII, Herod. IV, 17, 6
2. Education was to be in the Christian mould, but he encouraged the pagans Nicagoras and Sopater
3. Priscian rates Apollonius as the greatest grammarian. 4 of his 29 works survive, very little by his son
4. Pseudo-Dionysus, *Techne*; cf. two second century *Technai* (Pseudo-Aristides), by different authors. "Longinus", *On the Sublime*, is likely to be Augustan, and not the work of Zenobia's minister of that name
5. Greg. Thaum. *Orat. Paneg. Ad Orig.* 5
6. M. P. Nilsson; G. S. Kirk
7. E.g. good Neoplatonist mathematics: especially Iamblichus, Diophantus of Alexandria (*c.* 250, algebra), Pappus (*c.* 300, geometry)
8. Pergamum (superior now to Cos), Smyrna, Laodicea ad Lycum, Ephesus
9. Galen, *De Fac. Nat.* III, 10 (tr. A. J. Brock)
10. *Id.*, *De Usu Partium* (the hand)
11. C. J. Singer
12. Seven Liberal Arts (*Trivium, Quadrivium*), (cf. Martian. Capella, fifth century A.D.): probably of third-century origin. Physical education did not long survive official Christianity
13. P. Oxy. XII, 1467; Ulp. *Dig.* L. 5, 2, 8; *JHS.* XXIX, 1909, 30ff.
14. *Hermeneumata Pseudo-Dositheana* (one section dated A.D. 207), *Corp. Gl. Lat.* III, 381 *seq.*
15. Fables of Babrius (? second century A.D.) were also popular
16. Eumenes was sent to Augustodunum: *Pan. Lat.* IV, 14, 15
17. Commodus-Hercules was identified with Celtic gods. Cf. widespread cults of Belenus, Epona, Atargatis the "Syrian goddess"
18. *Syria*, XXIII, 1942–3, 178f. (A.D. 216)
19. Aug. *CD.* XVIII, 18; *Ep.* 136. 1,138
20. Apul. *Apol.* 55. Apuleius was a Middle Platonist
21. "Milesian Tales"—Tale of the Tub, Baker's Wife, Lost Slippers, Fuller's Wife
22. Cf. Catacomb of Domitilla, Rome: painting of Cupid and Psyche gathering flowers
23. Apul. *Met.* 1, 1
24. An attempted identification with Lucian is unlikely
25. P. Berlin 2041 f.
26. The girl's name does not appear in the surviving fragments
27. Pap. Michaelidae, Aberdeen (1955) no. l: cf. 156 P.
28. Aegialeus and Thelxinoe
29. Partially echoed by the *Story of Apollonius King of Tyre*, Latin version of early Byzantine date (model for Shakespeare's *Pericles*): from a Greek original, probably early second century A.D.
30. A. Vogliano, *Stud. Ital. fil. class.* XV, 1938, 121
31. Ach. Tat. III, 21

32. *Ibid.*, I, ix, 3–4 (tr. S. Gaselee)
33. *Ibid.*, II, xiv, 9–10 (tr. S. Gaselee)
34. *Ibid.*, IV, iv, 7 (tr. S. Gaselee)
35. Lucian, *Ver. Hist.* (tr. P. Turner; model of Rabelais, Swift, Voltaire), parodying *Marvels beyond Thule* of Antonius Diogenes (first/second century A.D.)
36. Longus I, 10 (tr. M. Hadas)
37. *Ibid.*, IV, 37f. (tr. M. Hadas)
38. G. Thornley (1657)
39. Xenophon of Ephesus had at first suggested that his hero Habrocomes wished to rise above Eros
40. Longus, II, 6f. (tr. M. Hadas)
41. Michael Psellus (eleventh century). The pagan emperor Julian had forbidden his priests to read novels
42. French: Amyot (1559). English: Day (1587). Cf. Shakespeare's *Winter's Tale*, Corot, Ravel
43. Heliod. *Aeth.* I, 1ff. (tr. W. Lamb)
44. Heliod. *Aeth.* I, 5f. (tr. W. Lamb)
45. The Egyptians also claimed Aesop. Homer was Syrian according to Meleager
46. Heliod. *Aeth.* IV, 3 (tr. W. Lamb)
47. *Ibid.*, VI, 9 (tr. W. Lamb)
48. Aphrodite in Charito, Pan and the nymphs in Longus, Artemis and Isis in Xenophon, Serapis in Achilles Tatius; cf. Isis in Apuleius
49. *Acts of Paul and Thecla, Acts of Xanthippe and Polyxena* (? third or fourth century A.D.). The French *roman courtois* owed a great deal to Byzantine romantic novels
50. Shakespeare knew Heliodorus (*Twelfth Night*, V, I, 121f.)
51. P. Lubbock
52. Wilkie Collins; Q. D. Leavis; D. H. Lawrence (against Hugh Walpole)

7

Gospels of Self-reliance

The Meditations *of Marcus Aurelius*

There is the sharpest of contrasts between these imaginative amusements, flavoured with religion, and the unique sense of duty (despite a desire for withdrawal) of the emperor who was ruling during the epoch when the novel developed to maturity, namely Marcus Aurelius. Against the ills and anxieties of the age, the remedy of novelists and their readers was to note their existence obliquely, and ride triumphantly over them in the imagination; the remedy of Marcus was to do all in his power to put them right, with utter conscientiousness.

The dramatically intimate disclosures of his deepest thoughts, entitled by editors 'his writings to himself' and later called his *Meditations*, are written in Greek and show a literary cast because he had a literary training, but they were private notebooks not intended for publication. Nor do they form a connected unity. The notes and reflections which they contain are a highly personal confidential diary—a work of self-consolation and self-encouragement, an unparalleled self-scrutiny, each separate passage reflecting its own mood. The unpretentious and mundane letters which Marcus had written to his friend and tutor Fronto (who attempted a reform of Latin style) contain his thoughts from the age of seventeen to forty-five. The *Meditations* take up the story, with greater profundity, during the last ten or fifteen years of his life.

The writings of Marcus convey the necessity and difficulty of moral and social effort in more comprehensible and urgent language than had ever been used to clothe such ideas before. This, in terms of decent behaviour, is the climax of pagan Rome. But it is an austere creed, without consolations except its own performance. For man must just strive onward, and continue his unremittingly laborious efforts as best he can. When Marcus gratefully praises his predecessor and adoptive father Antoninus Pius, what emerges is the patient long-suffering endurance of Antoninus.[1] And the central, practical, point of Marcus' demands upon himself and others is the same: turn inward; strengthen yourself, find the courage to complete your job—and his was almost intolerably burdensome. Life is short, he says, and all that is required is that you should think and act responsibly and unselfishly.

> Hour by hour resolve firmly, like a Roman and a man, to do what comes to hand with correct and natural dignity, and with humanity, independence, and justice. . . . If you do the task before you, always adhering to strict reason with zeal and energy and yet with humanity, disregarding all lesser ends and keeping the divinity within you pure and upright, as though you were even now faced with its recall—if you hold steadily to this, staying for nothing and shrinking from nothing, only seeking in each passing action a conformity with nature and in each word and utterance a fearless truthfulness, then shall the good life be yours.[2]

Conformity with nature and with the divinity inside oneself are ideals which go back to Zeno of Citium in Cyprus, the founder of Stoicism in c. 300 B.C. "Nature" is the providential divinity that governs the universe, and according to the Stoics, drawing in part upon the idealism of Plato, a spark of that divinity is present in each one of us. Such is the religion of Marcus Aurelius. "This intelligence in every man is God, an emanation from deity. To be a philosopher is to keep unsullied, unscathed, the divine spirit within oneself."[3] Marcus was also a pious worshipper of the Roman gods, for such ritual was necessary for the survival of the state and cohesion of its people (p. 214). But he saw those divine powers as aspects of a universal deity. He himself believed, like Stoics before him, that this deity is immanent in the world in such a way that it and the world make a single whole, like the soul and body. That is why man must be true to himself—to the highest part of himself, the heavenly force which has lodged this spark in his soul. Call this god or gods, it does not matter. Occasionally, twice for example when he was giddy or spitting blood, he felt their strength help him— through dreams. "It is experience which proves their power every day, and therefore I am satisfied that they exist, and I do them reverence."[4]

Accordingly Marcus believed there was something infinite in human experience itself. His is a more sombre version of the joyful resignation to transcendent Divine Providence which had been the creed of that other Stoic missionary and physician of the soul, the Phrygian slave Epictetus (d. *c*. A.D. 135). Marcus owed a very great deal to Epictetus. But he owed nothing to the hopes of salvation conferred by a host of contemporary religions (p. 240), for he did not share those hopes. Death, to him, is an unanswerable riddle; it is impossible to see where any consolation or remedy for it can be found. And yet, failing in health and facing the enemy, Marcus thinks and writes often of dying, and advises that each day should be lived as if it were your last.[5] He needed all his Stoicism to prevent such thoughts from overcoming him. Nor, even if the divine power occasionally seems present, did there appear to be any hope of influencing it by prayer.

For these reasons, the *Meditations* have been called the saddest of all books. Dedicated but far from optimistic, their writer looks for heavenly guidance but is only rarely conscious of receiving it, and tries to do his best though more than doubtful of a reward in the hereafter, let alone in this world. He was not a free-thinker (there were none) or an unbeliever or, according to the modern atheistic use of the word, a humanist. But Marcus did not share the irrational, unprovable assumption, common to all major religions, that the supra-sensible can be influenced by the activities of man. The rhythm of the universe is monotonous, meaningless and predestined. "Whatever may happen to you was prepared for you in advance from the beginning of time. In the woven tapestry of causation, the thread of your being had been intertwined from all time with that particular incident."[6]

Nevertheless, he believed that very much still does lie within our power, and inside the bounds of our own strength and capabilities. This Stoic theme had meant all to Epictetus. "Under our control are conception, choice, desire, aversion. If you think only what is your own to be your own, you will blame no one, nor is there any harm that can touch you."[7] This is the essence of Marcus' creed too: although much is predestined, much else is determinable by our own will, and from such decisions no man has the power to hold us back. They are ours, for us to make the best of them. So "keep yourself the friend of justice and godliness; kindly, affectionate, and resolute in your devotion to duty".[8] The prime duty of the soul is to realize its moral perfectibility by arduous discipline. Moreover, even if there are no posthumous rewards, men are capable of behaving well. And indeed, because of the divine spark which they share, it is natural for them to do so. For the suggestion that moral principles should not be identified with a deity's commands would have seemed wrong to Marcus—at least if the deity is interpreted as the natural unity of the universe: in this sense, "the gods" have given us full power not to fall into evil.[9]

For Marcus there were no oriental sensualities, but a rigorous asceticism typical of the age. He questioned the classical principle of a link between physical and moral beauty, and nowhere can one find a more relentlessly destructive analysis of the pleasures of eye, ear, food and sex, "twitchings of appetite" which he describes in the coarse and sordid terms also used by many other pagans and Christians of this changing, later Roman world. The last password of Antoninus had been: Equanimity. To guide one's will successfully through the batterings of Fortune is only possible by avoiding these alleged pleasures, and indeed by maintaining absolute calm.

Never to be flustered, never apathetic, never attitudinizing—here is the perfection of character. Be like the headland against which the waves break and break; it stands firm, until presently the watery tumult around it subsides once more to rest. "How unlucky I am, that this should have happened to me!" By no means; say rather "How lucky I am, that it has left me with no bitterness: unshaken by the present, and undismayed by the future." The thing could have happened to anyone, but not everyone would have emerged unembittered.[10]

These ideals, and Marcus' manful and continuous endeavours to live up to them, are more noteworthy because he had to fight continuously, with melancholy resignation, against tortured convictions of his own personal shortcomings[11] and those of the entire world. In such a fog and filth, what can be respected and pursued with enthusiasm he often no longer knows. "What do the baths bring to your mind? Oil, sweat, dirt, greasy water, and everything that is disgusting. Such, then, is life in all its parts, and such is every material thing in it."[12] It is all a mere service to the flesh. Hellenism's bright incentives encouraging material achievement have now been left behind. True, man is still the measure, for he must and can forge ahead. He is still to that extent captain of his own spirit, but with no sunny, classical sense of unlimited power. For Marcus echoes

Epictetus' belief in the essential insecurity of the human condition.[13] Not only is life disgusting, but it is transient:

> Yesterday a drop of semen, tomorrow a handful of spice and ashes. In the life of a man, his time is but a moment, his being an incessant flux, his senses a dim rushlight, his body a prey of worms, his soul an unquiet eddy, his fortune dark, and his fame doubtful. In short, all that is of the body is as coursing waters, all that is of the soul as dreams and vapours. . . . An empty pageant; a stage play; flocks of sheep, herds of cattle; a tussle of spearmen; a bone flung among a pack of curs; a crumb tossed into a pond of fish; ants, loaded and labouring; mice, scared and scampering; puppets, jerking on their strings—that is life.[14]

Just as Tolstoy felt like an orphan, isolated in the midst of all these things that were so foreign, so Marcus also saw life as a temporary visit to an alien land (p. 288).[15] From now on, as one tormented year followed another, these promptings of doubt and inadequacy became ever stronger, verging on stupor and despair.

So what can be done except to withdraw into one's own resources and draw strength from the inner life, that little domain that is the self? "Men seek for seclusion in the wilderness, by the seashore, or in the mountains—a dream you have cherished only too fondly yourself. But such fancies are wholly unworthy of a philosopher, since at any moment you choose you can retire within yourself. Avail yourself often, then, of this retirement, and so continually renew yourself."[16] Therein is the only chance of a more reassuring reality. "Withdraw into your own self. Dig within. There lies the well-spring of good: ever dig, and it will ever flow."[17]

Preoccupied with this introversion, which was to receive even greater emphasis from Plotinus (p. 193), Marcus felt that you should "leave another's wrongdoing where it lies".[18] Such a suggestion has been criticized for carrying tolerance to the point of becoming antisocial. But that is by no means his intention. On the contrary, "men exist for each other. Then either improve them, or put up with them."[19] In any case, the detachment which he advocated must never be allowed to produce a neglect of social obligations. "Injustice is a sin. Nature has constituted rational beings for their own benefit, each to help his fellows according to their worth, and in no wise to do them hurt. . . . The aim we should propose to ourselves must be the benefit of our fellows and the community."[20] Since, then, we are brothers by virtue of our shared divine spark, the social instinct like the moral instinct is inherent in our personalities. However difficult, therefore, this may be—and Aurelius often found it difficult[21]—we must be kind to our fellow-creatures and tolerant of their faults; we must make allowances for their ignorance, and come to their help. Since men are made to work together, the theme of service is incessant. To act otherwise is against nature, and despite all the sustenance to be derived from inward withdrawal, "the man who dissociates and severs himself from the laws of our common nature by refusing to accept his lot is an excrescence on the world".[22]

As ruler of the Roman empire, Marcus sought unremittingly to bring his principles into effect—thanking heaven that he had not succumbed to the temptation to remain academic. Plato enunciated the theme of the philosopher king, and later Greek monarchs had been influenced by their Stoic advisers to put into words and practice the "glorious slavery" which this role involved. Marcus, although without false modesty,[23] was unimpressed by imperial grandeur. He hated the life of the court, felt an acute distaste for many of the people he had to deal with, and understood deeply the moral dangers that lie in wait for the ruler. "Be careful not to affect the monarch too much, or to be deeply dyed with the purple; for this can well happen."[24]

He was forty when he came to the throne—the disenchanted age, he said, when a man of average intelligence will have experienced everything that has been and is to come. And this believer in contemplation had to spend the greater part of his reign commanding armies on the remote frontiers of the Roman empire. Yet, when he captured Sarmatians, he felt that any self-satisfaction to be derived from this was no better than the exultation of a robber, or of a spider that has caught a fly.[25] Indeed what, after all, is the imperial purple itself? Only the gore of a fish.[26] Fame, he reminds himself over and over again, is not everlasting.[27]

Yet Marcus also felt the strongest possible association between his philosophy and his emperor's task. For the closest analogy on earth to the ideal Stoic Brotherhood of Man seemed to him the Roman empire. "I became acquainted with the conception of a community based on equality and freedom of speech for all, and a monarchy concerned primarily to uphold the liberty of the subject."[28] And the answer, later echoed and transformed in Augustine's City of God, was the world of Rome. "There is a world-law, which in turn means that we are all fellow-citizens and share a common citizenship, and that the world is a single city. Is there any other common citizenship that can be claimed by all humanity?"[29] He would have approved Caracalla's declaration, whatever its motives, that all free men should become citizens of Rome (p. 112).

For half a millennium nearly every philosopher, of whatever creed or allegiance, had thought it his task to give practical guidance in the major problems of life. With Epictetus and now Marcus Aurelius, the quest became more intense and compelling. Marcus has received too little attention in the twentieth century because he was so fulsomely praised in the nineteenth—and some of this praise was for the wrong reasons. True, in spite of a certain grimness in the *Meditations*, Renan was right to call them the most purely human of all books that have come down to us; John Stuart Mill even judged their writer to stand at the summit of all previous attainments of mankind. But when Matthew Arnold finds Christian grace and sweetness in Marcus' thoughts, this is the mistake of a liberal Christian, such as could be found also in antiquity, attributing all pagan excellence to an unconscious yearning for the Christian faith (p. 270).

And yet, since the calmness which was Marcus' ideal required a man to avoid attitudes and excitements and to be unassuming,[30] he was disconcertingly far from sympathetic towards the deliberate martyrdoms of the Christians—persecuted during his reign (p. 289). For in his opinion, preparedness to die "must be the outcome of its own decision; a decision not prompted by mere contumacy, as with the Christians, but formed with deliberation and gravity, and, if it is to be convincing to others, with an absence of all heroics".[31] The words "as with the Christians" could conceivably be a later insertion, but in any case they are clearly the people to whom he is referring. His closest advisers were hostile to those forms of the faith that they had encountered; Fronto wrote a treatise against Christianity. And Marcus himself, as a Stoic believing (despite every personal temptation to the contrary) in the individual's duty to the state, took an unfavourable view of their unconcern for this worldly life. But what he particularly deplored was the readiness of Christians to die because they were trained to do so, without apparently exercising their choice as individuals. Love and pity were not lacking in Marcus' beneficence towards his fellow-man, yet his temperament and tradition and office alike caused them to assume a cerebral, unemotional form which could not include sympathy for the Christian martyrs.

But his exceptional significance lies in something else: in the lofty standard which he proposed and attained without the insistent prompting of any personal kind of religious inspiration or encouragement. He was a religious man, but the Stoic Nature and Brotherhood from which he deduced his goodness were impersonal; nor did he feel able to believe that salvation must reward goodness in the hereafter. Although there is much that we cannot change, he believed that there is also much that we can. And so human life has a meaning—whatever meaning we ourselves, we alone by our own unaided efforts, are able to give it. We are responsible to the nature of things for realizing and achieving all our potential worth and dignity. Marcus Aurelius is the noblest of all the men who, by sheer intelligence and force of character, have prized and achieved goodness for its own sake and not for any reward.

Plotinus

The outstanding philosopher of the age was Plotinus, of whose life we learn from his pupil and biographer Porphyry (Malchus) of Tyre or Batanea. Born in A.D. 205, perhaps at Lycopolis in Upper Egypt, Plotinus turned to philosophy at the age of twenty-seven, and worked for eleven years at Alexandria under Ammonius Saccas. A self-taught mystery man and renegade Christian, whose claim to reconcile Plato and Aristotle was characteristic of the age, Ammonius was reported to have interested Plotinus in Persian and Indian philosophy, so that he joined a Roman military expedition against Persia (242-3), hoping to come into contact with eastern philosophers.[32] The endeavour was unsuccessful, and Plotinus settled in Rome to teach philosophy, remaining there—in favour with Gallienus and his cultivated court—until a short time before his death, when he retired to Campania (269-70).

His instruction, which extended beyond philosophy to music and mathematics, took the form not of preaching but of investigation through seminar and discussion. During the last seventeen years of his life, Plotinus began to record these tutorials in a series of philosophical essays written in Greek and intended primarily as guidance for his pupils. Porphyry collected the essays together and eventually published them in *c.* 301. His arrangement, in six books or *Enneads* (groups of nine), is rather unnatural and confused; to find Plotinus' full thought on any subject one has to go through the whole work, and even then, though no apparent chronological development of thought emerges, there are unresolved tensions and variations of emphasis, as he continually rehandled the great central questions, always from different points of view and in relation to different types of queries and objections.

Plotinus saw living reality as a complex, ordered hierarchical structure which continuously proceeds from its transcendent First Principle, the One or Good, descending in an unbroken succession of stages or realities from this supreme power through the Divine Mind and then the Soul to the last and lowest reality, the Body. All these are intimately connected in the equilibrium of a great and ultimately homogeneous Whole, comparable to a series of concentric rings surrounding the parent One.[33]

Within this living, organic cosmos, in which none of the parts are cut off from one another by any insuperable barrier, there are two great movements—an outgoing downward surge from the One, and an upward return. All Being comes from the overspill and automatic creativity of this infinite immaterial One, ground of all existence, which is also the Good and the source of all values. Perfection, by a necessary reflex act, emits radiations and emanations which determine and generate the lower realities, and continually bring their different, ordered levels of activity into being.

> The activity of life flows from the One as from a spring. Picture a spring that has no origin, that pours itself into all rivers without becoming exhausted of what it yields, and remains what it is, undisturbed. The streams that issue from it, before flowing away each in its own direction, mingle together for a time, but each knows already where it will take its flood. Not a plurality, it is the source of plurality.[34]

This procession moves on its majestic, everlasting path by self-contemplation. It is by contemplating itself, like Aristotle's Mind which becomes what it thinks, that the One generates a spontaneous self-giving and outpouring that makes Plotinus' spiritual world "a place boiling with life, where infinite power surges eternally in a carefree spontaneity, without plan or need, into a splendid super-abundance of living forms".

Nor is this only a downward rush from the One. In the eternal dance of the universe there is always a double momentum: and this downward surge and radiation and procession are accompanied eternally by a simultaneous upward impetus—an uprising towards union and simplification within the One.

This is the dynamic metaphysical landscape of the universe. It is also the pattern of the individual human being whose condition is the counterpart of the cosmic order and procession. Men's life, like the universe, is an upward yearning urge; the religion of Plotinus is the endeavour to actualize within ourselves the universal impulse of return to the One. "I am striving", said Plotinus on his deathbed, "to give back the divine which is in me to the divine in the universe." Man can realize his true self by voluntary self-identification with the source. Plotinus' levels of human consciousness and achievement are the equivalents or projections of cosmic reality on the psychological plane.

Plotinus, marking a new stage in Plato's six-hundred-year-old inheritance of idealism, is known as the first of the Neoplatonists. But he owed much to an earlier philosophical movement which we know as Middle Platonism. For centuries the principal preoccupations of philosophy had been ethical, especially under the influence of the Stoics, whose tradition Marcus Aurelius still upheld (p. 180). But shortly before A.D. 100 the Middle Platonists, absorbing influences from a wide variety of different systems, had begun to restore metaphysics, instead of ethics, to the pride of place it had enjoyed before the age of Stoic primacy.[35]

But this was Platonism with a difference of emphasis, for what was now stressed was its religious element, its thoughts of a supreme, transcendent principle or God or Good at the head of the hierarchy of being. This supreme principle was quite separated from the world, which it neither contacted nor controlled. In order, therefore, to introduce controlling and linking forces the Middle Platonists followed up older ideas that there is an intermediate power or powers (p. 270): and it was in this general tradition that Plotinus created his own four-fold hierarchy of One, Mind, Soul and Body.

But these heritages are welded together into vivid coherence by the powerful stamp of his own genius. The One, as he conceived it, is beyond thought or definition or language: it inhabits "summits where reason, bewildered as in a storm, forsakes even thought". This is Platonic transcendence, but it has a unique ultimate otherness beyond Plato's Good. Since, however, the One exceeds human understanding, its descriptions are often phrased in terms of what it is not. The One is unmoved, without origin or quality or quantity or intelligence; it is unworldly, infinite, the negation of all number, outside movement or space or time.[36] "As the One begets all things, it cannot be any of them." And yet, by a supreme paradox, the One is also the very opposite to negation, for it is super-abundant reality; absolute, single, pure and simple goodness. "When you think of it as Mind or God, it is still more. It is not thought, for there is no other-ness in it. For what would it think about? Itself? But then it would need thought to know itself, it which is self-sufficient!"[37] Plotinus' One, seen sometimes as impersonal and sometimes almost as a personified deity, is nearer than anything else in Greek philosophy to the Christian God. Yet, in contrast to Christianity, this is not a power that concerns itself with human beings or the world, except in so far as It is man's ultimate goal.

He surpassed even Middle Platonism by the thoroughness which he removed the One beyond and outside all categories and orders of being. To express its limitless perfection, Plotinus, averse from mechanistic conceptions of the Universe, made use of symbols and images of brightness and colour. The One is described in terms of Light; and in these very same years the fundamental principles of Mani were Light and Darkness (p. 257). To explain the action of the One, Plotinus draws and enlarges upon Plato's metaphors of a refulgent luminosity. The Stoics, too, had thought of a single organic unity held together by the Divine Fire, and he owed much to their dynamic vitalism. "Fire is beautiful in a pre-eminent degree beyond all other bodies"; it is "light above light", and "a parable of the One may be found in the Sun".[38] The One's eternal engendering and emanation is like the Sun which generates its own encircling light, while itself remaining unchanged and undiminished (p. 226).

And yet, in accordance with Plotinus' insistence that the structure of the Universe is the structure of human beings as well (p. 187), the One is not only at large, but individual human beings have the potentiality of unification with it. For the One is not only the infinite enlargement of each individual, it is also "within him, at the innermost depth[39] . . . The One is absent from nothing and from everything. But it is present only to those who are prepared for it and are able to receive it, to enter into harmony with it, to grasp and to touch it by virtue of their likeness to it."[40] Remote though he is, man is capable of the effort of climbing to this height and uniting himself with the One; and the whole philosophy of Plotinus seeks to animate man's dulled sense of the supernatural and bring us back to our true nature and our source.

The next principle below the One in the eternal procession is Mind. Plotinus' conviction that this material world is ordered by divine intelligence was the religion of the cosmos founded by Plato—for half a millennium some variety of the belief has been the faith of most thoughtful men of religion. But, rather as St. Thomas Aquinas recast Aristotle, Plotinus rewove the various strands of Plato's thought,[41] and the Platonic Mind emerges from this process as distinct from the One. Instead it is the highest of the realities derived from the One's everlasting creativeness—a new version of the intermediary which current doctrines needed in order to associate transcendency with lower realms. By the analogy of the self-contemplation of the One, Mind is likewise both thought and the object of thought, thinking ever at unity with what it thinks, thought thinking itself. And this, like Plotinus' other realities, takes place at the two levels of the universe and the human being. Mind is an eternal lucidity of intellect as a single pure thought-force of timeless apprehension; and yet it is also split into the multiplicity of mortal minds, a plurality in unity, individual as well as universal, minds expressing themselves in the highest cognitive process of intuition or spiritual perception.

Below Mind is the universal Soul, which being weaker (though still eternal) must apprehend its objects not as a whole but successively and severally—and this creates the Time and Space that are the framework of our own world. Since it is beneath Mind and above Body and forms the link between them, Soul, looking upwards, is the order and intelligent direction emanating from Mind; and looking downwards it becomes the immanent principle of living organisms, the framework of universal sympathy. It is to Plotinus more than anyone else that we owe a definite doctrine of spiritual existence, and his super-corporeal world is intensely real and vivid.

And yet, when we have come down to this reality that is below the One and the Mind, there is already a lack of the sparkling momentum of the heights. Like One and Mind, Soul contemplates and is contemplated by itself, subject at one with object; but its contemplation is of the last and lowest sort, a kind of dream.

Yet its dual pattern is the same as Mind's. It is again universal, but there is also again a plurality of individual souls. The sphere of these, however, is not the high intuitive thought practised by mind, but thought of a less elevated, discursive type—reasoning and sensation, imagination and the world of ideas. Soul informs and unites the whole human organism. It is the most significant part of man, who in his normal state exists on the level of the soul; and this Plotinian assertion has found its way into the Christian tradition.

So has the emphasis on the plurality and autonomy of every individual mind and soul. For each individual is himself in his own right.[42] Analysis of this self is the heart of Plotinus' doctrine and the field of his most original discoveries. "What am I?" For there was a crisis of identity in the vast, tumultuous Roman empire as in the teeming communities of our own western world. Plotinus' answer is based upon the two-way stance of the Soul. In the universal sphere, this was not only the author of nature's life and growth below but the direct emanation of mind above; and as individuals, too, we at our highest are soul perfectly formed after the likeness of mind,[43] operating with conscious and self-conscious determination. This tract of personality, beyond the every-day reach of lower purposes, is what Plotinus discovered and cherished in man. To him the individual is not a helpless product; the Will emphasized by Marcus Aurelius is now seen in a new philosophical and psychological setting.

Yet he was also, as far as we know, the first philosopher (or psychotherapist) to explain how the individual soul, at its lower level or sub-division analogous to the dreamlike downward looking aspect of the universal Soul, operates unconsciously. Anticipating Freud's distinction between the Psyche and the Ego, Plotinus knew that there are some motions of our souls which "remain in the appetitive part and are unknown to us",[44] and that we possess, moreover, permanent dispositions which can pull strongest when we are least aware of them. Intellectual, conscious life is not our only life. Our personal identity is unstable, and fluctuates with the ebb and flow of consciousness; we live on the border-line between two worlds.

That is to say, our souls in their higher and self-conscious phase reflect our divine minds, whereas in their lower role they generate and combine with body.[45] Individual souls are heavenly entities, but in this inferior capacity they inhabit visible corporeal matter. When this happens, when soul is lodged in body, it is a misfortune. Plotinus has come a long way from the classical idea that man lives in the material world in order to master it; man is in it because he is obliged to be, whereas his real concerns are with higher things. Although there is the continual, Plotinian two-way traffic between soul and body, this sharp division between the spiritual and corporeal worlds had never been so clearly expressed and so strongly felt by a philosopher before. Porphyry noted that his master "seemed ashamed to be in a body".

Plotinus' notes, as they have come down to us, betray a hesitation whether the universal soul's descent to form matter, and the individual soul's corresponding descent into body, come about from necessity or from choice; and whether such a process is a Fall or, on the contrary, a good and necessary factor of the universal order. This hesitation is part of a fundamental conflict in his thought. At times Plotinus appears to be a dualist like his contemporary Mani, asserting that matter is darkness and the principle of evil, cause of the weakness in the good light inhabiting the soul (p. 257).[46] But Plotinus only sees matter as evil because it is negative. This low, last reflection of the soul is the mere principle of want and negation, absolute formlessness, and abstract receptacle of corporeal events. That is why the soul, on becoming subject to matter, suffers "the impact of the shapeless". And so evil, too, in anticipation of Karl Barth and existentialists, is not a Gnostic, Manichaean second power, but non-Being, chaotic, the dead end of the creative process: a lack, a privation, a nonentity. It is not only unreal but the very essence of unreality; unordered, formless disintegration.[47]

Given this negative nature of evil, it was possible for Plotinus still to hold that human bodies need not be entirely submerged and restricted by the evil that they contain, and are not, in fact, wholly evil themselves.[48] For however distinct and remote the two may have become, the body is still the emanation of the soul and therefore, more indirectly, emanation of the mind and the One from which it comes. The body is part of the living organic Whole to which all these higher realities belong, a reflection and image of the intelligible pattern it unconsciously strives to imitate.

So this world of the senses is essential to the nature of things, regrettable and vexatious no doubt, yet requiring to be accepted without impatience or repulsion or denial.

> The body is a living being, but a very imperfect one, which makes its own life difficult since it is the worst of living things, ill-conditioned and savage, made of inferior matter, a sort of sediment of the prior realities, bitter and embittering. Then are the evils in the Whole necessary? If they did not exist, the Whole would be imperfect. Most of them, even all of them, contribute something useful to the Whole—poisonous snakes do, for instance—though generally the reason why they exist is obscure. Even moral evil itself has many advantages and is productive of much excellence, for example all the beauty of art, and rouses us to serious thought about our way of living, not allowing us to slumber complacently.[49]

Since, therefore, matter and the body for all their defects are part of the general harmony, Plotinus attacks the thoroughgoing, pessimistic Gnostic dualists who, adopting the doctrines which Plotinus so narrowly avoided, regarded the entire material universe as evil. He declares their beliefs irrational, inconsistent, arrogant and subversive, a tragedy of terrors. These are the strong words with which a man criticizes those who go only a little further than himself. For Plotinus was entirely at one with the Gnostics in believing that our most urgent task is to escape from the darkness and evil that matter contains. Granted that the visible world contains goodness and nobility, it must none the less be renounced for a better.[50] This is possible just because human bodies are images of this better, higher existence. Plotinus' whole moral teaching is directed towards leading the soul, emancipated and purified, out of the material world and back to its original state of awareness, where it will live as though out of the body.

The process by which this can be done is contemplation, which is not only the machinery of the universe but the means by which the individual can realize himself (p. 186). "Turn from the things without to look within. The sum of things is within us."[51] We can only know the spiritual universe by finding it inside ourselves. Earlier philosophers had already understood that the need for contemplation is present in every human being. Plato stressed that our aim should be the contemplation of absolute beauty, Aristotle

The new achievements of portrait sculpture:
1 (*left*) Marcus Aurelius as a priest: the
philosopher king, responsible and resigned. 2
(*below*) Caracalla (211–17 AD) affects
Alexander's sidelong pose, but the flamboyant
sculptor unflinchingly portrays his tiresome,
dangerous personality

3 Agmat, daughter of Hagago, shortly before 200. In the special style of Palmyra in Syria, meeting place of the eastern and Mediterranean worlds

4 The new sort of spiritual interpretation: a sensitive study of an imperial woman, probably Julia Domna, wife of Septimius Severus

5 (*above left*) A brief return to the Hellenic
spirit. Gallienus (253–68 AD), who began to
restore a collapsing world, and liked
philosophers

6 (*above right*) The tormented features of
Philip the Arabian (244–9 AD) are rendered
with uncanny insight

7 (*right*) The formidable Danubian giant
Maximinus I (235–8 AD) inspired sculptors to
works of great expressiveness

9 (*above*) Diocletian (284–305 AD) and
Maximian, or other rulers of their Tetrarchy.
The nightmarish pseudo-naiveté of late
Roman art has left classicism far behind

8 (*left*) A late example in the wonderful series
of Roman portraits of old women. From
Tripoli in Libya, near the end of the third
century

Coins and medallions: 10 (*above*) Decius'
depiction of the two Pannonias, his own
Danubian homeland, illustrates the new
supremacy of this reservoir of soldiers and
emperors (249–51 AD). 11 (*left*) Probus
(276–82 AD) with the Sun-god his Companion
(COMIS): now the most revered deity in
the pagan pantheon. 12 (*below*) Coin
portraiture can still be individual under
Aurelian (270–5 AD). Close-cropped and with
unshaven military jowl, he celebrates the
recovered unity of the Empire by a figure
of Concordia. 13 (*above right*) Constantius I
Caesar has suppressed the dissident British
state of Carausius and Allectus, and is seen
entering London as *Restorer of the Eternal Light*
(296 AD). 14 (*centre right*) Constantine, at his
new capital Constantinopolis (CONS). The
standard, bearing the letters XP (Christos)
and inscribed 'The National Hope' (SPES
PVBLICA), crushes the serpent of evil (*c.* 333).
15 (*below right*) Shapur I (*c.* 239–70 AD), the
scourge of Rome and captor of its Emperor
Valerian. On the reverse is the Fire-Altar of
the Zoroastrian state religion

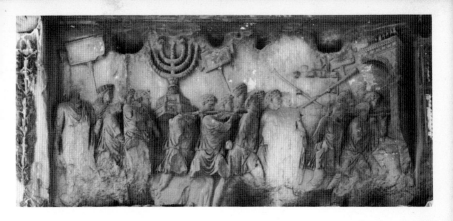

Relief sculpture: 16 *(left)* The Column of Marcus Aurelius, completed after his death, shows a new feeling for the horrors of war and the suffering of German prisoners. 17 *(above)* Jewry has now lost its national home: Arch of Titus in Rome, Roman soldiers carrying spoils from Jerusalem. 18 *(below)* The tombs of the early Christians stress not Christ's Passion but Old Testament tales of Deliverance: such as the story of Jonah, seen here with the Sea Monster

19 (*left*) Greco-Egyptian mummy portrait of a woman of the early fourth century, gazing out at her family (who kept its mummies in the house) and at the Unseen

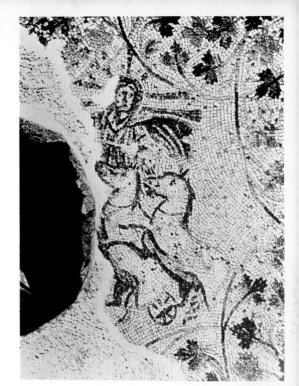

Mosaics: 20 (*right*) Christ, as the Sun-god, driving a chariot of four horses, symbols of the Gospels and the Resurrection, from a vault in the Vatican necropolis under St Peter's (*c*. 25–75 AD). 21 (*below*) As other provinces flagged, Britain prospered: villas abounded in fourth-century mosaics, of which this is an example, discovered at Sparsholt near Winchester

22 (*left*) The third- and fourth-century 'House of Cupid and Psyche', Ostia, where the brick arches rise straight from the columns, without horizontal entablatures

23 (*below*) A typical underground shrine of Mithras at Rome: successive churches dedicated to S. Clemente were built over it

24 Like other cities, Rome had to be fortified in the later third century. The Wall of Aurelian (271–5 AD), completed and remodelled by later emperors

25 The Porta Nigra at Trier (Augusta Trevirorum) on the Moselle (c. 300 AD). The gateway of an imperial capital, and almost a fortress-palace in itself

26 The Basilica of Trier is now a church, but
during Roman times the emperor sat
enthroned beneath the apse of the spacious,
timber-roofed hall

27 **Salonae** (Split in Yugoslavia). The Palace of Diocletian, who received homage beneath the central arch leading to his audience hall. Drawing by Robert Adam (1728–92)

28 The Basilica Nova at Rome, the work of Maxentius (*d.* 312) and Constantine. The massive vaulted aisles were lit by huge rounded windows that anticipate Romanesque cathedrals

29 In Constantine's Basilica of St Peter, here
shown on a sixteenth-century fresco, apse was
divided from nave by a noble transept over the
Saint's traditional burial-place. In the church
of S. Martino ai Monti, Rome

saw contemplation as the blessed life,[52] and Marcus Aurelius felt strongly the personal necessity of such withdrawal (p. 182). But it was Plotinus above all who drove men in upon themselves and shifted emphasis from the beauty of the heavens and the world to the need for habitual contact with the inner being. Inward-turning contemplation is the only true reality. "If one does not look in this way, one finds nothing."[53]

By means of dynamic, all-powerful contemplation, corporeal opaqueness and space-time are thought away into irrelevance and nothingness, and we do not only see and know the higher, true realities, but we become at one with them and the same. This is not only vision, it is union. "Anyone who attains to this contemplates himself and everything else and is the object of his contemplation; he does not look at it any more from outside." Consequently, to ask whether this ultimate perfection is transcendent or immanent becomes meaningless, because the two words are now indistinguishable. Just as the universe at large shows each level of reality creating emanations when it contemplates itself (p. 186), so likewise this occurs in the individual also; here too there is no longer any distinction between subject and object. "We ought not even to say that he will see, but he will be that which he sees. There is nothing between: they are no longer two, but one."[54] And this is the very essence of life, because Plotinus, in one of philosophy's most violent paradoxes, sees contemplation as creation.

Plotinus believed that he personally experienced this mystical union, alone with the lone. In the words of Porphyry,

> So to this godlike man, who often raised himself in thought (according to the ways Plato teaches in the *Symposium*) to the First and Transcendent God, that God appeared who has neither shape nor any intelligible form, but is throned above intellect and all the intelligible. Four times while I was with him he attained that end, in an unspeakable actuality and not in potency only.[55]

And so there came to Plotinus this sudden instantaneous, unplanned, unexpected, unforeseeable, impersonal *feeling of a presence*.[56] First he was drained empty of everything; and then, after a premonitory shock, he was overrun by a blessed fullness—a joyous stupor. Yet his self was not possessed or replaced or obliterated, but seemed instead to have been awakened or reawakened to what it really was. For this is no dualist, Manichaean liberation from one world into another but a discovery or rediscovery, no Christian supernatural grace or redemption but a natural event. Indeed the power to become aware of the presence "belongs to all men—though few use it",[57] and the condition is only occasionally and momentarily achieved. It is not merely a deep absorption, a very high form of contemplation, but an unmatchable "other kind of seeing, a being out of oneself, a simplifying, a self-surrender".[58] Plotinus appears to be the first to have used the term *ecstasis*, a being out of oneself, for this transformation. But the term could be misleading, for it might seem to deny the unitive effect of the experience, which Plotinus also called *enosis*, the momentary revelation of an eternal, potential Oneness.

He has risen beyond the abstract propositions of the philosophers to attain the heights about which they had hinted for so long. Out of eight hundred pages of his teachings, only twenty or thirty touch on this mystic theme. In these passages he tries again and again to find some form of words for what has happened to him. "There, in the solitude of self, one beholds simplicity and purity, the existent upon which all depends, towards which all look, by which reality is, life is, thought is. For the Good is the cause of life, of thought, of being."

How can one describe the absolutely simple? It is enough if the intellect comes into contact with it: but when it has done so, while the contact lasts it is absolutely impossible, nor has it time, to speak; reasoning about it comes afterwards.

One must believe one has seen, when the soul suddenly takes light; for this light is from him, and he is it. The soul which does not see him is without light: but when it is enlightened it has what it sought, and this is the soul's true end, to touch that light and see it by itself. It must see that light by which it is enlightened; for we do not see the sun by another light than his own.

How then can this happen? *Take away everything.* . . . There were not two, but the seer himself was one with the seen; for it was not really seen, but united to him. He was one himself then, with no distinction in him either in relation to himself or anything else; for there was no movement in him, and he had no emotion, no desire for anything else when he had made the ascent, no reason or thought; his own self was not there for him, if we should say even this. He was as if carried away or possessed by a god, in a quiet solitude, in the stillness of his being turning away to nothing and not busy about himself, altogether at rest and having *become* a kind of rest.[59]

The motive power of this transfiguration is understood by Plotinus, not as curiosity or self-interest, but as Love—the deep-seated desire of the soul for its source, its striving after contact and conjunction. "It is that union", he says, "which earthly lovers imitate when they would be one flesh; the soul merges with the divinity in an upward rush of love."[60] This yearning movement towards coalescence derives from the sympathy naturally existing between the different parts of the universe—the pervasive bond which establishes the continuity between all things. It is true and perfect Love, because it no longer limits itself to an illusory fixed object—we have limitless love for the Good because *it* is limitless. This is the Greek Eros (p. 168) raised to a supersensual sphere, Plato's ineffable intuition of the beautiful and "madness of love", experienced in all its purity and blazing strength.[61]

> Seeing, with what love and desire for union one is seized—what wondering delight! . . . flooded with an awesome happiness, stricken by a salutary terror! All loves but this he must despise and all that once seemed fair he must disdain. All other beauties are imports, are alloys. They are not primal. This is true and primal beauty that graces its lovers and makes them worthy of love. The one who does not attain to it is life's unfortunate—not the one who has never seen beautiful colours or beautiful bodies or has failed of power and of honours and of kingdoms. He is the true unfortunate who has not seen this beauty and he alone.[62]

When in that state, the soul would exchange its present condition for nothing in the world, though it were offered the kingdom of all the heavens. For this is the Good, and there is nothing better.

But the dialectic of love is not only an aesthetic and mystic experience; it is the intellectual basis of a philosophy.[63] Plotinus' ecstasy is the climax of intense thought, ascending upwards and flooding inwards by the most strenuous cerebration. Although the borders between a philosopher and a mystic and man of religion had become blurred, in his approach Plotinus is neither physiological like easterners, nor sacramental like Christians, nor based on drugs like modern seekers after psychedelic experience, but intellectual in the rational Hellenic tradition. Any revelations that might be achieved by other means, for example the "special" miraculous illuminations of the Gnostics, had no value for him.[64]

Mystical union is not the substitute for intellectual effort, but its crown and goal. Only by rigorous mental exercise and inward effortful self-discipline shall we realize our potential likeness and amalgamation with the One.

If it comes to contemplation purblind with vice, impure, weak, without the strength to look upon brilliant objects, the soul then sees nothing even if it is placed in the presence of an object that can be seen. For the eye must be adapted to what is to be seen, have some likeness to it, if it would give itself to contemplation. No eye that has not become like the Sun will ever look upon the Sun; nor will any that is not beautiful look upon the beautiful.[65]

We advance towards the Good by "the sternest and uttermost combat".

And then, the almost unimaginable reward. As the upland air becomes ever more rarefied and brilliant, the aspirant comes close to his destination. The One is just above him, already shining over the whole intelligible world. Then, letting all study go, he is carried out of that which he is by the very surge of the wave of Mind, and, lifted high by its swell, suddenly sees without knowing how. "Have you become like this? Do you see yourself, abiding within yourself, in pure solitude? Does nothing now remain to shatter that interior unity, nor anything external cling to your authentic self? Are you entirely that sole true light, greater than all measure and something more than all quantity? Then you have become vision itself. Be of good heart. Remaining here, you have ascended aloft. You need a guide no longer. Strain, and see."[66]

These are not merely rhetorical or poetic descriptions of contemplation at its highest pitch. They are authentic accounts of the overcoming, or believed overcoming, of all barriers between the individual and the absolute, by a process of transfusion and communion and identification. This mystical conviction presupposes and asserts a deeper harmony and unity in the world and the universe than science recognizes, a supreme Oneness to which reason and the senses cannot penetrate—an intimate interlocking of everything in an interdependence comparable, say, to the attraction of gravitational fields. Mysticism affirms the possibility of making a supraconscious contact, indescribably intimate and direct, with this seemingly ultimate reality—time, space and self obliterated, all passions spent, and the multiplicity of things reduced to the merest shadows. The experience can take two forms: extroverted nature mysticism, looking outward to the One behind phenomena and annulling their external separateness so that the One shines through them all; and introverted activity, looking inward into the mind and shutting off the senses to plunge into the depths of self. To Plotinus, the two processes go together: expansion is the accompaniment of concentration.

Every person is potentially Mind at large. True, we must during normal circumstances, in order to survive, exercise the eliminative function of our senses and reduce our awareness. But at rare times an occasional individual can regain the archetypal world of Mind, and recapture the rhythm which has been escaping him. "Our normal consciousness is only one special type: all about it lie potential forms of entirely different consciousness, parted from it by the filmiest of screens."[67] Entry into these normally inaccessible regions may come, as it came to Plotinus, with a shock, quick and sharp, without the mediation of discursive intellect or of the subject's aims, interests or feelings. The mystic is like the captain of a ship with sealed orders. "But when the moment arrives and he tears the envelope open, he only finds an invisible text. Now and then a word becomes visible . . . then it fades again. He will never know the exact wording of the order."[68] Yet he now thinks and acts as he did not before; he will never be the same again.

To some limited extent, this sort of experience can be brought about by chemical means. Visionary and mystical states have been induced by prolonged shouting and singing and by long suspensions of breath leading to high concentrations of carbon dioxide in the lungs and blood. Other agents of mystical experience are starvation, causing low blood sugar and vitamin deficiency; flagellation, producing histamine and adrenalin intoxication; focal infections and resultant protein decomposition; and any condition productive of insomnia and fever. There is also a very ancient connection between exaltation and hallucinogenic drugs,[69] of which lysergic acid (LSD) is at present the most favoured among youthful seekers after the depersonalizations, disintegrations of the ego, and time-disturbances which such chemical holidays can supply. As discussion rages today concerning the attitude which society should adopt towards these drugs, a second and even more fundamental controversy is likely to separate those who see, and those who deny, a clear dividing line between the mystical or hallucinatory experiences induced by drugs on the one hand and by religion on the other (with or without mental sickness as an auxiliary in either case).

The position of Plotinus in this dispute is highly significant and topical, because he shows that there is a further possibility. He is the pioneer of psychedelic experience for the west, but he achieved his end by purely cerebral, intellectual discipline—not by schizophrenia and not by drugs; and not by religion. For Plotinus illustrates the fact that, even if the characteristic condition of mysticism may be linked with any religion, intrinsically it is not religious—the unity it seems to grasp is undifferentiated, and no dogmas or creeds are required. But what is this unity? Has the recipient of the experience really contracted something *outside* himself, or has he only touched hitherto unplumbed well-springs within himself? Most believers in religion will, if they can overcome a suspicion of mysticism, take the former view. So will at least some of those adherents of the Perennial Philosophy[70] who, though not believing in established religions, maintain that beyond the world of matter and consciousness there is a Divine Ground, which a few human beings can now and then apprehend by direct intuition. Others who believe in no divinity, even in such general terms, will agree with Freud that the whole phenomenon is an inward one; and will conclude, like Delacroix, that St. Teresa's God was the product of her own sub-conscious mind. But whether mystic union goes outward or inward, those to whom the experience has befallen, whatever their religious or social background or time or place, display incontrovertible agreement that a marvel denied to others has been theirs: a vast, luminous and ineffably enchanting splendour has shone upon them. And it is in the tortuous, urgent, exciting work of Plotinus, striving to express the inexpressible, that the western world, racked by all conceivable political and economic disturbances, was presented with this marvel that made them irrelevant.

However, the moral and social implications of his doctrine have sometimes inspired repugnance. Marcus Aurelius did not suffer fools gladly, and yet he deduced from the Brotherhood of Man, with its universal sharing of the divine spark, an absolute, overriding obligation to serve his fellow-men (p. 184). He would have agreed with Plotinus that the self-discipline he teaches is not for the many. But Plotinus has in mind the additional consideration that mystic union is quite clearly beyond the generality. This was an age that believed in Gnosis, knowledge by revelation to small bands of the initiated and to them alone (p. 252). Plotinus did not accept the

Gnostics' elevation of evil matter to a positive and often equal power, but he did agree with them that only an élite could attain the heights.

"This is what the command given in those mysteries intends to proclaim, 'Do not reveal to the uninitiated'. Because the Divine is not to be revealed, it forbids us to declare it to anyone else who has not himself had the good fortune to see."[71] And consequently, using anti-democratic tones that are not heard in modern parliamentary elections, Plotinus wrote of "the vile crowd, mere machines, destined to minister to the first needs of virtuous men". Very possibly, he added, their rulers are villains, but if so that is the fault of the ruled, because of their lack of courage.[72] Human suffering receives this apparently unfeeling treatment because, until the soul rises to a higher plane, such misfortunes form an unavoidable part of the evil which is in the world (p. 192)[73]—a necessary element in the great pattern. And yet, according to Porphyry, Plotinus showed much personal and practical kindness; he was a man who cared efficiently for the children of his friends, and whose wise counsel saved Porphyry himself from suicide. And yet, Plotinus maintained, no one has a right to expect good men to help him—any more than God is likely to.[74]

But suffering, in any case, is something which does not affect true happiness. For the whole sphere of action is merely a shadowy and inferior counterpart of contemplation, suitable to the weak-minded[75]: statesmen and artists are only philosophers manqués, who project their dream because they cannot live it. Plotinus wanted Gallienus to let him found a Campanian community where people should live under Platonic laws: his ideal is "a life which takes no delight in the things of the world—escape in solitude to the solitary". Marcus Aurelius would have liked to live that sort of life, but believed that duty called elsewhere. Nor could he have approved Plotinus' deduction that public calamities are mere stage shows and comedies.[76] "The wise man will attach no importance to the loss of his position or even to the ruin of his fatherland",[77] and Plotinus, unlike Plato, was unconcerned with the paramount necessity of imperial defence, even advising his friends to withdraw from public office.[78] Moreover, to assert the full paradoxical force of what he meant, even personal bereavement was pronounced acceptable and welcome.

All this is a corollary of the need to concentrate on what is important. Like a sculptor, you must cut away everything that is inessential.[79] Yet this withdrawal from society meant no weakening of moral endeavour, for the self-discipline of Plotinus' path to divine union demanded intense moral as well as intellectual effort. Virtue, as well as knowledge, is needed before the One will be revealed. Teilhard de Chardin, like many earlier Christian mystics and Zen Buddhists, has urged a dedicated, integrated absorption in the world, agreeing that the opposite ideal of withdrawal is "a deadly pleasure, inferior in all respects to the joys of action, or to the sacred savour of accomplished duty".[80] To Plotinus, on the other hand, the way of Martha is submerged in the way of Mary; like Pascal he might have added that the world's evil would be much diminished if men could only learn to sit quietly in their rooms. Evidently, too, the order and breadth of Plotinus' teaching, and his perception of the harmonious sympathy of the universe, were no bad foundation for the virtues which he himself undoubtedly practised. Moreover, his quest for mystic union needed continual self-abnegation to drive out the folly and ignorance which are barriers to awareness. The mean, the drab and the trivial were far removed from his wondering openness to new ways and possibilities of life.

For Plotinus' world was no ivory tower but reality at its highest level, raised to its most exalted plane by the intensest concentration on what seemed to him the most real. Plotinus is no unhealthy, sick refugee from the world: to search, as he did, for union with the One is to tackle life with a daring and dedicated brand of realism.

The mystic experience of Plotinus was founded upon an intellectual construction which sprang from the Hellenic past. Plato's eloquent reachings-out to the indescribable impressed Christians as endeavours "to see God face to face",[81] and the idea that God is incomprehensible, only attainable in rare flashes of intuition, has a pedigree in the Platonic school.[82]

But how far, before Plotinus, such experiences had already been identified or claimed is uncertain. In the fourteenth century B.C. the Egyptian Akhnaton said he had embraced Aton through a personal revelation, apparently several times. The Hebrew prophet Ezekiel (c. 580 B.C.) has a hallucinatory quality, perhaps due to epilepsy or long spells of exposure to intense heat. This sort of prophetic vision inspired a mystic rabbinical school in the first and second centuries A.D.[83] "Like persons possessed and corybants, be filled with divine frenzy, even as the prophets are inspired", urged the Hellenized Jew Philo (d. A.D. 45); "Sometimes I have become full, ideas being in an invisible manner showered upon me ... an enjoyment of the light, a most manifest energy." Writing on *The Contemplative Life*,[84] Philo seems to anticipate Plotinus by his belief in our capacity to transcend ourselves. Yet his use of the word *ecstasis* suggests not so much mystic union as the common ancient phenomenon of dissociation and trance-mediumship, with the supernatural seeming to come into the human body (not vice versa), while normal consciousness either still persists unaltered or is temporarily suppressed.

Accounts of the life of Jesus contain no mystic suggestions, but St. Paul declared that the Saviour *appeared* to him.[85] This again seems mediumistic, downward visitation rather than upward and inward union; and Paul's conversion on the road to Damascus again does not sound mystical. But Paul was "ravished out of fleshly feeling" and believed himself to have entered the third heaven and heard the unutterable[86]: "I live, yet not I but Christ liveth in me." This might be a Christ-centred equivalent of the impersonal and not specifically religious experience of Plotinus (cf. p. 278)

In any case, however, from the first century A.D. onwards, the knowledge that such experiences could take place received abundant testimony; and tributes to mystical union, bestowed upon an elect, were becoming a substitute for the exhausted or flagging creeds of the Greco-Roman and Grecized worlds. "Through His marvellous mysteries my eye has gazed upon the eternal Being—a saving knowledge which is hidden from the man of knowledge (in the ordinary sense), a wise insight which is hidden from the sons of men; the well-spring of righteousness, the reservoir of strength and the place of glory. ... Among mortals God gave it as an eternal possession to those whom He has chosen."[87]

The Mystery religions, too, were fertile ground for similar experiences: sarcophagi with Dionysian scenes evoke the overpowering joy, the sense of being merged with the god, which was remembered by votaries as life's richest promise for the hereafter (p. 241). In the apocryphal *Gospel of Eve* a voice of thunder says, "I am Thou and Thou art I"—in the terms of a common formula of Christian, Moslem and Indian mystics. "Where thou art", the

Gospel continues, "there am I also. I am dispersed in all things: wherever thou wilt, thou dost assemble me, and in assembling me thou dost assemble thyself."[88] This is the description of a mystic philosophy or even experience. So is the assertion of another writer that he "has been in *the place of rest*. If one is called, he is wont to turn to him who calls, and go upward to him." And "let us rejoice! let us rejoice! let us rejoice!", proclaims another: "We have seen! we have seen! we have seen that which truly was in the beginning!"[89] Likewise the Hymn of the *Robe of Glory* (?c. A.D. 180) sings lyrically of the soul's return to the heavenly kingdom where it is restored to its original purity.

> At once, as soon as I saw it,
> The Glory looked like my own self.
> I saw it all in all of me,
> And saw me all in all of it—
> That we were twain in distinction,
> and yet again one in one likeness . . .
> And now with its kingly motions
> Was it pouring itself out towards me,
> And made haste in the hands of its Givers,
> That I might take and receive it.
> And me, too, my love urged forward
> To run to meet it, to take it.
> And I stretched myself forth to receive it;
> With its beauty of colour I decked me.[90]

We read in the Hermetic Corpus (p. 255):

The vision of the Good shines forth much or little according as he who gazes upon it is able to receive the inflow of the incorporeal radiance. The beauty of the Good bathes his mind in light, and takes all his soul up to itself, and draws it forth from the body, and transforms it wholly into the essence of God. . . . If you do not make yourself equal to God, you cannot apprehend God, for like is apprehended by like. Outleap all body and expand yourself to the unmeasured greatness; outstrip all time and become Eternity; so shall you apprehend God. Embrace in yourself all sensations of all created things, of fire and water, dry and wet; be simultaneously everywhere, on sea and land and in the sky; be at once unborn and in the womb, young and old, dead and beyond death; and if you can hold all these things together in your thought—times and places and substances, qualities and quantities—then you can apprehend God.[91]

Such threads were gathered together late in the second century A.D. by the Middle Platonists, with their personal quest for the divinity (p. 187). But particularly influential upon Plotinus was

Numenius of Syrian Apamea (c. A.D. 150–200), who called himself a member of the Pythagorean sect, and yet, since the borders between the schools were ill-defined, heralded much in Middle Platonism. To Numenius, the Supreme Being was indeed remote. Nevertheless very rare and short-lived direct intuition of its presence was possible, by sudden illumination like a blaze of light; and Plotinus often echoed Numenius' striking account of this process.

> One must withdraw far from the things of sense and enter into solitary communion with the Good, where is no human being nor any other creature nor body great or small, but only a kind of divine desolation which in truth cannot be spoken of or described, where are the haunts and resorts and splendours of the Good, and the Good itself at rest in peace and friendliness, the Sovereign Principle riding serene above the tides of Being.[92]

Numenius may have experienced the mystic exaltation which Plotinus later analysed in even more comprehensive and many-sided terms.

There are detailed analogies between Plotinus and the mysticism of the Hindus. The writers of the *Upanishads* in the eighth and later centuries B.C., searching for an ultimate reality more satisfactory than the Vedic gods of earlier times, had claimed to know by direct intuitive insight the supreme and universal principle. And knowing meant becoming: *Thou art that*. God is the creator and sustainer of the world, yet the kingdom of God is also within us, underlying, incommensurable, yet attainable by man, who can thus realize his essential instead of merely his superficial nature. "Having seen his own self as the Self, he becomes selfless. ... When everything is One Self, who can see another, how can he see another?"—or smell, hear, speak, think, know?[93] Brahman is the godhead, "all this is Brahman". The Brahman in man is Atman, and purpose of life, according to Hindu philosophy (from the Vedas onwards), is to eliminate the boundary lines of the particular and realize the Atman within oneself. The experiencer is also the experienced, and *Samadhi*, beyond the states of waking, dreaming and dreamless sleep, is a fourth kind of consciousness.

Plotinus' self-discipline is like the psychological exercises prescribed as the very centre and heart of spiritual life by Hindus and the Vedanta movement which continues this mystic trend.[94] And Hindu mysticism, herein resembling original Buddhism which was mystic in its very essence,[95] appears when there is no conception of God at all, or when his existence is a matter of indifference.[96] The third and fourth centuries A.D. were the classical age of Hindu art and literature, and we must ask whether Plotinus' similarities to these ways of thinking were due to direct contacts. His teacher Ammonius Saccas was said to have interested him in Indian and Persian philosophy (p. 185). Recently, too, writers such as Philostratus, like contemporary novelists, had stressed the importance of Indian lore (pp. 165, 236), introducing his saintly hero Apollonius of Tyana to Hindu sages.[97] Nor was it so very long since the *Bhagavad Gita*, the Hindu Song of God expressing the mysticism of action and faith alike, had assumed its final form.

Indeed, such ideas had been filtering through to the west since the time of Alexander the Great and before. Their *direct* influence upon Plotinus seems to have been slight—since so many of his ideas are explicable from Hellenic traditions, themselves now imbued with eastern thought. Yet in some ways the turn of his thinking has more in common with the Hindus than with later western developments. The *Upanishads*, like Plotinus, had continually stressed the identity of Supreme Self with individual human selves. Moreover, the mysticism of Plotinus resembles much Indian thought because it is natural and not supernatural and the unity which it apprehends is undifferentiated and not a personal God.

Despite the difficulties which have made them so inaccessible, the *Enneads* of Plotinus form the vastest and richest synthesis in the whole history of philosophy, and Plotinus himself was the most powerful thinker between Aristotle and Descartes.

During the second half of the third century A.D. he and other philosophers influenced the climate of opinion sufficiently to inspire two art-forms, the philosophical portrait bust—an ancient ideal revived with a new accent on spirituality—and the philosopher-sarcophagus, bearing reliefs on which the after-life is symbolized by philosophical discovery rather than religious salvation. When Plotinus was dead, his disciple Porphyry, who was more of a theologian, drew upon his words with the conviction that properly interpreted they would add up to an entire system. Hierocles helped to transform Neoplatonism into a comprehensive militant religion with its own saints and miracle-workers, and then Iamblichus of

Syrian Chalcis (d. 330), despite insight into mathematics as a physical science,[98] added an abstruse, phantasmagoric occultism, based on the "higher" magic known as theurgy and supported by fanatical mobs.

At first Plotinus' doctrines had been less valued in the east than in the west where they were translated into Latin; but subsequently the centres of the Neoplatonist sect were in Syria and at Alexandria and Athens. The emperor Julian the Apostate (d. 363) embraced the cult as part of his sentimental Hellenism. Its influence was greatest among the conservative aristocracy. But it was also popular in wider circles, for, while allowing cultured minds to soar above the old gods, it retained their worship for ordinary people. Neoplatonism was comfortably receptive and comprehensive, justifying all heathen religions, and seeking out and satisfying all needs—except inquiry and observation.

But in the next generation there was serious trouble between Neoplatonists and Christians. Although accepting salvation by philosophy, Plotinus seemed implicitly to criticize the Christian Saviour who had come down to earth to liberate man and was martyred. He saw the real man as incapable of suffering; and sin too assumed in his doctrine an insubstantial, irrelevant appearance. Accordingly the conflict with Christianity gradually became embittered. Porphyry attacked it violently, and Hierocles, Diocletian's governor in Bithynia and Egypt, played an active part in persecutions. The Neoplatonists had now become the most determined enemies of the Christian religion; and yet they could not, in the end, compete with its claims because of the over-complexity of their doctrines and the absence of a rival to the dramatic, historical Jesus. Though given a more emotional content by Plotinus' successors, theirs remained a too intellectual reply.

And yet in spite of this gulf between Neoplatonists and Christians, Plotinus, by a paradox, has made a more profound contribution even than Plato to the philosophy and theology of Christianity: he has influenced its thought more than any other pagan writer. This was partly because St. Augustine used him as the bridge from Manichaeanism (which had temporarily converted him to a dualist view of good and evil, p. 259) to Christianity.[99] He felt liberated from dualism by Plotinus' more exhilarating and apparently rational view of evil as the mere absence of the divine—so that there is one true reality only, and that is wholly spiritual.[100] Augustine borrowed from Plotinus many beliefs about the Soul and Providence,[101] and accepted his emanations (by an effort) as the equivalent of Christian creation; and the One, Mind and Soul seemed pagan previsions of the Trinity.

Augustine also derived from the *Enneads* at least a glimpse of mystical experience.[102] Although this is only a minor thread in Christianity, no single man outside the Bible so inspired Christian mystics as Plotinus. The main intermediary and fountain-head of subsequent developments is the fifth century "Dionysius the Areopagite".[103] His daring fusion of Christianity with Neoplatonism, more philosophical and less Christ-centred than later mystic thought, urges the annihilation of self-hood and carries to extremes Plotinus' *via negativa* which asserts that no words or qualities can describe the Supreme Being (p. 188). The influence of "Dionysius" on Catholicism was enormous, and his vision of the divine light as an object of desire also inspired later mystics of the Orthodox Church.

Neoplatonism came to the west through Augustine, Dionysius and Syrian Christians who translated Aristotle and other works from Syriac or Greek versions into Arabic (750–900).[104] From the twelfth century onwards the ideas of Plotinus became influential in the west through medieval Latin translations of these Arabs and later Neoplatonists.[105] Western mysticism then developed, partly as a challenge to the official religious establishment and a call for non-ecclesiastical salvation.

In the thirteenth century there was a powerful Plotinian pattern. St. Thomas Aquinas (d. 1274) found immaterial Neoplatonist spirit and thought more real than the physical and material world; and towards the end of his life he, too, underwent a mystic experience beside which all else "was no better than chaff or straw".

Eckhart (d. 1327), whose negative way of describing the One was derived from Dionysius and Plotinus,[106] combines with the God- or Christ-mysticism characteristic of Christian mystical feeling a more generalized, Neoplatonic attitude: "what a man takes in by contemplation, that he pours out in love". Dante often echoes Plotinus, and his last Canto is a final portrayal of mystic apprehension and, perhaps, experience. Supreme among medieval Neoplatonists was Jan van Ruysbroeck (d. 1381), who describes the introspective union in Plotinian terms of love which is radiant light and yet is also the pure "dark silence", in which all lovers lose themselves. "Here, beyond the Polar circle of the mind, the midnight sun reigns over that rolling sea where the psychology of man mingles with the psychology of God."[107]

During the Renaissance, Plotinus continued to elevate men's minds to the eternal. Marsilio Ficino's translation of the *Enneads* into Latin (1492) influenced not only his compatriots but Edmund Spenser's Platonic Hymns. Through Ficino, Plotinus is still active in the words of Henry Vaughan (d. 1695):

> I saw Eternity the other night
> Like a great Ring of pure and endless light,
> All calm as it was bright.

Cambridge Platonists of the same epoch grafted Plotinus upon Calvinism, but the Catholic church, between 1700 and 1900, almost purged itself of mystical trends for fear of the undifferentiated godhead. Midway in that period Novalis came upon Plotinus (1798) and admired his belief that matters had no independent reality, and William Blake, who hated Churches but was dogmatically Christian, conveyed urgently through his writings and visionary landscapes that "if the doors of perception were cleansed, everything will appear to man as it is, infinite". But such rare exceptions apart, the fountains of mysticism have steadily diminished everywhere for centuries; the Age of Reason supported ecclesiastical influence in keeping the western world away from these areas of experience.

And yet

> Ever and anon a trumpet sounds
> From the hid battlements of Eternity,
> Those shaken mists a space unsettle, then
> Round the half-glimpsed turrets slowly wash again.[108]

More than eight hundred years ago an Arab called mystics the world's sustainers, the ultimate source of our spiritual knowledge and the salt which preserves human societies from decay; and now, when the power of reason again seems inconclusive, there have been voices suggesting that the need for this higher reality is greatest, both within and outside the Christian pattern, when the domination of nature and ordering of life have reached their height. An Indian thinker sees mystics as the future's principal hope, about to inaugurate an epoch in which this superior form of consciousness, evolved in the east by Hindus and Buddhists and in the west by Plotinus, will become a gift far more abundantly utilized by mankind.

NOTES

1. M. Aur. *Med.* VI, 30; I, 16
2. *Ibid.*, II, 5, III, 12 (tr. M. Staniforth); cf. VIII, 41
3. *Ibid.*, XII, 26, II, 17 (tr. M. Staniforth)
4. *Ibid.*, XII, 28 (tr. M. Staniforth)
5. *Ibid.*, VII, 69
6. *Ibid.*, X, 5 (tr. M. Staniforth)
7. Epict. *ap.* Arr. *Enchir.* I, 13
8. M. Aur. *Med.* VI, 30 (tr. M. Staniforth)
9. *Ibid.*, II, 11; cf. VI, 13
10. *Ibid.*, VII, 69, IV, 49 (tr. M. Staniforth)
11. M. Aur. *Ad Front. Epist.* I, p. 216 Loeb
12. M. Aur. *Med.* VIII, 24 (tr. M. Staniforth): VI, 28
13. Epict. *ap.* Arr. *Enchir.* III, 13
14. M. Aur. *Med.* IV, 48, II, 17, VII, 3 (tr. M. Staniforth)
15. *Ibid.*, II, 17
16. *Ibid.*, IV, 3 (tr. M. Staniforth)
17. *Ibid.*, VII, 28, 59
18. *Ibid.*, IX, 20
19. *Ibid.*, VIII, 59
20. *Ibid.*, IX, 1; XI, 21 (tr. M. Staniforth); cf. XII, 20
21. *Ibid.*, XI, 9, etc.
22. *Ibid.*, IV, 29
23. *Ibid.*, I, 17
24. *Ibid.*, VI, 30 (tr. M. Staniforth)
25. *Ibid.*, X, 10
26. *Ibid.*, IX, 36
27. *Ibid.*, II, 17, etc.
28. *Ibid.*, I, 14 (tr. M. Staniforth)—learnt "from his brother Severus"
29. *Ibid.*, IV, 4 (tr. M. Staniforth)
30. *Ibid.*, VI, 30, etc.
31. *Ibid.*, XI, 3 (tr. M. Staniforth)
32. Porph. *V. Plot.* 3
33. Plot. *Enn.* VI, 5, IV, 23
34. *Ibid.*, III, 8 (tr. E. O'Brien)
35. Maximus of Tyre (*c.* 125–85) blended all systems except Epicureanism. Albinus saw the Platonic Supreme Principle as unmoved, like Aristotle's, but not as the Mover; he called Plato's Forms (Ideas) "Thoughts of God"
36. Plot. *Enn.* V, 5, 6
37. *Ibid.*, VI, 9, 6 (tr. A. H. Armstrong)
38. *Ibid.*, VII, 1, cf. V, 3, 12, I, 6, 3, V, 1, 6, etc.
39. *Ibid.*, VII, 18

40. *Ibid.*, VI, 9 (tr. E. O'Brien)

41. Plato's Idea of Good becomes immanent in Plotinus' Universal Mind, which thinks the Ideas and is their location

42. Plot. *Enn.* III, 1, 4. Contemplation of Soul generates the Forms or Ideas of individuals, which Plato's Doctrine of Ideas had not envisaged

43. Sometimes Plotinus instead suggests that at our highest we attain Mind itself. Plotinus' Soul is Plato's Soul and World Craftsman and more

44. Plot. *Enn.* IV, 8, 9

45. *Ibid.*, II, 3, 9

46. *Ibid.*, IV, 8, 14; cf. Numenius of Apamea (rational and irrational soul), Plutarch

47. Plot. *Enn.* I, 8, 3; cf. Aristotle: matter a mere potentiality and receptacle of Form. Aristotle's greatest commentator, Alexander of Aphrodisias, was active early in the third century

48. Plot. *Enn.* I, 8, 8

49. *Ibid.*, II, 3, 17f. (tr. A. H. Armstrong). Cf. conflict between Pl. *Phaedo* and *Timaeus-Laws*

50. Cf. Ar. *EN.* x, 7, 8: man, because of inherent divinity, can live as if not mortal

51. Plot. *Enn.* III, 8, 4

52. Ar. *EN.* x, 8, 7; cf. Pl. *Symp.* 211, *Phaedr.* 249 51, *Phaedo* 67c, 79c, 81A

53. Plot. *Enn.* VI, 9, 11, 22

54. *Ibid.*, VI, 7, 34, 12 ff., cf. VI, 10, 11

55. Porph. *V. Plot.* 23 (tr. A. H. Armstrong). Porphyry claimed to have had the same experience once

56. Plot. *Enn.* VI, 7, 34; IX, 4

57. *Ibid.*, I, 6, 8

58. *Ibid.*, VI, 9, 11 (tr. A. H. Armstrong)

59. *Ibid.*, V, 3, 17, VI, 9, 11 (tr. A. H. Armstrong)

60. Cf. sources in P. Hadot, *Plotin ou la Simplicité du Regard*, pp. 63 ff.

61. *Ibid.*, VI, 7, 21, 30 ff: cf. Pl. *Phaedo, Symposium*

62. *Ibid.*, VI, 7, 34 (tr. E. O'Brien)

63. *Ibid.*, VI, 7, 19, 24 ff.

64. *Ibid.*, II, 9, 1. Plotinus did not deny magic, but regarded it as a selfish application of the universal sympathy. He saw stars as perhaps indicating but not determining the future

65. *Ibid.*, I, 6, 9 (tr. E. O'Brien)

66. *Ibid.*

67. William James; cf. H. Bergson, C. D. Broad

68. Arthur Koestler

69. E.g. peyote yielding mescalin (Aldous Huxley)

70. First so called by Leibnitz

71. Plot. *Enn.* V, 3, 17

72. *Ibid.*, III, 2, 9, cf. II, 9, 9

73. Man's lot also depends upon previous existences (cf. Pythagoreans)

74. Plot. *Enn.* III, 2, 9

75. *Ibid.*, III, 8, 4

76. *Ibid.*, III, 2, 5
77. *Ibid.*, I, 4, 7; cf. VI, 7, 34: the "heresy of the half life"
78. Middle Platonists such as Celsus had not favoured this withdrawal from public life; cf. Angela of Foligno and Zen Buddhism
79. Plot. *Enn.* V, 3, 17
80. H. F. Amiel (1821–81)
81. Justin, *Dial. Tryph.* II, 3–6
82. E.g. Plato's pupil Speusippus
83. The Merkabah (Chariot Rider) rabbis; cf. the later *Book of Creation* (Sefer Yetsirah)
84. This, however, is to follow, not replace, the practical life
85. *Gal.* I, 12
86. *II Cor.* XII, 9
87. *Manual of Discipline*, XI, 5, 7
88. Epiphanius, *Haer.* XXVI, 3, 1. The Gospel is of the Ophite sect (dualists who emphasized the serpent)
89. *Gospel of Truth*, XXII, 3 Grobel; and *Revelation of Dositheus*. Both from Chenoboskion
90. *Hymn of the Soul* (*Acts of Thomas*) (tr. G. R. S. Mead)
91. *Corp. Herm.* X, 4–6, XI, 20 (tr. E. Dodds). Philostratus suggested that Apollonius of Tyana had had mystic experiences
92. Numenius, *fr.* 11 Leemans (tr. E. Dodds)
93. Maitryana and Briharadaranyaka Upanishads
94. Swami Prabhavananda
95. To the Buddhists Nirvana was attainable in this life, but union and metaphysics were repudiated
96. An-isvara-yoga
97. Philostr. *V. Apol.* III, 18
98. Iambl. 27 (86.4). Plotinus saw mathematics as a means of overcoming the indeterminacy of matter
99. Aug. *De Ver. Rel.* IV, 7
100. *Id.*, *C.Ac.* III, 20, 43; cf. 19, 42; 18, 41: from Marius Victorinus' Latin translation of Plotinus
101. Aug. *De Quant. An.* 76
102. *Id.*, *Conf.* VII, 10, 17. He misleadingly identified Plotinus' Mind with the Word of St. John's Gospel
103. Neoplatonic ideas had passed into theology in E. (St. Basil and St. Gregory of Nyssa) and W. (through Boethius)
104. *Theologia Aristotelis*=passages of Plot. *Enn.* IV–VI; cf. Alfarabi of Baghdad (d. 950) (illumination of Mind by Ideas, fusing with Aristotelianism), Avicebrol (Ibn Gebirol) (doctrine of Creative Reason)
105. Especially Proclus of Constantinople (d. 484)
106. Tauler and Suso tacitly dropped his Neoplatonism. Eckhart's mysticism is like Sankara's
107. Maeterlinck. Ruysbroeck's description of mystic consciousness is close to that of the Mandukya Upanishad
108. Francis Thompson (1859–1907), *The Hound of Heaven*

PART IV

From Paganism to Christianity

8

The Climax of Paganism

The Patriotic Gods

During this whole period most official pagan worships were fading into the background. Pliny the younger, on his arrival in northern Asia Minor early in the second century, had already found the temples becoming deserted and neglected,[1] and the withdrawal of paganism continued. During the third century its shrines in north Africa were abandoned, and at Rome, too, the cults lost ground. The public treated their annual ceremonies as occasions for carnival,[2] and even the official coinage shows markedly diminished attention to most gods and goddesses. An inscription reveals that the funds allocated to a religious foundation in A.D. 241 only amounted to one-quarter of the figure of earlier years.[3]

This failure of enthusiasm was one of the prices paid for war and disaster. As Julian the Apostate later remarked, "It was the sight of their undeserved misery that led people to despise the gods."[4] Another reason for waning interest in the old religion was the growth of monotheistic feeling. Throughout this period the Olympians were coming to be regarded as branches or aspects or symbolic representatives of a single unknowable divinity (pp. 179, 225).[5] A move in this direction was taken by the coinage of Commodus, on which Jupiter is described as *Exsuperator* or *Exsuperantissimus*—the chief god, but also something more.[6] This attitude made the deities of Olympus acceptable to the more advanced thinking of the day, but it also weakened their hold on the minds of the Roman people as autonomous, individual entities.

However, the eclipse of the ancient divinities was limited by two important exceptions. First, the Mystery religions which promised individual salvation were still powerful (pp. 240 ff.). The second exception, which found greater expression on the coinage, comprised deities concerned with the protection of the state. As the members of the Olympian pantheon mostly faded into an amorphous background, national propaganda concentrated upon those who fulfilled the time-honoured role of protectors of the ruling emperor and the Roman people.

While amid crisis and emergency Plotinus counselled withdrawal into contemplation (p. 192), many an emperor invoked these gods and goddesses as an emotional rallying-cry. For they, men still felt, were the divine guarantors of the military success on which the empire's security rested; there remained a strong instinctive conviction that Roman power depended upon proper cult-acts performed towards the traditional deities. Citizens and subjects, and above all soldiers, associated their support for the ruling power with recognition of the gods of Rome. That is why Dio Cassius, in the speech which he attributes to Augustus' adviser Maecenas, suggests (though a Greek himself) that the emperor should make worship of the Roman gods compulsory, "according to the customs of our fathers".[7] For this historian, like many others in governing circles, believed that the veneration of foreign cults implied an undesirable non-Roman way of life. Christians were atheists because they did not revere the gods who guarded the empire; and conversely the worst and most dangerous enemies to Christianity, in the eyes of its protagonist Tertullian, were not the Mystery religions but still the national gods of Rome.

Clearly the most Roman and patriotic of all cults was the worship of Rome itself. As the city began to lose its political and economic importance (p. 131), the emotional inspiration of its name remained as great as ever; the heavily charged slogan *Roma Aeterna* preserved and intensified its power. Imperial coins embroider upon the theme in many ways. They identify the city's fortunes with those of the ruling emperor, just as Tiberius, long ago, had been declared "born for the eternity of the Roman name".[8] Moreover, the festival of the Birthday of the City was given added grandeur by its association with Hadrian's magnificent temple which linked Rome with the divine founder Venus (p. 217).[9]

One of the army's annual celebrations, listed in the military Calendar of Dura, honoured the goddess Rome; and Aurelian's refoundation of her temple was connected with the strength of the cult in his native Balkan region which dominated the army and court. Another son of these Danubian provinces, Diocletian gave even more massive and widespread publicity to the idea of Rome than any other ruler. For he and his fellow-emperors expressed this idea, without variation, on millions of the silvered bronze coins of their universally circulating reformed currency. These enormous and uniform issues, issued at many mints from *c.* 294 onwards for more than two decades, represent one of the largest outbursts of numismatic propaganda in the whole of Roman history. By such means, every household in the empire was repeatedly reminded of eternal Rome for many years.

But the slogan of Diocletian and his colleagues was not simply concerned with Rome itself; instead it celebrated the Genius of the Roman People—GENIVS POPVLI ROMANI. The Genius was represented by a youthful male figure, carrying a cornucopia and wearing the turreted (mural) crown which was characteristic of the Fortune (Tyche) of cities. Since Genii, in very early days, had often been represented by snakes, they have conjecturally been regarded as a survival of totemism. The word means the begetter, and personifies that particular divine characteristic, some masculine principle beyond human eyes, which enables the line to continue for generation after generation; thus Hercules, manhood personified, was associated with Genius under Commodus (?) and Septimius,[10] and joined him as a patron of Diocletian's regime. In a crisis of the war against Hannibal (218 B.C.), the religious rites decreed by the state had included the sacrifice of five human victims to Genius—a magical measure by which Rome would increase its male population and win the war. During the further emergencies which heralded the end of the Republic, the Temple of Genius beside the Forum attracted attention for miraculous prodigies.

The idea had meanwhile developed that gods had Genii of their own—essences of their numinosity. Under the influence of the Greeks, whose *daimon* was a related conception, this doctrine came to be applied to individuals also: everyone had a Genius, who was his productive element and at the same time his protector. This meant that Roman emperors, although public worship of their own persons was contrary to tradition, could more readily be venerated through their Genii, by rather the same sort of cult-acts as were performed in honour of the *daimon* or *fravashi* of a Parthian king.[11]

Moreover, Genii belonged not only to people and gods but to institutions. Among these were military groups such as Decius' Army of Illyricum (p. 32). Cities also had their own Genius, and the concept had long been linked with Rome itself. For on the Capitoline Hill, as ancient calendars record, there was an annual festival of "the public Genius" (Genius Publicus) united with Rome's special goddess Venus,[12] and a shield on the Capitol was dedicated to the Genius of the City of Rome.

The Romans had never attributed human form to their deities with the same facility as the Greeks, and this dedication included the additional precautionary words "whether masculine or feminine". However, it became established that the Genius of the Roman People—for such was the formula which emerged—was, as might be expected, male. Supervision of the cult belonged to the family of the Cornelii, one of whose late Republican representatives had placed the head of the Genius on a coin—bearded at this stage and not clean-shaven as in later centuries.[13] Beside the head are globe and rudder, indicating that this is the power which guarantees Rome's universal rule. Then, after several subsequent appearances on coins, a relief of Septimius depicted the Genius of the Roman People wearing the turreted or mural crown of city Fortunes.[14] Genius again wears that crown, sometimes combined with the rays of fashionable Sun-worship, on the obverse of one of the last large bronze coins ever to be issued at Rome, and one of the very few, within the past two hundred and fifty years, to show any head at all other than some portrait explicitly ascribed as to an imperial personage. The coins may date from a short period of interregnum immediately following Gallienus' death (268).[15]

Then, after Aurelian had restored the Temple of the City, Diocletian, as has been said, singled out the Genius Populi Romani as the main publicity theme of his coinage. In the days when many earlier slogans no longer carried weight, here was one which, like the massive uniformity of the coinages themselves, would stress the Romanness and unity of the entire military and civil commonwealth, and marshal paganism to fight its decisive battle against the Christians (p. 298). Before long, certain additional coins referred to the Genii of the rulers themselves—GENIO AVGVSTI, IMPERATORIS, CAESARIS. It was these leaders, then, who guaranteed the success of the Roman world and cherished the creative spirit immanent in its people.

The principal issues with GENIO POPVLI ROMANI, diversified by a more varied range of *Romanità* from Maxentius whose principal asset was his control of the capital city, declined and came to an end in A.D. 316, when Christianity was beginning to offer new watchwords (p. 233). Yet the appeal of Rome did not cease. A large painting, apparently of Constantine's reign, shows a frontal seated figure of the goddess.[16] When Fortune (Tyche) and other gods vanished at this time, the Fortunes or spirits of cities were retained and interpreted as entities at God's gift and will. Indeed Constantine himself, despite his Christianity, gave Constantinople a temple of Fortune, and placed in this shrine a statue of the Fortune of Rome.[17] Coins and medallions of the new city honour not only CONSTANTINOPOLIS but also VRBS ROMA and POP(*ulus*) ROMANVS. For although the eternal was now believed to be the real, the majesty of the city reflected this eternity. In an age of provincialization and barbarization, when the capital had been removed elsewhere and emperors rarely set foot in Italy, the most urgent of rallying cries still was Rome.

The Temple of the City established by Hadrian and rebuilt by Maxentius associated Rome with the goddess Venus, who through her son Aeneas was the divine mother of the Roman race. As the other Olympians faded, Venus had retained her glamour as one of the founders of Rome. Her worship kept an emotional strength which confirms that these survivals of traditional paganism went deeper than merely official and superficial levels. The place which the goddess still held in the souls of Romans is revealed by the outstanding Latin poem of the whole singularly unpoetic epoch. This is the *Pervigilium Veneris* or Vigil of Venus (?*c.* A.D. 307). Its ninety-two exquisite, melodious, sensuous lines, with their unclassical lilting rhythm and recurrent refrain, blend official and personal cult, patriotism and nature and romance. The subject is the three-nightly Sicilian festival of Dione who is Venus.

> Then from the blood spilled from above and the glistening
> Sea-foam, among hosts of sea-urchins, sprang
> Creation's goddess—Dione: a wave, breathing her spirit
> Everywhere, sowing her seed-track over the hidden seas,

Through all skies and lands; man's heart and the veins of the earth
Received her way of creation.
Tomorrow let there be love for him who never has loved
And love for the lover tomorrow . . .

As it glows, she tinges the ripening year with jewelled
Sprays, pushing the buds to fertile
Clusters under the west wind's warmth, and sprinkles
Dew-beads left by the night breeze. Tears as they quiver
Hanging at bursting-point sparkle; the clinging dewdrop
Falls, a rounded pearl.
Tomorrow let there be love for him who never has loved
And love for the lover tomorrow . . .

She sings: I am silent. When will my spring come?
When shall I be as a swallow and stop being silent?
In this silence the Muses have left me—Apollo is gone.
So did the city Amyclae meet her end in silence
Without a word.
Tomorrow let there be love for him who never has loved
And love for the lover tomorrow . . .[18]

The pageant ceases with a sob, it has been said; and behind the
passion thuds the tramp of the barbarians along the roads to
Rome.[19] The days of the Olympians are nearly over, and there is
nostalgia for the glorious past. But since the world is still unthinkable
without Rome, Venus must survive, because Venus, as another part
of the poem recalls, was the mother of all Rome's glory; and
Hadrian and Aurelian had linked them in the resplendent temple
which sought to pilot paganism into new and unfamiliar epochs.

Another patriotic goddess who defied the decline of the Olympians
by her continued impact on the later Roman world was Vesta. Her
shrine in the Forum is repeatedly shown on coins and medallions of
Septimius and subsequent emperors, and the neighbouring courtyard
devoted to her service contained many dedications persisting right
up to the fourth century A.D. The fire-cult of Vesta (Hestia)
corresponded to contemporary Sun-worship and to the fire-altars of
Sassanian Persia; and her Vestal Virgins suited contemporary tastes
for asceticism and monastic seclusion. As the ancient, everlasting
guardian of Rome and its rulers, Vesta in these dangerous times
received more devoted veneration than ever.

So, for a time, did the great Roman emperors of the past, called *divi* to distinguish them from the *di* of Olympus.[20] Drawing upon Greek ideas of deification as a reward for merit, the Romans had fostered similar legends relating to Hercules and their own founder Romulus.[21] And just as those had been human beings whose mighty deeds raised them to be gods after their deaths, so also Augustus and some of his successors and their wives and relatives were posthumously appointed to this honorific godhead by a grateful state. They were hardly objects for prayer, but upon important occasions ordinary people probably thought of them as next and nearest to Jupiter.

As polytheism became unfashionable, the *divi*, like the Olympians, lost their personal identity and tended to become a generalized conception, representing the glorious past and the concept of eternal Rome embodied in the continuity of the throne. After the time of Marcus Aurelius, no new individual temples were given; but they received places in a general Temple of the Divi (275-6). They also enjoyed special honour at the headquarters of armies and were prominent in the cults laid down for soldiers. The military calendar of Severus Alexander found at Dura contains forty-one entries, of which no less than twenty-one are concerned with *divi* and *divae*; and when Aurelian received barbarian envoys, he set out the effigies of the *divi* at the place where the interview was held.

At almost all periods of the empire coins were issued with the heads of some of these deified personages. A characteristic accompanying design is the funeral pyre of consecration, a many-storeyed cenotaph still found centuries later in Asian lands. Usually not more than a single *divus* or *diva* is celebrated at a time, and usually these were personages who had not been dead for long. Some issues are exceptionally large; for example Antoninus' output of coinage for his deceased and deified wife Faustina the elder is enormous, and Marcus Aurelius' commemorations of the younger Faustina are scarcely less extensive.

But on a few occasions the government, looking into the past as it often did, produced a series of coins honouring simultaneously a whole range of such imperial deities. The most significant of these multiple issues is a "consecration" series of base silver issued in the mid-third century. Stylistic considerations and the evidence of hoards identify their issuer as Decius (249-51).[22] The series has been variously ascribed to Rome and Mediolanum (Milan), while local bronze pieces of similar types were minted at Philippopolis (Plovdiv) in Thrace. There in the Balkan territories, from which Decius the first Illyrian emperor had come, belief in immortality was ardent. But the appeal and circulation of the major series comprehended wider circles of the Roman world. Decius was fighting desperately against the Germans, not on behalf of the old Olympians but for the survival and perpetuation of Rome, whose finest representatives were these venerated emperors of the past, their virtues proved in action. The array of deified rulers on Decius' coinage, like the parades of ancestors at Roman funerals, were part of the crisis-propaganda which accompanied his persecution of Christians (p. 293). At a time of supreme stress he was closing the ranks behind patriotic tradition.

And yet the appeal to the *divi* was a failure, for except in some countries such as Africa, where their worship was especially strong, this cult did not outlast the third century; in the revivals of paganism under Diocletian it played only a very minor part. Nevertheless Maxentius deified his own son, who had died in boyhood (*c.* 310), and Constantine honoured Divus Claudius Gothicus, a fellow-Illyrian emperor and Sun-worshipper from whom he claimed descent (p. 232). Moreover, the Christian Constantine himself became Divus after his death. Poets could still call Christian emperors immortal, but now there was a new shade of theological meaning; coins issued in posthumous celebration of imperial ladies show their chariots beckoned up to heaven by the hand of God or Elijah.

The reigning emperor, unlike those who were dead and consecrated, had never in his lifetime officially become a god. But his status was a good deal more than human. For as the Olympians increasingly failed to satisfy religious aspirations, the ruler gained in stature at their expense. Before Rome had possessed emperors, the Greek monarchies which succeeded to the heritage of Alexander the Great saw their monarch to be a deity—and indeed the most efficacious of them all, because he was present in the flesh (*epiphanes*) and could therefore be of some use. Following these and other regional and historical traditions, people throughout the Roman empire likewise thought of their ruler as some sort of a divinity.

Caligula let his godhead be inferred, for example when he dressed as Mercury; and the theme of comparison with this or that Olympian was re-echoed for hundreds of Augusti by a million flattering tongues and pens. As the imperial role became more and more autocratic, informal ascriptions of divinity to the reigning monarch grew in frequency and explicitness. Things pertaining to him had already for some time been described as Sacred. The mint, with its vital responsibility of supplying money for the army's pay, was called by this epithet early in the second century A.D.[23] A hundred years later, an imperial pronouncement is described as *sacrae litterae*.[24] There was also increased emphasis on the Perpetuity and Eternity of successive rulers, and the frontality of their representations on reliefs had divine implications (p. 120). Yet for centuries the official coinage, while offering every other conceivable form of adulation, scrupulously refrains from declaring the living emperor to be a god. He was never named *divus* in his lifetime, and it was not until the later third century that a few rare issues of Serdica (Sofia) in his homeland call Aurelian *deus*. But that was an untypical, almost isolated, flight of fancy (cf. p. 262, n. 20); the empire was not a theocracy.

The most frequent and nearest approach to hailing the ruler as a god was to compare or identify him with one of the gods. A preferred model was Hercules, who embodied many of the chief ideas of enlightened monarchy and had himself, after death, supposedly risen to heaven because of his great deeds (p. 219). Trajan, of Romano-Spanish origin, was devoted to the gods of Gades (Cadiz) and particularly to Hercules Gaditanus, whom he emulated as conqueror of barbarians and the world. Hadrian saw Hercules as the pioneer and forerunner of his journeys; Marcus Aurelius interpreted him as the prototype of self-sacrifice and devotion to humanity; and Commodus, the last of the line, gathered together all the threads and identified himself publicly with Hercules, whose lion's skin he wears in portraits on his coins. Much to the disapproval of Dio Cassius, Commodus loved Hercules' occupation of killing animals[25]; like many a Persian and Parthian monarch and Alexander the Great and his own predecessors, he was the Royal Huntsman. A coin which shows Commodus attacking a lion is inscribed "to the Courage of the emperor" (VIRTVTI AVGVSTI), for the ruler's daring in the hunt symbolizes military victory, and the slaughtered beasts stand for the powers of evil.[26] The last bronze medallions of the reign boost his role as Hercules, and this was also made prominent in army shrines. The terms "conqueror" and "unconquerable" (*victor, invictus*), which henceforward become official designations of the ruler, again imply a comparison with Hercules, and with Alexander the Great as well.

Commodus used to appear dressed as other gods also. His coins present a dedication to "Jupiter the youthful" (IOVI IVVENI), and in order to point this comparison the god is endowed with the imperial features. Similarly, on the Arch of Septimius at Lepcis Magna, the emperor's Triumph no longer leads him to Jupiter on the Capitol; in his own person, he is not only the victorious general but Jupiter as well. Although emperors were not officially deified in their lifetimes, there was now little more that could be done to emphasize their elevation to the rank of the gods.

Nevertheless, in an increasingly spiritual age, these pretensions began to ring false. In spite of the ruler's growing autocracy and magnificence, he was not the same as the quasi-monotheistic transcendent divine power in which people of this epoch believed (p. 213). And so while the adulation of reigning Augusti continued and intensified, a different and indeed contradictory interpretation of their relationship with the deity gained ground. This was the idea that the emperor was *not* one of the gods, but was instead their favoured and chosen delegate and regent upon earth. Such a belief went back to ancient Persia, where Darius had declared "by the grace of Ahuramazda, I am king"[27]; and the Parthian and Sassanian monarchs whom Rome saw beyond its eastern borders maintained that they, too, were the gods' elect. The conception was familiar in Egypt; and Semitic countries had likewise seen their rulers as messenger or angel (*mal'ak*) of the deity, borrowing his character, becoming his emanation and substitute, and rising to his lofty height. Similar ways of thinking are found in the *Iliad*, in Plutarch's biographies of Roman kings and leaders, and in Greco-Roman theories of divine monarchic right.[28] The success of Roman emperors had always been attributed to heavenly guidance, and the view gained ground that, whatever their own qualities, they needed this guidance in order to prosper.

Thus a medallion of Marcus Aurelius shows him as a minute form standing beside Jupiter's huge figure. Commodus, too, when not identifying himself with the gods seeks to claim them as his protectors. Jupiter is not just made to resemble the emperor but is described as the defender of his safety. Commodus not only identifies himself with Hercules but calls him his Comrade or Companion (HERCVLI COMITI). From now on, coins and medallions increasingly concentrate on displaying the gods in this light—not, that is to say, as themselves, but as the patrons and protectors and comrades of the emperor. The divine comrade was a sort of double, a friend beyond phenomena. Godhead was one, there were many telephone lines, different switchboards; a *comes* gave you a private line.[29] Even poetical flatterers had sometimes recognized that there was a natural hierarchy in which the emperor, though superior to mankind, was below the gods.[30] His higher position than mere humans was stressed by the epithets declaring his unequalled piety and good fortune (*pius*, *felix*), which first appear jointly in 184 and come to form an essential part of a ruler's titles. But the emperor's lower position than the gods is indicated by his heavenward look, which is also a feature of sculptural representations (p. 125). Pertinax (A.D. 193) shows Providence raising her eyes and hands to a star, and the head of the ruler is sharply upturned on portrait busts and medallions from the time of Gallienus.[31] Man's gaze into the skies had long been a Greek commonplace, and became a symbol of the aspirations of Alexander the Great; and Roman Republican coin-portraits may already have shown traces of the same heaven-directed emotion.[32]

This, then, was the spirit in which Aurelian, while describing the divine power as his consort (*consors*), explicitly rejects the deification attributed to him on one of his coins (p. 221); it was more in keeping with the spirit of the times to claim divine grace. The god, he said, had given him the purple and fixed the length of his rule,[33] and his coins stress various aspects of the concord between the emperor and this divine power. It was again as elect of the gods, rather than as gods themselves, that Diocletian and his colleague Maximian attempted to renew and restore the pagan worship to which they had been devoutly brought up in their Balkan peasant homes. The endeavour was proclaimed all over the empire by coins and medallions, reliefs depicting pagan sacrifices and vows, and inscriptions. The publicity of Diocletian and his colleagues leans heavily upon the past; and orators pronouncing the eulogies of these rulers again assert that success comes by correct acts of worship.

For the emperors were not, themselves, officially gods,[34] but their dominion was the earthly counterpart of heaven. "We must practise ourselves", says a writer of the time, "by praising earthly kings and so habituate and train ourselves for adoration of the deity."[35]

The link was made still more explicit when Diocletian and Maximian founded their whole theology on the specific comradeship and protection which they received from Jupiter and Hercules respectively, and which led them to assume personal titles of Jovius and Herculius. Although there were later continuations and revivals of paganism, this was the last great official manifestation of the Olympian cults. But the culmination of this whole tendency to treat the emperor as the elect of pagan deities was reached under Constantine, when he devoted his coinage throughout the empire to proclaiming that his comrade was the Sun-god.

The Worship of the Sun

About fifteen years after Diocletian had mobilized all his bronze-currency mints for a uniform proclamation of the Genius of the Roman People (p. 215), Constantine likewise concentrated all the resources of this coinage upon the single theme and figure of the Sun-god, inscribing each piece *To the Sun, the Unconquerable Companion:* SOLI INVICTO COMITI (*c.* 309). These uniform, multitudinous issues, like Diocletian's, represented a huge-scale operation unmistakably intended to implant an idea in the minds of the populations of the empire. Sun-worship, at that moment, was the state-cult of the Roman world, and the god was accepted by millions of its inhabitants. If the solar cult had not succumbed to Christianity a few years later, it could well have become the permanent religion of the Mediterranean area.

Only a few peoples in the hottest regions of the world have regarded the Sun as pestiferous and diabolical.[36] Elsewhere men from the remotest periods of antiquity concluded from their divinization of nature, and confirmed afresh each day, that they should greet its orb as a beneficent deity. The life of our planet has its source in the Sun, of which every force is a product.[37] In Egypt, for example, where this worship abounded, the rising Sun appears upon reliefs of Amenhotep IV (Akhnaton) who in the fourteenth century B.C. instituted a revolutionary new cult of his Sun-god Aton,

224

including novel emphasis upon its light-giving and life-giving properties, accompanied by a claim to have achieved personal revelation through the embrace of the god's caressing hands (shown as the termination of his golden disc). In Asia Minor and the near east, all-seeing Marduk, who became supreme in the Babylonian pantheon, had at first been a solar divinity. So had Shamash, who was originally secondary to the Moon-god; but experts on the heavens reversed their roles.

The learned cult of the Sun which these men evolved became, in subsequent stages of Semitic paganism, the solar theory of the "Chaldaeans", Babylonian priests of the Greco-Roman epoch who turned all Baals into Suns or into an aspect of the single Sun. For this was recognized as the heart of the universe and master of its divine energy. Through the influence of astrology, the Sun's power to attract and repel the stars, whose revolutions determined the course of events, was seen as the arbiter of men's destiny and the animator of their minds and bodies alike.[38] Fire, endowed with Reason, becomes the creator of the particular reasons which direct the human microcosm. This was a central and basic form of the monotheistic religion, uniting man with the cosmos, which spread throughout the ancient world (p. 213).

In the Old Testament, Elijah's horses and chariot have sometimes been held to represent the Sun[39]; the synagogue of Beit Alpha in Israel had a picture of the Sun driving his horses in the sky. But the classic solar theologian of the Jews is Malachi (c. 460 B.C.), the last in the prophetic section of the Old Testament canon, who foretells how a Messianic Sun of Righteousness will rise for the faithful.[40] In Persia, too, the Sun and Moon were very early worshipped as emanations and almost synonyms of Ahuramazda, the god of Light (p. 249); there are still Sun-worshippers in Persia, as well as Parsees (whose principal centre is Bombay). The quality of kingly glory in the *Avesta* (p. 251) is described as lustre or light, and the Persian Great King was called the One rising together with the Sun.[41] There were fire-cults in his palaces, and then at the fire-altars and fire-temples of his Parthian and Sassanian successors.[42] The Parthian court of justice at Babylon may have had stars painted on its dome, and the Sassanian ruler was partner of the stars, brother of the Sun and Moon.[43] When Plotinus takes an interest in Persian philosophy, what he has in mind is its solar theology, which likened the Supreme

Being to a luminous source emitting rays that pierce and illuminate the darkness of matter.[44] St. Augustine, when he broke with the dualist Manichaeans, criticized their habit of worshipping the Sun and Moon.[45]

The Sun had also played its part in much Greek literature, beginning with the *Iliad* in which it was appealed to as a witness.[46] Aeschylus' lost play the *Bassarae* tells how Orpheus was torn to pieces by Dionysus, because he believed the greatest deity to be not Dionysus but the Sun[47]—who was also Apollo. The disciples of Pythagoras identified the Sun as the creator of individual reason, author of generation and god of the dead.[48] Plato saw the solar deity as author of all light and life in the material world, and described how Socrates offered it a prayer.[49]

Then the Sun figured largely in the astronomical speculations which grew in Plato's circle, and soon after the death of Alexander the Great a certain Alexarchus declared himself to be its incarnation.[50] Monarchs of the successor-states began to wear its crown of rays,[51] and solar hymns were written; one was perhaps Alexandrian,[52] and a later example, from Susa in Persia, identifies the Sun with Dionysus and greets him as the universal lord. Indeed, almost every writer now agreed that the Sun, Moon and stars were gods, with the Sun as their leader. Or, if they were not divinities, they were at least visible signs of the divinity and channels by which man could attain it[53]—that is to say intermediaries (demiurges) between god and brute matter (p. 270).

Although few people were prepared to join Aristarchus of Samos in asserting that the earth revolved round the Sun,[54] the next two hundred years witnessed the spread of the Sun-cult throughout the Mediterranean world. As Semitic, Iranian and Greek theology, astrology and philosophy intermingled, there was an ever-growing tendency to explain the traditional gods in solar terms. Mixtures and blendings of deities were now universal;[55] the gods are of many names, but one nature, and their common factor is the Sun. Funeral art shows its heavenly shield,[56] the image of the Revolving All, and upon a gold diadem found in Syria the god is the central figure among thirteen deities. Posidonius of Syrian Apamea (d. *c.* 50 B.C.), who summed up the state of the world's knowledge in his day, saw the Sun as the burning heart of the world and its intelligent light.[57]

Metaphors of its emanations and rays were constantly used to describe the relations between the deity and mankind. But this was only one of many ways in which solar literature continued to proliferate at every level. The poet Statius ended the first book of his *Thebaid* with a hymn to Apollo, who is also the Sun and Titan and Osiris and Mithras (p. 237). Hadrian's Cretan freedman Mesomedes wrote a metaphysical hymn to the Sun-god, and there is a Latin litany hailing it as the cosmic orderer and master of the four elements and seasons (p. 243), bringing heat, fecundity, joy and science in its train.[58] Light-symbolism was at home in many eastern cultures, and one of its most vivid exponents is Philo the Hellenized Jew of Alexandria (p. 201). During the third century, this way of thinking reached its height in the simultaneously evolved systems of Mani and Plotinus.

Sun-worship appealed to the learned, with their taste for the abstract, but less erudite invocations to local manifestations of the god shows that these intellectuals had no monopoly.[59] There are also magic papyri, offering a personal introduction. One such document, recommending an almost mystical self-hypnotism, indicates the magic which will at last enable its exponent to see the opening of the solar disc and the golden beams of the everlasting light.

Upon the mainland of Greece, Helios had not normally possessed local cults of his own. But it was different in Italy, and early bronze coins from the south of the peninsula show the deity's radiate facing head (*c.* 200 B.C.). At Rome, devotees of the Sun went back, it was said, to the legendary days of King Numa.[60] Apparently native to Rome, Sol had its festival on 9 August, and was linked in inscriptions with the fire-goddess Vesta (Hestia), who was analogous to the power worshipped at Persian fire-altars (p. 218). An antique Roman shrine of the Sun still existed in Nero's reign. The god's radiate-crowned personification appears on Republican and early imperial coins.[61] Upon the summit of the Temple of Apollo on the Palatine, which stood for the régime of Augustus, there was a magnificent sculptural group showing Sol the Charioteer, whose old identification with Apollo the Augustans repeated and stressed. Caligula and Nero were hailed as the New Sun; Nero set a precedent for centuries by giving his coin-portraits the radiate crown of Greek monarchs

(p. 226), and a colossal statue at Rome apparently represented him in solar guise.[62]

During the Civil Wars of A.D. 69, the Third Legion saluted the Rising Sun, since "that is the way in Syria".[63] Literary and official symbolism, particularly in relation to emperors, now concentrated on this *ascent* of the Sun, which had received religious attention from the earliest times (p. 225). Dawn (Aurora) accompanied Sol on the breast-plate of Augustus' statue from Prima Porta, and Statius obsequiously tells how Domitian "rises with the new sun—himself shining more brightly". Before long, an important publicity slogan of the Roman state is ORIENS and then in the third century ORIENS AVGVSTI, the Rising of the Emperor, a daily event of salvation for Rome like the Sun's resurrection from the night in which his glory had been hidden. Hadrian's radiate ORIENS is the ever-renewed god of Sunrise, with an implied imperial analogy appropriate to the personal relation with the god which that emperor claimed.[64]

A medallion of Antoninus Pius strikes the same note of victory over the powers of darkness. A later figure of Sol has the features of Commodus, whose father Marcus Aurelius, on his deathbed, had compared him with the Rising Sun. A relief from Ephesus shows the deified Marcus ascending to the sky in the god's chariot which returns dead souls to their heavenly element[65]; and it was the family of the Aurelii that had traditionally been charged with the Roman cult. The Sun is called Discoverer of Light, and its characteristic title "Unconquerable" (INVICTVS) now finds increasing expression and is applied directly to emperors.[66]

Under Septimius Severus and his family solar worship almost took charge of the entire pantheon. His building the Septizodium displayed him as Sun-god with seven planets around him, the seven spheres of which the deity was Lord. In this Septizodium, the emperor acted as judge, just as Parthian contemporaries may have dispensed justice in a star-studded hall (pp. 134, 225). Septimius' politically powerful wife Julia Domna and her sister Julia Maesa were daughters of the high priest at the Syrian Sun-temple of Emesa (Homs), and Domna was patron of Philostratus who gave a pronouncedly solar emphasis to his fictitious life of the sorcerer Apollonius of Tyana (p. 235). In this atmosphere, designs on imperial coinage show advances upon their customary conservatism.[67] In particular the boy Geta, son of the Unconquerable and Pious Septimius, not only appears as Sol himself, portrayed in a novel half-length representation with radiate crown, but his right hand is raised in the Sun's magic gesture of benediction (*c.* A.D. 200). This gesture, which warded off evil influences as well as conferring blessings, was very ancient, and had appeared in statues of Roman orators.[68] Court-poets wrote of the holy or divine hand of their emperor, and Sol's arm is similarly lifted on Alexandrian coins of Trajan. This symbol, still the sign of episcopal blessing today, was to become frequent on sarcophagus reliefs and in the catacombs of Christians, where Jesus outstretches his hand in the most popular of all Christian themes, the Raising of Lazarus from the dead (p. 275).

When Geta's brother Caracalla became ruler, the emphasis on Sun-worship became even stronger. He claimed, not entirely in jest, that he used the god's method of chariot-driving.[69] A lion on his coinage indicates the derivation of his régime from Sol, and a little bronze portrait in the form of a shield endows him with its rays.[70]

And then Elagabalus, though he adopted the names of Marcus Aurelius Antoninus which Caracalla had used before him, swept aside any caution or tradition in his haste to incorporate Sun-worship into the Roman imperial theology (218–22). For this Roi Soleil imported his native, eastern local solar cult, unmodified, into the centre and headship of the religion of Rome. His god of Emesa was a black, phallic meteorite, also praised at this period by another who was attached to its cult by ancestry and temperament, the novelist Heliodorus (p. 173).

A huge temple was now built for this Sun-god at Rome, and the deity's Semitic name ELAGAB(*alus*) or Baal, identified with Sol, strikes an outlandish note amid the conservative traditions of the official coinage. In keeping, however, with an age which was beginning to call its rulers the comrades of divinities rather than actual divinities themselves, the emperor does not himself claim identification with the god, preferring to recall his hereditary position as priest of the cult.[71]

> He placed the Sun-god in a chariot adorned with gold and jewels and brought him out from the city to the suburbs. A six-horse chariot bore the Sun-god, the horses huge and flawlessly white, with expensive gold fittings and rich ornaments. No one held the reins, and no one rode in the chariot; the vehicle was escorted

as if the Sun-god himself were the charioteer. Elagabalus ran backwards in front of the chariot, facing the god and holding the horses' reins. He made the whole journey in this reverse fashion, looking up into the face of his god. Since he was unable to see where he was going, his route was paved with gold dust to keep him from stumbling and falling, and bodyguards supported him on each side to protect him from injury. The people ran parallel to him, carrying torches and tossing wreaths and flowers. The statues of all the gods, the costly or sacred offerings in the temples, the imperial ornaments, and valuable heirlooms were carried by the cavalry and the entire Praetorian Guard in honour of the Sun-god.[72]

Elagabalus was too rash, and was murdered. And yet in spite of this setback, the worship of the Sun did not cease to flourish and increase. The new emperor Severus Alexander, cousin to Elagabalus, repeatedly shows Sol on his coinage, but portrays him in classic form without Emesan accretions. For Rome required methods of integration and assimilation more subtle than Elagabalus' misguided attempt to outdo and subordinate every element in the traditional fabric of religion.

Nevertheless, forty years later, matters had advanced so far that Gallienus proposed to dominate the city, from the highest point of the Esquiline Hill, with a chariot-group including a colossal statue of himself as the Sun.[73] His successor Claudius II Gothicus (268–70) was devoted to the same deity, and then the logical, conclusive move was taken soon afterwards by the next emperor Aurelian. For he established, as the central and focal point of Roman religion, a massive and strongly subsidized cult of Sol Invictus (274), endowing him with a resplendent Roman temple, and instituting on the model of the ancient priestly colleges, and as their equal in rank, a new college of Priests of the Sun.[74] The birthday of the god was to be on 25 December, and this, transformed into Christmas Day, was one of the heritages which Christianity owed to the solar cult.

In such developments several threads are apparent. First, official religion had long been moving in this direction. Secondly, Aurelian came from the Danubian land of Pannonia, where Sun-worship is attested in the astral symbolism of many tomb-reliefs (p. 244); and his own mother was said to have been its priestess in their village.[75] And then again his own name fortuitously, but felicitously, suggested a link with the family of the Aurelii which had traditionally been in charge of the ancient Sun-worship of Rome (p. 228). Furthermore Aurelian was deeply influenced by the Syrian veneration of the Sun which the relatives of Septimius, coming from that land, had done so much to extend. The outstanding event of Aurelian's reign was his defeat of Zenobia and recovery of the eastern provinces of the empire (p. 37). During these campaigns Aurelian had visited both Emesa and Zenobia's capital Palmyra, which was another centre of solar theology, as its temple of the Sun-god Bel (Baal) still indicates today; Zenobia's husband Odenathus had been called the city's Sun-sent priest.[76] Aurelian now restored this temple at Palmyra, and, interpreting its deity as a form of Sol Invictus, adorned his own Roman temple of the Sun with statues not only of Helios-Sol but also of Belos or Baal.[77]

Like Elagabalus, Aurelian was importing into Roman cult the vigorous beliefs of partially Hellenized Syria, which were now so pervasively active in contemporary speculation. But his tactics were more statesmanlike than those of the earlier emperor. In this determined effort to revivify and concentrate paganism, Aurelian was not overturning the Roman cults; he was adding to them, and thereby changing their emphasis and balance of power, so that Sol now stood at the head of the pantheon.[78] This was not only an integration, it was a creative, novel deed of religious statecraft, like the act of the Ptolemies of Egypt when they had imported a minor god Serapis and made him into a new divinity of state. But Aurelian's decision was even more comprehensive, because it sought to weave the main religious strands of east and west into a united, cosmopolitan universal faith.

The strongest part of Aurelian's army came, like himself, from Sun-worshipping Pannonia (p. 32). The religion of this Danubian army is revealed by hundreds of little votive tablets or amulets found in the area; they show that the men venerated the Sun as chief of the gods. In Syria, too, homeland of the soldiers who came next in importance to those of the Danubian region, the cult had long possessed a military character. It was the Syrian way for troops to worship the rising Sun (p. 228). His statues in eastern frontier areas are clothed in armour, with shoulder clasps ornamented by the eagles which stood not only for Rome's emperor and army but also for the solar religion.[79] In the same spirit, a new coin-type of Aurelian shows a personification of Loyalty (Fides) holding two standards and facing a figure of Sol, who with globe of world domination in hand commends the emperor to the fidelity of the legions. The cult was now officially prescribed for the army, and its symbols were added to military insignia.

In pursuance of a concept that had been developing for over a century, the Sun was the emperor's special comrade and companion (p. 223). The Danubian Probus (276–82) displays his own portrait on a bronze medallion, and together with it is a radiate head of the Sun-god, described as his comrade. Something of what people now felt for the Sun's ever-renewed Light is indicated by the Neoplatonist Iamblichus (p. 204), who gave it the place of honour among 360 deities. Moreover, when Constantius I Chlorus took London from the usurper Allectus (296) and brought England back into the empire, a medallion hailed him as Restorer of Eternal Light (REDDITOR LVCIS AETERNAE). This language, although replete with pagan traditions, is on the way to the terminology of Christian hymns. It is also solar language, for Constantius was a monotheist who revered the Sun,[80] like his forebears before him in their Sun-worshipping Balkan homeland.

Then in *c.* 309 Constantius' son Constantine the Great began his vast, homogeneous series of coinages inscribed SOLI INVICTO COMITI (p. 224).[81] Thereafter, for a decade, he continued to concentrate upon this design and theme. Indeed Constantine, before finally turning to Christianity, stressed the worship of the Sun more frequently and emphatically than any of his predecessors. Formerly, he had been officially attached to the cult of Hercules sponsored by Diocletian's colleague Maximian "Herculius" (p. 224). But when Maximian continually sought to return to the throne from which he had abdicated, Constantine broke with him (308) and, adhering to an ancient custom of claiming physical or spiritual descent from deified past rulers, attached himself to the memory of a hero-emperor who had come from his own Illyrian home country, Claudius II Gothicus (d. 270).[82] Claudius II had been a solar devotee (p. 230), and in 310—the year of Maximian's final political collapse and death—Constantine's birthday at Augusta Trevirorum referred to the young monarch having been vouchsafed a vision of his "comrade and ally" Apollo at that god's sanctuary in the Vosges. The speaker greets the rising emperor as personification of Apollo, who is bringer of salvation and the universal Sun.[83] Constantine felt a strong need for a divine companion and sponsor, and for a time the Sun, whose worship had been ancestral in his family, was his choice.

Nor did Constantine's victory over Maxentius at the Milvian Bridge (312), which the emperor and his eulogists later attributed to a Christian vision, terminate his allegiance to the cult. It was athwart the Sun that he claimed to have seen the Cross (p. 301), and on the sculptures of the Arch of Constantine at Rome (c. 315) the old gods have gone but the Sun still remains: the emperor is represented between the rising Sun and Moon, and the victory-giving figure is the Sun-god, whose statuettes are also carried by the army's standard-bearers. An inscription describes Constantine himself as the Sun who sees all.

It was not until 318–19, when the Christianization of the empire had gathered force, that the Sun disappeared from the coinage. With him went the radiate crown and the title *invictus*, now replaced by the less characteristically pagan *victor*. The coins, conservative as ever, had not been very quick to turn Christian. They were intended for the whole empire, which was still predominantly pagan; and so, no doubt, was the administration of the imperial mints. Even as late as 321, when official Christianity was forming deep roots, Constantine forbade legal proceedings on the day of the week "celebrated by the veneration of the Sun". Since the second century the choice of the seventh day for Christian meetings had been justified by its interpretation as the day both of the Creation and Resurrection,[84] but Constantine, apparently, believed that Christians observed the day because it was already sacred to Sol. Moreover, in the east, his fellow-emperor Licinius was still seeking the loyalty of his Danubian troops by a solemn profession to "the Highest Holy God".[85] But the future did not belong to Licinius, who soon afterwards succumbed to his colleague. Constantine was now sole ruler of the Roman world and arbiter of its religion, upon which he had already begun to impose such revolutionary changes. Yet his panegyrist still sees him "with a circumambient halo resembling rays of light"; and when his great statue was erected at the central point of the new capital at Constantinople (328–30), it portrayed him as Apollo-Helios, wearing the Sun's radiate Crown. This crown, however, was also fashioned from the nails of the True Cross, for he now saw himself as the Vicegerent of Christ. In his own mysterious way, Constantine seems to have worshipped Sun and Christ at the same

233

time, or regarded them as interchangeable, assimilating the Christian faith into an inherited solar tradition as Aurelian had assimilated the Sun into the traditions of Rome.

Indeed, there was nothing novel about such an association between Sun-worship and Christianity. The solar theology contributed to the Old Testament by the prophet Malachi had been Christianized, and so had the Ascent of Elijah which was also the Ascent of the Sun (pp. 225, 220). In the time of Marcus Aurelius, Jesus' baptism had been described as the Bath of Helios.[86] Christians in east and west, in their public and private prayers, turned to Oriens, the rising Sun, in order to glorify its resurrection from the prison of the dark, which they identified with the Resurrection of Christ. Origen (d. 254/5) linked Christ with the rising of the Sun[87]—and in the same period a mosaic beneath St. Peter's showed a composite Christ-Helios (p. 280). Some people confused the two deities: fourth-century Christian writers criticized co-religionists for their veneration of Sol, pointing out the superiority of the Christian Sun of Justice to the pagan Sun.[88] Owing to such links and analogies, the solar cult acted as a bridge by which many people were converted to Christianity.

That is partly why devotees of the Sun, in spite of all these connections, were among the fiercest enemies of the Christians. When Julian the Apostate (361–3) temporarily brought the official religion of the empire back to paganism, he was moved by a prophecy to choose the worship of the Sun, the religion of his Illyrian ancestors, and censured his relative Constantine for deserting it. Julian himself proclaimed this faith in his Hymn to Helios. The Sun-god, common father of all mankind and object of our longing, seemed to him, in the fashion of contemporary philosophical thought, intermediary between the One and the material world from which it is so remote (p. 187); for our own eyes can see the solar power changing and swaying the cosmos.[89] As late as A.D. 400, when the empire had become Christian again, Macrobius observed that almost all gods are the Sun, for he is the Mind of the Universe.[90]

St. Leo the Great (d. 461) complained that Christians still worshipped the Sun. Acclamations of Byzantine emperors continued to compare them to the rising Sun-god, and solar and lunar images were long retained in the rituals of Christmas and Epiphany, the Feast of Lights.[91]

Why then did Sun-worship fail to remain the religion of the empire? Its most attractive features were simplicity and obviousness and ready justification: the Sun was there for all to see, and everyone could appreciate its indispensable, beneficial, creative activities. Moreover, although its abstract and learned side proved convenient to rulers as a theology on which to base their own domination, the cult was not limited to intellectuals and the governing classes; for there were no more passionate Sun-worshippers than the ordinary unintellectual soldiers of the Roman army. And yet the creed was deficient in profundity, emotional intimacy and heartening humanity. It did not grapple with the root problem of evil like the Manichaeans. It was weak in the appeals which endeared the mystery religions to millions. It also lacked two allurements which were the strength of Christianity: the explicit promises of immortality which cheered poor people in desperate times, and the excitement of a Messiah who was believed to have been an actual historical figure.

Some of the advocates of Sun-worship were aware of these disadvantages and attempted to remedy them. For example, a historical Saviour was provided. Septimius' Syrian women-folk who gave official prominence to their family's worship of the Sun (p. 228) also took the initiative by adding this further attraction of a solar Messiah. For the cosmopolitan-minded writers and scholars (mainly Greeks or Hellenized orientals) who gathered round Julia Domna included Philostratus,[92] who at her prompting wrote a descriptive eulogy (c. A.D. 217–18) of Apollonius of Tyana in eastern Asia Minor. That man, who had lived by the first century A.D., acquired the reputation of being a wizard, and may have possessed mediumistic powers. But Philostratus transforms Apollonius into a holy man who practises and preaches a religion of the cosmos based upon the Sun. Apollonius declares, in tones suggestive of mysticism, that the air is his chariot, and that those who would sing his praise must rise from the earth and soar aloft with the god (p. 204).[93] The writer is also careful to inject Sun-worship with the human interest which was its most serious deficiency. For every kind of spicy out-of-the-way anecdote is utilized to represent the solar devotee Apollonius as a virtuous, saintly, ascetic, miracle-working paragon leading a dramatic life in which he loved and helped his fellow-men, following

Pythagoras (whose life he wrote) in his detestation of blood sacrifices. This career, echoing the Gospels and parodying Christian martyrologies, could be set against Jesus' life in rivalry—or even with a claim to superiority, since Apollonius' alleged defiance of the tyrant Domitian seemed more comprehensible than the humiliation of Jesus (p. 274).

The faith ostensibly propounded by Apollonius, and subsequently associated with his name, was a philosophical Sun-worshipping paganism possessing its own historical Messiah and approximating to a religious system. Eastern influences were also freely admitted. Indeed, in accordance with Julia Domna's tastes and a current fashion for oriental travel-romances (p. 165), Philostratus deliberately stressed the debt of Apollonius to Indian thinkers who had anticipated even the Egyptians in the wisdom with which they practised mysticism and avoided the sacrifice of animals.[94] In recognition, moreover, of strong Babylonian elements in contemporary thought, Philostratus suggested that information about Apollonius had come to light from a memoir by Damis, a native of that country.

Caracalla built an important temple of Apollonius, and along with Christ, Abraham and Orpheus he was said to be represented in Severus Alexander's private shrine.[95] Apollonius was also reported to have appeared to Aurelian in a vision; and anti-Christians pointed to the sage of Tyana as their model.[96] Christians retaliated by charging him with irresponsible and immoral fatalism, demonology and black magic.[97] But his religion succumbed to theirs, in spite of imperial patronage, because it fell between the two stools of philosophy and religion, and achieved little more than a fashionable donnish artificiality.

Gospels of Salvation

Meanwhile another, very different attitude to Sun-worship, more deeply rooted in religious feeling, enjoyed far greater success in providing the personal, emotional, dramatic satisfaction which the Sun cult, for all its imposing simplicity, lacked. This was Mithraism, which also linked solar theology with the other outstanding pagan movement of the time, the dualism of good and evil powers (p. 248). The religion of Mithras contained this dualism in its ancient

Persian form—or rather in the popular Iranian versions of the belief which were current on and beyond the Persian borders. But Mithras, although the Romans regarded his origins as Persian,[98] came to them, as his Phrygian cap shows, by way of Asia Minor, taking on Hellenistic elements there, and other accretions in the Balkans as the cult expanded towards the west.

In origin, he was an ancient Indo-European god dating back even before the legendary Zoroaster. Throughout Iranian lands he attended upon Ahuramazda, in eternal opposition to the evil power Ahriman, and was the ally and agent (or even sometimes the off-spring) of the all-powerful Sun, who is shown feasting and riding with him in the chariot that at the last conveyed Mithras up to heaven. A sacrament celebrated his Last Meal, which he shared with the Sun. Mithras himself was god of the Morning Light: a small marble altar of his cult is inscribed "to the Rising One" (p. 228).[99] And indeed from about the first century A.D. he and the Sun were identified with one another.

Mithraism, then, could seem to be a specialized form of the Sun-worship which was soon to assume increasingly official shape (p. 229). But the religion of Mithras always retained its private character. Certainly it received state approval. Otherwise there would not have been a large Mithraeum in the substructure of the Baths of Caracalla, nor (though Mithras figures sparsely in imperial sculpture) would there have been a bust of Mithras-Sol within the folds of Rome's veil on a relief of Diocletian in the Roman Forum. Moreover, if approbation by the authorities had been lacking, a dedication at Carnuntum (Petronell) in the Danubian region— where Mithraism was very strong—could scarcely have described Mithras-Sol as the favourer of the tetrarchs' rule (A.D. 307).[100] But the private nature of the cult, even if other evidence had been lacking, is confirmed by numismatic information: or rather, lack of information, because the imperial coinage shows a remarkable unanimity of silence. Among the hundreds of official coin-designs that venerated the Sun (and not a few which celebrated the Mystery faiths), there is not one single specific reference to Mithras. This total contrast cannot be accidental. Even the local bronze coins which cities were allowed to issue for purely regional circulation include few representations of the god. In his characteristic bull-slaying role (p. 239) he only appears on a single isolated city-issue under Gordian III at Tarsus in Cilicia, a land of famous sanctuaries of the Sun and Moon where the Romans perhaps first encountered Mithraic devotees.[101]

In contrast to the intense, increasing publicity for its official counterpart the Sun-cult, Mithraism was not a court religion. Out of all the long list of emperors, only four are known to have had any direct interest in this faith.[102] Moreover, the epoch in which Aurelian elevated the Sun to official supremacy (p. 231) comprises the very years when Mithraic inscriptions happen to be exceptionally infrequent; they are at their height before 250 and after 284. Despite its kinship with the religion of the Sun, Mithraism presented a contrast because it had no public ceremonies and no professional priestly class. Though loyal to the government, it was personal, supplying the intimate element which Sun-worship lacked.

Yet it had gone ahead very rapidly. This advance was less apparent in Asia Minor, from which the cult had originally spread, than throughout the great cosmopolitan ports and trading centres, in the west even more than in the east. Nearly fifty shrines of Mithras are identifiable in Rome and its suburbs alone, and eighteen more have been discovered at Ostia—eleven from the later second century A.D., and seven after 200. Mithras was also venerated at Alexandria and the Piraeus, and at Carthage, Puteoli (Pozzuoli) and London, where the Walbrook shrine is sixty feet long.

The worshippers included numerous merchants and imperial civil servants, members of a middle-class urban society which was prosperous in the earlier part of the period; and many freedmen and educated slaves. But it was the army, and particularly the officers, who more than anyone else diffused these beliefs. For Mithras had displayed unsparing, heroic, Herculean effort: like the Sun with whom he came to be assimilated, he was Unconquerable (p. 228). In grim times these were the qualities needed, and they spurred men to an active and militant form of the asceticism characteristic of the age (p. 181). Mithras had, indeed, much to offer. He provided a strong ethical basis that was lacking in Sun-worship and was weak or equivocal in the other Mystery religions (p. 241). His worshippers must resemble him in purity and continence; moreover, as god of Light he became the business man's patron of truthful dealings and obligations. Light must kill Matter, in dualist fashion (p. 257), and so Mithras, in the most familiar and typical of his sculptural representations, has to slay the first of living creatures, the Bull, in order that its blood and seed may create the world. But the god was also compassionate, for artists imprint upon his features the reluctance and emotion with which he did the deed that represents the tragedies of the whole world.

His worship also contained in melodramatic and even violent form all the excitement inherent in the initiation of an elect, which was such a prominent aspect of contemporary religion (p. 253). These secret initiations (*mysteria*) included rigorous and sometimes deliberately horrifying tests, ordeals and expiations aimed at developing by harsh means that imperviousness to circumstances which had long been an ideal (p. 180). In order to be at one with Mithras, who had risen to heaven, the would-be initiate had his hands bound with chickens' intestines, and, before these could be removed, he was thrown across a pit filled with water. A cell equipped for inflicting extremities of heat and cold has been found at Procolitia (Carrawburgh). There were also tortures and brandings and the shedding of blood. But after these pains came supremely rewarding privileges and promises for the hereafter. Another strength of Mithraism was its readiness to offer a welcome and an assimilation to other religions. For example, the statues, reliefs and emblems of a variety of Mystery cults were found in the London temple, where they may have been collected together and hidden to avoid Christian wreckers.

The worship of Mithras, then, had ideas, moral urgency, emotional intensity and receptive breadth. It also possessed considerable superficial resemblances to Christianity. Mithraic baptisms, sacrifices, communal meals and martyrdoms seemed to the church a sinister mimicry of its own rites and sacraments.[103] Yet Christianity won the day. In part this was because the story of Mithras, although the subject of a "biography" recounting his ostensible exploits, sounded too mythical for his devotees really to feel that they had ever happened upon this earth: he seemed much more distant than Jesus, whose life as a historical figure kindled the imagination of millions. Moreover, the cult of Mithras was a stern one. Even if he showed pity, it was the pity which accompanied an act of killing. His religion lacked the tenderness and sympathy which alone could solace the poor for their misfortunes; the socially indiscriminate popular appeal of Christianity was not there. Besides, Mithraism was a masculine creed and had no place for women—who form the basic element in most successful religions—whereas Christianity incorporated them as its most faithful element.

Mithraism was only one of the Mystery religions of initiation which promised and bestowed upon their elect salvation from the miseries of their lives. This salvation was effective already, if only symbolically, in this world, but more particularly in the next. For when people were initiated, they were progressively raised beyond the reach of fate and hostile heavenly bodies. Neither these nor the troubles and demons of this earth can touch the initiate any longer.

Although some of the Mystery religions were very old, it was during the first three centuries A.D., when the corporeal world increasingly seemed evil, that they spread with particular rapidity throughout the Roman empire. Their magical purifications promised escape and rescue through personal union with a Saviour God who was believed, in many cases, to have died and risen again. The initiations which carried the worshipper along this path of immortality provided sharp emotional experiences conveying a new conception of other-worldly power and holiness; and every device of elaborate organization and stage-management was exploited to intensify the excitement.

Participation in the ancient worship of Demeter (Ceres) and Persephone (Proserpina) at Eleusis ensured the favour of the subterranean deities who have power over the after-life. This blessed state was achieved by three stages of initiation. To the end of paganism, the Eleusinian Mysteries were the most venerated institution in Greek religion, and Roman emperors still participated in their rites. One of them was Gallienus, whom an official coinage strangely feminizes and turns into one of these goddesses as GALLIENA AVGVSTA, personified with corn-ears and wreath.

Another cult of extreme antiquity was that of Cybele and Attis. "Be of good cheer, initiates", cried their priests, "since the god is saved! Because we too, after our labours, shall find salvation!"[104] For just as Attis, according to this primeval cult of Asia Minor, dies and is reborn annually with the vegetation of the year, so amid hysterical, orgiastic pageantry and the din of cymbals, horns and flutes his initiates are likewise saved. And this worship of Cybele and Attis was often accompanied by the sacrifice of bulls and goats, their blood pouring down into underground chambers to drench the initiates and confer upon them rebirth for ever.[105] Even the sensible, serene Antoninus Pius was a devotee of the cult of Cybele. So was his wife Faustina the elder; unlike Mithraism, it was a religion particularly successful with women, and from that time onwards the official coinage confers upon many empresses, including especially the second Faustina who was the wife of Marcus Aurelius, implicit identification with the goddess.

But it was the initiation and resplendent cult-drama of the Egyptian Isis, though less prominent in numismatic propaganda, which gave the most glowing and exciting promises of escape from this world into a glorious life to come. At the Finding every November of her counterpart Osiris, god of the year's birth and death and of the underworld, the initiate passed symbolically through all the elements, visited the lower world, and met the gods face to face in triumph. Plutarch identified Isis with the wisdom that confers a knowledge of the highest, and the novelist Apuleius, though he scoffs at the old gods, believed passionately that Isis was his salvation (p. 159). He clothes his belief in moving, shimmering words which, across the centuries and gulfs that separate our ways of thinking, make it almost possible to understand why countless men felt the same. And especially women: for Isis, even more than Cybele, exercised powerful feminine appeal.

Dionysus (Bacchus) too, whose worship was linked with the Sun-cult (p. 226) and other moods and currents of the time, punishes unbelievers, and as a host of funeral reliefs testify, dramatically rewards men and, women initiates alike in the world to come. But the weakness of this faith, in an age when thoughtful people hankered after austerity, was a too easy conception of the next world as a jolly, sensual place. In the long run this facile appeal meant unsuccessful competition with more ascetic convictions. Yet Dionysus mobilized countless adherents. Funeral reliefs show them in the company of their Saviour, celebrating for evermore a sacred reunion and marriage, and the eternal banquet of the blessed.

These numerous depictions of the immortality attained through Dionysus are only a small proportion of the sarcophagus reliefs illustrating people's urgent desire for salvation from the evils of this world. Such sarcophagi, reviving a widespread Mediterranean custom which had spread from the orient to Greece in classical times, created one of the major art-forms of the later second and third centuries A.D. The Roman world had experienced a massive, revolutionary, reversion from cremation to the long-since obsolete rite of burial.[106] The change was due to the desire for an after-life which attracted so many to the Mystery religions. That other world was envisaged in terms of human experience; there was an inarticulate but almost universal feeling that the future welfare of the soul depended upon comfortable repose of the body, which is its temple and mirror. This involved a contradiction. No doubt the dead dwell with the gods and heroes—or in some other spiritual sphere. Yet they also sleep in their sarcophagi, upon which their reclining forms are often depicted. What lies in the sarcophagi seems to possess something more than a purely symbolic significance, and the well-being of the dead still needs to be secured by reverent devotion to their material remains.

These remains were individual, and the receptacles and other attentions dedicated to them must be individual too. For the after-life was now understood to be a personal affair. Men must expect a posthumous reward or judgement; death was not the fullstop which it had often seemed to Marcus Aurelius (p. 180). There must therefore be a gentler, more respectful emphasis upon the dead man's autonomous personality. In order that his remains should not be scattered, they were buried, and to do them honour the monuments of burial—steles, altars, chapels, pyramids, towers, but especially sarcophagi—were often adorned with sculptural reliefs that are the finest work of their time. They strike various tactful balances between terrestrial recognition and posthumous salvation. The human features are usually depicted with particular care and skill (p. 122), because they reflect the soul's survival as a personal entity that has won its right to paradise.

These sarcophagus reliefs exhibit a bewildering, endlessly ramifying multiplicity of doctrines indicating the manner of escape from this world's evils that the next world is to bring. This multiplicity is reflected in an equally massive diversity of aesthetic methods and attitudes. At Rome, the typical sarcophagus is carved on three sides, the fourth being intended to stand against a wall. These Roman sarcophagi are primarily intended as display-surfaces for narrative pictures; according to the Assyrian-Babylonian formula of overall composition favoured by the Columns of Trajan and Marcus Aurelius (p. 119), their long front side is often covered with a single, intricate, many-figured relief. Sarcophagi from the eastern provinces show less interest in narrative, and greater structural sensibility. They are carved not on three sides only like their Roman counterparts, but on all four. These monuments are free-standing eternal dwellings, and so their reliefs display architectural frameworks founded on the classical Orders and sometimes intended to represent the tomb itself. Within these frames are niches containing human or mythological figures, in high relief or partly in the round.

While Attic workshops prefer austerer treatments, the rich forms of this recessed, columnar decoration occur frequently in Asia Minor. And it was there that the revival of decorated sarcophagi seems to have begun. One of the earliest known examples, found in Lydia (c. A.D. 170), has twisted columns, and round and pointed niches hollowed out in the form of shells.[107] But the Asian sarcophagus reached its zenith of diversity and technique in c. 220, when architectural designs achieve an elegant elaboration dissolving in strong plastic effects of light and shade.[108]

A predominant theme of sarcophagi in this period is the animated, elaborate scene of battle, standing for the annihilation of death and evil by the victorious dead. Pictures of the chase, reminiscent of an ancient Mesopotamian tradition which was revived in contemporary Persia, have a similar meaning;[109] and certain artists make the hunted lion display a pitilessly grinning mask of death. Sometimes the hunters of these animals are Erotes or Cupids, symbols of Love representing Good triumphant over Evil,[110] as in Platonic and contemporary philosophers and the romantic novelists (pp. 195, 168).

The Four Seasons, too, are seen on the wing. In the first century A.D., these Seasons had been shown as women, but then they were changed to masculine shape. Ovid had compared them with the four ages of man, yet on sarcophagi they are vigorous children or youths, because they stand for rebirth and immortality. A sarcophagus shows them beside this central Gate of Heaven of which they are the guardians[111]; the design inspired Michelangelo's first plan for the tomb of Julius II, just as other sarcophagi had guided Italian sculptors from Niccolà Pisano onwards. A sarcophagus of c. 220–40 shows the Four Seasons with Dionysus,[112] from whom the pious dead receive the gifts of prosperity and bliss that the Seasons symbolize. The static foreground, displaying the calm assurance of salvation, is skilfully contrasted with an animated backcloth which illustrates the teeming life beyond the tomb.

Often there are frameworks of cosmic symbols, suggestive of nature's continuity. Castor and Pollux, the Dioscuri who preside over the alternations of night and day, represent the passage from this world to the light hereafter; and similarly at Edessa in Mesopotamia a series of mosaics which depict the soul's future life includes a Phoenix symbolizing resurrection (235-6). Later in the same century, a sarcophagus portraying Prometheus' creation of human beings, which foreshadows their rebirth in another world, adds a new subtlety by showing the image of a dead child as if life is only suspended, not extinct.[113] Moreover, as philosophy attained a new fashionable stature during and after the time of Plotinus, the philosopher-sage is frequently seen on sarcophagi, and so are the Muses. These are restrained Hellenic representations expressing the soul's freedom from the passions and oppressions of matter, and its nostalgic hope of joining the lofty spirits of the past after the appropriate guidance and initiation (p. 204).

Reliefs showing boys at school are likewise reflections of this instructional, initiatory motif. They came from Noviomagus (Neumagen) on the Moselle, and throughout the western provinces there are local variations and elaborations upon the Roman and Attic and Asian funeral themes. In addition to the school-scenes, Germany and Gaul provide a number of other attractive realistic studies (imitated by Romanesque sculptors) of the living man at his daily work—compliments to his worldly activities, which at the same time allegorize his soul's struggle in this world to happiness in the next.

All such examples of funeral art reflect religious views which promised their initiates escape in the afterlife from the evils inherent in our world. Others preferred the even more ancient methods of astrology and magic. For example, sarcophagi of the Danubian area specialize in solar and astrological signs, and north African monuments abound in magical symbols to ward off evil. Moreover, magic had the further advantage of being able to alter one's lot in this world without waiting for the next.

In previous centuries certain Greeks, and even occasionally a few Romans, had made valiant attempts at rationality, but these had not usually been very widespread or lasting. Adrift in the vast, impersonal world of later Rome, people lost their nerve when they considered the hopelessness of working out their own futures by themselves. And so they fled from the thought into total unreason. Fortune had long seemed to many the only governor of the universe (p. 162). Or was it Fate? As a third-century philosopher pointed out, you could not consistently believe in both at the same time.[114] In this religious age, an interfering Fate seemed on the whole more likely than a capricious and inconsistent Fortune. Besides, belief in Fate was less discouraging because, although it was impossible to influence Fortune, surely Fate could somehow be turned.

This must be done through the heavenly bodies; for an enormous majority of the people in the Roman Empire identified Fate with these celestial powers. Since universal sympathy binds heaven to earth, movements of the Sun, Moon and stars must direct the fates of mankind, predestining all that will happen (p. 225). There were dissentients,[115] but few thinkers questioned the influence of the heavenly bodies upon human affairs. And yet countless men and women found acceptance of this mechanistic destiny unendurable, and sought means whereby its oppressiveness could somehow be mitigated. The first step was to investigate what heaven was intending; and then to determine and time one's own activities so as to avoid its most hostile influences. But these difficult tasks could only be performed with the help of professional astrologers, who consequently became an extremely influential class in the ancient world. Reliance upon their powers was almost universal.

Astrology was an easy and pseudo-scientific way of escaping the intolerable burden. And there were other "solutions" where the veneer of rationality was thinner still. For throughout the whole of this period magical practices of all kinds, always strong, waxed still more abundant and powerful. Dreams, too, seemed to offer counsel; even Marcus Aurelius believed in them, and Tertullian's Christianity allowed him to say that most people obtain their knowledge of God from dreams.[116] The novelists of the time bear repeated witness to an intense faith in oracles and prophecies. Such beliefs received fresh impetus from the "Chaldaean oracles". This theosophical hotch-potch of horoscope-making, which purported to provide translations from Zoroaster, throve upon popular interest in Babylonian antiquities after Trajan's conquests, and developed further in about the time of Marcus Aurelius when a certain Julianus evolved a higher or religious form of magic known as theurgy, later favoured by Neoplatonists such as Iamblichus (p. 204). There was also an ever-increasing use of private spiritualistic mediums, especially boys.[117] Egypt had always sought to influence events by magic,[118] and before developing a national literature the Coptic language was an adjunct of magicians. They and they alone seemed able to prevail against the miseries of the times, as well as performing a variety of special tasks: in Africa for example, inscriptions employ witchcraft for the doping of race-horses. As these primitive irrational elements surged up to drown the man-centred self-assertion of the classical age, there was a ready belief in miracles. Nor was it always officially discouraged. The Column of Marcus Aurelius shows a military engine on the enemy side struck by a thunderbolt as a result of prayer, and then illustrates the salvation of Rome's armies by the Miracle of Rain (c. 173), weirdly depicted in ghostly, semi-personalized form. This event was later attributed to the prayers of Christian soldiers of the Twelfth Legion. But in pagan and official circles it was ascribed to invocations of Thoth (identified with Hermes or Mercury), offered by an Egyptian magician Arnuphis, a companion of the emperor (p. 255).

Why, it was asked, are serious men interested in lies about miracles, and why do sick people long to invent them and make them plausible?[119] Because the age had lost all hope or prospect or desire of solving its problems by common-sense means; this was an epoch in which hardly anyone any longer had his feet on the ground.

But who could have asked such a question as this?—for it shows precisely that note of unbelief which had become so unfamiliar. Its author was the man who also made fun of contemporary "travel" literature, Lucian of Samosata on the Euphrates (p. 166). His native language was Syriac, but his books are in Greek which he had learnt at school[120]; and he wrote with penetrating adroitness throughout most of the later second century A.D. During an epoch of gravity, tension and unreason, "the steady advance of the irrational in the form of an escapist mysticism or banal superstition is accompanied by the laughter of a man whose outlook was scepticism and whose trade ridicule".[121] Many a sparkling, scoffing dialogue or literary letter of Lucian hits hard, if sometimes superficially, at these overwhelming tendencies of his time. Religion is the target of a number of his pamphlets. He tells how the sensible philosopher, following the anti-conventional Cynic principles of Diogenes, flies to heaven in order to rise above the confusion of contradictory dogmas. Jupiter, and elsewhere Minos the judge of the dead, is hard put to it to understand his own relationship with Fate. The gods are upset—because they have been proved not to exist. And one of their spokesmen deplores the large influx of new members to the Olympian club.[122]

These entertainments are more or less in the realm of literary religion, but then Lucian turns to some of the peculiar hysterical phenomena of his own day. He writes scathingly of the wandering, abusive preacher Peregrinus, an amorist, temporary Christian, flagellant and suspected parricide, called after the shape-changing Proteus because of his versatility, whose morbid craving for notoriety impelled him to throw himself in the fire at the Olympic Games (A.D. 165)—whereupon his memory became the object of devotions attracting numerous pilgrims.[123] Next Lucian shows up an even more disgraceful adventurer who had long battened on contemporary credulity, Alexander of Abonutichus in northern Asia Minor. The quack prophet of a snake, whose macabre, sheep-headed, human haired image has recently been found at Tomis (Constanţa in Rumania), Alexander used every kind of sleight of hand, confidence trick and lechery to win a considerable following, in which upperclass female supporters were prominent; his daughter married the governor of Asia, and the cult even survived its founder's death.

Lucian analyses the methods by which a rascal like this comes to the top.

> Just as Alexander was beginning to grow a beard, his master died and left him without any means of support—for he couldn't live on his looks any more. However, he now had more ambitious plans, so he teamed up with an even lower type, a ballet-dancer from Byzantium—I think he was called Cocconas—and the two of them went round cheating and fleecing "fatheads"—a technical term used by magicians to denote people with money. While they were so engaged, they came across a Macedonian heiress who was past her prime but still liked to be thought attractive. They lived on her for some time, and when she went back to Macedonia, they went too. . . .
> There they saw some enormous snakes, which were so tame and domesticated

that women used to keep them as pets, and children even took them to bed with them. They didn't mind being pinched or trodden on, and would actually take milk from the breast like babies. The couple bought a magnificent specimen for a few coppers, and that, as Thucydides would say, was how it all started. For those two unscrupulous adventurers put their heads together, and decided "that human life is ruled by a pair of tyrants called Hope and Fear", and if you treat them right, you can make a lot of money out of them. They saw that the one thing people want, the one thing they must have when they're oppressed by either Hope or Fear, is information about the future. That was why places like Delphi, Delos, Claros (Colophon) and Branchidae (Didyma) had become so fabulously wealthy—because the tyrants I mentioned made people keep going there and paying exorbitant prices, in cattle or in gold, for any sort of prophecy. Having turned these facts over in their minds, they finally cooked up a plan to establish an oracle of their own. If all went well, they expected it to show an immediate profit—and in fact the results surpassed their wildest dreams. . . .[124]

But Lucian's scepticism about such impostors, like scepticism in general (p. 252), was out-of-date—an almost isolated survival from a past age in which intellectual penetration had been more widespread and more highly regarded. Nowadays the problems that racked people's minds were spiritual, and their solutions ranged all the way from the charlatanism of Alexander of Abonutichus to the profundity of Plotinus or Mani.

Mani: The Good and Evil Powers

The last section showed how millions of people sought various means of religious escape from the evils of the times. But, many more especially if they were thoughtful, were tormented by the eternally topical problem: why does such evil exist? If the world was created or is controlled by a beneficent and all-powerful God or gods, how can this be? Browning in his *Mihrab Shah* called it the most issueless and tragic of all the dilemmas of mankind:

> Wherefore should any evil hap to man—
> From ache of flesh to agony of soul—
> Since God's All-mercy makes All-potency?
> Nay, why permits He evil to Himself?—

If a bullet causes apparently pointless evil by mistake, asked William James, should God (1) prevent this, (2) deflect the bullet, (3) undo the injury? Each of these causes involves reversals of the law of nature, and (3) also implies by the initial error a doubt of

God's sovereign power. And (1), (2) and (3) alike deny the freedom of the human will, a cardinal belief of Christianity which had also been stressed by Epictetus and Marcus Aurelius (p. 180). If the world were forced to be good and happy, said Berdyaev, "man would have lost his likeness to God, which primarily resides in his freedom". The arguments of Catholic Theodicy defend the justice and righteousness of God in the face of this fact of evil.

> Those dark, deadly, devastating ways,
> How do you bear them, suffer them? I praise![125]

Christian Scientists respond by dismissing evil, not exactly as the supreme unreality like Plotinus (p. 191), but still as an illusion. Other modern thinkers speak of an internal dualism locating opposition to good within a single divine nature. When, however, this question why the world contains so much evil preoccupied the people of late antiquity, they sought different solutions. The deplorable and ever-present facts of life, it was felt, cannot be harmonized with the supposition that the world is made and managed by an all-powerful and all-beneficent god or gods, for if they were all-powerful and all-beneficent there would not be evil. This can, therefore, only be explained by the existence of *two* powers, not only a good one but an evil one—which must have created this world.

A dualist view of the divine power is found in the earlier Egyptian legends which tell of the struggle between Horus and Set, day and night, good and evil; and the problem of evil is discussed in the *Dialogue of a Misanthrope with his own soul* (*c.* 2000 B.C.). But the classic formulation of the dilemma is Job's. "The earth is given into the hand of the wicked. God covereth the faces of the judges thereof: if not, where and who is he? . . . God hath shaken me to pieces." Job does not venture upon a dualist solution. Nor does the Preacher (*Ecclesiastes*), who considers the same theme. Yet during the successive stages of the composition of the Old Testament, Satan changes from an over-zealous member of the heavenly court, not indeed into a second principal power, but at least into a bad spirit who entices man to disobey divine commands.[126] Satan appears more frequently in the later than the earlier books of the Old Testament. The change is partly due to Persian influence, for the Persians, influenced by the legendary Zoroaster, had developed a thoroughgoing dualism. Although they believed in many gods, their basic theological fact was the strife between the good power of Light, Ahuramazda (Ormuzd), and the power of Darkness, Ahriman. Even if an ultimate optimism was justifiable—and Zoroaster is lyrical in praise of Creation[127]—the mentality which dominated western Asia was pessimistic as far as the measurable future was concerned. Ahriman, the older of the two gods, controls the world, and the fight must go on until victory is eventually achieved by Ahuramazda—his counterpart on earth being the Persian Great King whose seals represent the god and himself as twin images.

Such dualism seems inherent in the Indo-European languages, in which the root "two" stands for badness—dishonourable, dyspepsia, dubious, bévue, Zweifel. The Buddhist epic the *Dhammapada* asks, "How is there laughter, how is there joy, as the world is always burning?" To the Hindu sage Yajnavalkya, existence is "this patched together hiding-place".

In Greece, Athenian tragic dramatists had been preoccupied by the problem of evil. The contrast between celestial and terrestrial worlds was stressed by Plato, who anticipated modern theologians by claiming that Zeus was not wholly responsible for evil happenings.[128] Then Epicurus formulated the problem in timeless terms: is the divine power impotent or malevolent? If neither, whence comes evil?

In later Greek and Roman times, the dilemma was restated in the ancient terms of the two powers, of good and evil. Within this dualistic framework the restatement assumed a thousand different forms, which added up to a dominant religion of the age. There were many reasons why this came about. Among them were the increasing preoccupations with morality and individual salvation, displayed respectively by Marcus Aurelius' *Meditations* and by a thousand sarcophagi. But dualism was also encouraged by the obvious proliferation of evil—visible in civil war and economic collapse—and the failure of the traditional Olympian religion to provide an explanation. To the Jews, as well, the catastrophe of their risings against the Romans seemed to show that God had failed to act and could not act.[129] Philosophers such as Epictetus and Marcus had stressed the utter instability of the human condition; another writer described it as no better than a nightmare.

Moreover, Persian ideas had been seeping towards the west for centuries, particularly through Mesopotamia, the cockpit of empires and faiths; and Greco-Roman dualism recognized Zoroaster among its prophets. The forty treatises found at Chenoboskion (Nag Hammadi) in Egypt include an *Apocalypse of Zoroaster*, and one of the texts found at Qumran on the dead Sea, the *Manual of Discipline*, explains the origin of evil in terms of Zoroastrian dualism. This had begun to come westwards in the second century B.C., through the Greek writings of Persian priests in Asia Minor. These "Magi" produced a purified text of their holy writ the *Avesta*, which was rendered into Aramaic characters in Parthia and thus became more accessible. There were traces of Buddhism in the dualists' dismissal of material nature as illusion; and sorcery and demonology made their contributions. Many dualists also drew heavily upon Christianity, and indeed believed themselves to be Christians.

Throughout all this phantasmagoric variety of beliefs ran the general theme that the world, created by the evil power, must be condemned, and that man, to escape the imprisoning vileness of the body, must purge what is non-spiritual within him. For the spirit is in him, too, waiting for realization; seeing that human spirits are fragments, incarcerated in the body, of the vast luminous divine light beyond the sky (p. 226). Some drew positive and optimistic conclusions from this situation, and there were thorough pessimists who believed that the material universe ought not to be there at all. Yet the purpose of all their faiths was to rescue and uplift a being who is good but fallen, the visible universe being an evil prison. From Time also man must obtain deliverance. The official Persian (Sassanian) religion of the third and later centuries A.D. regarded Time as the original Principle producing the good and evil spirits alike,[130] but to many dualists it was a defilement, an enemy and a horror. "In this world (of Darkness) I was living for a thousand myriads of years, *no one knowing that I was there.*"

But escape from the world and its evils is possible: man possesses the consciousness of good which allows such an escape. There is a way out of the prison, while we still remain in the body. We must give expression to what is spiritual in us and "flee to our own country". A fresco painted soon after A.D. 200 at Rome (Viale Manzoni) shows this idea in terms of the return of Odysseus—the soul's return to the land where it belongs.

But how are we to get there? The answer is provided by the second characteristic feature of dualist doctrine, which has given it the synonym of Gnosticism. For escape can only be effected by knowledge (*Gnosis*). But this is not the rationalist sort of knowledge for which the leading thinkers of the ancient world had been striving; this is neither science nor common sense. The last great theory of knowledge, formulated by Chrysippus the director of the Stoics in the third century B.C., had been shattered by Carneades (d. *c.* 128 B.C.), who was founder of the New Academy in Plato's line but a sceptic above all else. Carneades had denied all possibility of knowledge,[131] and his tradition was maintained in the later second century A.D. by the physician Sextus Empiricus, who has given us our only complete account of ancient Scepticism. His chief principle is *suspense of judgement*: "there is no agreed opinion on justice, courage or religion".[132] Like Carneades before him, Sextus was attacking knowledge acquired by supposedly rational means. Neither of them meant to imply that reverence for wholly irrational "knowledge" should instead be encouraged; but such was the result when they discouraged the rational kind.

Sextus' contemporary, Lucian of Samosata of Cynic leanings, tried jeering at the ever-increasing irrationality of the times, and did so very amusingly (p. 247), but he was kicking against the pricks. Daylight reality was ceasing to be trusted.[133] The dualists or Gnostics are not intellectuals. Their "knowledge" of the secrets of the universe is acquired through piety and inner vision. This is the illumination bred not of reasoning or dialectical struggling but of proclaimed revelation: what premises were to the philosophers, revelation was to the dualists.[134] *Gnosis* was given its name by Persian Magi practising in Babylon and Egypt. But its attitudes recall beliefs in the magic liberating power of knowledge that had already been apparent in the early Vedic philosophy and then the early *Upanishads* (from the eighth century B.C.) and the *Bhagavad Gita* which originated some six hundred years later. Meanwhile the followers of Pythagoras supplied the Greco-Roman world with the idea of knowledge, acquired under instruction and discipline, as at once the condition and the end of sanctification (*c.* 500 B.C.).

The knowledge attained by the Gnostics gave its recipients special privileges not only here but hereafter. A stele-relief shows how life's choice of good and evil is repeated in that next world: the possessors of *Gnosis* are redeemed not just now but for ever. In reaction against the egalitarian tendencies of the age (p. 111), the Gnostics were an elect, raised above the rank and file. Yet they were not a single religion, but a scattering of small intimate spiritual aristocracies each with elaborate scriptures of its own. These were esoteric movements shrouding the names and rituals of their deities in an atmosphere of determined secrecy, enforced by maledictions. Their messages and scriptures were therefore often complex, too complex. A divine revelation had to make some sense to its recipients, but complicated solutions looked elevated and inspired, and showed that only a true initiate could attain first-class status. Gnostics gathered together endless and often contradictory speculations and mythologizings by anonymous seers, conjuring up ever new cosmic patterns—and reinterpreting previous revelations as hitherto mistaken and misunderstood. Christianity, in particular, was subjected to these reinterpretations. But Christians such as Irenaeus and Eusebius replied that Gnosticism's outstanding weakness was its bewildering variety and absence of a Canon. For it was not a system, but a collection of diverse materials, a mythological attitude, a climate of opinion, a state of mind.[135]

Yet throughout all these fantastic structures of the imagination ran the thread of alienation and recoil from man's physical environment, which was incurably corrupt because it was the creation of an evil power.

Most surviving texts of Gnosticism range from the later third to the early fifth century A.D.[136] But there are also earlier ones, including moving hymns lamenting over our banishment in matter, and it was in the time of Antoninus Pius and Marcus Aurelius that the most talented and influential exponents of these doctrines flourished.

The first beginnings of the movement may be placed earlier still. Legend later ascribed a founder's role to Simon Magus, a sorcerer regarded by his devotees as a god; he is mentioned in the *Acts of the Apostles*.[137] Simon came from Gitta in Samaria, and it was perhaps to those regions that the origins of the Gnostics can be traced. Then the deacon Nicolaus of Antioch was said to have formulated the distinguishing doctrine of Gnosticism indicating that the visible world, being evil, had been made not by God but by a "demiurge". Next, in Hadrian's time, there were Gnostics in Egypt, where many of their texts have been discovered—and after the middle of the second century A.D. the largest of their groups, the one expressly calling itself Gnostic, appeared at Rome.[138]

Marcion of Sinope in northern Asia Minor, who abandoned Christianity in *c.* 138 and perhaps died in *c.* 170, seems to have organized something like a dualist church. Perhaps partly Iranian in culture, Marcion was struck by the contrast between the Old and New Testaments, and made their irreconcilable opposition the basis of his dualism. He hated the Old Testament, and set up the mercy of Jesus against its justice, his love against its rigour.[139] The New Testament was purged of Judaism, only St. Luke's Gospel and ten letters of St. Paul being retained. Pauline teachings were welcomed and carried to extremes, for Marcion had a pathological distaste for the world. His beliefs, endowed with an arresting simplicity so often lacking in Gnosticism, were backed by an efficient organization which, although it did not gain a footing at Rome, lived on elsewhere and outlasted its founder by centuries.

On a less organized and unified basis there were also both eastern and western disciples of Valentinus, an Egyptian who was active in Rome during the middle years of the second century A.D. The dualism of Valentinus, though too complicated and scholarly, was daringly speculative, with a psychological, indeed almost psychoanalytical, freshness and originality of its own. In his world-order Jesus played a part but was little but an incident. Evil had originated when the Fall took place before men existed; it was a Fall of Wisdom (Sophia). The demiurge, maker of the world, is of imperfect understanding—he believes he is the only god—but not wholly evil. Valentinus may also have been the author, or more probably the inspiration, of the *Gospel of Truth*.[140] The theme of this meditative work is humanity's deliverance from its plight, which, contrary to St. Paul, is due not to sin but to ignorance. The New Testament is referred to, yet this is not a specifically Christian but a Gnostic vision, showing "whence man has come and whither he is going".

To Valentinus also has been ascribed another treatise explaining the purpose of the universe, known as the *Poimandres*. Here it is man himself who has Fallen, not the abstract pre-human Wisdom of Valentinus. The *Poimandres* is the earliest and best of a collection of holy books, more literary than liturgical, which are deeply concerned, in differing ways, with revelations based upon the dualism of the good and evil forces. These writings, composed in Egypt by men of Greek speech during the second and third centuries A.D., bear the name of Hermes the Thrice-Greatest (Trismegistos), the equivalent of the god Thoth, reputed author of ancient sacred writings kept in Egyptian temples (p. 246). The wisdom of Egypt, with the prestige of its remote antiquity, seemed best able to provide revelations which would give the keys to knowledge and the after-life.

The Hermetic treatises were varied, and their collection under this single heading may be fortuitous. Every contemporary influence is present in them, with strong overtones of current Platonism and Judaism. The Hermetists, like the Gnostics, seem to have been a proliferation of small quasi-religious groups or sects; and their scriptures have something of the common Gnostic attitude according to which all research is subordinated to revelation to the elect, and revelation is designed to explain the conflict between good and evil. Some of the solutions are popular and magical, others breathe an elevated, tranquil grandeur. There are pessimistic conclusions such as the plea of the *Poimandres* that the world should be totally shunned. But there are also more hopeful arguments holding that the world of matter, being penetrated by the divinity, is good. The demiurge, who relieves God of responsibility for creating the world, is often interpreted not as an independent deity hostile to God but as an emanation or intermediary or subordinate, through whom ritual may establish communication with the deity itself and thus bring about individual redemption. According to another fertile idea, regeneration would take place not by means of any personal redeemer but through the replacement of the old self by a new divine personality. As in Plotinus' union with the divine (p. 194), the stress is on personal experience mediated by private instruction. The Hermetists influenced the Jewish Kabbala, and their lore also passed into western iconography of the fourteenth and later centuries.

By the time of Marcus Aurelius, the dualists had gained a substantial following. At Alexandria Basilides taught that men have a good and an evil soul, and that all evil is the result of personal sin, from which, however, the elect are able to escape. His curious scheme of 365 heavens—the sort of over-complexity which ultimately proved fatal to Gnosticism—represents yet another endeavour to place God out of range of the material universe, for which he is therefore not responsible. There were still followers of Basilides in fourth-century Gaul; and linked with him, perhaps, were various groups attributing revelations to Adam's third son Seth, who is no longer (like the Pharaonic Set) an enemy to the other principal gods, but the recipient of revelations at the Gates of Paradise.[141] This tradition was still retained in an eighth-century Syriac chronicle,[142] in which "Adam imparted revelations to his son Seth, and showed him his original greatness before the Transgression and his going out of Paradise."

The culminating period in the history of dualism, a decisive stage in the religion of the Roman empire as well as its eastern neighbours, began in *c.* 240 when the young Mani started to preach at the Persian (Sassanian) capital Ctesiphon, and Seleucia which lay opposite it across the Tigris. A contemporary of the other outstanding spiritual personality of the century, Plotinus, Mani taught for thirty years. By the time of his death, the Persian empire was filled with Manichaean doctrines, and within the following century they had permeated huge regions of the Roman empire. Mani's intention was to found a religious community which for the first time would embrace the entire world.

He combined first-class organizing ability with high artistic and poetic gifts, comprehensive mastery of oriental literature and Greek philosophy alike, a talent for staging ceremonial, and a reputation for miraculous acts such as levitation and the healing of demons. Brought up in a Christian community, Mani called himself the "Apostle of Jesus Christ", but among his divinely sent forerunners he included Buddha and Zoroaster as well as Jesus. Their place was on the periphery, while he himself stood in Babel or Babylon, the centre of the earth, as the Redeemer's latest and last Incarnation and the Seal of the Prophets.

The religion and philosophy of Mani can be reconstructed from writings in Greek, Latin, Arabic, Syriac, Turkish and Persian of central Asia, and the Coptic of upper Egypt. His teaching conveys a basic dualism in which both Persian and Greco-Roman strands converge. He is an eclectic unifier of doctrines from many sources,[143] a theosophist, a speculator in numerical patterns, but he is also heir to Marcion and the last of the great Gnostics, terminating one epoch and inaugurating another. Yet his doctrine is even more radical than Marcion's, and goes far beyond Christianity in its outspoken,

256

comprehensive claims to synthesize contemporary thought and employ inspiration to solve the problems of the universe.

Mani's fundamental principle is the distinction between Light and Darkness. Light-symbolism was prominent in the philosophy and religion of the day (p. 227), but Mani probably derived his particular attitude towards the opposition of the two principles from a Mesopotamian who, like himself, claimed to be an heir of Christianity, Bardaisan (p. 297).

> Light and Dark are two absolutely different eternal existences. In the past the Dark made an incursion on the Light and some of the Light became mingled with the Dark, as it is still in the Present, in this world around us; nevertheless in the Future Light and Dark will be happily separated. To Mani with the idea of Light was conjoined with everything that was orderly, peaceful, intelligent, clear, while with the Dark was conjoined everything that was anarchic, turbulent, material, muddy, a region of suffocating smoke, of destructive fire, of scorching wind, of poisonous water, of "darkness that might be felt".[145]

This damage, from which we are still suffering, began when Darkness invaded Light. Then Primal Man was called into being to repel the invasion, but he failed; the suffering of this Redeemer in need of redemption is a central theme, since his failure and Fall created the world in which we live. When he was thus temporarily overcome by the Demons of the Dark, for the time being Primal Man lost his Divine Light. Adam, who was then born, contained both Light and Darkness together, and through him and his son Seth are descended our corrupted selves (p. 256). As the world thus pursues its weary way, there is ground for final optimism, because its dirt is, all the time, slowly being blotted out by the distillation of the particles of Light into their true realm. When this has been completed, Jesus will return[146]: man will cease to exist, and the imprisoned fragments of God will return to their home. Meanwhile the body is an encumbrance. "Woe, woe to the creator of my body", laments Adam. "Woe to him who has bound my soul to it and to the rebels who enslaved me!"[147] Manichaeans often quoted St. Paul's antithesis of spirit and flesh, seeking to increase the Light in themselves by abstaining from sex and meat and wine. Except for those who interpreted the unimportance of material life in the opposite sense—as an invitation to uninhibited sensuality[148]—asceticism seemed necessary to win the cosmic conflict and attain redemption from this loathsome world.

Mani had his apostles, bishops, priests, teachers, monastic communities, rules of fasting, and confessions. He preached in Persia and north-west India, where Buddhism impressed him. But his movement had its heart in Mesopotamia and Syria and western Asia, and it absorbed the mass of dualistically, Gnostically minded people in those lands. His crusading zeal enjoyed the favour of the Persian monarch Shapur I, who knew him personally. But as time went on Mani was eclipsed in state favour by another. This was Kartir, architect of the Persian state religion which, although Mani owed it so much, claimed to need no prophet like himself for its interpretation; the King of Kings was sufficient leader for the faith. Recently discovered inscriptions in Middle Persian show how Kartir (later chief Magus and judge of the whole empire) became guardian of patriotic orthodoxy and founder of traditional fire-altars. Jews, Buddhists, Brahmins, Christians and Manichaeans were alike the objects of his persecution: the national church was to be made safe from the Euphrates to India. Shapur I found it possible to encourage Kartir and Mani at the same time. But when Shapur was dead, royal favour was withdrawn from Mani, for why, asked Bahram I, had the revelation come to him and not to his king? Mani was arrested and charged, and at Gundeshapur, under the weight of his heavy fetters, he collapsed and died (c. 274/7).

But within the next twenty years his doctrines continued to spread so rapidly, westwards as well as eastwards, that the emperors Diocletian and Maximian saw them as major dangers to the national religion of Rome. A savage imperial edict against Manichaeans was forwarded to the governor of Africa (c. 297). Like Rome's pronouncement against the Jews in 139 B.C., the edict denounces poisonous witchcraft and the abominable books with which the people had been seduced. But the Manichaeans may also have been involved in an Egyptian rebellion.[149]

To the Roman government such risings, and indeed eastern ideas in general, assumed a pro-Persian aspect. Persia was Rome's enemy, and the Manichaeans had originated there. At the very least, they were an unstable and even a socially revolutionary element on the sensitive Persian frontier, and among the suspected immigrants who filtered through its barriers into the world of Rome. And indeed these formed only a part of a larger problem, created by the many believers in Manichaeanism who wandered about and lived on charity, despising the world too much to do any work or abide by secular regulations.

Nevertheless during the century after Mani's death his doctrines became a world religion: nearly *the* world religion. Their churches extended from Turkestan to Carthage. Yet they were too pacifist and non-resistant to stand up well against repression by the Roman and Persian states: and their martyrs lacked the dramatic appeal of the Christians. When Christianity became the national religion of Rome, again the Manichaeans could not compete. For if they were too passive to form a good opposition, they were too anti-social to create a national church. Christianity made its pact with the government, but Manichaeanism meant irresponsibility, ascetic withdrawal, and potential race suicide. Nor did it fully satisfy the spiritual emotions of the time. This is reflected by the experience of its most distinguished convert, St. Augustine. For nine years he embraced the creed of Mani (373–82), because he could not believe that a good God had created evil. He was also fascinated by the apparent completeness of Manichaeanism's doctrines, which seemed to have a reasonable and consistent answer to everything. But a turning-point in world-history came when Augustine decided, partly through his studies of Plotinus (p. 205), that it was, after all, "a shocking and detestable profanity to make the wedge of darkness sunder the very nature of God".[150] Besides, if Satan created the world, how and why did God allow any good to be imprisoned in it?—the dilemma was unexplained, and the alleged scientific outlook dissolved into myths. Augustine felt it nobler and more rewarding to make the effort of faith demanded by Christianity.

A further advantage possessed by Christianity was that it had preceded Mani: and had been launched by a series of alleged historical happenings which the vague myths of the Manichaeans could not rival. Another cause of their failure to win over the generality was that, in spite of Mani's world aspirations, he preached a perfection to which only an elect of initiates could aspire. Christianity, too, went through such phases of esotericism—there are many signs of them in the New Testament—but it outgrew them and universalized its appeal (p. 267).

And yet Manichaeans continued, through a wide variety of channels, to play a vital part in world affairs. In the east, despite the passivity of its devotees, Persian persecution could not keep them down. Related to Manichaean doctrines were those of the Mandaeans, who believed in a Great King of Light, contrasted by them with the Zodiac and Seven Planets which are the creations of evil spirits. The earliest texts of the Mandaeans go back to *c.* A.D. 400, but seem to originate from an unorthodox Judaism of a date several centuries earlier. There are still today people of similar beliefs, the Sabians, in southern Iraq.[151]

Mani was translated in Arabic, and the Manichaeans were persecuted by Caliphs. Persian writers came under criticism as dualists, and dualist missionaries were denounced by the Chinese whose court they visited—though their beliefs were allowed for western barbarians. Bugug Khan (760–80), prince of the Uigurs, was converted, and proclaimed Manichaeanism as his state religion; it continued in eastern Turkestan until the end of the millennium. From the eleventh to the fourteenth centuries the doctrines of Mani gained favour in the province of Fukien, and two Manichaean works are represented in the Taoist canon. There were still Chinese Manichaeans up to modern times; perhaps there still are today.

Meanwhile the Byzantine empire, despite the strength of its church, saw the same rich Gnostic tradition kept alive by evangelical dualists. This group, following Basilides' belief that men have two souls of which one is the dwelling of a demon (p. 255), was accused of immorality because its members held that until initiation a human being is at the disposal of the devil. But its supporters became numerous in an Armenian principality on the Euphrates, which troubled the Byzantines and was persecuted by them in the ninth century. When these heretics were deported to Thrace, dualism was maintained there by the powerful Bogomil sect. In the twelfth century its numerous adherents at Constantinople were treated with hostility by the government; but two hundred years later they still flourished in the monastic centres of Mount Athos. And meanwhile Bogomilism had become the national religion of Bosnia, where it remained strong after 1400.[152] Many a popular legend and fairy-tale has kept the tradition alive.

Such sources in eastern Europe brought dualism to Italy, where Gnostics known as the Cathars (the Pure) made their appearance in the tenth and eleventh centuries. From there the doctrines spread to France, Flanders and Germany. "So it was that one great confederate dualist church arose, stretching from the Black Sea to Biscay."[153] The strength of this new, persistent Manichaeanism was mainly in Lombardy, Provence and Languedoc, where the severity of the Albigensians—as these Cathars were called from their centre at Albi—suited the melancholy gaiety of the troubadours' civilization. But St. Louis IX of France (1226–70) employed every means to detach dualists from their cause, and then misused the name of Crusade to stamp them out. Catharism seemed a major menace to the social structure, because it brought together in one group and theology most of the current elements of heterodoxy and potential subversion—revulsion against worldly materialism, an ascetic, fervent elect and *élite*, private and peculiar religious practices, and an appeal to the disaffected poor.

But even St. Louis' knights could not eradicate beliefs that have a fundamental hold upon the mind of man. It was correct Christianity to believe that there is a Devil who is powerful but did not create the material world. But it was Manichaean heresy to believe that he is the creator, and that evil is the product not of God but of him. Such dualism has exerted strong temptations upon our own times. Karl Gustav Jung, for example, regarded the Devil as "a most valuable and acceptable psychic possession"—we enjoy criminal fiction, and when the lion roars, we know where old Harry lurks. Already amid the disruptions of the third century, it needed exceptional faith to believe that a single all-powerful all-beneficent power was responsible for all that happened, or even to conclude with any conviction that the battle between two powers, a good and evil one, will surely be won by the good. Amid the unspeakable horrors of twentieth-century persecutions, dualism is even more tempting. "If God much stronger", said Man Friday to Robinson Crusoe, "why God no kill the devil?" Personification of the powers of good and evil may be out of date; but the age when millions found it easy to believe that the two forces exist on more or less equal terms is with us once more.

NOTES

1. Arnob. *Adv. Nat.* I, 24
2. Especially the Quinquatria, Neptunalia, Saturnalia
3. The Arval Brethren
4. Jul. *Ad. Theodor.* 362
5. Max. Tyr. XXXIX, 5; cf. Plutarch
6. Grant, *Roman Imperial Money*, p. 229
7. Dio Cass. LII, 35f.; cf. XL, 47, 3
8. *ILS.* 157
9. The festival was on the day of the Parilia (21st April)
10. *CIL.* VI. 30738; Porta Argentariorum
11. *CRAI.* 1930, 208 ff. (Susa). ? Phraates IV
12. Venus Victrix and Fausta Felicitas (9 October)
13. Cn. Cornelius Lentulus Marcellinus, *c.* 76–74 B.C.
14. Porta Argentariorum. Coins of A.D. 68–9; medallic piece of Hadrian
15. The alternative attribution to Aurelian is stylistically less probable
16. Barberini Roma (? *c.* 326–30)
17. Zos. II, 31
18. *Perv. Vigil.* (tr. P. Jay). Date disputed (? *c.* 307, ? early second century, ? *c.* 283–4, ? mid-fourth century)
19. J. W. Mackail; F. L. Lucas
20. Gallienus' large gold piece with DEO AVGVSTO is exceptional (cf. p. 221)
21. The monument of the Secundini (Igel) displays the ascension of Hercules
22. Hungarian finds have suggested an alternative attribution to Gallus (251–3)
23. *ILS.* 1638
24. *Ditt.*[3] 881
25. Dio LXXVI, 16, 3
26. Dio Chrys. *De Regn.* III, 125
27. Behistun inscription
28. Hom. *Il.* II, 205, Plut. *Num.* 6, Sen. *Clem.* I, 1, 2, *Corp. Herm.* XVIII, Orig. *C. Cels.* VIII, 63
29. A. D. Nock
30. Stat. *Silv.* III, 3, 48 ff.
31. E.g. head in Mus. Naz., Rome; medallion at Milan (with diadem)
32. Xen. *Mem.* I, 4; coin-heads of Scipio Africanus (?) and Pompey; third century A.D. medallions of Alexander the Great
33. *FHG.* IV, 197
34. Though *ILS.* 629 calls them gods and the creators of gods
35. *Corp. Herm.* IX (*c.* A.D. 300)
36. E.g. Atarantes (Ethiopia), Mela, *De Chor.* I 43
37. E. Renan
38. Cens. *De Die Nat.* 8
39. *II Kings*, II, 11. Cf. white horses sacrificed to the Sun, Hel. *Aeth.* X, 36
40. Malachi IV, 2; cf. Zech. III. 8, VI, 12

41. Pseudo-Call. *Hist. Alex. Magni* I, 36, 2; 38, 2. The term in the Avesta is *hvareno*. Shubbiluliuma (Hittite) called himself the Sun-god
42. Late fire-temple now discovered at Tang-i-Chak-Chak
43. Philostr. *V. Apol.* I, 25, Amm. Marc. XVII, 5, 3
44. Plot. *Enn.* VI, 4, 3 (criticized in VI, 5, 8)
45. Aug. *C. Faust.* XIV, 11; cf. *De Haer.* 46
46. Hom. *Il.* III, 277
47. Cf. Soph. *Ter. fr.* 582 Pearson: Thracians prayed to the Sun
48. *CIL.* VI, 29954. But Anaxagoras regarded the Sun as a stone
49. Pl. *Symp.* 220D; cf. *Laws* 887 E.
50. Cassander's brother; he founded the City of Heaven (Uranopolis)
51. Ptolemy III Euergetes, Antiochus IV
52. *Hom. Hymn* XXXI
53. As Plut. *De Os. et Is.* 6
54. Seleucus of Seleucia on the Tigris (*c.* 150 B.C.) was his follower
55. Syncretism by juxtaposition, superposition and pantheistic amalgamation
56. Cf. Tert. *Apol.* 16
57. Cf. Cic. *Somn. Scip.* 4, Pl. *NH.* II, 5
58. Baehrens, *Poet. Lat. Min.* IV, p. 543
59. E.g. at Talmis (Kalabsha), Preisigke, *Sammelb.* 4127
60. Jul. *Or.* IV, 155 D
61. Antony, Augustus; cf. Vespasian, Trajan
62. Dio LXII, 6, 2 (meaning disputed)
63. Tac. *Hist.* III, 24
64. P. Giess. 20
65. Vienna; cf. *Klio*, VII, p. 278 (Trajan); and coins
66. Invictus and Discoverer of Light: Guarducci, *Rend. P. Acc. Rom. di Arch.* 1957/9, 161 ff.
67. The Sun-god is shown with Septimius' beard (197)
68. E.g. Arringatore (Mus. Arch., Florence)
69. Dio LXXVIII, 10, 3
70. Brendel, *Die Antike*, 1936, p. 275 (Berlin)
71. SACERD. DEI SOLIS ELAGAB.
72. Herod. V, 6, 6–8 (tr. E. C. Echols)
73. *SHA. Gall. Duo* XXIII, 18
74. *ILS.* 210 etc.
75. "Callicrates of Tyre" *ap. SHA. Aurelian.*, IV, 2
76. *Or. Sib.* XIV
77. Zos. I, 61
78. Since Aurelian reconquered Gaul as well as the east, his cult of Sun-Apollo may also have echoed the Gallic worship of gods of light and healing identified with Apollo
79. Kantorowicz, *Proc. Am. Phil. Soc.* 1961, p. 379, Harat; cf. Palmyra
80. Eus. *V. Const.* I, 17
81. Maximinus II imitated this coinage in the east
82. For date, cf. the Montbouy hoard. Licinius likewise claimed to be related to Philip

83. *Pan. Lat.* VI (VII), 21: *salutifer*
84. Eus. *V. Const.* III, 10
85. Lact. *De Mort. Pers.* 46; cf. for Constantine. Eus. *V. Const.* IV, 20
86. Melito of Sardis. Clement of Alexandria called Jesus the Sun of Righteousness, after Malachi
87. Orig. *In Libr. Ind. Hom.* VIII, 1, 2
88. Tert. *Adv. Nat.* I, 13, *Apol.* 16; Eusebius, Zeno of Verona
89. Jul. *Or.* IV, 130C, 134D, 135D, 137D. As mediator the Sun is "offspring of Zeus"
90. Macrob. *Sat.* I, 19, 9 (a Neoplatonist like Julian)
91. Prokypsis Hymns. Cf. St. Ephraim the Syrian (d. 373), *Fest. Epiph.* II, 1: joint rule of Semha (? Claritas) and Denha (Sunrise)
92. Probably the second of three, or even four, writers of that name (? *c.* 170–244/9). Perhaps from Lemnos. Others who attended her salon were Oppian (perhaps two), Aelian, the future emperor Gordian I, Sammonicus Serenus, Galen
93. Philostr. *V. Apol.* VI, 11; cf. I, 10
94. *Ibid.*, VI, 11; VII, 12. Cf. Pythagoras
95. Dio LXXVIII, 18, 4; *SHA. Alex.* 2
96. E.g. Porphyry, Hierocles; Soterichus wrote an epic about him
97. Eus. *Vs. V. Apol.* 31
98. Stat. *Theb.* I, 719. Perhaps the religion came west via Aquileia
99. M. J. Vermaseren, *Corp. Inscr. et Mon. Rel. Mithr.* 206 no. 518 (Tiber)
100. *ILS.* 659
101. Plut. *Pomp.* 24 (inconclusive). Several Black Sea mints shew a rider-god who is identified with Mithras
102. Nero, Commodus, Diocletian, Julian
103. Orig. *C. Cels.* I, 9, etc.
104. Firm. Mat. *De Err. Prof. Rel.* 22 ff.
105. *ILS.* 4271; cf. 4099, 4152 (*taurobolium*, cf. *criobolium*)
106. Exception: gens Cornelia
107. Melfi (Pal. Pubblico), found at Alberi
108. E.g. Sidamara and Seleucia ad Calycadnum (Silifke) sarcophagi (Instanbul mus.)
109. E.g. from Attaleia (Antalya) and Xanthus
110. E.g. Diocletian's Mausoleum at Salonae
111. Vatican
112. Badminton sarc. (New York); cf. coins of Caracalla
113. Mus. Cap., Rome
114. Alex. Aphrodis., *De An. Mant.* p. 182, 18 Bruns
115. E.g. Favorinus of Arelate *ap.* Gell. *NA.* XIV, 1
116. Tert. *De An.* 47, 2
117. Cypr. *Ep.* 16, 4; cf. Min. Fel. *Oct.* 27
118. E.g. *The Book of the Dead*
119. Lucian, *Philopseudes*: a mocking collection of ghost stories and enchantments
120. *Id., Bis Accus.* 27
121. A. Lesky. Lucian was influenced by popular Cynic "diatribes" of Menippus of Gadara

122. Lucian, *Icaromenippus; Juppiter Confutatus; Mortuorum Dialogi; Juppiter Tragoedus; Deorum Concilium*

123. *Id., De Morte Peregrini;* cf. *Adv. Indoct.* 14, Athenagoras, *Leg.* 26

124. Lucian, *Alexander.* The snake was the mouthpiece of Asclepius (Aesculapius)

125. R. M. Rilke (tr. J. B. Leishman)

126. *I Chron.* XXI; cf. *Zech.* III, 1–5

127. E.g. *Farvardin Yast*

128. Pl. *Rep.* 379c; cf. *Theaet.* 176A, *Polit.* 269E, *Tim.* 28c

129. A.D. 66–70, 115–16, 132–5

130. Eudemius Rhodius (Damascius, *De Prim. Princ.* ed. Ruelle, I, p. 322)

131. Sext. Emp. *Math.* VII, 159–65

132. *Id. Pyrrh.* II, 218–38

133. S. Eitrem

134. Alexander of Lycopolis

135. G. I. Gurdjieff and his followers are the modern successors of the Gnostics

136. Hippol. *Philosophumena*, Bks. V, VI *frs.*; Epiphanius

137. *Acts* VIII, 9 ff. Dr. Faustus owes some features to Simon Magus

138. Iren. *Adv. Haer.* I, 35, 6 (mid-second century), arising from the sectaries of Carpocrates

139. His followers less subtly identified the Old Testament with Evil

140. From Chenoboskion; translation from Greek into the Subakhmimic dialect of Coptic

141. E.g. *Gospel of Nicodemus* (in which there are also *Acts of Pilate*). Also called Agathodaemon, Baal, Typhon

142. from Zuqnîn; cf. a widely circulating *Book of the Cave of Treasures.* Seth survived in Shi'ite lore

143. He knew Vologeses I's (?) new edition of the Avesta, and running commentary in Pahlavi

144. Mani's Fall is also based on Bardaisan. The overcoming of Primal Mind is told in Turki in the *Khuastuanift* (Confession)

145. F. C. Burkitt

146. After 1,468 years

147. Theodore bar Konai *ap.* Pognon, *Inscr. Mandaites*, p. 193

148. But dualists were also known as *bougres*, since they believed it better not to propagate the race

149. P. Cair. Isid. 62 (Domitius Domitianus)

150. Aug. *In Man.* XXIV, 26; cf. *Conf.* V, 10, VI, 5

151. *Manda* means something between reason and revelation. The Yezidis of N. Iraq regard the devil as the creative agent of the Supreme God.

152. Byzantine dualists: Messalians or Euchites. Armenians on Euphrates: Paulicians. Bosnia: Patarenes

153. Steven Runciman

9

The Triumph of Christianity

The Saviour of the Christians

The first two centuries of our era produced a great number of writings which offer descriptions of the life and teaching of Christ that diverge in various ways from the canonical four Gospels. One such work of comparatively early date, the popular *Gospel of Thomas*, names that apostle as the Saviour's special heir and confidant, and records one hundred and twenty sayings and incidents attributed to Jesus.[1] Many other writers, too, assign to him sayings that are not found in the four Gospels.[2]

Yet meanwhile little by little these four, although two of them did not bear the names of apostles, obtained special recognition. The Gospel attributed to St. John, despite a Greek as well as Jewish approach and a date not earlier than the second century, was gradually included, because the author, mistakenly identified with the apostle of that name, was believed to have been a direct witness of Jesus' life and death and then to have lived to a great age and passed on the tradition. Accordingly this Gospel was already united with the other three in the writings of Justin of Neapolis (Shechem) in Samaria (d. 165/7).[3] Justin's Syrian disciple Tatian, pioneer of Syriac-speaking Christianity at Edessa where apocrypha abounded, wove all four Gospels into a composite work with a title stressing its fourfold origin (*Diatessaron, c.* 170). Acceptance of the remaining books that came to be known as the New Testament was piecemeal, but before the end of the second century A.D. plenary inspiration was generally ascribed to the *Acts of the Apostles* and a selection of Epistles; most churches also accepted the Book of the "Revelation of St. John the Divine".[4]

The establishment of this united canon was vital to the subsequent development of Christianity. The New Testament now possessed a manageable size which was lacking in the multitudinous, confusing scriptures of other religions. Moreover, although subsequent appeals to canonical authority would inevitably produce much artificial interpretation, the canon made further rewriting impossible. Certainly, there were discrepancies in what was retained. The outstanding theologian of the next century, Origen, admitted this, and Christianity's most dangerous enemy Porphyry, much to the indignation of St. Jerome, criticized the New Testament as contradictory, incoherent and illogical (p. 205). But the canon achieved its main purpose of eliminating certain doctrines which could well have changed the whole direction of the church and faith.

In particular, much of the apocryphal literature excluded by the purge was of dualist character, attempting to diminish the omnipotence of God by declaring that evil in the world was not of his creation (p. 249). To admit this would have conflicted with Christianity's thorough-going Jewish monotheism, and that is why theologians became impatient when members of deviant sects and philosophers kept on asking, 'Where does evil come from, and why?'[5]

Vigilant though the compilers of the canon had been, there were still passages in the New Testament which could lend themselves to dualist interpretations. The Word (Logos) of Greek philosophy, which St. John's Gospel envisaged as an actual historical person who is also divine, could be thought of as the intermediary or demiurge that enabled the god of the dualists to create and contact base matter. Moreover, although St. Paul maintains the monotheistic Jewish doctrine of Adam's Fall into which the whole human race was plunged by God until its redemption, there seemed to be dualist implications in his continual opposition between the flesh, with its ingrained bias towards evil, and the spirit. Besides, Paul also reflected the second main tendency of dualism, its concept of *Gnosis* (private knowledge) to be taught only to the elect of fully initiated: a doctrine which, though not wholly absent even from the Gospels, undermined the universal appeal of the faith (p. 293). Although he concludes that grace is accessible to all by means of Christ, it took the Christians centuries to outlive ideas of an elect. And meanwhile, Christianity and dualism continued to influence and stimulate one another, so that pagans such as Porphyry even saw the dualists as a Christian sect or sects; and so they often did themselves (p. 256). An enormously diverse apocryphal literature assimilates and amalgamates the two approaches.[6]

Irenaeus of Smyrna, who became bishop of Lugdunum (Lyon) in Gaul, attacked the dualists in his *Five Books against Heresies* (*c.* 185). This comprehensive work, of which only part is preserved, argues strongly against their view that an intermediary power, other than the Creator, has to be introduced to explain evil. However, the writer equally differs from those who believe that Adam had Fallen and had thereby caused the whole of mankind to fall with him. For mankind, according to Irenaeus, is God's raw material still in the dynamic process of creation: God is working his purpose out, towards the supreme future good which was foreshadowed by the apostles.[7]

Irenaeus has deeply influenced the Orthodox Church. There were also modern Irenaeans until war seemed to destroy the upward curve, and recently Teilhard de Chardin and Austin Farrer, like non-religious thinkers, have favoured this same evolutionary view. Two hundred years after Irenaeus, in an age when human self-sufficiency had declined, his optimistic opinion was superseded by St. Augustine's Pauline doctrine of man's Fall and consequent desperate ignorance, sin, guilt and helplessness[8]; a plight from which not evolution but only divine grace can rescue him. Augustine's British or Irish contemporary Pelagius disagreed, discarding the Fall and original sin, and teaching, like Irenaeus, that man is able to win eternal life by his own natural powers: 'if I ought, I can'. But throughout the ages it is Augustine's view to the contrary which western theologians and churches have made to prevail.[9]

The arguments of Irenaeus and Augustine were sharply opposed, and yet their starting-points were the same; for each of them was attempting to refute the dualist belief that God could not be omnipotent because evil must have been created by some other power. Both thinkers, for all their differences, saw that the denial of omnipotence to God struck at the roots of Christianity.

Another essential feature of the faith, and a difficult and unique one, was the blend of divinity and humanity in Jesus.

To believe fully in these two parts of his nature at the same time needed great faith; and that is why faith fulfilled so exceptional a role in early Christianity. It required a faith exceeding any pagan standard to believe in a Saviour who, fully retaining his divinity, had lived a human life upon earth. At first there was no attempt to assert that reason or learning or *Gnosis*—other than knowledge of the Old Testament prophecies—could in any way support or prove belief in the human, yet divine, life of Jesus. "A man", said St. Paul, "is justified by faith without the deeds of the law", and Tertullian (p. 290) specifically explains that nothing else is needed. "The first article of our faith is this: that there is nothing beyond this that we need believe"—anything short of it, or beyond it, is "knowledge falsely so called". As Karl Barth declared, the majesty of God is beyond the scope of our petty rational discussion; and so a man must commit himself totally to the affirmation that Jesus is Christ, both human and divine. It was an affirmation which needed physical courage, because of persecution: and spiritual courage, because it had nothing but faith to rely on. St. Augustine later explained that there are many other things also in our lives which we have to accept on trust—for example, facts about countries and cities we have never seen—and "unless we believed these things, we should get nothing done at all in this life". But, as he was aware, pagan opponents had regarded such neglect even to attempt rationality as extraordinary. The physician Galen, in spite of his own not wholly scientific approach, deplored the contempt of the Christians for empirical knowledge (p. 155), and their professional enemies dwelt critically upon this strange, unreasoning reliance upon blind faith—this attitude of *Ask no question but believe*.

Before long a different feeling appeared among a small but increasing number of Christians who had received the traditional Greco-Roman philosophical education. These men wanted to reconcile their education with their faith. They found they were only able to do so by excluding Christ from truly divine status. For their philosophies could not accept the idea of God on earth; the transcendent Supreme Power, of which they like most thinkers accepted the existence (p. 213), was single and indivisible in nature, and was not therefore able to comprise a divine Son on earth in addition to a Father in heaven. Since Jesus then, living in this world, could not comprise part of this God, he must be wholly or mainly man—a more glorious successor of other great men, somewhat in the evolutionary fashion proposed by Ireneaus, and in pursuance also of the classical, humanist idea of men achieving greatness which had sometimes won a final place in heaven (p. 219).

One of the pioneers of these attempts to harmonize Christianity with pagan philosophy was Justin (p. 266), though this did not save him from martyrdom at Rome, where he had taught during the wave of anti-Christian feeling under Marcus Aurelius (c. 165/7).[10] For he was more courageous than tactful in attacking pagan idolatry, legends, and deifications of emperors who did not seem to him great enough men to merit this fulfilment. "Whatever had been nobly said by anybody really belongs to us Christians"; and yet Plato and Platonists and others had unwittingly played an integral, preparatory part in the Christian achievement. Jesus was not altogether unique, since the Word (Logos) of God, a sort of Stoic Divine Mind, had already appeared in various forms—as a man to Abraham, as fire in the bush to Moses. The Word in contemporary philosophy was a mediating principle between the Supreme Power and the phenomenal world (p. 187), and that is what Jesus seemed to be; not indeed separate in the sense of a dualist second power, but nevertheless distinct from the Creator and not therefore divine in the same sense as he, but requiring worship "in the second place".[11]

Meanwhile, a certain Pantaenus, after visiting India which exercised so much fascination at this time, started the Christian School of Alexandria (c. 170?). Then for two decades, terminating with his flight from Septimius' persecutions, its head was Clement of Alexandria. He was a convert from paganism, like so many of these apologists—whose writings were thus a personal defence of their own life's choice. Justin and men of his persuasion, known as the Greek Apologists, had sought to commend their faith to educated pagans and Jews. The Alexandrians, belonging to an old, rich and cultivated Christian community, went further and collaborated with Aristotelian logicians in order to construct a whole intellectually satisfying philosophy of Christianity. Clement was not satisfied with faith alone, which he regarded as a summary of urgent truths suitable for people in a hurry. He wanted to endow the New Testament with a rationalist basis: to use knowledge and learning to build a faith that was scientific, employing philosophy as "an evident image

of the Truth, a divine gift to the Greeks"—though a somewhat
esoteric gift (in the Gnostic tradition), especially as the *élite* would
remain an *élite* in the world to come. Polytheism had been wrongly
imposed by demons; but Clement's monotheism is more Hellenic
than Hebrew in spirit, and his explanation of sin, not by dualism
but by free will, was given humanistic overtones (p. 249).[12] Like
Justin, he saw Christ as the final expression of the Hellenic Word or
Divine Reason, and Plato as Attic Moses and forerunner of Jesus.
Yet Clement expressed his Christian idea of the function of philosophy with jubilant vigour.

In Origen (d. 254/5), the most prolific author of antiquity, the
church for the first time found a theologian who had really mastered
Greek thought and particularly Plato, and had been in close contact
with the head of a philosophical school—Ammonius Saccas, who
taught Plotinus as well (p. 185). An ascetic of poetical insight and
fine character, Origen succeeded Clement in the headship of the
school at his native Alexandria, making it into an institute of
advanced Christian studies (202–231/2). His sophisticated refutation
of Celsus, whose Platonism had been anti-Christian (p. 289), is
second only to Augustine's *City of God* as a landmark in the struggle
with paganism. Origen's work *On Beginnings* presented a Christian
system of theology to the educated opinion of his time as an intellectually respectable advance on other beliefs. Tackling or
ignoring the pitfalls which awaited those who justified the story of
Jesus by rationality instead of faith, Origen instead maintained the
Alexandrian tradition that a reasoned belief is a firmer belief, more
worthy of God, and brings one nearer to Him. He would not have
agreed with Karl Barth (p. 269), or with Pascal's cry that the God
he needs is no God who can be proved.

This cerebral inquiring approach, however, was only practicable
because Origen allowed himself wide latitude in interpreting the
tradition. For he believed that the scriptures must not be accepted
literally but should be interpreted symbolically or allegorically for
the inner meanings that, when properly considered by philosophical
methods, they will be found to contain—"the forms or figures of
hidden and sacred things". There was ancient philosophical precedent in allegorical commentaries upon Homer, and Origen quoted
St. Paul, "we have this treasure in earthen vessels".[13] His imaginative
attitude towards holy writ was given free rein in the Biblical com-

mentaries that were the most influential of all his works. Origen's pagan critic Porphyry saw this process as a "clever reading into the falsehoods of foreigners the beliefs of the Greeks". Certainly, like Bultmann and others in our own day, he boldly interpreted away many parts of the Bible, overlaying them with a grandiose construction of Platonic and Stoic ideas. In the manner of Justin and Clement, but with a more impressive array of arguments, Origen saw the Son of the supreme, incorporeal God as a vision of the divine which had also manifested itself in other forms at other times, progressively liberating the human soul.[14] The Son was not only subordinate to God but even potentially multiple; and the philosophical tendency to deny the New Testament's unique historical importance and the godhead of Jesus had become more pronounced.

Yet Origen was an enthusiastic Christian missionary who gave his life for his beliefs, since he died at Tyre soon after being tortured in the persecutions of 250-1 (p. 293). This martyr's death helped to perpetuate his way of thinking, not so much in Alexandria (where he had become estranged from his bishop) as in Syria and Palestine —where he spent the last two decades of his career—and particularly in Asia Minor. Philosophers, pagan and Christian alike, were now in fashion; and in the latter half of the third century, just as pagan sarcophagi pictured the after-life in terms of philosophical tranquillity (p. 244), so too their Christian counterparts show Jesus in the guise of a philosopher. While paganism reached its climax in Marcus Aurelius and Plotinus, Christianity attained intellectual status from their contemporaries Irenaeus and Origen—though the views of neither commended themselves to all Christians of subsequent ages.[15]

Nor did those of another thinker on similar lines, the Alexandrian priest Arius (d. 336). The emphasis of these philosophically trained apologists on the humanity of Jesus, with consequent depreciation of his divinity, reached its culmination in his work. Brought up on Origen's doctrine of the singleness of God, Arius, like Unitarians of later times, regarded Christ as distinct from God and inferior and, although created before all time, in a sense posterior: he could even have sinned—although, because of his free-will, he did not. The influence of Arius was strong at Licinius' court, which turned against the church when that took a different view (320). Constantine called the Council of Nicaea (325) and promoted its Creed in order to achieve a consensus, but the result was Arius' excommunication: though his doctrine became temporarily dominant after both he and the emperor were dead,[16] and later prevailed in the leading Germanic kingdoms of Italy and the west.

This underlying tendency to treat Jesus as more human than divine, despite its imbalance, was at least rooted in a determination not to lose sight of Christianity's claim to a concrete place in history. For it was unique among the religions of the ancient world because its Saviour, unlike Mithras and Isis and the rest, was believed to have been a historical figure who had lived and died at a certain place at a certain time. In Jesus, God and man were one, spirit and matter cohered, and it seemed that a new dimension had been added to the world when the eternal Creator once for all disclosed himself in the concrete stuff of our life. And belief that this had happened, and could be pinned down to a precise moment of history, gave Christians a solid basis for their faith far more exciting than the tenuous mythical fabrics provided by other religions.

And yet at the same time there were strong, and much more passionate, Christian forces endangering that very doctrine from motives of a different kind. In contrast to the Alexandrians and other apologists who stressed the humanity of Jesus to the detriment of his divinity, there were many who preferred to think of him as divine rather than human. First, there was much vigorous hostility to the whole philosophical approach, for example from Tertullian (p. 290) and his fierce fellow-African Arnobius (c. 305).[17] Belief in divine Saviours was easier and more familiar than the concept of a Saviour both human and divine. And so the narration of what was claimed to have happened in Jesus' life on this earth sometimes took on an altogether subordinate position.

There were powerful external pressures towards these conclusions. Anti-Christians concentrated their attacks upon the unjustified presumption that limited decisive history to such a narrow focus, and denounced the Incarnation of Jesus as a clumsy attempt, incompatible with the Platonic transcendental divinity, to repair the gulf between the divine and human spheres which Christian doctrine had sundered. Moreover, within Christianity itself there were similar strong tendencies to minimize the Incarnation. This is clear from the urgent plea of St. Ignatius (d. c. 117) to the cities of

Asia Minor *never to abandon belief in Jesus' humanity*. Yet this is what some sects continued to do—notably the Monarchians, who followed a north African preacher Sabellius (*c.* 250–60).

The "Christian Cicero" Lactantius (d. *c.* 317) summed up the whole attitude of these men who believed that Jesus had never really been man at all, but was merely a temporary manifestation of God on earth. "They say, in short, that it was unworthy of God to be willing to become man, and to burden himself with the infirmity of flesh, since the majesty of heaven could not be reduced to such weakness as to become an object of contempt and derision, a reproach and mockery to men."[18] The conception of a suffering god—Orpheus, Attis, Osiris, Adonis, Baal, Isaac—whose death stands for the death of the year and whose resurrection brings its devotees rebirth and immortality had long been familiar in many lands where agriculture was the source of human livelihood (p. 240). But in the New Testament story the theme takes on a new and harrowing emphasis because of its actual location in history. This is what made it too difficult a doctrine for many to accept. People wanted a Saviour, and if the acceptance of Christ's humanity itself needed a superlative act of faith, it was even harder to believe in the subtle idea that their Saviour had suffered painful ignominy and humiliation.

For such reasons, early Christianity, in contrast to a few Greek and Alexandrian intellectuals, does not emphasize the earthly life of Jesus. Except among the exalted who drew inspiration from martyrdom (p. 294), it dwells on his sufferings even less. The reliefs on sarcophagi say little about his human trials. They were influenced by pagan thought, and in times of trouble they wanted to stress not Christ's weakness but his *power to save*. It is only fairly late that Christ begins to appear as Sufferer rather than as divine Teacher and Wonder-Worker; and even then this is shown as a triumph in disguise, without humiliation. The Crucifixion is rarely depicted before the fourth century. As to Constantine's alleged vision of the cross in the sky, followed by his employment of the cruciform *labarum*-monogram XP (= Christos) (p. 301), the cross meant magic more than anything else to him, and in any case it stood not so much for the Passion as for the Resurrection—a new era and a new stage in the divine plan. Those wishing to see Jesus as god rather than man could rely on the Gospel according to St. John. For this, despite its Hellenism, had concentrated in mystical and allegorical fashion on the divine nature of Jesus, seeing him not as a man but as a personified idea (pp. 273f.).

The wall-paintings in the catacombs of Rome and elsewhere are strongly influenced by this Gospel, and again have little to say about the humanity of Jesus. As among pagans, burial and not cremation was the custom, in order to permit the Resurrection of the body (p. 242). Early Christians had at first preferred to bury their dead in open-air cemeteries above ground, but from c. 200, when space grew short and persecution increasingly threatened, they buried them instead in these underground corridors and cells. At Rome such catacombs evolved from subterranean graves of the Jews and other western and eastern traditions. The dark, soft, volcanic rock, strong but easily cut, was hollowed out first into a simple Greek cross or grid in the Catacomb of St. Calixtus—to whom pope St. Zephyrinus (d. c. 217) entrusted the administration of "the cemetery"[19]—and then into miles of several-storeyed mazes, containing between half and three-quarters of a million tombs. During the persecutions, some catacombs may have provided temporary places of refuge, and after Christianity became official, although burials continued until the end of the fourth century, they were turned into centres of pilgrimage.

The catacombs are lined with religious paintings, which reflect all the tendencies of the time, ranging from the artistic traditions of Rome to those of Alexandria and Mesopotamia, and from natural classical style to impressionistic or illusionistic baroque on the one hand and the simple severity of popular art on the other. This is a dogmatic narrative art, owing debts to the crowded reliefs of Roman tradition, and it uses much symbolism and shorthand, not from any desire for secrecy (the intention was to instruct rather than conceal) but because supernatural truth defies analysis. The paintings seem to reflect cycles of instruction partly derived from Jewish sources; there are echoes of prayers from the liturgy and from writings attributed to the great saints, and reflections of Christian poems and paraphrases of the Resurrection story.

The artists of the catacombs reveal an almost complete lack of emphasis on the humanity and suffering of Jesus. What they stress instead is his power as a divine Saviour. For the most frequently represented scene from his life is the Raising of Lazarus of Bethany from the Dead, of which the only account is in the Fourth Gospel.[20] Already a good many years ago no less than fifty-three portrayals of this theme, accompanied by a gesture of benediction found also on the imperial coinage (p. 229), were noted in the catacombs of Rome. For what most Christians really wanted from their faith was that they, like Lazarus, should be saved when the time for their Resurrection comes. The Raising of Lazarus meant the Resurrection of themselves. The doctrine of a general Resurrection and bodily survival or ascension of the dead is present in Ignatius and again in the oldest versions of the Creed, of late second-century date. For Christianity satisfied more specifically and invitingly than any other religion the almost universal craving for escape and salvation in the next world from the evils of this (p. 240). Man, says Arnobius, has received the gift of immortality unknown before[21]—that is the decisive fact, and the relief from a dreadful fear. His pupil Lactantius declares that he himself became Christian because conversion guaranteed him immortality.

This salvation in the world to come is represented upon many sarcophagi,[22] and most explicitly by a praying figure, the Orans, who is the human being or personified human race begging for admission to the Christian paradise.[23] For example hundreds of steles from Terenouthis (Kom Abou Billou) in Egypt reflect the theme. Some show the Resurrection as self-abandoning surrender to the transcendent power: the Orans is carried off by the ship of salvation, or awaits its arrival. Other Terenouthis reliefs more materialistically depict the self-sufficient repose of a reclining figure admitted to a banquet in the afterlife. A Christian woman at Thabraca in Africa envisages her eternal peace under the protection of Mother Church. Constantine, too, tells the Council of Arelate that he expects a judgement upon his deeds after his death. Much of this is confused theology (an eternal reward for good living seems to make the Redemption unnecessary), but shows overwhelming devotion to Jesus as a Saviour.

It was from the troubles of this world that people wanted to be saved. The idea of salvation from sin also existed (p. 243), and there was a clear idea of the need for a saviour from demons—malevolent active evil spirits which were supernatural beings though below divine rank (p. 271).[24] As Christian writers abundantly testify, one of the most popular and powerful assets of the church was efficient exorcism of demons. Lactantius points out that these are terrified by the symbol of the cross, and Eusebius asserts how well we know, by experience, that troublesome and evil *daimones* beset men's bodies and souls. Just as philosophers believed in intermediary powers, so too the church saw demons pressing in from all sides: and Jesus was the Saviour from their terrors. Exorcism, the healing of the sick by expulsion of demons "without manipulations or the use of drugs",[25] was a Christian curative activity which impressed the popular imagination—and it was a deliberate activity of the church, not as in other religions a private commercial pursuit for profit. This reflects the common Christian view, expressed by Justin, that the Son of God had become man in order to destroy demons: that was his task as Redeemer.[26]

Accordingly anti-Christians saw Jesus as one of the many charlatans of the period who professed magical powers (p. 245). Magic was much spoken of in Christian circles. In Egypt, where it had always been strongest, the Coptic tongue developed from magical papyri to become the language of the church. Constantine, without the church's approval, made a concession in favour of white magic, but action against sorcery was vigilant—the Synod of Laodicea (Denizli, 360) moved against Christian clergymen who were magicians, charmers, soothsayers, astrologers and makers of amulets. Prophetic visions likewise played an immense part in the early church. In the fanatical movements of rural Christianity this was a particularly strong element: revivalist sects like Montanism originated from prophecy (p. 305) and continued to stress this aspect of the New Testament among Christians. Montanism owed its attention to women, which was even greater than that in the parent church, to their success as mediums; one such person saw a vision of Christ in female form.

Another way in which devotees claimed to have possible contact and communion with the Christian Saviour was by means of the mystic association and union which also underwent so remarkable a development at this time in paganism (p. 193). For Christianity added to its belief in the personal deity (of the Old Testament) faith in the Kingdom of God experienced in men's own souls. The continued earthly presence of the Holy Spirit after Jesus' death had been stressed by St. Paul as the principle of the new life. And then the Gospel according to St. John spoke of a personalized Advocate or Comforter who would be sent to confirm the revelation.[27] Whether or not its author and those of comparable apocryphal writings experienced mystical exaltation (or alternatively trance-mediumship), the fourth Gospel became the charter of mystic Christianity (p. 201). Origen, too, an older contemporary of the mystic Plotinus, often felt that the Bridegroom was "as far as may be" with him, but "then he suddenly vanished and I could not find what I was seeking".[28]

However, there were other and far more widespread Christian means of seeking union with the Saviour. After the Lazarus miracle, easily the most popular New Testament scene in catacomb paintings is Jesus' miraculous Feeding of the Four or Five Thousand by the multiplication of loaves and fishes. Moreover, this tale had already been recorded no less than six times in the four Gospels—more often than any other incident or miracle. It was given this special emphasis because it stands simultaneously for both the sacraments: the Eucharist (Thanksgiving, Lord's Supper), and Baptism. Christianity was by no means alone among contemporary religions in relying upon sacraments, but owing to the special, personal nature of the Saviour, with whom sacraments united the believer, these played a peculiarly large part in Christian life. The scene of the miraculous Feeding stands for the Eucharist because this was "the true bread and fish of the living water". And the fish, besides spelling out in Greek the initials of Jesus' titles, recalls the sacrament of Baptism because "we little fishes too are born in the water".[29]

Christianity's greatest asset was that these sacraments could bring union with God at all times. Christ had himself been baptized by John the Baptist, and the predicted baptisms with the Holy Spirit by his own agency were held to have been fulfilled in its outpouring at Pentecost described in the *Acts of the Apostles*. These were the glorious precedents for the baptism of individual Christians, whose sins it would wash away. Since men had to live in the world and wished to avoid sin after baptism, they often did not take this sacrament until they were on their deathbeds (p. 302), though the christening of infants had already become common in the third century. Baptism, even more than the initiations of pagan faiths, was a direct, personal, intimate contact with the divinity, blending the sacramental with the transcendent, combining splendour with simplicity. Above all, the rite was believed to effect escape from damnation into immortality; it was a second birth, a birth-giving wave, a calm pure light which came from above and flooded the cleansed heart of its receiver.[30] Yet there were stern conditions imposed and demanded—repentance and faith.

The bond forged by this initiation was constantly renewed by the sacraments and sacrifice of the Eucharist. The symbolic act by which Jesus had made his disciples willing partners in his death became the re-enaction of that event. "The bread which we break, is it not the communion of the body of Christ?"[31] At first this solemn Last Supper was associated with the Love-Feasts (*agapae*) or charity dinners. But after these, during the course of the third century, had gradually become ordinary banquets, the Eucharist remained as a separate rite, endowed with peculiar and wonderful efficacy. Its culmination, after a long recital of God's mercies, was the distribution of bread and wine. This Eucharistic meal, depicted in catacombs by the Tree of Life,[32] was the central mystery and highest spiritual expression of Christianity, renewing baptism's initiatory promise of immortality, signalizing the brotherhood of Christians throughout the world, and bestowing personal union with Christ.

The conferment of these gifts was peculiarly necessary, because the belief in an imminent Second Coming, characteristic of the earliest days, was fading as Greco-Roman ideas overlaid Jewish doctrine. Puritan revivalist movements such as Montanism still expected an immediate end of the world, and persecutions and hardships encouraged the idea, but only among an uneducated minority.[33] Already by *c.* 200 there was a feeling that the Roman empire could postpone the end of the world (p. 289). Consequently the sacraments, uniting believers with Christ here and now, had to play the consolatory part that had previously been played by belief in the Second Coming.

The artists of the catacombs reveal how Christians of the time regarded their Saviour. They do not, normally, portray him direct, since Christianity inherited from Judaism an abhorrence of attempts to depict God, and there is literary evidence that this idea persisted during the third century A.D. A Christian chapel at Dura shows its remoteness from central trends by exceptionally depicting Christ in a painting as early as A.D. 232-3 (some writers interpreted the Old Testament as attacking sculptural rather than painted representations). The Mausoleum of the Julii under St. Peter's at Rome, redecorated by Christians in *c.* 250–75, displays a less direct approach, for its vault-mosaic identifies Jesus with the Sun-divinity who was now emerging as the principal official god of Rome (p. 234). Christ is shown driving the Sun's four horses, symbols not only of the four Gospels but the Resurrection, against a golden background which anticipates Byzantine colour-schemes and stands for the celestial Light Everlasting that the Resurrection will herald. Another favourite idea, displayed on the floor-mosaics of rich men's villas as well as the painting of catacombs, was the assimilation of Jesus to Orpheus, the martyred charmer of nature and mythical originator of the ancient religious movement of Orphism. This identification seems to come from a poem attributed to David which alludes to the Orpheus myth[34]—and Orpheus, represented on a mosaic of Edessa (A.D. 227–8), looks like David in a synagogue at Dura. There was a conviction, shared by many Christians, that Orpheus and other founders of faiths were philosophers using symbols which later generations could unfold. Since their own founder was claimed to be a figure of history, they felt able to show, as paganism could not, a *true* Orpheus or Odysseus or Hercules. Orpheus is displayed in Christian as in pagan art as the singer: as Christ he became the Prince of Peace prophesied by Isaiah, and assumed divine patronage of the liturgical chanting which is the earliest traceable Christian form of common prayer or praise.

Obstacles still had to be overcome before the Byzantine custom of directly portraying Jesus became widely prevalent.[35] In 306 the Council of Elvira in Spain was still critical of art in churches, and Eusebius rebuked Constantine's half-sister Constantia for desiring to see and copy a representation of Christ. During the preceding century the Virgin Mary, who had been written about in the *Protevangelium* (*Book of James*) and stood for Christianity's conspicuous emphasis upon women, had for the first time been depicted by catacomb painters.[36] Yet like contemporary sculptors they continued to represent Jesus indirectly. He is shown particularly often as the Good Shepherd, who redeems his flock by rescuing and saving them "from the mouth of the lion". These pictures appear more than twice as often as the Raising of Lazarus, more than three times as often as the miraculous Feeding. The Shepherd carries his ram or lamb across his shoulders like many a pagan herdsman in Greek sculptures going back to archaic times. Sometimes it is uncertain whether the representation is pagan or Christian, whether it symbolizes pagan kindness (*philanthropia*) or Christian Love. This curly-haired youth is not only a David but an Apollo or a Hermes, conductor of souls, rescuing the lamb which is a soul snatched from destruction. But he is also bringing the Paschal Lamb to sacrifice, the divine Victim which unites past deliverance with present fellowship and hope for the future.

The Good Shepherd appears on one of the earliest known Christian sarcophagi, between portraits of the departed among the trees of paradise. From the mid third century to *c.* 280 he is a predominant and central subject, evoking the best artistic achievements and setting a style and iconography that lasted for many centuries. Occasionally he wears imperial robes which are a reminder that the theme is again not Christ's humanity or pain but his power to save.[37] Although martyrs encouraged themselves by believing that their sufferings were modelled upon his, believers as a whole saw him less as a pattern for imitation than as a Saviour: a deity brought into the world to complete the divine plan by bringing the faithful to salvation.

The same message is again conveyed by the phase of catacomb paintings which, in a change of fashion, superseded the Good Shepherd in *c.* A.D. 280. The serene, static compositions in which the Shepherd had appeared were replaced by a series of lively, rapidly moving narrative scenes. These concentrate upon the marvellous power of God to intervene in history, against all odds, to deliver those who have trusted in him. But, with the single exception of the Raising of Lazarus which speaks directly of salvation (p. 276), the selected incidents are not from the life of Jesus or from the New Testament at all. They are from the Old Testament, and tell of mankind's deliverance in the time of the Hebrews and their prophets. This theme is illustrated by the stories of Noah, Abraham, Moses, Susanna, Daniel, Shadrach and his fellow-heroes, and Jonah.[38] Out of 233 of these Old Testament scenes that were counted, 68 of them show Moses striking the rock, and 57 and 39 the stories of Jonah and Daniel respectively. As in Arabian and pagan traditions, Moses, under God's guidance, gave his people the water that saved their lives; and Jonah and Daniel were preserved from terrible fates by God's intervention—Jonah from the sea-monster to which the great persecutor-states were likened[39] (his three days and nights in the belly of the whale being prophetic of the time before Jesus' Resurrection), and Daniel from the lion's den of the Persian oppressor. These, then, were the themes which now overshadowed all others in the minds of Christians. The Old Testament is stressed as the demonstration of God's power to save his loyal followers. Under the pressure of persecution, Christianity returned to its Jewish origins in which this salvation had been so strongly and prophetically declared.

Another result of these pressures was total physical, geographical withdrawal from the world which was applying them. In this age, when asceticism and contemplation were both counted as supreme human virtues (pp. 257, 192), there were many people, of numerous faiths, who believed that these virtues must be practised in solitude.[40] The Greek world had a Pythagorean tradition of monastic seclusion. Moreover, already in the times of the Ptolemies there had been recluses in Egypt[41]; and round Lake Mareotis, in the same country, lived Jewish hermits called Therapeutae.[42] In Palestine the Essene sect dwelt in retirement upon the mountains near Hebron.[43] During the second and third centuries A.D. such tendencies were increasing. Christians justified them by the contempt for the human body and condition shown by St. Paul and even, so it was argued, by Jesus who had watched and prayed and taught to sell that thou hast. His own disciples could be called 'solitaries' (*monachoi*) since they, like him, had belonged to the flesh on a transitory basis.[44]

A sheer distaste for humanity was one dominant motif. Another was an intense and widespread guilt, which was a further feeling characteristic of the age. Some withdrew from the community because of their disgusted incomprehension of learned Alexandrian Christianity. The earliest known Christian hermit (*anchorite*), Narcissus in the second century A.D., went into retreat to escape from slander; and others wanted to get away from family quarrels. But many fled from social wrongs, oppression and conscription, and from the tax-collector, and many, too, were escaping from persecution (pp. 293 ff.). Fanatically puritanical movements such as Montanism stimulated this urge to shun the world.

And so in the third century the monastic movement was born in

Egypt. The idea was encouraged by the exile of Christian leaders, such as St. Dionysius of Alexandria whom the persecution of Valerian forced to withdraw to the Kufra oasis. But already the persecution by Decius (250) had allegedly compelled a young ascetic, Paul of Thebes, to flee into the desert, where he stayed until he died, reputed to be 113 years old. Soon afterwards St. Antony began his life of seclusion which was to make monasticism famous. Born in upper Egypt in *c.* 251, he found a much older solitary already living near his native village.[45] Antony abandoned his worldly property (*c.* 270), and then visited Paul of Thebes and began a hermit existence. Fifteen years later he went to live a life of total isolation, in an empty tomb at the top of a hill in the desert.[46] But many people wanted to follow his example and to be with him, and during the last great persecutions he organized his followers into groups, who lived in separate and scattered cells and met only for common worship (*c.* 305–6).[47] During the final years of the persecution St. Antony helped its victims who were interned in the mines and prisons of Alexandria. But then, apart from brief absences, he spent the rest of his life in his desert retreat near Mount Quolzoum, where he was said to have lived on until the age of 105. People continually flocked to join him, no longer in fear of persecution since persecution had ended, but hankering for a substitute—martyrs for mortification in an age when blood-martyrdom was no more. This self-torment, pursued even to extreme forms such as castration (forbidden in the fourth century by canon law), seemed to such men the only way to be soldiers of Christ and to avoid worldly temptation and the eternal damnation that followed in its wake. This movement of escapist unworldliness was alien to contemporary ecclesiastical spokesmen, but gained remarkable impetus within a short time.

Although he came of a prosperous family, Antony was illiterate, and knew no other language but Coptic. He taught a very simple Biblical faith, asserting with indifference to speculation and doctrine that the scriptures are enough for salvation.[48] Such men adhered to the Sermon on the Mount and to correct forms, but paid little attention to Jesus. They were more concerned with demons (p. 277). The desert was the demons' haunt, and Antony spent his life fighting them off and teaching the other solitaries, of whom he was the pioneer, how to do the same. As many a painter fond of demonology has shown with gusto, he believed that they tortured and wounded him until he could no longer stand: he saw them in the shape of lascivious women, and he also watched the four walls of his cell opening, and demons rushing in as lions, bears, leopards, bulls and scorpions, with a terrifying noise.

Amun, who died before Antony, founded groups of three or four similar scattered cells, half-hermit and half-monastic.[49] There was no Rule, but deference to the personal authority of the elders was expected. Amun did not agree with Antony about the need to concentrate on the Bible, which he felt to be eerie and incomprehensible because of its divine origin; he found it safer to use *Sayings of the Fathers*.[50] Another Egyptian on the other hand, St. Pachomius (*c.* 292–346), encouraged the study of the scriptures, and incorporated this in the elaborate and strenuous programme of meditation and discipline which he established for his recluses. Pachomius was also the first to bring these together in a truly communal existence by establishing a monastery at Tabennisi, an island in the upper Nile (*c.* 320). This centre soon contained 1,400 monks; and before he died he had founded nine such monasteries and two convents as well, with a total of 7,000 monks and nuns.[51] To asceticism and isolation and vague deference was now added formal obedience: every institution was directed by a Superior, and each of these received orders from Pachomius as Abbot-General.[52] Like hermits in earlier times, the inmates earned their subsistence by the labour of their hands; the monasteries were factories and economic units on a considerable scale, bastions against the miseries of the times. Many monks and nuns wove mats, visiting cultivated areas to collect rushes and sell what they had woven, and in season to till the soil.

Before very long the Egyptian deserts harboured between a hundred and two hundred thousand monks. This monastic movement, which had so rapidly achieved enormous dimensions, was among Egypt's most remarkable gifts to the world, expressing all that is best and worst in the national temperament; it was also one of the most influential of all the phenomena that arose during this climactic period of the Roman empire, and one of the supreme achievements of eastern Christianity.

In *c.* 307 St. Hilarion of Tabatha near Gaza visited Antony and then started a new colony of monks near his own home.[53] Eugenius, a pupil of Pachomius' monasteries, transmitted the institution to Nisibis (Nüsaybin) in Mesopotamia. St. Basil the Great of Caesarea

284

in Cappadocia (c. 330–79) gave articulate formulation to the ideals of communal monastic life; his rulings took root throughout the east, and are still followed in Orthodox monasteries.

Gradually monasticism grew closer to the church. Hitherto its exponents had generally been hostile not only to the state and its urban civilization but to the largely urban Christian hierarchies. Monks were often thorns in the flesh of the episcopacy—from whose power some of them were in flight. Pachomius did not want them to become priests, and some deliberately had their ears cut off in order to avoid consecration. Fourth-century monks were still disrespectful to clergy and bishops.[54] But they had to have the services of priests, because a good monk was meant to take the sacrament daily,[55] and in due course the eastern monasteries became nurseries of the priesthood. From now onwards they were launched on their long career, not only as critics of the church, but as its powerful auxiliaries as well.

St. Jerome, who founded a religious house at Bethlehem (389), was one of the chief popularizers of the extreme brand of austerity of which the practitioners were disliked by Gibbon and Hume, with an eighteenth-century hatred, as gloomy hare-brained enthusiasts, delirious and dismal. But already when Jerome was a boy St. Athanasius had written one of the most influential best-sellers of all time, his *Life of St. Antony* (356–62). Mingling fantasy and fact according to an established pagan genre (p. 161), this work provided a model for many later biographies of saints, and in its Latin version carried the tradition to the countries of the west. In Ireland, the Antonian, semi-eremitical custom long remained dominant; in Gaul on the other hand St. Martin founded a monastery at Ligugé near Poitiers (c. 360).[56] It remained for St. Benedict to stamp western monasticism with its peculiar and permanent shape. His *Rule* (c. 515) superimposed upon oriental asceticism the Roman virtues of gravity, stability and moderation, which made western monks into missionaries, explorers, cultivators and preservers of inherited culture.

Jews, Christians and the State

In spite of all Greco-Roman accretions, the fundamental theology of the Christians had always remained Hebrew; and their reputation among the Romans was greatly affected by their Jewish origins.

The position of the Jews in the Roman empire was ambiguous. Since they did not worship the gods of Greece and Rome, they seemed atheists. They were also exclusive, both in regard to their customs—circumcision, diet of the Mosaic law, sacredness of the family—and in their conviction of being the Chosen Race. This exclusiveness endangered their survival by making them unpopular with their neighbours, whom they, in turn, appeared to dislike. "They regard the rest of mankind", said Tacitus, "with all the hatred of enemies." Their relations with the Greeks, especially, were always strained, particularly in Alexandria where the Jews for a long time possessed a large colony. Moreover, Roman and Greek feelings of alienation from the Jewish communities were intensified by their two rebellions in Palestine preceded (A.D. 66–73, 132–5), on the latter occasion, by the renewal of earlier revolts of the empire-wide Dispersion in Egypt, Cyrenaica and elsewhere. And yet the isolation of their society was not only a source of moral strength to the Jews but also helped their position with the Romans, because it made their God seem a national deity—and that the government could understand and even tolerate. Early emperors protected the Jews and their right to follow their own religious law. Although the circumcision of anyone not of their race by birth was strictly forbidden, a Jew could not be brought into court on the sabbath, or be conscripted into the army, where he would have been unable to follow his prescribed way of life. This uneasy balance between protection and suspicion continued. The later second century A.D., during which the Mishnah (the earliest part of the Talmud) took shape, was a period of success for the Jews. The name of Antoninus was popular in their tradition, for between the times of Marcus Aurelius and Caracalla—who both bore the Antonine name—they flourished and gained official recognition under their Rabbi Judah the Prince I (135–217).[57] The Rabbi's privilege of riding in an official carriage seems to be shown on the sculpture of a synagogue at Capernaum; and in spite of Septimius' suspicion (p. 287), there were many magnificent synagogues in Galilee. Important schools also sprang up at Sura on the Euphrates and elsewhere.[58] For Palestine, owing to bad economic conditions and epidemics, was giving way to Mesopotamia as a Jewish cultural centre. The polyglot Mesopotamian city Dura has a synagogue with paintings which allegorize the destruction and resurrection of Israel's national life, stressing, as Christians did, the continuity of Jewish history as a witness to God's rewards and penalties for observance or breach of the law (c. A.D. 235). The building at Dura reveals in its decorative scheme how Hellenization had led the Jews—who like early Christians very often spoke Greek rather than Hebrew—to defy the Talmudic prohibition of representational art. Elsewhere, too, synagogues show Victory, the Sun-god, and even Leda and the swan. At Dura, amid a wide variety of artistic models, the Greek tradition is clearly perceptible in three nymphs attending the infant Moses. Ezra reading his scroll is like a Greek orator, and David with his harp too, although the picture is oriental in posture and arrangement, resembles Orpheus—whom Christians also equated with Jesus (p. 280).[59]

Yet it has seemed likely, to the excavators of Dura, that its Jews were attacked; perhaps Rome believed them to be sympathizers with Persia. Their salvation cycle on the walls may thus have had a contemporary significance. Only a few years earlier Septimius Severus had prohibited Jewish missionary activities, and Philostratus (p. 235), repeating ancient criticisms, had voiced an opinion of the Jews as rebellious against Rome and humanity, living irreconcilably apart, and 'separated from ourselves by a greater gulf than divides us from Susa or Bactra or the more distant Indies'.[60] And conversely there is a strong Jewish tinge in the numerous anti-Roman and anti-Greek oracles which were in circulation. Nevertheless, Jews were exempted from the major persecutions of Christianity, or at least did not feel their full force.

When the empire became Christian, this ambiguous pattern somewhat worsened. Constantine used forcible language against the Jews, forbidding them to circumcize their Christian slaves or molest those who had abandoned the Hebrew faith for Christianity. Yet he also allowed their rabbis exemption from municipal duties.

It had been a long time before people clearly distinguished Christianity from its Jewish parent body. Although the Roman authorities had apparently seen some difference between the two faiths as early as Nero's persecution (A.D. 64), the tendency to treat the Christians as an extremist branch of Judaism persisted.[61] Moreover, if the Jews were excusable because they followed their ancestral religion, there was no such excuse for the Christians; and so they were even more unpopular. Besides, the appeal of Christianity to the lower classes and slaves, and its promises of a classless salvation,[62] could easily be interpreted as subversive, especially in times of national emergency (p. 294).

Indeed, Greco-Roman society felt provoked by the whole way of life of the Christian communities. Without the Jewish justification of a national sect and custom, they too lived apart, worshipped apart, considered themselves Chosen, and set up values and standards opposed to those normally and traditionally current. Even after an immediate Second Coming was no longer expected (p. 279), their instructions were to love not the world, neither the things that are in the world. For "while a Christian is honestly serving God, he is a stranger even in his own state. We have been enjoined as strangers and sojourners to sojourn here but not to dwell here."[63] This was likewise the feeling of many thoughtful pagans of the time (p. 182), but it is easy to see how it aroused misunderstandings about Christianity; and these resulted in outbursts of violence. Already under Nero, Christians were made scapegoats, allegedly for arson but really, as Tacitus points out, because they seemed to 'hate the human race'—a charge that was also brought against the Jews.

And yet for another century or more the emperors, concerned as always to lower the temperature, were more inclined to protect Christians from the hostile public than to convict them of any crime. Early in the second century Pliny the younger, governor of Pontus and Bithynia, felt alarmed by their refusal to deny this perverse and excessive superstition. He therefore sought guidance from the emperor Trajan, who replied: "They are not to be hunted out; any who are accused and convicted should be punished, with the proviso that if a man says that he is not a Christian and makes it obvious by his actual conduct—*namely by worshipping our gods*—then, however suspect he may have been with regard to the past, he should gain pardon from his repentance."[64] Nevertheless, although other emperors did not institute persecution, they felt obliged to allow it from time to time, on a limited scale. For otherwise popular agitation would have become too vigorous, to the detriment of law and order.[65] Yet it was a remarkable privilege—indeed unique where criminal action against the state was concerned—that recantation brought a free pardon. For to act as a Christian could be interpreted as making a man liable to sanctions by provincial governors, under their general authority to protect the state religion. But enforcement was sporadic, and at times completely abandoned.

Under Marcus Aurelius, however, things took a turn for the worse. In both Gaul and Asia Minor the population rioted against the Christians as scapegoats for military, economic and natural disasters; and the Gallo-Romans hated the oriental Christian businessmen in the Rhone and Saone valleys, immigrants who were always vulnerable to xenophobia. In order to placate inflamed public opinion there were arrests and sadistic executions; and under Commodus the persecution spread to north Africa.

In the time of Marcus one of the victims was Polycarp, bishop of Smyrna, whose examining judge could not understand his refusal to swear by the Genius of the emperor (p. 215).[66] Yet Polycarp was able to point out that Christians had been taught to render honour, "if it hurt us not, to princes and authorities appointed by God,"[67] and by the same token his fellow-Christian Irenaeus (p. 268), one of the founders of western medieval political thought, claimed that government is necessary because of the vices and shortcomings of mankind. It was also widely held by Christians that the simultaneous appearance of the Saviour and the Pax Augusta had not been fortuitous; thus Melito of Sardes, writing to Marcus, was full of praises of the imperial régime.[68] But Marcus' tutor Fronto was against the Christians, and a full-scale attack on them by the philosopher Celsus (? c. 177–8; 271), known to us from his refutation by Origen, treated their saying "no man can serve two masters" as plain rebellion. Celsus regards the Christians as uneducated, stupidly anti-traditional, barbarous people, who contravened the laws governing secret societies. Why do they not shoulder their share of responsibility and hold office and fight as fellow-soldiers of the emperor? If everyone took your pacifist line, he told them, there would be an end of everything sensible—and of your kind of religion too.[69]

It was perhaps in the later second century that Minucius Felix, apparently a north African, wrote the first extant defence of Christianity in Latin. In doing so he quotes, for purposes of refutation, a representative hostile view, which shows how easily the wildest fabrications of obscenity and even cannibalism could be read into the little-known morals and customs of the Christians.[70]

And from their ranks the Syrian Tatian retaliated by writing of pagans who ate Christian flesh to prevent its resurrection.

Septimius Severus directed the first coordinated, empire-wide sanctions against the Christians, forbidding both them and the Jews to proselytize, and subjecting converts to severe penalties (201-3). In north Africa, where executions are recorded, hostility to the Christians was displayed by the priests of the Egyptian deity Serapis, whose high favour from the emperor (p. 125) encouraged them to bring accusations and induced the governors of Africa and Egypt to give way to their pressure.

"We are besieged," cried Tertullian (c. A.D. 160-228), "hunted down, taken by surprise in our secret congregations!" But this impetuous, argumentative, learned African, who infused forceful conviction into his flashing, scathing Latin, had already struck a note which, far from conciliatory, showed a new aggressive confidence. For his *Apologeticus* attacked the pagans with novel directness and violence (197). He loathed the defiled tongues of their prophets, and the filthy heathen sacrifices; the blood, the smoke, and the stinking holocausts of dead beasts. For their sins they are condemned already to a far more frightful holocaust on the Day of Judgement, they and all their works.[71]

All the same Tertullian, a lawyer who adapted Roman judicial concepts to Christian doctrine, was at that time not lacking in temporal loyalty, which he still regarded as strongly in the Christian interest. "We know that the great force which threatens the whole world, the end of the age with its menace of hideous suffering, is delayed by the respite which the Roman empire means for us. We do not wish to experience all that; and when we pray for its postponement we are helping forward the continuance of Rome."[72] But as Tertullian developed the increasingly puritanical convictions which led him to fanatical Montanism (p. 305), his former patriotic feelings decreased to vanishing point. For now he turned right against the culture and tradition upon which the empire rested. Christians are instructed not to participate in any pagan functions, even family festivals, and mixed Christian-pagan marriages are denounced as idolatrous. Religious coercion by the state is deplored. He no longer troubles even to affirm formal loyalty; there is not a glimmer of compromise. No official position is tenable by a true

Christian, and the sword is rejected as an anti-Christian tool of which the bearer will come to a nasty end. The only permissible military service is the army of Christ. Tertullian now felt that a Christian must not only refrain from sacrificing to the emperor—he must even avoid sacrificing *for* him.[73]

As attitudes continued to harden, Maximinus I, coming to the throne after a period of toleration, exiled rival Christian bishops to Sardinia (235), and, while anti-Christian animosity was being fomented by military and economic crises and earthquakes, began to enforce the existing regulations against the sect, and particularly against its clergy. Another lull followed. But when Origen wrote his refutation of Celsus (? A.D. 248–9), he knew that further troubles awaited the Christians, and that there would be terrible upheavals throughout the empire. And yet Origen now feels able to make conditions more confidently than Tertullian. The empire has smoothed the way for the Gospel, and "we defend it by praying for empire and emperor alike": but only if he is a good ruler, and only for soldiers engaged in a just war. For Christ is stronger than the emperor and all his officers, and stronger than the senate and people of Rome.

Origen sees the church as parallel to the empire,[74] and it was indeed a state within a state. Its organization, more efficient than that of any other religion, had suppressed the oligarchic and democratic elements of its origins in favour of episcopal autocracy. The earliest Christians had followed the Jewish custom by which each synagogue not only possessed scribes and priests but also a body of ruling elders (presbyters); and that is still the system upon which Presbyterian Calvinism bases its government. New Testament writers often use the words elder and bishop (*episcopos*) as synonyms, but during the second century a distinction becomes evident. Ignatius (d. *c.* 117) was already able to praise the system of episcopal control, and by *c.* 140 Roman bishops (popes) were special officers with spiritual and liturgical functions and care of the poor. With the support of Irenaeus' demonstration that they were direct heirs of the apostles, the holders of other major bishoprics also emerged into the light (*c.* 190).

The growing importance of bishops meant a loss of power not only by elders but by the mass of lay members. In conformity with the idea of the universal Royal Priesthood of all Christians, these had earlier played a vigorous part in ecclesiastical government. In the time of Origen we still hear of decisions ratified by the whole assembly, including its lay members.[75] This active participation of the laity was to remain a feature of eastern churches, in which educated laymen were more numerous (p. 309), but the west was now taking the lead in a gradual movement to revert to older ideas by which the clergy were separated from the laity. By the fourth century all church functions and services were clericalized, and this was claimed to have a basis in law.

Already in the 250s the uniqueness and consequent sacramental purity of the Ministry was being stressed. This, for example, was the attitude of the first important north African bishop, St. Cyprian (d. 258). A pacific, prudent man (though he fell victim to the Roman government), Cyprian believed that the abolition of more democratic methods in favour of episcopal power was more than compensated by gains in harmonious strength. For his *Unity of the Catholic Church*, communicated to the Council of Carthage (256), emphasized that, while the bishops were individual vehicles of the divine purpose, they embodied a *single* episcopal office. Cyprian was thus at pains to stress the united, dynamic solidarity of Christians. This was unrivalled in contemporary religions, and the strong leadership on which it was based served as a necessary counterweight to imperial and municipal bureaucrats. For example the freedman St. Calixtus, pope or bishop of Rome 217–22, was himself a wealthy banker who could stand up to them.

Efforts were made to compensate for the loss of democracy by welfare measures that knew no social distinction. These had precedents in Jewish charities and the mutual assistance projects of Greco-Roman social and burial clubs and orphanages. But all such previous arrangements were comprehensively exceeded by the imaginative care taken by every Christian community to look after its old people and widows and poor and oppressed, and victims of the plague and other illnesses. In mid-third-century Rome, the community was supporting more than 1,500 widows and poor persons; and, stimulated by the exciting fellowship of common danger, parish organization continued to improve.

All these endeavours were solidly based on a bank, developed in the time of Commodus and Septimius. Priests received salaries, and the church began to own property. Christians had long regarded its philanthropic activity as fundamental, unlike deviant sects which "have no care for love, none for the widow, none for the orphan, none for the distressed, none for the hungry or thirsty".[76] Look, cried Tertullian, how true Christians love one another. Their social services impressed even enemies such as the sceptically inclined Lucian; and two centuries later the emperor Julian attributed Christianity's success, not only to an ostensibly strict way of life and meticulous burial of the dead, but to the feeding both of Christian poor people and non-Christian as well—while pagans neglect their own.[77] Such measures and the human warmth behind them, in a terrifyingly impersonal world, contributed to Christianity's eventual dominance. Moreover, slowly but steadily, this same humanity led to the condemnation of gladiatorial games, parents who exposed their babies at birth, and suicide (p. 113). But meanwhile Christian social services were the visible sign of an outstanding strength. For although ninety per cent of Christian ethics had already appeared in Judaism, Christianity was the only religion to profess and practise total, revolutionary, unrestricted love, charity, compassion and consolation, without distinction of birth, sex, occupation, race or education, embracing in its promises of immortality even the sinner and hopeless and destitute whom society had rejected. The beggar Lazarus was on Abraham's bosom, and the rich man left to be tormented in hell, because "Happy, you that are poor: for yours is the Kingdom of God. Happy, you that hunger now; for you shall be satisfied." Moreover, the cult of a Saviour who had actually appeared among mankind proved a singularly powerful attraction (pp. 239, 280).

Although the church was still relatively small and uninfluential, its effective administration seemed a provocation to the troubled government. And so Decius, when he now turned against the Christians, first singled out their leaders (250–1). Maximinus I had done this too, but Decius saw with even greater clarity the organized nature of the institution he opposed. For after executing their Roman leader St. Fabian, he is said to have remarked, "I would far rather receive news of a rival to the throne than of another bishop in Rome."

The state devoted its machinery to the task of securing reasonable uniformity. The universality of Roman citizenship (p. 112) did not exactly stimulate persecution, but it brought to the fore the idea that citizens should pay respect to the gods upon whom the national welfare depended. Decius did not ask Christians to give up their religion, but he would not tolerate their refusal to join in communal corporate observances. Decius was a soldier, and this was a soldier's order. It was also a psychological gesture of policy, in a time of crisis when confidence was breaking down—an act of state to distract attention from people's miseries and anxieties. Moreover, these same months seem to have provided the occasion for a unique issue of coinage in honour of earlier, deified emperors (p. 220): all citizens of Rome, their religious deviations forgotten, were to rally round these venerated figures of the glorious Roman past. Decius only required a single religious performance from the Christians. When this was done, the local Sacrificial Commission handed over a Certificate of Sacrifice (*libellus*), of which specimens have been found in Egypt. The church, being mainly urban, was dangerously vulnerable. Nevertheless, many Christians probably evaded the tests quietly. Others bribed the commissioners to give them certificates without sacrifice; and large numbers of Christians at least momentarily lapsed.[78] Those who refused to do so were put to death.

Martyrdom (from *martus*, a witness) was not a new phenomenon. The executions under Marcus Aurelius had strengthened the faith at a juncture when tolerance would have fostered all manner of off-centre sects, and led to disintegration. Moreover, though Marcus and other pagans might deplore these recalcitrants as exhibitionists (p. 184), their deaths were recorded by their fellow-Christians (in pursuance of Stoic and other pagan models) as precepts and examples.[79] This self-immolation was inspired by a death-wish founded upon a desire to purge all guilt by imitating the suffering of Christ. They believed also that their sacrifice, founded upon his, would speed the reconciliation between God and his people. Until the Second Coming, martyrs will be in paradise, and none but they. Happy is the man whom God has devoured, declared Tertullian. "*The blood of Christians is seed!* That very obstinacy which you execrate is a lesson to the world. As there is enmity between the things of God and the things of man, we know that, when we are condemned by you, we are acquitted by God."[80]

In Rome, artists and congregations preferred pictures of Christ as powerful Saviour rather than suffering martyr (p. 275). But in more austere circles, particularly in north Africa, Christianity was interpreted as an ordeal which brought triumph against the Devil and the demons who incited the government to persecute. "O feet blessedly bound", cried Cyprian, "which are loosed not by the smith but by the Lord!"[81] And the faithful threw their clothes on the place where Cyprian himself was to be executed, in the hope that they would soak up his blood. Origen, too, was a zealot for defiant martyrdom as the best means of showing that we aspire to heaven by our deeds.

By this time, shrines of the martyrs had been established, on the analogy of pagan heroes. In Asia Minor, such cults go back to the second century. But most venerated of all was the Roman Martyrium of St. Peter, who by at least A.D. 100 was believed to have been executed by Nero; a shrine (c. 160–70) recently discovered under the Vatican Basilica dedicated to Peter (p. 146) has been identified with the Trophy celebrating his victory over death and paganism, which was seen by a priest at the turn of the third century. From then onwards, liturgical celebrations and memorial services for martyrs became continually more prominent. For "where their bones are buried, devils flee as from fire and unbearable torture".[82] The demonstration that Christianity had been found worth dying for made it seem worth living for as well.

A few years after the measures of Decius, Valerian launched a new anti-Christian plan (257–8). He no doubt repeated the patriotic appeal, especially as the military situation was growing even worse— and the loyalty of Christians was suspect after desertions to the Goths who had invaded Pontus. But his motives may have been primarily financial. Church property was an inviting temptation, and the holders of salaried priesthoods had become marked men. When, therefore, Valerian moved against the organization and corporate life of the church, he not only banished its bishops but also, for the first time, confiscated its meeting places, churches and cemeteries; and he seized the property of prosperous Christians.

But after Valerian had been captured by the Persians, the anti-Christian policy was brought to an end by his son Gallienus.[83] That may be why ancient pagan sources regard Valerian as a good emperor and Gallienus a bad one. However, Gallienus' reversal of the persecution was not due to any personal inclinations towards Christianity; he was more interested in the pagan teachings of Plotinus. But there were Christians at court, and in desperate times of community strife and near-anarchy Gallienus felt it better to conciliate factions than to identify scapegoats.

Gallienus' policy of toleration lasted for forty years, and during this time Christianity established itself on an increasingly solid basis. While extension to the rural east produced dissident, fanatical converts (p. 307), the main strength still lay in the lower and middle classes of cities, where shopkeepers, sailors, clerks, small traders, artisans and labourers were members of the faith. The Greek historian Dio Cassius failed to note the growth of Christianity. Tertullian, on the other hand, declared "we Christians are only of yesterday, and yet we now fill the world", and specifically that the Christians already formed almost a majority of the urban populations.[84] This was an exaggeration, or a generalization from a few places, but important gains could be reckoned. At the Carthage Council of 256 there were 87 north African bishops: fifty years later their number was trebled. Even earlier there were members of the faith—though not very many—in high posts of the imperial and civil service; there was a sprinkling of Christian intellectuals at Alexandria and elsewhere (p. 270), and by the end of the third century provincial governors belonged to the religion.[85] All over the southern and eastern Mediterranean, and especially where there was a noticeable Jewish or Semitic element, the balance was shifting slowly but perceptibly in this direction. The Christians were growing together with Greco-Roman society.

Asia Minor was the land of religious longings where their churches had most quickly established the impetus that led to other successes elsewhere. This Christianity of Asia Minor began in the Greek cities of the western sea-board, and then spread eastwards to the upland peoples. St. Gregory the Wonderworker of Neocaesarea (d. *c.* 272), converted by Origen, used intelligent missionary methods in Pontus and Cappadocia, where he unmasked the spurious character of pagan oracles and cures, and superseded local festivals by equally festive commemorations of Christian martyrs. Yet here, as in Egypt and Syria, expansion into the villages also produced a non-conformist religion of dissent (p. 305). The Egyptian population may have been more than fifty per cent Christian by 300, and these numbers were swollen by new populations of monks (p. 284). Syria and the Levant had expanding churches (piloted by Antioch, Caesarea and Tyre) which for the first time gave Christianity a strong regional cast, founded on new Syriac and Aramaic literatures. Syria was also active in the missionary field, and when a bishop of Antioch consecrated his first colleague at Edessa (Urfa), capital of Osrhoene in Mesopotamia (c. 200), the stage was set for a church which was not only regional but national. For soon afterwards the monarch of that Roman client-state became a Christian convert, and created an ominous precedent by persecuting pagans (p. 304).[86] The king was a friend of another convert, Bardaisan (Bardesanes) (154–222). This intellectual Syriac-speaking astronomer and astrologer, who influenced Mani (p. 357), professed so peculiar a form of Christianity —including the doctrine that Christ's body was an illusion—that he was said to have "a legion of demons in his heart and Our Lord on his lips".[87] But in an advanced piece of political thinking, dedicated to Caracalla or Elagabalus, Bardaisan argued that Christian liberty —by which he meant free will—expresses itself through a people's national characteristics; and although he was not necessarily hostile to Roman imperial ideals, that was the pattern which he superimposed upon them.[88]

Edessa was prolific in its own brands of theology, and its priests established a bishopric at Arbela (Erbil) across the Tigris. An Armenian poet praised Edessa as "the betrothed of the Son of God".[89] For towards the end of the third century Armenia, too, had been converted, by St. Gregory the Illuminator, a member of the former Parthian royal family. The king of these disputed Armenian territories who adopted the faith, and endowed it with pagan temples, raised Christianity to the status of an international problem.

Latin-speaking Christianity was comparatively slow to emerge. Then at Carthage it produced the outstanding works of Tertullian (p. 290). Half a century later the north African church, in spite of many a deviant movement, was tolerant, highly organized and supported by wealthy members and a well-travelled clergy. Subsequently, under St. Augustine, it was in and through this community that Christian religion took a firm hold upon the western Mediterranean world.

British Christianity was making headway soon after 200. Early in the following century the Spanish church, already foreshadowing its powerful future, provided Constantine with his religious adviser, Ossius of Corduba, and with an ecclesiastical Council (Elvira, 306). In Gaul, second-century Christians had still mainly been Greek-speaking orientals, whose alien origin contributed to their persecution by the Gallic population. At Rome, too, the church used Greek until the third or even fourth century. There may have been about ten thousand Christians at Rome in A.D. 200, rising to thirty or forty thousand a hundred years later, and perhaps twice the latter total under Constantine.

That seemed nothing like a large enough figure to take over the empire; and the same years witnessed the most formidable of attacks upon the basis of Christianity, launched by Plotinus' chief pupil Porphyry (d. *c*. 305).

The quotations that have survived from his fifteen-book work *Against the Christians* show a force and thrust much superior to previous indictments. St. Jerome, one of many who tried to refute his attacks, took them so seriously that he called their author a scoundrel, sycophant, lunatic and mad dog. Nevertheless, Porphyry was a religious man as determined as the Christians to find revela-tion, redemption and immortality, and prepared even to jettison pagan worship in order to do so.[90] Less concerned than his predeces-sors with Roman patriotic motives,[91] Porphyry, being the best orientalist of antiquity, was preoccupied with higher criticism. Here his targets include the genealogy of Jesus, the canon of the New Testament, alleged distortions by the Evangelists, and the theology and personality of St. Paul.

Porphyry's colleague Hierocles was one of the principal instigators of the Great Persecution which now followed (A.D. 303–13). This was launched by Diocletian and his Caesar Galerius. Either because the government underestimated the strength of the faith or because Christianity possessed friends at court, a start was not made until Diocletian had been in power for nineteen years and Galerius for ten. But when persecution came, its purpose was annihilation. This was a death-struggle of faith against faith, of the old order against the new.

After Diocletian had consulted the Roman gods, the Sibylline books, and the oracle of Apollo at Branchidae (Didyma), edicts began to be announced. The first of them forbade all assemblies of

Christians for purposes of worship, and ordered the destruction of their churches and sacred books. Known adherents were dismissed from state employment, including the army in which emperor-cult was a requirement of military discipline. Then followed two further proclamations limited in operation to the eastern provinces. These were directed solely against the clergy: one edict ordered their arrest, and the other commanded that they should sacrifice to the gods of the state. Finally, a fourth edict extended this order to every member of the Christian faith (304).[92] Soon afterwards, Diocletian abdicated his eastern throne in favour of Galerius. Thereupon the latter and his nephew and subordinate Maximinus II Daia called upon governors to enforce upon all men, women and children their obligation to sacrifice to the gods. The suppression of recalcitrants was intensified, and Maximinus II decreed that everyone, even babies at their mothers' breasts, should be present at these sacrifices and should taste the victims' flesh (309).

Yet resistance was unprecedentedly resolute and defiant. There were, inevitably, many renegades, but a considerable number of people were executed. Few of these casualties took place in the west, where Constantine's father Constantius I Chlorus was no persecutor and took no action except to demolish certain churches. But the main stress fell upon those African and eastern provinces where the tougher peasants, as well as townsmen, were now firm adherents of Christianity. In Palestine, eighty-three executions are recorded, including thirty-two Palestinians and fifty-one Egyptians. In Egypt itself, though we do not possess any such detailed account, there had been political unrest and rebellion, and here the successive blows fell most heavily of all. Perhaps the total number of those who died in all parts of the empire was about three thousand.

In eastern provinces bureaucracy and army joined forces to carry out the anti-Christian measures, which continued, with a few pauses, for ten years. But these were the final bloody acts of the tragedy.[93] For as these harrowing years passed, it became clear that the persecution was spent. Times had changed. The pagan communities no longer egged on the authorities with the same ferocity as before. On the contrary, they now regarded the victimization as exaggerated,[94] disliking the Christians (who were not so eccentric as they used to be) rather less than they disliked the totalitarian government which tyrannized the entire population. And so, in circumstances which we cannot reconstruct, Galerius, mortally ill, issued an edict granting freedom of worship to all members of the Christian faith (311). Persecution, declared the dying emperor, had only made them obstinate or caused them to cease worshipping any god at all.

> So, in view of our benevolence and the established custom by which we invariably grant pardon to all men, we have thought proper in this matter also to extend our clemency most gladly, so that Christians may again exist and rebuild the houses in which they used to meet, on condition that they do nothing contrary to public order. . . . In view of this our clemency, they are in duty bound to beseech their own god for our security, and that of the state and of themselves, in order that in every way the state may be preserved in health and they may be able to live free from anxiety in their own homes.[95]

For the first time, that is to say, Christians were given a measure of legal recognition. Nor does this edict merely allow them to exist: by enjoining them to pray for emperor and state the authorities implicitly recognize their God as a divine power. Nothing definite is said about church property, but Maxentius, the ruler at Rome (306–12), although himself a devoted adherent of patriotic cults and the banisher of two Christian bishops, restored to the church its property that had been confiscated during the persecutions.

In the east, however, Maximinus II Daia, who had now succeeded Galerius, fought a strong rear-guard action against the encroachments of Christianity. He had at first grudgingly accepted the edict of Galerius. But then his attitude changed, and persecution began again. Petitions were received from the municipal authorities at Nicomedia and Tyre and from provincial organizations requesting that their Christian residents should be expelled; and Daia graciously agreed.

> If they persist in their damnable folly, let them be thrown out as you requested, and driven right away from your city and neighbourhood, in order that thereby, in accordance with your praiseworthy enthusiasm in this matter, your city may be purged of all contamination and impiety, and in pursuit of its set purpose may with due reverence give itself to the regular worship of immortal gods. . . . We permit your Dedicatedness to ask whatever munificence you wish in return for this your devout purpose. The fact of its being granted to your city will provide evidence for all time of your devoted piety towards the immortal gods.[96]

To encourage this repressive action, Maximinus Daia obtained and circulated confessions from prostitutes that they had taken part in Christian orgies. He also directed that spurious anti-Christian

Acts of Pilate should be included in school curricula. Executions took place, but they were few, for Maximinus preferred tortures to death-penalties, in order to improve his statistics of apostasy: the obstinate were blinded in one eye and had one leg ham-strung, and were then sent to mines and quarries. But what interested Daia more than such penal measures was the positive establishment of a pagan organization which would rival and outdo its efficient Christian counterpart. And so he created an elaborate, homogeneous, pagan ecclesiastical system with its own priestly hierarchy.

While this was happening in the eastern provinces, Constantine defeated Maxentius at the battle of the Milvian Bridge outside Rome, and became sole master of the west (312). Constantine was in the midst of his determined but rather confused transition from Sun-worship to the Christian faith (p. 233). Later in life, he told Eusebius that while marching in Gaul, some time before his conquest of Italy, he had seen a cross of light superimposed upon the Sun,[97] with the injunction to "conquer with this sign" written in stars about the cross. What he saw may have been a rare natural phenomenon, in which the Sun's rays look like a cross. Or he may have had one of the trance-like experiences with which the age abounded. But whether it was the one or the other, or a combination of both, or a sign from heaven, the vision stimulated the boldness that Constantine showed in his successful campaign against Maxentius. And it was also reported by Lactantius that, before the Milvian Bridge, he was warned in a dream to inscribe the monogram XP (*Christos*) upon his soldiers' shields.

In the east, Constantine had two emperors to deal with—Maximinus Daia in the non-European part of the empire, and his rival Licinius (a friend of the late Galerius) in the Danubian provinces. Professing amicable relations with both, Constantine requested Daia to stop the persecution of the Christians—and gave Licinius his half-sister Constantia in marriage. At the wedding celebrations, Constantine and Licinius published the so-called Edict of Milan, which introduced universal religious tolerance. Constantine then left Maximinus Daia and Licinius to fight it out (313). Daia, defeated, agreed to a tolerant policy just before his death, and Licinius remained emperor of the east as Constantine's colleague for another eleven years. On the eve of his decisive battle against Maximinus, he too had claimed to have seen an angelic vision. But it was not explicitly Christian; nor was the monotheistic litany which his troops recited three times before the engagement,[98] since this was addressed to the Highest Holy God (p. 233).

On Constantine's side, too, there was still much vague mention of the supreme godhead. Yet before long he explicitly identified the Divine Power with Jesus, spoke of "the lawful and most holy" Christian religion, and initiated over a period of years a series of measures openly granting favour to the Christians. Their priests, other than those of dissident sects (p. 307), were, like those of the Jews, exempted from municipal obligations. But a more decisive step had already been taken when funds (presaging a heavy drain upon the national exchequer) were sent to subsidize provincial churches, for example at Carthage. The lodging of the bishop of Rome or pope changed sharply for the better when he was given the royal palace of the Laterani[99] and magnificent new churches. The liturgy borrowed imposing features from official and court ceremonial. Moreover, the church, in keeping with its new privileges, was entrusted with public responsibilities. In spite of the differences between Christian ideas and pagan legal traditions, episcopal courts were given jurisdiction in civil cases (318). People were permitted to bequeath their property to the church, which thus ranked as a civic corporation.[100] Finally Constantine himself was baptized, after postponing this, like many Christians, until his deathbed when he could sin no more (p. 278).

Church and state were to be run in double harness. But as the emperor increasingly became aware of his personal mission, the successive Councils of Arelate (314) and Nicaea (325)—the former attended by western, and the latter mainly by eastern bishops— showed that the master was Constantine, to whom the celestial will had committed the government of all things on earth. Consequently membership of the church now meant resignation to the claims of the state, and an extremely oppressive state it was (pp. 88 ff). Since, however, there was going to be an official church, nothing but this enforced subordination could produce the power-structure needed to guarantee that state and church, and the empire with them, would not fall apart. Eusebius, whose *Life of Constantine* framed the new theory of Christian sovereignty in terms comparing the relationship of the emperor to Jesus with that of Jesus to God the Father,[101] felt so anxious not to return to the relative ineffectiveness of earlier Christian institutions, whose persecution by Diocletian even seemed to him deserved and merciful, that he applauded the capitulation of the church to Constantine. St. Jerome (d. 420), on the other hand, felt that "as the Church increased its influence it decreased in Christian virtues". And St. Augustine, bearing in mind unsavoury aspects of Constantine's régime, could not fully accept Eusebius' eulogy of that ruler, reserving unqualified praise for the contemporary monarch Theodosius I (d. 395). It remained for St. Ambrose to introduce a new era of intrepid churchmen by rebuking Theodosius. Constantine, too, had been requested by Ossius of Corduba not to interfere in ecclesiastical affairs, but his church did not attempt to compete with the emperor who was the author of its revolutionary transformation.

Constantine felt an impulsive, emotional, exalted need for divine support—of which this faith, with its most satisfying of Saviours, gave a better promise than the various forms of paganism. He or his advisers may also have experienced a growing conviction that Christianity was the only force which could effectively bring together the conflicting social elements of the empire. Nevertheless, this conversion of the state was a rash and remarkable personal venture—one of the apocalyptic acts of history which deny the modern doctrine that everything happens impersonally through tendencies.

A tendency towards the spread of Christianity had existed, but on too small a scale to exercise great effects without vigorous impulsion from above. At Rome the Christian population, although larger than before, still numbered no more than seventy or eighty thousand (p. 298), and relatively few of these people were of political or social significance. The empire became Christian because of the unlikely emergence of a Christian emperor. Without such a Christian ruler on the throne, and a singularly forceful and determined one at that, the conversion of the Roman world, if it had ever happened at all, would have taken a very long time. For example Persia, though its population included many Christians, never had a Christian monarch and consequently never became a Christian state.

The vast majority of Constantine's subjects were still pagans, and he insisted, in the interests of unity, that his mission was not only to Christians but that he was also bishop of those outside the church. Yet towards these pagans, still firmly entrenched in important positions, his attitude underwent a predictable change. At first he proposed to "let those who are in error be free to enjoy the same peace and tranquillity as those who believe". They were, it is true, required to recite a general monotheistic prayer, and pagan terminology was gradually abolished from official vows. Yet only a few well-known heathen temples were closed down,[102] and in two cases this action was ascribed to their unacceptable practice of ritual prostitution. However, the violent antipagan tone of Lactantius' *Deaths of the Persecutors* (c. 316) suggested that co-existence could not last for long. When Licinius became irritated by the Arian controversy (p. 272) and reintroduced sanctions against Christians in general (320–1), his relations with Constantine grew strained, and the latter retaliated by showing increased hostility to the pagans. In the year of Licinius' downfall (324) Constantine passed a severe law against divination. In the eastern regions, which Constantine now added to his western realm, there were in future few provincial governors who did not belong to the Christian faith. Temple treasures were confiscated (331); and finally pagan sacrifices were banned. Nevertheless, it took two more generations for all this pressure to deal paganism its death-blow.

Meanwhile, the pagans presented Constantine with a less intractable and ominous problem than disobedient fellow-Christians. In 314 he wrote to a high official in north Africa that divine favour was only procurable by united worship which must rise above quarrels and contentions distasteful to the Highest God.[103] The church must not only be united with the emperor, but Christians must be united with one another. As Eusebius pointed out, disharmony was a direct invitation to divine chastisement—nothing angers God so much as the division of the church, which is the cutting up of the body of Christ.[104]

Constantine's ecumenism was not a defensive closing of the ranks, like its modern counterpart, but a universal missionary attack launched at a time when he had estimated that the tide was running in Christianity's favour. Moreover, unlike most modern ecumenists, Constantine, as King James I of England appreciatively noted, was influenced by a political motive. For heretical and schismatical deviations, besides calling down the wrath of God, would also by opposing and disobeying the official church which was Constantine's

own instrument create communal anarchy and chaos and consequently thwart the imperial will.

To prevent such divisions the emperor summoned and presided
over the Council of Nicaea (325). Its purpose was to reconcile the
conflicting interpretations of the godhead by Arius and his enemies
(pp. 272, 304) which were disrupting the unity of the church. When
agreement had been reached, Constantine did not much care, or
perhaps understand, how bishops interpreted it.

And yet unity was still prevented by other grave obstacles, which
went far beyond the purely theological field. One of these obstacles
was dissenting puritanism. This expressed itself most dramatically
in mass-flights into hermitages and monasteries (p. 282). But such a
movement, although in its early days hostile to bishops and rulers
and society, was not powerful enough to meet with severe official
disapproval. Subject to certain controls, monasticism was tolerated
as a legitimate outlet for unavoidable tendencies of the day. Nevertheless, even those who remained in their homes were not all pleased
by Constantine's unification of state and church. At the Council of
Arelate (314), there was still a feeling that the emperor's service
was hardly compatible with membership of the church.[105] The
assembled clerics finally decided to the contrary; but it had indeed
required a mental and spiritual about-turn to belong to a church
which instead of being perpetually proscribed was subsidized and
directed from the Lateran palace under the guidance of the emperor.
St. Jerome's doubts about the desirability of such a situation echoed
a feeling of disquiet that went wide and deep.[106]

This feeling had ancient roots. Before the official recognition of the
church, many Christian writers had detested not only the Roman
state but the whole philosophical education in which the Apologists
had tried to dress Christianity's Jewish doctrines (p. 270). For
instance, the easterner Tatian in the second century A.D. gloried in
Christian "barbarity".[107] And he was echoed by Tertullian, how
after initially attacking all deviations from official doctrine (c. 197)[108]
later identified himself with their most extreme version, Montanism. This New Prophecy was a product of the apocalyptic
hysterical cults of Phrygian villages (p. 277), where there had
formerly been penitential inscriptions to the pagan god Men. The
movement was a rural one rejected by the majority of Christian
believers in Asia.[109] Yet it spread vigorously to the rustic populations

of Syria, Egypt and particularly north Africa, where Tertullian was converted to its ideas.

Hitherto Christianity had been mainly urban, and its extension to country areas raised new problems. The peasantry of the empire, although they provided the bulk of its income, had always been subordinated to town-dwellers, and there was a complete lack of sympathy between the two (p. 85). To them, therefore, the new faith meant not only hatred of imperial persecutors but social discontent, and dislike of the establishment. This meant that they were also impatient with Christianity in the towns. They found it too formalized, institutionalized and centralized; and they felt that its growing official hierarchy, in order to achieve unified and peaceful progress, had made too many improper and deplorable compromises with the world.

Tertullian's harsh eloquence also contains a Semitic revulsion, Punic as well as Jewish, from Roman and Greek attitudes towards a burning desert fundamentalism which was the heir of fierce local pagan cults.[110] This is a backward plunge to an austere, prophetic church, taking its stand on the Word of God, enthusiastically loathing the world, and yearning for the martyr's crown. Christianity in northern Africa had never stressed love and mercy. Certainly Montanism did not, since it was more concerned with propitiating divine wrath and with the terror of Judgement. The basis of salvation, said Tertullian, is Fear.[111]

A breach between these puritans and the main Christian church in north Africa was caused by the persecution under Septimius. St. Calixtus, pope and bishop of Rome, was opposed for allowing renegades, who had given way to official pressure, to return to the fold. And then again after the persecution of Decius, Novatian—no doubt to the satisfaction of the government with its policy of divide and rule—led a schismatic Roman congregation which refused to be polluted by such apostates (251). He gained powerful backing at Antioch and elsewhere in Syria and was substantially supported by Asia Minor's humble populations who, being inconspicuous and having little to lose, had not been so severely tempted to fall away from their faith, and were therefore out of sympathy with the urban middle-classes who had done so. Elderly Montanists supported Novatian, and both his sect and theirs continued to maintain their primitive martyr-worshipping churches for centuries.

While the persecutions of Decius and then Valerian were followed by four decades of tolerance, these dissenting rural Christians in the oriental provinces and north Africa increased markedly in numbers. As in the days of Tertullian, north Africa was the scene of the next outburst, and it was caused by a wave of official repression. A newly elected bishop of Carthage was denounced by his colleagues from the less sophisticated regions of Numidia, because he was opposed to the deliberate seeking-out of martyrdom. The second of two rival bishops successively put forward in his place was Donatus. Like a contemporary sect in Egypt, the Donatists to whom he gave his name completely denied humanist, urban, traditional culture, and at the same time rejected the sovereignty of the church. Constantine, regarding these Donatists as irreconcilable enemies of the unity which was his aim, excluded them from the subsidies distributed to Christian churches. In spite of endless argument, the attitudes of the two sides took irreversible political shape, for and against the government (316). After Constantine's dismissal of repeated appeals, the Donatists asked the new and crucial question of the day: *what has the emperor to do with the church?* And he for his part, tougher against Christian splinter-groups than against pagans, confiscated their churches and banished their bishops. The Donatists began to form a calendar of martyrs of their own.

Five years later military suppression was abandoned in favour of a scornful tolerance. For when his unfriendly eastern colleague Licinius was goaded by Arian defiance into reviving persecution (p. 304), Constantine thought it best that he himself, by way of contrast, should not punish disobedient Donatists, but should leave their punishment to God. Yet an ominous tradition was already established: Christianity, as soon as it became official, had begun to persecute Christians. In the east, too, Constantine confiscated the churches of the various sects, and forbade them to hold services.[112] The doctrine of the church as a unity meant that, unlike Judaism, it was a universal and missionary institution; and this in turn indicated that it must forcibly absorb nonconformists. However, far from achieving the desired unity, these measures of coercion which Constantine felt obliged to initiate produced as their heritage many centuries of hatred between one Christian and another, exploding often into lethal bloodshed.

Despite further persecutions,[113] Donatism continued to flourish until, after the Arian interlude which intervened in every principal barbarian kingdom in the west, Arab conquests during the eighth century suppressed all forms of Christianity in north Africa. The Donatists had not, like Constantine's church, set out to be universal proselytizers. But they claimed the right to defend their separate identity as preservers of a divinely given law. They were also a social-revolutionary movement, attracting fugitive slaves and destitute peasants. Inscriptions from village churches in Numidia repeat texts hailing Christianity as a refuge from the toils and sorrows of the world. There was a Donatist left-wing composed of anarchic, millennium-seeking Vagabonds (Circumcelliones). The Donatist leaders, it is true, spoke and wrote in Latin. But on the whole the sect flourished less in the towns, where its persecutors were too strong, than in country areas such as the high plains of Algeria, from which puritanical brands of Islam likewise came to draw their strength. The Donatists were jealous of civilized towns; and, because they also felt hostility to the ruling cultures, they were strongest in regions where the native Berber and Punic elements prevailed.

This then, in a variety of ways, was a religion of protest. Towards its adherents Constantine had at first shown patience. But when that was exhausted, the more forcible methods that followed contradicted his unifying intentions, pointing the way instead to the Protestant tradition which came to its full stature twelve hundred years later.

Another fundamental breach in this unity, however, had already begun to take effect not in the sixteenth century but in the fifth and sixth: namely the rupture between the Catholic Church, centred upon Rome, and the Orthodox Church based on Constantinople. And this division too, though it had perhaps become inevitable by the time of Constantine, was involuntarily hastened by him—when he founded Constantinople.

While this was being planned, the Council of Nicaea declared Rome, Alexandria and Antioch to be patriarchal sees (325). The eastern centres contested Roman supremacy; but Rome had long enjoyed particular respect. Already, before A.D. 100 its pope or bishop had intervened, for example, in the affairs of Corinth. In the following century the church at Carthage was conscious of dependence on Rome, and the Roman community felt aware of its own special significance.[114] One reason why other churches looked to the church of Rome was because of its fateful and responsible position in the imperial capital. And yet, as the empire began to change its character and Rome gradually lost political and economical power, its abstract, eternal status, among Christians as among pagans, was not diminished but enhanced (p. 214). Already in the later second century Irenaeus put forward the superior claims of the church of Rome on grounds of the apostolic succession. Pointing out that the main body of the church owed its supremacy over deviations to a direct chain of authority extending from the apostles to bishops of his own day, he indicated that in Rome this unbroken continuity went back to St. Peter, who was Christ's leading apostle, and to St. Paul; and that at Rome, accordingly, will be found the pure doctrine with which other communities should agree.[115] A much revered martyr's shrine of St. Peter dates back to the same period (p. 295).

Eastern communities admitted the special distinction of the church of Rome, but they were much more reluctant to admit that this body had any right to legislate for them on doctrine or organization. They did not share the increasing western tendency to eliminate laymen from church government. It was also their belief that ecclesiastical authority is not vested in any one person, but belongs by scriptural direction to *each* bishop (in spite of "precedence of honour" to a few holders of historic sees), and expresses itself through all of them united in their general councils (c.f. p. 292).

But Romans and Greeks, in many matters beside religion, had never liked each other or understood each other's attitudes. The admiration which educated Romans such as Cicero professed for past Hellenic culture was rarely extended to its living exponents, and most Greeks of all periods detested the richer, more powerful and coarser Romans whose financial aid they so often sought. In spite of conciliatory efforts by a few imaginative thinkers such as Virgil on the one side, and by pro-Roman Greek leaders on the other, the gap widened. Moreover the bilingual educated man was becoming very rare (p. 157). These difficulties extended into ecclesiastical affairs. The Roman church had at first been thoroughly Greek. But after Hippolytus (d. *c.* 236) there were no more spokesmen of this Greek-speaking Christianity at Rome; Novatian wrote in Latin, and by the fourth century Greek had ceased to be the language of the liturgy. Few eastern churchmen spoke Latin at all—and they did not see why they should, since the New Testament had been written in Greek and they felt themselves to be the repositories of its truth.

There were, accordingly both psychological and linguistic reasons why western and Greek Christians should fail to understand each other's point of view. A quarrel over the celebration of Easter impelled a Roman bishop (pope) St. Victor (d. *c.* 199), contrary to the wishes of Irenaeus, to break with the churches of Asia Minor. Matters came to a head when St. Stephen (254–6) was prompted by a dispute regarding baptism to claim subordination of all churches to Rome in view of the primacy conferred upon St. Peter, whose tradition had now become fully established at the capital (p. 295). Firmilian of Caesarea replied denying any legal pre-eminence to Peter or his successors, and maintaining that *every* bishop is the successor of the Apostles.[116] For the Greeks could not share the legal centralized autocratic approach which the Romans owed to their training and to the juridical moulding their faith had received from lawyers such as Tertullian. Nor did the Romans, for their part, appreciate the Hellenic, philosophizing tendencies of the Apologists (p. 271) which were so strong in Greek lands. The east enacted creeds; the west discipline.[117]

Aurelian strengthened the church of Rome by supporting it in a dispute relating to the bishopric of Antioch. But the differences between east and west were accentuated and perpetuated by Constantine's foundation of Constantinople. The removal of the imperial government away from Rome had already given the head of the Roman church far greater opportunities for independence and civil authority than he had possessed hitherto. But now the presence of the emperor at Constantinople began to raise the patriarch of that place also to a peculiar importance of his own, which, although the initial privileges of the new city were limited (p. 133), was in due course recognized by a precedence second only to Rome (381). Already two decades earlier, the new city had been described as "a bond of union between east and west to which the most distant extremes from all sides come together, and to which they look up as the common centre and emporium of the faith".[118]

But this was too optimistic in view of the disputes which followed. They were concerned with clerical celibacy, the Fall of Man, and the nature of the Holy Ghost. The east, as always, stressed the singleness of the supreme deity, and the west emphasized the divinity of Jesus (p. 272).[119] Constantine's elevation of Constantinople to be the imperial capital had sharpened long-standing cultural, psychological and linguistic differences. The result was not the religious unity for which he had hoped, but a major breach between Catholicism and Orthodoxy which has lasted until now; just as his attitude to the Donatists, and their attitude to him, foreshadowed that other major breach which was to result in dissident Protestant churches. The effect of Constantine's ecumenical drive was, paradoxically, not unity but lasting Christian division—productive of all the weakness of disunion, and all the devout vigour of separate loyalties.

NOTES

1. From Chenoboskion; and 3 MS. strips from Oxyrhynchus
2. St. Clement I of Rome, Polycarp
3. Cf. Irenaeus: as natural as the four winds and four quarters of the earth
4. But disputes continued (Eus. *EH.* III, 25, 1) until Athanasius (367)
5. Tert. *De Praescr. Her.* 8. Cf. conquest of evil (lion and boar hunts) on Christian sarcophagi
6. E.g. traditions of Jesus passing on his secret knowledge to James, John and Peter; or to Philip, Matthew and Thomas, twin brother of Jesus. Cf. *Pistis Sophia (Apocryphal Acts of John*, P. Berlin 8502), Syriac *Acts of Philip the Apostle and Evangelist*
7. Cf. *Hebr.* II, 10. Irenaeans regard the doctrine of eternal hell as invalidating the Christian explanation of evil
8. Cf. *Gen.* III; VI, 1, 8; and St. Paul. Augustine rejected Platonic praise of human intellect
9. Unsuccessful opposition by Arminius in seventeenth century Holland
10. Earlier Apologists: Quadratus to Hadrian, Marcianus Aristides to Antoninus Pius
11. Just. *I Apol.* (he wrote two Apologies). Justin's attitude made the prophets unnecessary. He identified St. John's Word with Stoic Mind
12. Clem. *Paed.* I, 62, 70
13. *II Cor.* IV, 7; cf. Orig. *DCB.* IV, 119 (and Metrodorus of Lampsacus, fifth century B.C., on Homer)
14. He explained evil by adopting the Platonic, Pythagorean view of the soul's pre-existence, determining man's fortunes. He accepted Clement's esotericism, but refused to allow that this *élite* would continue in the next world
15. Clement of Alexandria was struck off the list of saints in 1748. Almost all Origen's works were condemned by Justinian (543), and he inspired a fear of Platonism in tenth- and eleventh-century Byzantines

16. Synods of Arelate and Mediolanum (355, 357). Arius, who denounced his opponents as dualists, had rejected the formula (*homoousios*, of one substance to the Father) agreed at Nicaea, since it seemed to imply the two Persons' identity. After *c.* 350 Arianism asserted that the Holy Spirit was a creature (Tertullian, following Justin, had laid down that the Trinity was one substance, three persons)

17. Tert. denounced philosophers (except Seneca) and professors; cf. *Apol.* 46, 18, *De Test. Anim.* 1. But Hippolytus' *Apostolic Tradition* (*c.* 215) does not ban the teaching profession

18. Lact. *Inst. Div.* IV, 22, 30 (tr. Fletcher)

19. Hippol. *Philosophumena*, IX, 12

20. John XI, 43 ff.

21. Arnob. I, 65

22. Symbolized by peacock and phoenix (cf. on pagan mosaic at Edessa, 235–6). The personal touches, relating to the dead, that are depicted on sarcophagi will be needed at the time of their personal Resurrections

23. Via Salaria sarcophagus; Coemeterium Majus *c.* 270–5 (female). Cf. PIETAS type on imperial coins

24. Cypr. *Ep.* 69, 15, Tert. *Apol.* 46, Min. Fel. 27, Eus. *EH.* VI, 43, Lact. *Inst. Div.* IV, 27, 1

25. Orig. *C. Cels.* VII, 4

26. Just. *II Apol.* 6

27. John XIV, 17, 26, XV, 26, XVI, 7–14

28. Orig. *Hom. in Cant.* I, 7 (*GCS.* VIII, 38, 16); preparing the way for the mysticism of Gregory of Nyssa.

29. Tert. *De Bapt.* 1; cf. Paul. Nol. *Ep.* XIII, 11

30. Cypr. *Ad Donat.* 3

31. The Mass is described by Justin. Origen took a figurative view of the rite

32. E.g. Cat. Praetextatus (third century)

33. Revived in the Great Persecution, discounted by Eusebius and Jerome. The fantastic apocalyptic poetry of Commodian, admired by Huysmans, may be of third, fourth or fifth century

34. Essene origin (?). Cf. parallels with Hercules

35. The Iconoclasts rebelled against this. A series of crude sarcophagi (*c.* 290) narrate, the lives of Jesus and Peter

36. E.g. Cat. Priscilla, mid-second century. *Protevangelium*: late second or early third century. Sometimes with Balaam (*Num.* XXIV, 17), who was held to have prophesied the Virgin Birth, and thus linked the two Testaments

37. Cat. Hermes

38. Noah also appears with his Ark on a coin of Phillip at Apamea in Phrygia

39. Jon. I. 17

40. Cf. Sen. *Ep.* X, 1, etc., on the blessings of solitude. Cf. third-century papyri, "The Kingdom is within you"

41. Serapis cult (Ptolemy VI Philometor)

42. Regarded with sympathy by the Hellenized Jew Philo

43. Jos. *BJ.* II, 119. 21

44. *Gospel of Thomas*

45. *PG.* 26, 84
46. Near Pirpir
47. Three nuclei near Memphis and Arsinoe may be regarded as the origin of the communal (coenobitic) monastic life
48. Ath. *V. Ant.* 44
49. In the Nitria area of Egypt (Wadi Natrun)
50. *Apophth. Amun,* II, p. 128
51. There are earlier records of virgins devoted to prayer and service (cf. pagan Vestals): Methodius of Olympus, *Banquet of the Twelve Virgins,* end third century. Nunneries are sometimes believed to have preceded monasteries
52. At Pabau (Fau-kebli)
53. Seven miles from Majoma
54. E.g. Sulpicius Severus
55. *Hist. Mon.* VIII, 56
56. St. Martin was from Pavia and became Bishop of Tours. Cassian's monastery and nunnery at Marseille (early fifth century) served as models for many others
57. R. Hezekiah and R. Abbahu, citing R. Eleazar. The Mishnah contains a collection of rulings on O. T. texts
58. Founded by Abba Arika (175–247). Also Nehardea under Samuel (180–250), sacked 258; then Pumbeditha under Judah ben Ezekiel (d. 299). The Alexandrian Jewish community seems to have been almost wiped out in 115–17
59. Cf. Hellenistic themes at Kahane, Avigad. At Beth She'arim Hebrew and Greek inscriptions are mixed. David in the Dura synagogue resembles Orpheus
60. Philostr. *V. Apol.* 33
61. In Asia, Christians were still observing the Passover in *c.* 170
62. Cf. Orig. *C. Cels.* III, 55. The early Christian *Didache,* however, recommends slaves to submit to their masters as to the images of God. But St. Calixtus (217–22) held that divine law authorized inter-class marriages not legally recognized at Rome
63. Pont. *V. Cypr.* II, Cypr. *De Mort.* 26, *Ep. Diogn.* 5, 5
64. Pl. *Ep.* X, 97
65. Bar Kochba's revolt under Hadrian seriously shocked the government
66. ? A.D. 155–6 ? 165–8 ? 177
67. Mart. X. 2; cf. I Clem. 60, 61
68. Mel. *ap.* Eus. *EH.* IV, 26, 7 ff.
69. Orig. *C. Cels.* VIII, 68; cf. 2
70. Min. Fel. IX, 1 ff.
71. Tert. *Apol.* XXIII, 14 ff.
72. *Ibid.,* XXXI, 4 f. (tr. T. R. Glover)
73. *De Idol.* (*c.* 211), *De Cor. Mil.,* cf. *Ad Ux.* II, 4, 9, *Ad Scap.* 2
74. Orig. *C. Cels.* III, 29, 30
75. *Library of Christian Classics,* Philadelphia, 1954. For Royal Priesthood, see *Rev.* I, 6, I Pet. II, 9. Constantine's recognition of the church ended the period of the laity as a true order

76. Ignat. *Ad Smyr.* VI, 2. Parochial organization at Rome developed further under Dionysius (259–68)
77. Jul. *Ep.* 84a; cf. Luc. *Peregr.* 12, 13
78. E.g. *libelli* from Theadelphia (Fayum)
79. From *Acta Martyrum Scillitanorum* (A.D. 180) onwards
80. Tert. *Apol.* 13, 15, 16
81. Cypr. *Ad. Nem., Ep.* LXXVI
82. John Chrysostom. Soldiers of Christ: Lact. *De Mort. Pers.* 31. Martyrdom rare in art: Isaiah at Bagawat, Kufra (fourth century) (cf. scourging of Aelia Afanasia, Cat. Praetextatus, *c.* 270–80). Pilgrimages to martyria: *Bordeaux Pilgrim* (333)
83. Eus. *EH.* VII, 13, 1
84. Tert. *Apol.* 37, 4, *Ad Scap.* 2
85. Eus. *EH.* VIII, 1, 2
86. E.g. followers of the Syrian goddess Atargatis. Missionary bishop of Antioch: Serapion. First bishop of Edessa: Palut. Its king: Abgar IX. The Syriac language of Edessa is still used by Nestorians
87. St. Ephraim
88. Athenag. *Leg.* 1, Tert. *Apol.* 24, Just. *I Apol.* 24, had sought to justify Christianity by the diversity of different cultures
89. James of Sarug. The converter of Armenia was king Tiridates III
90. Porph. *De Regressu, fr.* 10. He also attacked the Mosaic authorship of the Pentateuch and the authenticity of the Book of Daniel
91. Lact. *Inst. Div.* VIII, 15, 11, still shrank in terror from the thought that the empire might be not permanent
92. *Id., De Mort. Pers.* 16
93. W. H. C. Frend
94. Eus. *De Mart. Pal.* IX, 3
95. *Id., EH.* VIII, 17 (tr. G. A. Williamson)
96. *Ibid.,* IX, 7 (tr. G. A. Williamson)
97. *Id., V. Const.* I, 28, III, 3. Lact. *De Mort. Pers.* 45. Cf. cosmic Chi in Pl. *Tim.,* and tree of Eden with four fructifying rivers. Perhaps the interpretation was suggested to Constantine by his religious adviser Ossius of Corduba
98. Lact. *De Mort. Pers.* 46
99. Inherited by Constantine's wife Fausta from her father Maximian
100. *Cod. Theod.* XVI, 2, 4; cf. I, 27, 1 on jurisdiction. Constantine also allowed bishops to free slaves
101. The three sons of Constantine remind Eus. *V. Const.* IV, 40 of the Trinity. But Constantine, officially, was divinely protected, not quite divine (Firm. Mat. *De Err. Prof. Rel.* XXIX, 4): cf. heaven-gazing head on coins (as Alexander, Gallienus), interpreted by Jul. *Caes.* 329 as the Sun looking up lecherously at the Moon. Constantine's rule is based on the pattern of God who has committed earthly government to him (Opt. Milev. *App.* III)
102. Eus. *V. Const.* IV, 24
103. Opt. Milev. *App.* III (to Aelafius)
104. Cf. also John Chrysostom, *Ep. ad Eph. Hom.* XI, 5

105. Canon 3 (army) remains obscure. Fourth- and fifth-century popes were still critical of Christian soldiers, civil servants and lawyers
106. Jer. *V. Malchi*, init.
107. Tat. *Or.* 25; cf. *Didache*
108. Tert. *De Praescr. Her.*; cf. *Apol.* 46
109. Anon. *ap.* Eus. *EH.* V, 16, 10
110. Tert. *De Pall.* 2. Cf. Apul. *Apol.* 98 on hatred of Latin
111. Tert. *De Cult. Fem.* ii, 2
112. The ban on the Novatianists was lifted a year later
113. Constans persecuted the Donatists (345). At a disputation held at Carthage by imperial command (A.D. 411) they mustered 279 bishops out of 565. Four years later the death penalty was invoked against them. The Egyptian sect comparable to the Donatists were the Melitians
114. I Clem. (*c.* A.D. 95). The titles *pappas, papa*, at first used of all bishops, were gradually limited in the west to the bishop of Rome (by fifth century), though still used of priests in the eastern church
115. Iren. *Adv. Haer.* III, 2, 3, cf. Tert. *De Praescr. Haer.* 36
116. Cypr. *Ep.* 75; cf. *De Cath. Eccl. Un., Ep.* 45. 3, 55. 4
117. H. H. Milman
118. St. Gregory of Nazianzus
119. After disputes between St. Basil (d. 379) and pope St. Damasus I, Rome enforced clerical celibacy (385) and Constantinople did not. From 484 *de facto* division for 40 years. At the same time views on the Procession were becoming irreconcilable: did the Holy Ghost proceed from the Father only (eastern view—single and indivisible supreme deity) or from the Father and Son (western view—stressing divinity of Jesus)?

Epilogue

Have all these events any direct messages or warnings for ourselves?
The history of a remarkable period is an absorbing and rewarding
study even when it throws no direct light on today, but it may also
throw such a light, and there are reasons for supposing that the
years described in this book are indeed relevant to our own times.
The ancient Greco-Roman world, which has given us so many of our
own characteristics, is the only civilization or group of civilizations
which is spread out completely for our examination from its beginnings until its last years—after the years I have tried to describe in
this book. It produced artistic, literary, spiritual and political brilliance with unequalled lavishness. The Roman empire is unique for
the huge size of the territories of Europe, western Asia and northern
Africa—the matrices of modern nations—which it comprehended
under its single government. Although history does not reproduce
exact analogies, this convergence of circumstances makes it evident that so remarkable a civilization will illuminate subsequent
ages.

The later empire, of which part is discussed in this book, was
this ancient world's final and therefore most hereditable phase.
Certain suggestive links and resemblances become evident at once
(Part II). First, the continual *coups d'état* and politico-military succession struggles, which did more than anything else to reduce the
empire to financial crisis and encourage its enemies, are still with us
nearly two thousand years later. The newly created states of the
world have often during the past decade suffered from rapid sequen-
ces of governments lasting for as short a time as Roman emperors
and then coming to as violent an end. Very soon too, perhaps before
these words are read, similar discontinuities are likely to recur in
several countries of Europe and America, possibly with the same

grave effects of widespread dislocation as attended similar emergencies at Rome. This was the characteristic political problem of the later Roman empire, which it failed to solve, with disastrous results. Today, the solution continues to elude vast areas of the world, and its politicians and political scientists and political psychologists would do well, in the light of what befell the Roman empire, to study how a country can best increase the efficiency of its steps to secure peaceful continuity of control.

A second resemblance between late Rome and modern times lies in the military and financial situations and their political consequences. Like the states of the modern western world, the Roman government was faced quite suddenly, within a couple of generations, with foreign enemies or potential enemies far more menacing than for many centuries past. The resulting military efforts necessitated governmental expenditure on a hitherto unknown, astronomical, scale—as is again the case in western countries, and for that matter eastern countries, today. Thirdly, the collection of these funds from the subjects of the empire prompted the same trends towards egalitarianism that are a feature of the twentieth century; and there was a tendency for the levelling to be downwards rather than upwards. Fourthly, the levying of the necessary funds only seemed attainable by developing authoritarian rule to unprecedented lengths. This too is of concern in our own times. For our century too has witnessed the establishment of total autocracy in several great countries, and today many other governments too, including those with liberal democratic traditions, are tempted to feel that the only way to meet their financial needs is by constantly intensifying regimentation. The outcome of this tendency cannot be foreseen, but a scrutiny of the later Roman empire, of which the conditions were in many ways anticipatory of our own, will help us how to avoid some of the tragic paths which led to its iron compulsions and controls.

Rome's actions were based on certain hypotheses which deserve to be tested upon ourselves. For one thing, there was the conclusion that dangers beyond its frontiers could best be dealt with by increased expenditure on military operations. For reasons of prestige, diplomacy was never really seriously tried for long. After a while, it was too late; no diplomacy would have halted the Persians and Germans in the mid-third century. But earlier that was not so, and the opportunity was missed. In modern Britain there is much self-questioning whether we can afford not to retract our imperial role; and in the United States the obligations of a world-wide policy are also the subject of ever-continuing discussion. Like Britain, Rome found it difficult to grow out of old-fashioned expansive attitudes which were too costly and out of keeping with its major needs. On the other hand, it is also true that an occasional emperor rejected the policy of his predecessors, and the period even shows two examples of actual permanent withdrawals from an area. One of these, Gallienus' evacuation of the upper Rhine-upper Danube re-entrant, was the involuntary product of pressure. Aurelian, when he evacuated Dacia and moved back to the line of the lower Danube, provided the only example of a ruler who deliberately withdrew from a hard-pressed province for ever. What should or could Rome have done, in order to avoid a burden that had become unendurable? There were grave practical and humanitarian as well as prestige objections to drawing in its horns. Probably, while it had the chance, it should have relied more on negotiations; and ancient writers who unanimously scorned the subsidization of emergent peoples across the frontiers may well have been wrong.

The Roman government, in setting such high sights for its military and consequently also for its financial obligations, achieved a certain grand simplicity and potential (if unrealized) justice in the grant of universal citizenship. But meanwhile it was transformed into a totalitarian régime. Will that happen to us? It need not, since we can avoid certain evil results of Rome's backward economy. We, like the Romans, need a seller's market in order to meet our enormous financial needs: indeed we need it much more than they did, since they depended so largely on agriculture. Their external market, during most of the period covered by this book, hardly spread in any substantial degree beyond the frontiers, because of strained or hostile political relations with northern and eastern neighbours alike, which may be compared with the modern division imposed by the Iron Curtain. But in addition to such obstacles Rome's market, in its provinces as well as foreign lands, reached saturation point, because of the decentralization of industry itself. So perhaps will ours, as new countries develop their own resources. But when this happened in the Roman empire, most people were so poor that there was no internal market to expand instead. We on the other hand, not being bound to the stagnant technology and lack of incentives imposed on the Romans by their social system, can create material wealth and provide our own people with the resources for buying the products of their labour.[1]

So there are certain means by which we might escape slipping, like the Romans, into government by compulsion. We can avoid their foreign policies which cost more than they could afford and limited their external markets; and if external markets fail, we can profit from our superiority to Rome's social and technological structure and develop a sufficient internal market. These are not panaceas but they provide grounds for hope.

While, owing to circumstances not altogether unlike those pressing upon ourselves, Rome was falling under authoritarian rule, it also achieved a military recovery so remarkable that it seems today, as it must have seemed to many contemporaries, to disprove the theory that there are inevitable tendencies in history. The whole of an apparent process of disintegration and collapse was arrested in full flood and delayed for a century and a half. This was surely not the achievement of a decaying empire. After the stringent exactions which made survival possible had been enforced by the most in-fluential and perhaps the most talented lawyers the world has known, this military reassertion was stabilized by a series of the first annual budgets that any government had ever produced. And finally, by one of the most imaginative acts in history, a new capital was established at Constantinople, from which not only another of the greatest of the world's civilizations emerged, but a huge part of the classical heritage, reprieved and preserved by the third century recovery, was handed on (Part III).

These were portentous events, but I am doubtful whether in themselves they would have justified the title of *The Climax of Rome* which I have chosen for this book. (Although, witness Soviet Russia, a national climax may well be harsh.) That title, however, is deserved by a number of simultaneous or successive artistic, intel-lectual and spiritual developments during the same period. In spite of incessant military and financial crisis, fine arts developed along lines of exceptional novelty and excellence. The portrait sculpture of emperors, passing rapidly through diverse stages of development, attained a brilliance and depth of insight which have never been equalled in any earlier or later age; and then imperial architects made revolutionary use of older conceptions in order to develop the huge halls, domes, apses and vaults of the greatest palaces ever yet seen, and of equally magnificent and even more original Christian churches and shrines. Together with the lawyers and the last important ancient doctor Galen, these architects and engineers were the outstanding products of an educational system which had become sterile in its other higher branches. Yet it was more widely diffused than before, and in contrast, therefore, with the various traditional literary *genres* its characteristic product was the middle-brow romantic novel, which attained its zenith during this epoch and profoundly influenced the reading habits of many ages to come.

Meanwhile, however, amid a rapidly rising tide of irrationality, two philosophers of unique and eternal interest, Marcus Aurelius and Plotinus, had graver counsels to offer. Marcus is the noblest and most moving of all those guides to life who have drawn their principal strength from sources other than religious hope: in order to play his imperial part, he took his sustenance from within himself. The old classical world of self-reliance and courageous achievement is still there, but it has been turned inward into channels which led to medieval ideas. A long further step in the same direction was taken by Plotinus. His grand and compelling system, anticipating existentialism in its ethics and Freud in its original psychology of the unconscious, again concludes that the task of man is introverted contemplation. But now Marcus' classical dutifulness to public life has gone. And above all this inward contemplation brought Plotinus to the supreme experience, which he interpreted as mystical union with the controlling power and essence of the universe. Plotinus is at one with the portrait-busts of his day which gaze beyond the apparent realities of our day-to-day world to a truer reality beyond; and he is a pioneer of that rich tradition of mysticism which many believe to carry a powerful message for the modern world, in transcendental meditation or sterner forms.

While ancient philosophy thus came to its culmination and verged upon the Middle Ages, Rome's official world appealed for reliance upon traditional and imperial cult (Part IV). This patriotic feeling, which played its part in the military salvation of Rome, gradually became concentrated upon a revived and almost monotheistic version of the ancient Sun-worship which, with its noble and comprehensive simplicity, seemed to be taking control of the empire in the last days of official paganism. For those who wanted a more personal religion, the worship of the Sun provided an offshoot in Mithraism, a moral variant of the Mystery cults promising their initiates that personal immortality after death which had become the principal preoccupation of religion. But the outstanding spiritual leader of the age, living in Persia yet exercising profound effects upon the Greco-Roman world, was Mani, whose compelling Manichaean religion, handed down by one elect to another, held that evil exists because there is not one high God but two. The Gnostics had seen not only a good power but also, since good cannot create or allow evil, an evil creator of the world. Mani expressed this in the ancient Persian terms of a fundamental distinction between Light and its perpetual enemy Darkness: it is our millennial task to refine the Light from the Dark with which it has become mingled.

This dualism, which formed great churches in the Middle Ages and has continued ever since to attract those who think they see the Devil at work, was unacceptable to Jewish monotheism or to its offspring the religion of Christ. During the period under consideration in this book, the fateful decisions were taken by which the New Testament assumed its present shape. Varying blends of Hebrew and Greco-Roman ideas, possessing infinite significance for the spiritual future of millions of Christians who accepted or rejected them, were being moulded by speculative theologians of unprecedented calibre. Meanwhile other, less learned, contemporary interpretations of the faith and the immortality that it conferred were depicted by artists of catacombs and sarcophagi, illuminating the mentalities and preoccupations of the people whose belief and endurance and cohesion had begun to make Christianity into a world religion. Its message of love possessed a universality and simplicity which proved to have a greater appeal than the doctrines of any other faith. Christian communities expressed this conception—and thereby brought the humanitarian tendencies of the age into unprecedentedly practical effect—by their expansion of the welfare organizations they had inherited from Jews and Greeks.

This was also the age in which the attitude of the Roman state to this small but increasingly well-organized church underwent a revolution to which history can offer no parallel. Alienation between

Greco-Roman society and the Christians had erupted into repeated official persecutions. But Galerius, on his deathbed, called off these attacks; Constantine proclaimed his personal adhesion to this religion of a minority of his subjects, and the church, instead of being the enemy of the government, became its subsidized auxiliary. This apocalyptic empire-wide reversal did not extend to the Persian empire, whose Christian communities found no similar unexpected royal protector. But it transformed the future of Europe and the Mediterranean world. The ecclesiastical unity which Constantine championed was as universal as that of any modern ecumenicalist, but it was the ecumenism of a confident, aggressive advance—and indeed a single united church was nearer to achievement than it has ever been again.

Nevertheless, there were still many Christians who could not comprehend the identification of the church with the state. Instead they preferred to withdraw, creating from pagan precedents the monasticism which exercised so formative an influence upon medieval life. Moreover, Constantine's insistence upon ecclesiastical unity prompted another phenomenon which had an equally durable role to play in later Europe, the persecution of fellow-Christians. The victims of his forcible measures were members of dissenting puritan sects, and his inability to suppress these groups (since violence only encouraged their determination) sowed the seeds of future differentiation between Catholics and Protestants. Meanwhile the foundation of Constantinople was accentuating another division which had already been latent in the whole intellectual history of the times and has again lasted until our own day, the breach between the Catholic and Orthodox churches.

These are a few of the happenings which make the epoch between Marcus Aurelius and Constantine the most significant in the history of the Roman empire. Even the Augustan age had not seen such a variety of original talent and thought and productive events. Although Rome itself had now lost much of its practical importance and gave birth to hardly any of the chief actors on the world stage, this epoch of supposed decline, by a significant paradox which I mentioned in the Foreword, was the climax of Rome.

What, during the later Roman empire, was the general pattern of relationship, by correspondence or reaction, between cultural and religious achievements and contemporary political and social trends? Sometimes, as in the times of Augustus or Pericles, literary and artistic and spiritual developments are almost all in close harmony with national and official life. But during the period which begins with Marcus Aurelius intellectual schizophrenia prevailed. There were spheres in which late Rome directly inspired greatness. The lawyers produced most of their unequalled work in the service of the government, which they helped to make authoritarian. Portrait sculptors not only benefited from patronage, but were directly inspired by the flamboyance and anxiety and brutal virility of their imperial models. They moved with the tide rather than against it, and so did the imperial architects, who were prompted to achieve masterpieces by the magnitude of the emperor and the diminutiveness of man. Moreover, certain pagan religious movements, such as the traditional Roman cults and Mithraism, were patriotic, and at the very end of the period Constantine similarly brought the dominant trends of Christianity into line with the policy of the state.

Yet for the most part, during the hundred and fifty years before this happened, the greatest and most influential advances of the mind and soul give no comfort to an admirer of classical public spirit, for they were often escapist reactions against the miseries of the times. The bridge between those who devoted their gifts to serving the state and those who sought a means of escaping from it is provided by the complex personality of Marcus Aurelius. Though an emperor, he felt an urgent desire, characteristic of the epoch, to remain an individual impregnable to external pressures, and that is the tension which gives the *Meditations* their perennial and modern fascination. The characteristic literary men of the age, the novelists, saw and described, in symbolic fashion, the discomforts of the world, but wove phantasies which enabled people to forget them. Their outstanding contemporary, Plotinus, even more unmistakably teaches avoidance of the sordidness of this life; and it is in order to turn away from these mundane miseries that innumerable pagan monuments of many different creeds manifest a passionate desire for immortality. The supreme religious leader of the age, Mani, was again deeply influenced by the troubles of existence—and they moved him not only, like his contemporaries, to preach withdrawal, but to provide a uniquely imposing analysis of their basic causes. Finally the Christians too were prompted to other-worldly devotion by the unhappiness of their lives. Martyrs carried this rejection of the world to its extremity, and, after the church had become Constantine's instrument, monks and puritans continued in the same tradition of alienation.

Accordingly, there were two different and simultaneous relationships between daily life on the one hand and cultural and religious life on the other: a relationship of direct stimulus, perceptible in the lawyers and sculptors and architects and in the official versions of pagan and then Christian religion, and a relationship of stimulus by reaction, visible in the novelists and philosophers and most religious groups, including pre-Constantinian and then dissenting Christianity. By these two different and opposite processes the torments of the times produced not inertia but abundant greatness. The ruthlessness of the government did not reduce outstanding thinkers and believers to silence, but provided them with sources of energy. Here there is a contrast with modern times. In their most accentuated phases, the totalitarian governments of the twentieth century have evoked comparatively little original cultural or spiritual activity; artists and architects in sympathy with them are nearly always sterile; rebels are few and mostly ineffective or inaudible. That is because the governments of our own age, with their modern technologies, are capable of regimenting people with a thoroughness which all the efforts of the Roman state and its agents were unable to achieve. "Too much evil and too much suffering", as Aldous Huxley remarked, "can make it impossible for men to be creative; but within very wide limits greatness is perfectly compatible with organized insanity, sanctioned crime, and intense, chronic unhappiness for the majority."

Admittedly the later empire, for all its levelling tendencies, was a gloomy place for the majority. This was nothing new, but the exigencies of the times had made it worse. In this final phase of the ancient world, as in its earlier phases, achievements (other than mere endurance and survival) are due not to the many but the few. Despite egalitarian tendencies, this remained an undemocratic time, and its history cannot profitably be written from a wholly democratic standpoint.[2] It was the few who kept civilization going and handed it on, and during this period they presented subsequent ages with superlative creations of the mind and spirit. Despite all their anxieties and troubles and perils, certain men brought

325

into being, for themselves and for people who felt like them, their own worlds of thought and belief which are the ultimate monuments of a terrible but marvellous age.

NOTES

1. Cf. F. W. Walbank
2. Cf. V. Ehrenberg: "For our purpose, it will be sufficient to see society as that part of the population which, at a certain time, can be regarded as the necessary background for the creative individual"

Genealogical Tables

1. *The Family of Marcus Aurelius*

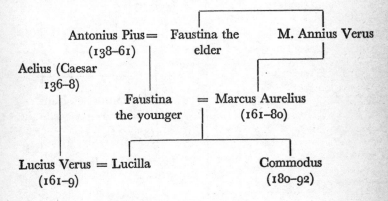

Antonius Pius= Faustina the elder   M. Annius Verus
(138–61)

Aelius (Caesar 136–8)

Faustina the younger = Marcus Aurelius (161–80)

Lucius Verus = Lucilla   Commodus
(161–9)   (180–92)

2. *The Family of the Severi*

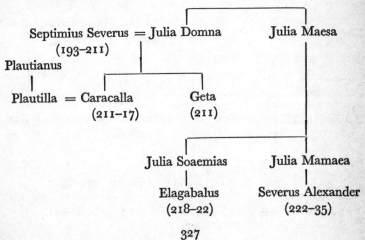

Septimius Severus = Julia Domna   Julia Maesa
(193–211)

Plautianus

Plautilla = Caracalla   Geta
(211–17)   (211)

Julia Soaemias   Julia Mamaea

Elagabalus   Severus Alexander
(218–22)   (222–35)

3. *The Family of Diocletian and Constantine*

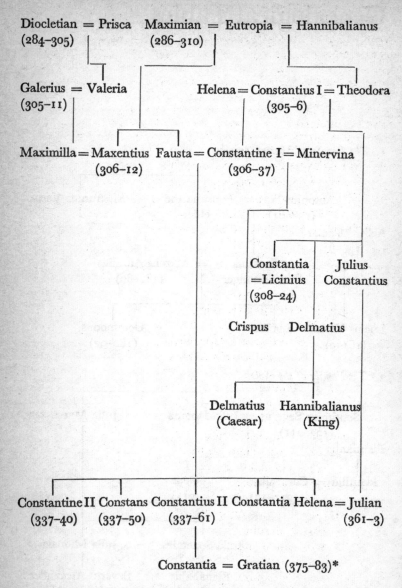

Diocletian = Prisca   Maximian = Eutropia = Hannibalianus
(284–305)

Galerius = Valeria   Helena = Constantius I = Theodora
(305–11)   (305–6)

Maximilla = Maxentius   Fausta = Constantine I = Minervina
         (306–12)   (306–37)

Constantia   Julius
=Licinius   Constantius
(308–24)

Crispus   Delmatius

Delmatius   Hannibalianus
(Caesar)   (King)

Constantine II   Constans   Constantius II   Constantia   Helena = Julian
(337–40)   (337–50)   (337–61)   (361–3)

Constantia = Gratian (375–83)*

*Son of Valentinian I and step-brother to the wife of Theodosius I.

List of Later Roman Emperors

<table>
<tr><td>A.D.</td><td>161–80</td><td>Marcus Aurelius</td></tr>
<tr><td></td><td>161–9</td><td>Lucius Verus</td></tr>
<tr><td></td><td>180–92</td><td>Commodus</td></tr>
<tr><td></td><td>193</td><td>Pertinax</td></tr>
<tr><td></td><td>193</td><td>Didius Julianus</td></tr>
<tr><td></td><td>193–211</td><td>Septimius Severus</td></tr>
<tr><td></td><td>211–17</td><td>Caracalla</td></tr>
<tr><td></td><td>211</td><td>Geta</td></tr>
<tr><td></td><td>217–18</td><td>Macrinus</td></tr>
<tr><td></td><td>218–22</td><td>Elagabalus</td></tr>
<tr><td></td><td>222–35</td><td>Severus Alexander</td></tr>
<tr><td></td><td>235–8</td><td>Maximinus I</td></tr>
<tr><td></td><td>238</td><td>Gordianus I Africanus</td></tr>
<tr><td></td><td></td><td>Gordianus II Africanus</td></tr>
<tr><td></td><td>238</td><td>Balbinus</td></tr>
<tr><td></td><td></td><td>Pupienus</td></tr>
<tr><td></td><td>238–44</td><td>Gordianus III</td></tr>
<tr><td></td><td>244–9</td><td>Philippus</td></tr>
<tr><td></td><td>249–51</td><td>Trajanus Decius</td></tr>
<tr><td></td><td>251–3</td><td>Trebonianus Gallus</td></tr>
<tr><td></td><td>253</td><td>Aemilianus</td></tr>
<tr><td></td><td>253–259/60</td><td>Valerianus</td></tr>
<tr><td></td><td>253–68</td><td>Gallienus</td></tr>
<tr><td></td><td>268–70</td><td>Claudius II Gothicus</td></tr>
<tr><td></td><td>270</td><td>Quintillus</td></tr>
<tr><td></td><td>270–5</td><td>Aurelianus</td></tr>
<tr><td></td><td>275–6</td><td>Tacitus</td></tr>
<tr><td></td><td>276</td><td>Florianus</td></tr>
<tr><td></td><td>276–82</td><td>Probus</td></tr>
</table>

282–3	Carus
283–4 {	Carinus Numerianus
284–305 {	Diocletianus
286–305 {	Maximianus
305–6	Constantius I Chlorus
305–11 (	Galerius
306–12 {	Maxentius
308–13† (	Maximinus II Daia
312–24 {	Constantinus I Licinius
324–37	Constantinus I sole ruler

*This list does not include transient claimants in the provinces or junior members of an emperor's family raised to the rank of Augustus (in a more or less honorary capacity) in his lifetime.

†This period also included the reigns of Severus II (306–7) and Maximian (306–8, second reign). Constantinus I and Licinius were declared Augusti from 306 and 308 respectively.

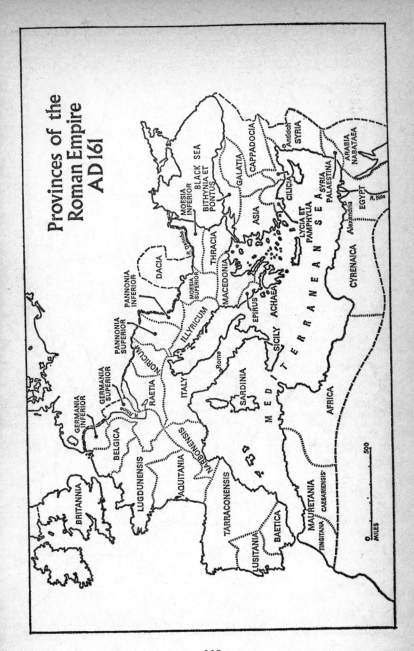

Provinces of the
Roman Empire
AD 161

BRITANNIA

GERMANIA INFERIOR
GERMANIA SUPERIOR
BELGICA
LUGDUNENSIS
AQUITANIA
NARBONENSIS
TARRACONENSIS
LUSITANIA
BAETICA

RAETIA
NORICUM
PANNONIA SUPERIOR
PANNONIA INFERIOR
DACIA
ILLYRICUM
ITALY
SARDINIA
SICILY
Rome

MOESIA SUPERIOR
MOESIA INFERIOR
BLACK SEA
THRACIA
MACEDONIA
EPIRUS
ACHAEA
R. Danube

BITHYNIA ET PONTUS
GALATIA
CAPPADOCIA
ASIA
LYCIA ET PAMPHYLIA
CILICIA
Antioch
SYRIA
ARABIA NABATAEA
SYRIA PALAESTINA

MEDITERRANEAN SEA

CYRENAICA
AFRICA
MAURETANIA CAESARIENSIS
MAURETANIA TINGITANA

EGYPT
Alexandria
R. Nile

Rhine

0   500
MILES

331

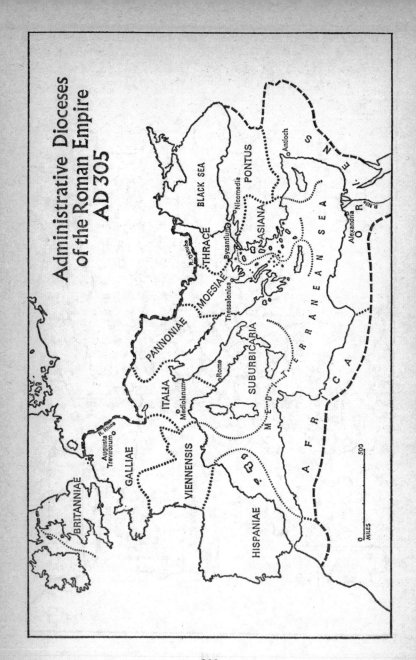

Administrative Dioceses
of the Roman Empire
AD 305

BRITANNIAE

GALLIAE

Augusta
Treviorum
R. Rhine

ITALIA
Mediolanum

VIENNENSIS

HISPANIAE

SUBURBICARIA
Rome

AFRICA

M E D I T E R R A N E A N   S E A

PANNONIAE

MOESIAE
Thessalonica

R. Danube

THRACE
Byzantium

BLACK SEA

ASIANA
Nicomedia

PONTUS
Antioch

O R I E N S

Alexandria
R. Nile

0   500
MILES

The West

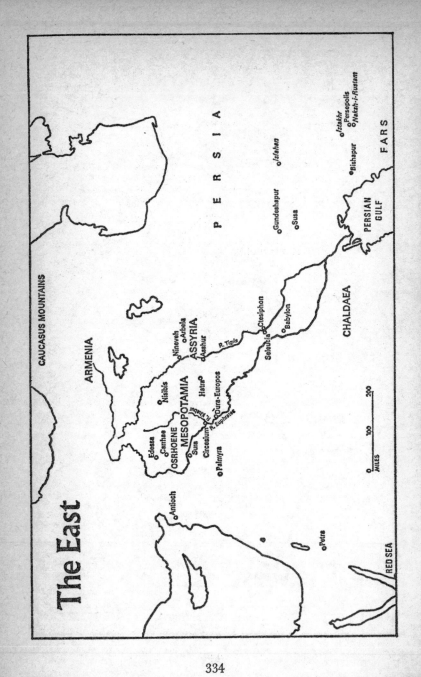

The East

CAUCASUS MOUNTAINS

ARMENIA

PERSIA

FARS

Istakh
Persepolis
Naksh-i-Rustam
Bishapur

Gundeshapur
Susa

Isfahan

PERSIAN
GULF

Nineveh
Arbela
ASSYRIA
Asshur

R. Tigris

Ctesiphon
Seleucia
Babylon

CHALDAEA

Nisibis

MESOPOTAMIA
Hatra
Dura-Europos
R. Khabur
R. Euphrates

Edessa
Carrhae
OSRHOENE
Sura
Circesium

Palmyra

Antioch

Petra

RED SEA

0   100   200
MILES

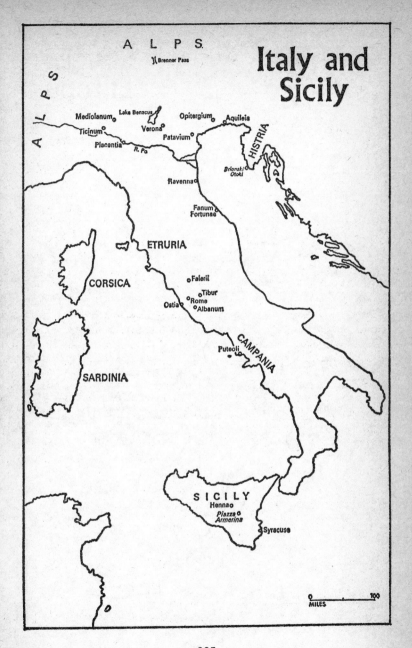

Italy and Sicily

ALPS

)(Brenner Pass

ALPS

Mediolanum Lake Benacus
Ticinum   Verona   Opitergium   Aquileia
Placentia   R. Po   Patavium   HISTRIA

Ravenna   Brionski
                                        Otoki

Fanum
Fortunae

ETRURIA

CORSICA

                Falerii
                    Tibur
Ostia   Rome
                Albanum

                              CAMPANIA
            Puteoli

SARDINIA

                    SICILY
                    Hennao
                    Piazza
                    Armerina
                              Syracuse

0   100
MILES

335

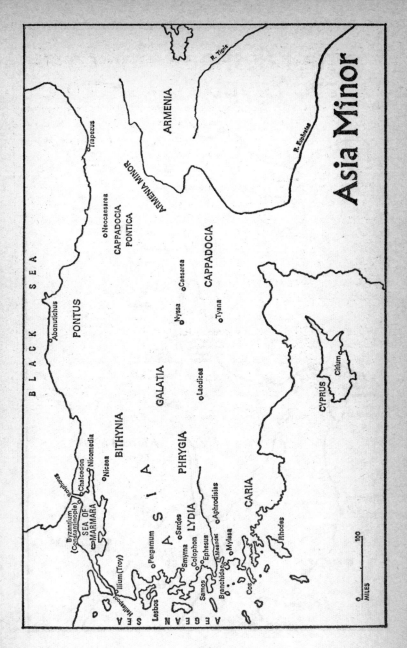

Asia Minor

337

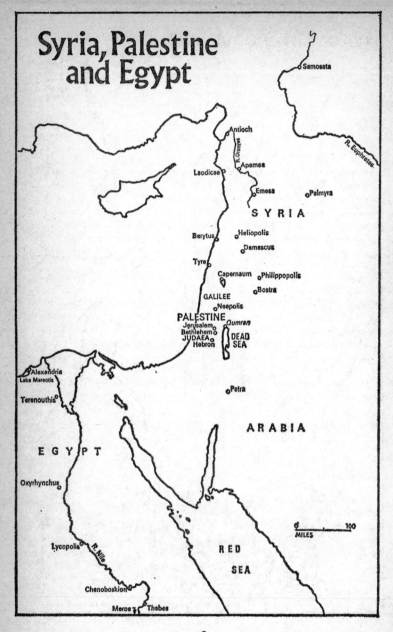

Syria, Palestine and Egypt

Samosata

Antioch

R. Orontes

Apamea

Laodicea

Emesa

Palmyra

SYRIA

Berytus

Heliopolis

Damascus

Tyre

Capernaum

Philippopolis

Bostra

GALILEE

Neapolis

PALESTINE

Jerusalem

Qumran

Bethlehem

JUDAEA

DEAD SEA

Hebron

Alexandria

Lake Mareotis

Petra

Terenouthis

ARABIA

EGYPT

Oxyrhynchus

0 ____ 100

MILES

Lycopolis

R. Nile

RED SEA

Chenoboskion

Meroe

Thebes

R. Euphrates.

Cyprus

Notes on Further Reading

I AND II: HISTORY. The fundamental works in English are *Cambridge Ancient History*, XI (1936), XII (1959), and A. H. M. Jones, *The Later Roman Empire* (1964), summarized in *The Decline of the Ancient World* (1966). Other convenient books include R. Rémondon, *La Crise de l'Empire Romain de Marc-Aurèle à Anastase* (1964), H. M. D. Parker, *A History of the Roman World A.D. 138–337* (2nd ed. 1958), A. Piganiol, *Histoire de Rome* (5th ed., 1962), F. Altheim, *Niedergang der Alten Welt* (1952), S. Mazzarino, *The End of the Ancient World* (1966), C. G. Starr, *Civilization and the Caesars* (1954), A. Alföldi, *Insignien und Tracht der römischen Kaiser* (*Röm. Mitt.* L, 1935), J. Vogt, *The Decline of Rome* (1967), L. White (ed.), *The Transformation of the Roman World* (1967), P. Brown, *The World of Late Antiquity* (1971). On special aspects: M. Hammond, *The Antonine Monarchy* (*Mem. Am. Ac. Rome*, 1959); R. MacMullen, *Soldier and Civilian in the later Roman Empire* (1963), A. Passerini, *Dizionario Epigrafico*, IV (1949), s.v. *Legione*, G. Forni, *ibid.*, *Limes*; M. Rostovtzeff, *Social and Economic History of the Roman Empire*, 2nd ed. (P. M. Fraser), 1957; Reports of Excavations at Dura-Europos, on many subjects; F. W. Walbank, *The Awful Revolution* (1969); F. Altheim-R. Stiehl, *Finanzgeschichte der Spätantike* (1957); Pauly-Wissowa, etc. (ed.), *Realencyclopädie für Altertumswissenschaften*, XXII (1954), ss. vv. *princeps civitatis* (L. Wickert), *praefectus praetorio* (W. Ensslin); R. Ghirshman, *Iran* (1956), M. Sprengling, *Third Century Iran* (1953); H. Mattingly, *Roman Coins* (2nd ed., 1960), M. Grant, *Roman Imperial Money* (1954), *Roman History from Coins* (1958), J. M. C. Toynbee, *Roman Medallions* (1944); F. Millar, *A Study of Cassius Dio* (1956), R. Syme, *Emperors and Biography: Studies in the Historia Augusta* (1970). Bibliographies in C. A. H., Piganiol, and G. Walser and T. Pekary, *Die Krise des romischen Reiches* (1962).

III: ARTISTS, ARCHITECTS, NOVELISTS, PHILOSOPHERS. J. M. C. Toynbee, *The Art of the Romans* (1965), G. M. A. Hanfmann, *Roman Art* (1965), R. E. M. Wheeler, *Roman Art and Architecture* (1964), M. Borda, *La Pittura Romana* (1958), D. E. Strong, *Roman Imperial Sculpture* (1961), H. P. L'Orange, *Art Forms and Civic life in the late Roman Empire* (1965), H. Kähler, *Rome and her Empire* (1963), M. Gough, *The Early Christians* (1961), R. Krautheimer, *Early Christian and Byzantine Architecture* (1965), A. Grabar, *The Beginnings of Christian Art* (1967).

The state of our knowledge of the Greek novel, after recent papyrus discoveries, is summed up by A. Lesky, *History of Greek Literature* (1966, translation of German second edition, 1963), cf. B. Perry, *The Ancient Romance* (1967), A. Scobie, *Aspects of the Ancient Romance and its Heritage* (1969). On the educational background see H. I. Marrou, *The History of Education in Antiquity* (1962), W. Stahl, *Roman Science* (1962). On Marcus Aurelius see A. S. L. Farquharson, *The Meditations of Marcus Antoninus* (1944), *Marcus Aurelius: His Life and his World* (2nd ed., 1952), A. Birley, *Marcus Aurelius* (1966). On Plotinus, H. R. Schwyzer in Pauly Wissowa etc., *Realencycl.* XXI (1951), s.v. *Plotin*, A. H. Armstrong, *Plotinus* (1953) and introduction to Loeb ed. of Plotinus (Vol. I, 1966), and other references there, P. Hadot, *Plotin ou la Simplicité de Regard* (1963), J. M. Rist, *Plotinus: the Road to Reality* (1967); S. Spencer, *Mysticism in World Religion* (1963), etc.

IV: FROM PAGANISM TO CHRISTIANITY. For religion in this period see A. D. Nock, *Conversion* (1933), E. R. Dodds, *Pagan and Christian in an Age of Anxiety* (1965), A. Momigliano (ed.), *The Conflict between Paganism and Christianity in the Fourth Century* (1963), M. Sordi, *Il Cristianesimo e Roma* (1965). On special aspects, R. O. Fink, A. S. Hoey, W. F. Snyder, *The Feriale Duranum* (*Yale Classical Studies* VII, 1940), F. Cumont on Sun worship, etc.—bibliography in *Mélanges F. Cumont* (1936)—and *Lux Perpetua* (1949); E. H. Kantorowicz, *Oriens Augusti* (*Dumbarton Oaks Papers*, no. 17, 1963), M. J. Vermaseren, *Mithras, the Secret God* (1963), G. Widengren, *Mani and Manichaeanism* (1965), K. Grobel, *The Gospel of Truth* (1960), J. Doresse, *The Secret Books of the Egyptian Gnostics* (1960), H. Lewy, *Chaldaean Oracles and Theurgy* (1956).

On the Jews: L. Finkelstein, *The Jews*, I (1949), M. Avi-Yonah, *Geschichte der Juden im Zeitalter des Talmud* (1962, Hebrew ed. 1946).

On Christianity: H. Lietzmann, *Geschichte der alten Kirche*, II (2nd ed., 1953), P. Carrington, *The Early Church* (1957), J. G. Davies, *The Early Christian Church* (1965), J. Danielou-H. Marrou, *Nouvelle Histoire de l'Eglise* (I, 1963), R. M. Grant, *Gnosticism and Early Christianity* (1959), J. Moreau, *Les Persécutions du Christianisme dans l'Empire romain* (1956), W. H. C. Frend, *Martyrdom and Persecution in the Early Church* (1965), J. M. C. Toynbee and J. Ward-Perkins, *The Shrine of St. Peter and the Vatican Excavations* (1956), A. Alföldi, *The Conversion of Constantine and Pagan Rome* (1948), N. H. Baynes, *Constantine the Great and the Christian Church* (*Proc. Brit. Ac.* 1929), A. H. M. Jones, *Constantine and the Conversion of Europe* (1948), H. Chadwick, *Early Christian Thought and the Classical Tradition* (1966).

INDEX

344

345

HISTORY OF CIVILISATION SERIES

THE WORLD OF THE PHOENICIANS

Sabatino Moscati

A comprehensive survey of the culture, history and social life of the Phoenicians, one of the most enigmatic peoples of antiquity.

£1 *Illustrated*

THE CELTIC REALMS

Myles Dillon and Nora Chadwick

The definitive work on the history and culture of the Celtic peoples, from their prehistoric origins to the Norman invasion of Britain.

£1·25 *Illustrated*

THE GREEK EXPERIENCE

C. M. Bowra

'To succeed in giving the Greeks a fresh life is a hard task, but Sir Maurice Bowra has achieved it'
Books of the Year, Sunday Times

75p *Illustrated*

THE WORLD OF ROME

MICHAEL GRANT

The historical background and astounding cultural and political achievements of the Roman Empire, resulting in a fascinating contribution to our understanding of the important role Rome played in the evolution of the modern world.

£1 *Illustrated*

THE BYZANTINE COMMONWEALTH

DIMITRI OBOLENSKY

'Outstanding ... Obolensky has provided what must, for many years, remain the most authoritative and comprehensive textbook on the history of Eastern Europe'
Times Literary Supplement

£1·25 *Illustrated*

THE MEDIEVAL WORLD

FRIEDRICH HEER

A brilliant and comprehensive picture of two and a half centuries of European civilisation, discussing all the facets of Medieval life, which laid the foundations for modern society.

£1·50 *Illustrated*